Las Románticas

Carolina Coronado

Las Románticas

*Women Writers and Subjectivity
in Spain, 1835–1850*

Susan Kirkpatrick

UNIVERSITY OF CALIFORNIA PRESS
Berkeley · Los Angeles · London

University of California Press
Berkeley and Los Angeles, California

University of California Press, Ltd.
London, England

Copyright © 1989 by Susan Kirkpatrick

Library of Congress Cataloging-in-Publication Data

Kirkpatrick, Susan.
  Las románticas: women writers and subjectivity in Spain,
  1835–1850 / Susan Kirkpatrick.
    p.   cm.
  Bibliography: p.
  Includes index.
  ISBN 0–520–06370-8 (alk. paper)
  1. Spanish literature—Women authors—History and criticism.
2. Spanish literature—19th century—History and criticism.
3. Romanticism—Spain.   4. Subjectivity in literature.   5. Self in
literature.   6. Literature and society—Spain.   I. Title.
PQ6048.W6K5   1989
860'.9'9287—dc19   88–22740

Printed in the United States of America

1   2   3   4   5   6   7   8   9

For Rosemary

Contents

Acknowledgments

This book has been for me an exciting voyage of discovery, but in no sense a solitary one. I have learned so much from so many and received nourishment and help of so many different kinds that I can here only acknowledge the most urgent of my debts.

I am grateful to the University of California, whose aid enabled me to carry out the research necessary for this project, and to the John Simon Guggenheim Memorial Foundation for financial support while I completed the manuscript. A section of chapter 7 appeared as "On the Threshold of the Realist Novel: Gender and Genre in *La gaviota*," *P.M.L.A.* 98 (1983): 323–340. Also, a portion of chapter 1 has come out in a different form as "Spanish Romanticism," in *Romanticism in National Context,* edited by Roy Porter and Mikulás Teich (Cambridge: Cambridge University Press, 1988), pp. 360–383.

For their sustained and unstinting help with all stages of this manuscript, for their wisdom and their loving encouragement, I thank Page DuBois, Lori Chamberlain, Julie Hemker, Stephanie Jed, and Kathryn Shevelow. I owe much gratitude also to Carlos Blanco, Alda Blanco, and Nancy Armstrong for their useful comments on parts of the manuscript. I want to thank too all those from whom I have learned through both the written and the spoken word: Bridget Aldaraca, Alicia Andreu, Nancy Armstrong, Edward Baker, Pepe Escobar, David Gies, Geraldine Scanlon, and particularly my dear friend Cora Kaplan.

Without the propelling faith of Darwin Berg, and his unflagging enthusiasm and support, this project would probably not have been attempted and certainly not completed. I thank him and also my son, Taylor, whose presence lit the writing of this book with joy. How shall I thank my mother? Perhaps she, who through countless maternal attentions brought me into social being, will glimpse somewhere in this book the dim contours of her own desire.

Introduction

The Romantic Self and Gender

In 1841, after centuries of silence broken only intermittently by exceptional voices—such as those of Saint Teresa in the sixteenth century and Josefa Amar y Borbón in the eighteenth—Spanish women began to make themselves heard. That year witnessed a small but noticeable burst of publication that was to grow during the next decades into a steady and broadening flow of writing by hundreds of female authors. Thus women began to assert themselves as producers of written discourse precisely at the peak of the Romantic movement and of a first wave of liberal reform in Spain: that is, precisely when a new language for representing the individual subject and defining gender offered women a justification for taking up the pen. My purpose in this book is to investigate the problematic of subjectivity and gender within which the beginnings of a Spanish tradition of women's writing took shape.

The emergence of female authorship depended on a complex of factors particular to Spain. Economic, political, and cultural forces all played a role in the coincidence of female authorship, Romanticism, and liberalism in Spain. As we shall see in chapters 1 and 2, economic pressures exerted by the Napoleonic War and the loss of Spain's colonial empire brought about liberal reforms that found cultural support in Romanticism and enabled the expansion of the Spanish press industry, which in turn incorporated female readers and writers as a way of expanding its market. This study, however, will focus mainly on the

1

representation of social relationships in written discourse, seeking in a broad spectrum of writing practices the elements that incited Spanish women of the 1840s to break their silence and present themselves as writing subjects. I will argue that the vast rearrangement of social structures in late eighteenth-century Europe brought with it a shift in definitions of gender difference and a new way of representing and experiencing subjectivity that opened a channel through which women could assert themselves as producers of print culture.

The model of female difference that emerged in a number of eighteenth-century discourses, ranging from medical science and conduct books to Rousseau's rethinking of the natural and the social, gave rise to a new bourgeois image of woman as the angelic arbiter of domestic relations. This norm, while it enclosed women within the patriarchal household, gave them an unprecedented though limited and strictly regulated authority in language.[1] The valorization of individual subjectivity and of imaginative self-expression that culminated in the Romantic movement combined with the rising feminine norm to encourage female writing. However, in the woman-authored texts inspired by this conjunction, the cultural model of femininity interacted with the Romantic paradigms of selfhood in complex patterns of concurrence and contradiction that put into circulation a distinct, feminized language of the self.

The early nineteenth-century discursive formations within which images of the self and of gender difference were constructed extended throughout Europe—throughout the West, indeed—even though national language and history modified them in each particular instance. Thus, while the late emergence of women writers in the Spanish press is a local fact of Spanish history, the representational forms that stimulated Spanish women to write derived from broad international social and cultural movements. It will be necessary, therefore, to start our study of subjectivity and gender in early nineteenth-century Spain with a discussion of the broader European context of the Romantic elaboration of subjectivity. The benefits of such a procedure will not go all one way, however: if general European social and literary paradigms enhance our understanding of Spanish writing in the 1830s and 1840s, so too does a particularly Spanish phenomenon—the late appearance of women writers in Spain—compel us to explore revealing connections among liberal ideology, Romantic images of the self, and gender difference in European culture as a whole. In such a context, in fact, the writing of Spain's women poets will itself be seen as a contribution to European Romanticism, supplying rare examples in the poetic genres of women's appropriation and rewriting of Romantic lyrical language.

CULTURAL REVOLUTION

The clash of radically different modes of daily life and thinking accompanied the decisive political and economic conflicts of the late eighteenth century, constituting what Fredric Jameson calls a cultural revolution.[2] The multileveled phenomenon we think of as the Western Enlightenment, Jameson observes,

> may be grasped as part of a properly bourgeois cultural revolution, in which the values and the discourses, the habits and the daily space, of the *ancien régime* were systematically dismantled so that in their place could be set the new conceptualities, habits and life forms, and value systems of a capitalist market society. (96)

The emerging social forms and ways of thinking, in fact, produced a new concept of the self, a new kind of subjectivity, one that lies at the heart of the literary phenomenon we shall be examining. For at the level of language, the revolutionary process produced intricately interrelated new ways of representing both the self and gender difference, in liberal discourse, in fiction, and in Romantic writing.

Of the cultural transformations that shaped subjective experience and the conceptualization of the self, one of the most important was the social atomization that followed from the breakup of traditional communities. New forms of production disrupted the older way of life, detaching people from guilds, peasant communities, and extended families and drawing them into wage contracts or competitive enterprise. The field of human activity was consequently reorganized into two distinct areas: the public arena of production, market, and the state, where human beings functioned as equivalent units interrelated by money and contract; and the private world of blood or love relationships, which contained those aspects of human experience cast out of the increasingly rationalized, reified productive and political processes.

The history of the family dramatically manifests this shift. According to Philippe Ariès, in earlier modes of family life, living space had been open to various kinds of work and social activity in which servants and guests mingled indiscriminately with members of the extended family, while children and parents, the nucleus we now define as "family," were frequently dispersed among different households for economic, educational, or political reasons. By contrast, when the modern form of the family emerged, the home became a privatized space, enclosing the nuclear group of parents and children in a bond defined as unlike other social ties. Lawrence Stone, in part 5 of his study of the family in England, pursues the issue of the affective ties within the family and argues that only with the eighteenth century did loving, intense, and exclusive relations between spouses and parent and child become firmly established as the norm in England; on the Continent it did not occur until even later. The socialization and daily life of a member of the middle or upper classes, then, separated a private realm of intimacy, nurturing, and feeling from the rest of social relations, which might come under such categories as work, business, political economy, public life, or "history." Such a separation promoted the tendency to think in terms of a distinct inner self containing emotions and fantasies that had no place in the outer world. The radical division of life into intimate and public spheres was also closely linked to an emerging system of sexual difference that identified femininity exclusively with the private world of domesticity.

The spread of the values roughly designated as the Protestant ethic also connected the economic forces leading to a new mode of production with how people throughout Europe felt themselves to exist as subjects. If the ethic of hard work, thrift, and honesty worked in synergistic harmony with early stages of capitalist development as Max Weber shows in *The Protestant Ethic and the Spirit of Capitalism,* another aspect of Protestantism—individualism—combined with the breakup of traditional social structures in shaping a new subjectivity. Although a set of quite diverse religious tendencies and movements are grouped together under the rubric of Protestantism, they are linked in their impact on cultural forms by an emphasis on the validity of individual conscience, personal judgment, and inner response in moral and religious matters. This focus on the individual led on the one hand to insistence on the autonomy of the inner self expressed as the demand for "freedom of conscience" and on the other hand to the cultivation of introspection as a means of assessing the authentic movements of the soul.

As changes in the family and the spread of Protestant values reinforced the construct of an autonomous inner self in the emerging bourgeois society, that construct became a basic principle of the theoretical systems that supported and promoted revolutionary change. The eighteenth-century economic and political writing that formed the basis of liberal theory postulated the individual as a primary unit in the description of social phenomena. Individual agents and their interests lay at the heart of classic liberal political economy, which conceptualized the market operations that determined value in terms of an impartial mechanism mediating the actions of individuals. The "rights of man," principles that would provide political protection for the self-motivated autonomy of the private self, seemed "self-evident" to the extent that a person's inner core was held to be separate and inviolable. While these concepts of individual autonomy and inviolability justified such fundamental aspects of capitalism as absolute ownership of property, they also generated radical arguments for universal liberty and equality that became widely influential in the various revolutions at the end of the century.

Liberal theory viewed the self as an essentially gender-neutral rational subject, subordinated by nature to no external social authority. Insofar as ideas of individual autonomy did not distinguish between the sexes, the same arguments that refuted a monarch's claim to divinely ordained sovereignty over peoples could be marshaled against the male sex's supposed authority over the female. Mary Wollstonecraft, uniting the liberal belief in rationality with the Protestant view of the authority of the inner self, asserted in A Vindication of the Rights of Women that

> I love man as my fellow; but his sceptre, real, or usurped, extends not to me, unless the reason of an individual demands my homage; and even then the submission is to reason, and not to man. In fact, the conduct of an accountable being must be regulated by the operations of its own reason; or on what foundation rests the throne of God? (53)

Thus the rhetorical terms of the struggle against absolute monarchy—"sceptre" and "homage" versus "reason" and accountability—were used to characterize the existing relations between men and women, as the feminism that emerged with the Enlightenment and the French Revolution applied the liberatory implications of the new concept of the individual to the female half of the human race.

Although feminists in revolutionary Paris extended this logic to claim for women the full political rights of the citizen, most eighteenth-century feminist writing confessed only to the more modest aim of seeking intellectual and moral independence for women. (Even the radical Wollstonecraft hedged on the issue of political representation for women: "I may excite laughter, by dropping a hint, which I mean to pursue, some future time, for I really think women ought to have representatives" [68].) The view that women had a right to develop their minds and express their ideas, backed up by the fact that in parts of Europe women were writing and publishing in considerable numbers, gained wide currency toward the end of the eighteenth century. Such ideas cropped up even in Spain during the strongly reactionary period that followed the French Revolution. A letter from the early 1890s shows the Cádiz merchant Nicolás Boehl von Faber trying to discourage his fiancée's interest in intellectual endeavor and begging her to burn her copy of Wollstonecraft's *Rights of Women*.[3]

Susan Moller Okin has shown in detail how sentimental ideals of the family and of women's "natural" domesticity made it possible for some of the most prestigious philosophers of the eighteenth century— Rousseau, Kant, Hegel, James Mill—to flout their own basic principles in justifying women's political subordination.[4] The intellectual grounds for deflecting the feminist bid for complete equality during this period of cultural revolution were also implicit in the Enlightenment's reinterpretation of the biological facts of sexual difference. Thomas Laqueur makes a persuasive argument that the eighteenth century significantly revised an earlier model of sexual difference. From antiquity onward, he argues, the female body was regarded as an inferior version of the male model of perfect humanity; women's physical inferiority mirrored their moral and intellectual deficits, which justified their subordinate position in society. Laqueur shows, however, that Enlightenment biology and thinking in general began to stress the differences between the sexes, seeing them as essentially unalike:

> [A] new model of incommensurability triumphed over the old hierarchical model in the wake of new political agendas. Writers from the eighteenth century onward sought in the facts of biology a justification for cultural and political differences between the sexes. . . . Arguments about the very existence of female sexual passion, about women's special capacity to control what desires they did have, and about their moral nature generally were all part of a new enterprise seeking to discover the anatomical and physiological characteristics that distinguished men from women. (18)

Londa Schiebinger documents in anatomical drawings of the human skeleton a striking example of this shift: only in the latter half of the eighteenth century were specifically female skeletons drawn, and these drawings exaggerated the differences between the male and female anatomy (58–59). The female body was represented no longer as an imperfect version of the male but as the perfect instrument of women's "natural" function—maternity. Jean-Jacques Rousseau, who was not only a fundamental source of liberal theory but also a prime exponent of the new concept of the self, articulated the new view of sexual difference as a moral and social imperative in his influential *Émile*: because nature made women inherently different from men, suiting them physically, morally, and intellectually to their primary task of reproduction, he asserted, their education, their activity, their place in society should reflect this difference by channeling natural feminine instincts into civilized domesticity.

The reinterpretation of the female body by Enlightenment medical science and by Rousseau and his followers legitimized the development of a characteristically bourgeois ideology of womanhood, with its corresponding social practices. Consonant with all the social changes and struggles that were in the process of producing the nuclear family as the dominant norm, Rousseau's image of the woman utterly devoted to the duties and joys of motherhood, to the physical and moral welfare of her family, quickly became the accepted feminine ideal. In France after the Revolution, even aristocratic women abandoned their formerly powerful public role of courtiers to become models of domesticity, partly to help restore the credit of the nobility during the French Restoration, according to Margaret Darrow. That powerful nineteenth-century stereotype of feminine identity, whose English version Virginia Woolf called the "Angel in the House" (58–60) after a poem by Coventry Pattmore, formed along lines set down in the late eighteenth century. The Angel's main characteristics stressed her subordinate complementarity to men: whereas men were capable of grand endeavors, intellectual, political, military, that linked their self-interest to the universal good, the true woman was finely, selflessly, and almost exclusively attuned to the needs and feelings of her domestic circle. The idea that while men were affected by sexual passion, women were designed to experience maternal tenderness but not sexual desire was one of the most universally accepted propositions of the new ideology of gender; as Nancy Cott observes in her essay on "passionlessness," both feminists and social conservatives found it advantageous to deny female sexuality.

The success of the burgeoning new ideology of female difference served as an effective justification for maintaining male political dominion over women, but it had rather ambiguous, even contradictory consequences in the emergent discourse of subjectivity that supplemented and concretized the abstract rational subject of liberal discourse. Within the eighteenth-century cult of sensibility and sentiment grew a language of psychological response, of sensation and feeling as individual experience, a language that supplied a representation of the complex experience of the newly important individual. As the ideology of difference between the sexes intersected with the various modes of representing the subject, it carved them into gender-associated fields. The ancient association of analytic and creative intellectual processes with male subjectivity and emotional processes with female subjectivity is well documented in the cultural history of the eighteenth and nineteenth centuries. To this, as we have just seen, the eighteenth century added another differentiation with important consequences for women writers in the early nineteenth century: the delegation of sexual passion to men, tenderness to women. Although this sexual division of the attributes of the psyche dovetailed with the broad tendencies of bourgeois culture to define women according to their reproductive function and confine them to the domestic circle, it nevertheless had the effect of granting a certain kind of female authority. If feeling was a feminine specialty, if the loving and restorative spirit of the home was identical with the female psyche, then women surely had something to say in the forging of a language to represent the full range of subjective experience. The authority conferred upon bourgeois women by the system of gender difference was limited and carefully circumscribed, but it was real.

The conjunction of forces that both preserved patriarchal power and opened a new space of authority for the feminine is nicely summarized in Terry Eagleton's study of *Clarissa*:

> The decline of the relatively open, impersonal system of traditional kinship, with its primarily economic and genealogical rather than affective bonds, has produced by Richardson's era a considerably more closed, "nuclear" family, whose patriarchal structure reinforces an authoritarian state and fulfills some of the religious functions traditionally performed by the church. The other face of this despotic patriarchy is a deepening of emotional ties between men and women, the emergence of new forms of subjectivity of which the birth of "childhood," the hymning of spiritual companionship within marriage and the proliferating cults of "sentiment" and "sensibility" are major signs. (14)

Referring to Jean H. Hagstrum's study of the cult of feeling and tenderness in the fine arts of the eighteenth century, Eagleton concludes that bourgeois culture adopts these "feminine" values in opposition to certain aspects of aristocratic culture:

By the time of Sir Charles Grandison, a wholesale "domestication of heroism" has been effected: the barbarous values of militarism, naked dominance and male hauteur, badges of a predatory public aristocracy, have been
mollified by the fashionable virtues of uxoriousness, sensibility, civility and
tendresse. Pity, pathos and the pacific, "womanly" qualities suppressed by
a warring nobility, become the hallmarks of a bourgeoisie whose economic
goals seem best guaranteed by political tranquillity. (15)

Bourgeois culture's revaluation of the womanly and domestic modes of
experience, arising with the nuclear family, possessive individualism,
and Protestant ideology, is also linked with the late eighteenth century's
turn to the subjective, as Eagleton notes (15). Cultural revolution, in
redefining gender differences as well as individual subjectivity, brought
multiple and sometimes dissonant forces to bear on the literary representation of the individual subject.

ROMANTIC SUBJECTIVITY

We can better perceive the elusive unity of Romanticism by approaching it from the perspective of its function in the cultural revolution initiated in the eighteenth century but continuing with the
massive social readjustments of the early nineteenth century. In no moment of transformation whose traces are still accessible to us has the
role of literary activity been so clearly implicated in the formation of
subjectivity. Despite the striking variations among individual writers
and national schools, the identifying feature of the Romantic movement is its grounding in the subjective. Indeed, writing of one of the
movement's earliest, trend-setting poets, Harold Bloom observes that
"Wordsworth's Copernican revolution in poetry is marked by the evanescence of any subject but subjectivity" ("Quest-Romance" 8). To be
sure, this is an extreme formulation of the Romantics' self-reflexive impetus, for their quest to integrate the subject and locate its sovereign
place in the total scheme of things necessarily and voraciously drew the
non-self of society or nature into their writing. But the center, the or-
ganizing principle, is the subject, conceived as an individual self. And
Romanticism's part in the formation of bourgeois culture was precisely
that: to figure subjectivity as individual self, in a form and content
through which readers could interpret their immediate and concrete experience in terms of the scheme that distinguished the perceiving, desiring subject from the surrounding social and physical world.

The appearance around the turn of the eighteenth century of the first of the artistic productions that we class together as the Romantic movement was, insofar as these productions adopted the expression of feeling as their objective, an extension of the "feminizing" trend in bourgeois culture. But the Romantic self was also built on aspects of the liberal subject that the redefinition of gender difference had subtly denied to women: both the implicit imperiousness of the liberal subject, arbiter of right, wrong, truth, and falsehood, and its liberatory interests were carried to passionate extremes in the Romantic "I." In articulating multiple elements making up the new individual subject, Romanticism claimed for its image of a whole self a range of psychological territory that included areas of desire proscribed to women by the emergent definitions of feminine subjectivity. The "gendered eighteenth-century psychic economy," Cora Kaplan observes, allows men "a roomier and more accommodating psychic home, one which can, as Wordsworth and other Romantics insisted, situate all the varieties of passion and reason in creative tension," whereas in women the appearance of any sexualized sensibility was the mark of a degraded and vitiated subjectivity ("Pandora's Box" 158). Consequently, the position of the female subject in relation to the Romantic elaboration of a language of subjectivity was contradictory: on the one hand, the new aesthetic movement seemed to encourage women's participation by valorizing feeling and individuality, but on the other hand, women found it difficult to assume the many attributes of Romantic selfhood that conflicted with the norm tying feminine identity to lack of desire. Before considering in what forms and with what results women writers of the early nineteenth century appropriated the paradigms of subjectivity that informed Romantic writing, however, let us characterize those paradigms in greater detail.

The Romantics' commitment to making the individual subject the standpoint from which the world was viewed gave the movement a deeply introspective character. In rewriting inward existence and self-identity, the Romantics discovered and described a myriad of psychological processes and effects.[5] Seeking to include within the single psychic space of the individual self the libidinous and irrational impulses that earlier psychological schemes had attempted to eliminate from the true self—soul or reason—Romantic literature provided the first in a continuing series of charts to represent the ever-deepening tides and currents of the psychic space. Indeed, Bloom makes a pointed parallel between Freud and certain Romantic writers: "I think that what Blake and Wordsworth do for their readers, or can do, is closely related to what Freud does or can do for his, which is to provide both a map of the mind and a profound faith that the map can be put to a saving use" ("Quest-Romance" 3).

But the Romantics' claim was not just that they brought the intricacies of inner being to light but that their maps of the mind were also somehow mirrors of the infinite. A corollary of their determinedly individualistic stance was that the universal could be reflected within the single subject. The self, then, must expand to encompass the outside. As J. H. Van den Berg describes the process:

> The inner self, which in Rousseau's time was a simple, soberly filled, airy space, has become ever more crowded. . . . The inner life was [by the nineteenth century] like a haunted house. But what else could it be? It contained everything. Everything extraneous had been put into it. The entire history of mankind had to be the history of the individual. Everything that had previously belonged to everybody, everything that had been collective property and had existed in the world in which everyone lived, had to be contained by the individual. (61–62)

As a rewriting of the distinction self/non-self, then, the self that the Romantics regarded as being both a center from which to understand the universe and a space requiring exploration was a heterogeneous and inherently unstable construct.

To say that the relations of self and non-self were constructed through artistic activity is simply to state a basic principle of Romantic aesthetics. Tilottama Rajan points out that "the ideals of the Romantic movement are . . . closely bound up with a belief in the transforming power of aesthetic activity. . . . Art, as the power to invent, is paradigmatic of man's capacity to take existence itself into his mind and rewrite it according to the images of desire" (13). But it is not only reality that the Romantic poet defines, transforms, creates in "his" texts, for the poetic process also brings the defining and creative self into being. The dominant and desiring center of consciousness that refashions existence in Romantic texts is the ultimate "image of desire" projected by the poem.

The self represented by the Romantic text, then, is inevitably the writing subject in the process of constructing itself. Indeed, the text's enactment of the struggle to subordinate all aspects of libidinal impulse to the subject of aesthetic activity becomes so intense in English poetry that Bloom can affirm that "the creative process is the hero of Romantic poetry, and imaginative inhibitions, of every kind, necessarily must be the antagonists of the poetic quest" ("Quest-Romance" 9). Even Geoffrey H. Hartman, a critic who does not see self-reflexivity as the final goal of Romantic writing, argues that much Romantic writing records the effort to surmount alienating self-consciousness through the powers of imagination—that is, the mental power to internalize and reconstruct the outer world: "To explore the transition from self-consciousness to imagination, and to achieve that transition while exploring it (and so to prove it still possible) is the Romantic purpose I find most crucial" (53). These critics see at the heart of Romantic literature the representation of the process that orders subjectivity and the world under the unifying power of the poetic self.

If Romantic writing textualizes the search for an autonomous, ordering self, it is underwritten by the assumption of an analogy between art and experience. Indeed, the complexity that permits the interdependent coexistence of Romantic sentimentality and Romantic irony arises from the double message of this assumption: impassioned Romantic sincerity proclaims that art can be the equivalent of experience, while Romantic irony plays with the gap between the two. Constructing a lack in experience as a being in art, the Romantic "identified" with the created textual image, sometimes with a high degree of self-consciousness, sometimes not. Consequently, the Romantic text encourages the reader to confuse the writer as a person with the text-created subject of writing or of action—the lyrical "I" or the protagonist. The openly autobiographical claims of *The Prelude* fomented the identification of the poem's subject with Wordsworth; other works more obliquely suggested that their protagonists were autobiographical projections of the authors, that René was Chateaubriand and Manfred Lord Byron. But at the same time, the irreducible gap between experience and art creates an area of slippage between the person of the author and the persona of the text. The residue of noncoincidence between actual individual experience and textual image permitted a certain fluidity of meaning for the figured subject: as a semi-admitted fiction, it could be read as the image of a collective desire, a generalized subjectivity, as well as the self-representation of an individual.

The relative openness of the Romantic representation of the subject, despite its identification with a particular individual's experience, can be illustrated with an example from the earliest phase of the movement. Discussing the trend-setting impact of *Die Leiden des jungen Werther*, David Morse observes:

It is of course true that Werther embodies a new type of personality. . . . But, as has often been recognized, Werther is not really a novelistic character, but rather the dramatisation of the state of subjectivity, in a manner which owes much to Sterne. . . . The recognition that such things as concepts of the self and notions of identity are not purely given in experience, but must of necessity be arrived at and worked through intellectually, is a precondition for reading this otherwise problematic work. (164–165)

This reading of the novel spells out very clearly for us the relationships among individual experience, general subjectivity, and the necessarily aesthetic construction of self-identity that make up the Romantic representation of the individual subject. In this sense, early nineteenth-century writing retained something of the social openness that, according to Marilyn Butler, characterized the eighteenth-century literature of sensibility, which, interested above all in eliciting reader identification, was "affective and emotional without seeming private" (30).[6] That openness disappears from the Romantics' late nineteenth-century successors, for whom the inner self has become utterly disjoined not only from external time and activity but also from any transindividual modes of desire.

Though tending toward solipsism, then, the Romantics represented the subject as something more than a completely particularized being whose generality consists only of its conformity to laws of psychology or physics. Jameson points out the fluid interplay of subjectivity among biographical, fictional, and narrating subjects in an early novel of Balzac, characterizing the constitutive narrative strategies of *La vieille fille* as "a wish-fulfilling or fantasy investment that dissolved the biographical into the Utopian" and characterizing a corresponding lack of a centered subject as narrative point of view (169). Arguing that such novelistic features corresponded to a moment of cultural history "before the full constitution of the bourgeois subject and the omnipresent effects of massive reification" (170), Jameson compares *La vieille fille* with the naturalist narrative of a later moment of history, which manifests "a decisive development in the construction of the subject, . . . the constitution of the latter into a closed monad, henceforth governed by the laws of 'psychology'" (160). Although Jameson concedes that Balzac's later novels move in the direction of this monadic subjectivity, his analysis of *La vieille fille* suggests that the earlier works, deeply imbued with Romanticism, show us a stage in the conformation of the bourgeois subject in which the inner self and the outer world were still conceived in terms of a paradoxical, difficult, but thinkable interdependence and in which the images of desire were simultaneously autobiographical, fictitious, and collective.

The underlying structure of the Romantic self was figured in three interrelated archetypes to which most heroes and poetic self-images of the movement corresponded: the Promethean transgressor of the barriers to desire, the superior and socially alienated individual, and the self-divided consciousness. Once we have outlined some of the social and political as well as the aesthetic and psychological meanings of these figures of the self, we will be in a position to consider their implications for the gendered writing or reading subject.

In speaking of the Romantic impulse to "rewrite" existence in the "images of desire" or of the "utopian investment" of a Romantic novelist, Rajan and Jameson are reiterating the crucial insight of the Romantic philosopher *par excellence*. In *Philosophy of Fine Art*, Hegel characterized Romantic art—by which he did not mean exactly the same thing we do—as the externalization of desire, consciousness's "appetitive relation" to the world of objects. Indeed, desire is fundamental to the Romantic representation of the self. Besides basing their map of the psyche on the contours of desire, the Romantics made desire the core of an archetypal figure of the self. Linked to Prometheus and Lucifer, this figure provides an identity, a center, for images of the appetitive impulse and its struggle against a resistant world. The Romantic rebel is one form of the Promethean self; the irrepressible energy of the rebel's desire, demanding liberty and power, bursts constraints of any sort, political, aesthetic, physical, and moral. This model, cast as the protagonist of Romantic works from *The Four Zoas* to *Prometheus Unbound,* was also the identity often adopted by the writing subject and indeed, given the tendency to conflate the two, by the biographical author.

In Lord Byron, the most notorious conflater of biographical and literary identities, we see the coincidence of the erotic and the political in Romantic Prometheanism. He also provides an excellent example of the porousness that allows the seepage of the collective and the historical into the individual in the Romantic subject. Bloom points out how Napoleon, considered the historical personification of Prometheus by most Romantics, inspired in Byron one of the clearest formulations of the Promethean self:

> there is a fire
> And motion of the soul which will not dwell

> In its own narrow being, but aspire
> Beyond the fitting medium of desire;
> And, but once kindled, quenchless evermore,
> Preys upon high adventure, nor can tire
> Of aught but rest; a fever at the core
> Fatal to him who bears, to all who ever bore.

Citing these verses from the third canto of *Childe Harold's Pilgrimage*, Bloom observes, "Clearly this is another portrait of Byron himself, as much as it is of Napoleon" (*Ringers* 82). Not only does this passage show the capacity of Romantic self-figuration to encompass a literary persona, a historical figure, and mankind as a whole, but it also reveals the negative aspect of the myth that is assimilated by the Promethean self: just as the rebellious overreaching of the Titan and his counterpart, Lucifer, condemns them to eternal pain and punishment, so the subject of quenchless Romantic desire bears a fatal fever. Indeed, the self figured as Prometheus/Lucifer incorporates desire's basic paradox: existing as a lack in relation to its object, desire can never coincide with its goal. So the Romantic desiring subject, represented as a rebel against the limitations of the objective world, fails ever in its quest to impose its own image on reality.

The modalities incorporated in the Promethean self, then, apply as much to the Romantic concept of the poetic process as to the figure of Napoleon or the self-image of Byron. Such a superimposition permitted the Promethean paradigm of subjective experience to be imagined and understood in English literature as a figure related to the shared historical experience of the French Revolution. In a study of this question, Meyer H. Abrams persuasively demonstrates the awareness of a cross section of English Romantics that "the characteristic poetry of the age took its shape from the form and pressure of revolution and reaction" (26). As Abrams goes on to show, that characteristic shape reflected the disappointment of the utopian hopes aroused by the French Revolution during the formative years of the first generation of Romantics. Abrams considers the master text of this connection to be the passage of *The Prelude* that narrates Wordsworth's departure from France in 1890 and the revelation he experiences in the Simplon Pass:

> Man's infinite hopes can never be matched by the world as it is and man as he is, for these exhibit a discrepancy no less than that between his "hopes pointed to the clouds" and the finite height of the Alpine pass. But in the magnitude of the disappointment lies its consolation; for the flash of vision also reveals that infinite longings are inherent in the human spirit, and

that the gap between the inordinacy of his hope and the limits of possibility is the measure of man's dignity and greatness. . . . In short, Wordsworth
evokes from the unbounded and hence impossible hopes in the French Revolution a central Romantic doctrine. (56–57)

And as an integrated image of subjective experience, that doctrine is
figured in the Promethean self that we have seen in Byron and that appears in Blake, Coleridge, and Shelley as well.

Whereas Byron turns to irony from the historical and personal failure of Promethean aspiration, however, the other English Romantic
poets sublimate disappointed desire into a further construction of the
poetic self. This accounts for the triadic movement of Romantic texts
noted by many critics. Hartman, for example, finds that in Romanticism "the traditional scheme of Eden, fall, and redemption merges with
the new triad of nature, self-consciousness, imagination; while the last
term in both involves a kind of return to the first" (54). In terms of
desire, this pattern corresponds to a movement from desire to frustration to a recuperation of the thwarted desire on a higher level, a process most fully described by Bloom in his reading of Romantic poetry
as the internalization of the traditional quest-romance. Bloom views
the Promethean self as a first stage in the quest of ultimate fullness
of being, a phase marked by the self's rebellious struggle against the
obstacles to its libidinal energy: "Generally, Prometheus is the poet-
as-hero in the first stage of his quest, marked by a deep involvement in
political, social and literary revolution" ("Quest-Romance" 11). A crisis ensues, during which the will-to-power over the external social or
natural world is renounced and the self turns inward, seeking a way to
transcend its limitations—its "Selfhood" in Bloom's terms. In the final act, the self discovers its capacity for "imaginative love" in which
"desire is wholly taken up into the imagination" (13). "[T]he outward turning of the triumphant Imagination . . . [completes] a dialectic
of love by uniting the Imagination with its bride, who is a transformed
ongoing creation of the Imagination rather than a redeemed nature"
(17).

In English male-authored poetry, then, the construction of the desiring self tends to follow a pattern that subsumes the personal, historical,
and cosmic possibilities of the Romantic Promethean figure within the
aesthetic aspirations of the writing subject, represented in the text as
the lyrical self. As we shall see shortly, this paradigm, which identifies
the female with the *object* of creative powers while centering the creative self on an "unfeminine" overweening desire, could not easily be

adopted by female writers. And even in male poets of the early nineteenth century, the triumph of subjectivity figured in the creative powers of a self that transcends external and internal limitations through
imagination rarely remained unqualified: when not presented as a
glimpsed potentiality, that triumph was represented as a discontinuous
moment of epiphany. Reservations about the artistic ego's ability to
transcend the barriers to creative desire were figured even more clearly
in Romantic archetypes of alienation.

Alienation is a fundamental aspect of the Romantic self, according
to Bloom:

> The figure of the Solitary, in *The Excursion,* is the central instance of the
> most fundamental of Romantic archetypes, the man alienated from others
> and himself by excessive self-consciousness. Whatever its poetic lapses, *The
> Excursion* is our most extensive statement of the Romantic mythology of
> the Self. (*Ringers* 91)

This version of the self emphasizes the radical distinction involved in
separating an inner subjectivity from an outer world of things. The self
is defined in terms of its difference from external reality—its acute sensitivity versus the insensitivity of the world (either social or natural),
its self-consciousness versus the simple existence of things or others, its
yearning aspirations versus the brute presence of reality. Whereas the
Promethean self centers on desire in relation to its object, the solitary
self is constructed upon the unbridgeable gap between them.

In English poetry, the solitary subject's alienation is often represented in relation to nature, but on the Continent the world from which
the self is alienated tends to be social or historical. Goethe's socially ill-
adapted Werther is certainly one of the earliest examples of the alienated, self-conscious mode of subjectivity embodied in the Solitary. An
early French counterpart can be seen in Chateaubriand's René, whose
loneliness, melancholy, and inexplicable uneasiness in society as it is
characterizes the paradigmatic ailment of the alienated Romantic self—
the *mal du siècle,* the aching dissatisfaction with the modern age. In
this formulation, the subject withdraws from the surrounding historical world, representing itself as both the victim of a hostile society
and the superior soul who rejects society's inadequacy. The self that
experiences *mal du siècle* becomes absorbed in introspection, for its
fascination with the interior play of fantasy, impulse, and emotion
compensates for the pain of its frustration and solitude. Such a characterization may become self-consciously perverse, as is the case with

Octave, Musset's self-fictionalization—again the Romantic conflation of aesthetic construct and personal existence—in *La confession d'un enfant du siècle,* of whom Lilian Furst observes:

> In spite of his frequent tears, he is so totally self-centered, so "renfermé dans ma solitude" that he is quite incapable of any real feeling towards other people and in this sense he becomes a victim of his own character, when his inability to give love, his cruelty, his capriciousness, his cynicism, his suspiciousness bring nothing but unhappiness. (110)

Furst notes that when Octave is compared with René, the deepened isolation of Musset's self-representation can be seen to correspond to a greater tendency toward exhibitionism. Both this perversity and this exhibitionism illuminate the connection of the *enfant du siècle* with the subjective impact of shared historical experience that is incorporated in Romantic self-constructions.

In his monumental work, *Balzac et le mal du siècle,* Pierre Barbéris demonstrates how the alienation of Musset's generation, the children of the new century, grew out of their dissatisfaction with the social conditions of post-Revolutionary France. By 1830 the gap between Revolutionary ideals and the emerging liberal establishment had become painfully apparent to a generation raised in hope of new individual possibilities and a transformed society:

> The *mal de siècle* is the consciousness of a dissonance between Man and History when History, the domain of energy, now called into question and liberated from the traditional imperatives, screens itself and lies. . . . Something important happened that mobilized hearts and minds, that gave energies a direction. And then, on the scene of the old exploits, a half-finished world established itself. Some men had established themselves, satisfied, dominant, complacent. But the youth in contrast held on to the memory of something intense. (112)[7]

When the Prometheanism of a past revolutionary moment appeared fraudulent, one course open to the new generation was to construct a self that emphasized the difference between a disappointing historical world and an interiority that preserved intensity even at the cost of perverse cultivation of unhappiness. The exhibitionism that Furst notes in Musset thus corresponds to the impulse to display to a degraded historical world the internalized forms of energy and intensity it has lost. This construction of the self, however, allows no transcendence through creative imagination; in denying the very possibility of unity between self and world, the subject retains only the desires and energies frustrated by History and condemned to dispersion and incompletion. The self-constructing activity of the alienated Romantic reveals the degeneration of the totalizing aspiration found in Wordsworth or Blake. As Barbéris puts it, "To live a great love, to have a splendid career: these derived from Promethean desires condemned to slip from the universal to the partial" (130).

Lord Byron comes to mind in this regard, in his aspect as the ironic narrator of *Don Juan*. Indeed, Byron's second persona perfectly illustrates how defining the poetic self in terms of its alienation leads to Romantic irony as an aesthetic mode in much the same way that a self that refuses to relinquish Promethean desire tends to adopt the Romantic doctrine of the imagination. A construction of the subject-object relationship that founds itself on separation, distance, incompleteness becomes an ironic consciousness when it attempts to transcend self-pity. Peter Szondi, explicating Friedrich Schlegel, succinctly describes how ironic consciousness is generated:

> The subject of romantic irony is the isolated, alienated man who has become the object of his own reflection and whose consciousness has deprived him of his ability to act. He nostalgically aspires toward unity and infinity; the world appears to him divided and finite. . . . In an ever-expanding act of re-flection he tries to establish a point of view beyond himself and to resolve the tension between himself and the world on the level of fiction. He cannot overcome the negativity of his situation by means of an act in which the reconciliation of finite achievement with infinite longing could take place. (Qtd. in de Man 201; trans. de Man)

The alienated subject who adopts the stance of the ironist, however, accomplishes a more positive self-creation than Szondi's interpretation would allow, according to Paul de Man, who points out that Schlegel gives the name of freedom to the potentially infinite progression of the mind from one "self-escalating act of consciousness" to another (202).

Thus the processes of consciousness utilized by the alienated self constructed as ironist have a function analogous to that of the imag-ination in the case of the Promethean self. Both serve the aspiration of the self to escape the dilemmas of its relation to the non-self, but with this difference: imagination seeks the illusion of wholeness and of rec-onciliation, while irony makes the potentially infinite regression of self-differentiation the basis of the self's creative freedom. Indeed, as de Man points out, the process of ironic disjunction takes place via lan-guage, which "divides the subject into an empirical self, immersed in the world, and a self that becomes like a sign in its attempt at differen-tiation and self-definition" (196). The ironic self, then, knows itself as a fiction and via the fiction of verbal representation. Not surprisingly, the form of irony we designate as Romantic is the form *Don Juan* exemplifies so well by calling attention to its own fictitiousness. Yet the Romantic version of the ironist resists that pure modality described by de Man: dissolution "in the narrowing spiral of a linguistic sign that becomes more and more remote from its meaning" (203). Even in the case of Don Juan, despite the poem's refusal to lay claim to any truth beyond its pleasureful self-invention, the narrating subject retains traces of an empirical self that will not recognize itself as only verbal sign. Rajan observes that "the point about Byron is that he too cannot be satisfied with irony, and approaches Juan through the eyes of a narrator whose occasional lapses into sentimentality keep unsettling the poem's commitment to [narrative] realism" (265). Such vacillation reflects the persistent force of Promethean desire at the core of the Romantic construction—no matter how self-conscious—of the self: the possibility of the coincidence of lived experience and history with the aesthetically created self cannot be relinquished.

We see, then, that the Romantics' efforts to articulate subjectivity into a structuring self lead via the alienated self and ironic consciousness to ever more heterogeneous and unstable figures of the self. Indeed, the self-duplicating process of irony is echoed in a third important configuration of the Romantic self—the internally divided subject. On the one hand, the duplication, or division, of the self is inherent in the dialectical process by which it distinguishes itself from the non-self. Hegel speaks in *Phenomenology of Mind* of the mind's breaking up into two regions in order to know itself as pure consciousness.[8] On the other hand, the dual existence of consciousness described in philosophical terms by Hegel emerges in experiential terms as a consequence of the Romantic search for the self in regions of subjectivity other than the processes of intellection.

Arnold Hauser, although unsympathetic with this search, writes suggestively of how it leads to internal duplication when he comments on the recurring Romantic image of the second self:

> The source of this *idée fixe* is unmistakable: it is the irresistible urge to introspection, the maniacal tendency to self-observation and the compulsion to consider oneself over and over again as one unknown, as an uncannily remote stranger. The idea of the "second self" is, of course, again merely an attempt to escape. . . . On this flight from reality, the [the romantic] discovers the unconscious, that which is hidden away in safety from the rational mind, the source of his wish-fulfillment dreams and of the irrational solutions of his problems. (72)

What Hauser characterizes as a flight from reality is not, in my view, finally escapism; it is a movement inward to find a standpoint from which the individual subject may dominate reality. However, Hauser's characterization pinpoints the effects of a search that treats the subjective as unexplored territory: the self-estrangement that creates the double when projected outward imagines inner space as a labyrinth housing unknown powers and mysterious alter egos.

Morse argues, in the chapter "From Protestantism to Romanticism," that the Romantics conceptualized the self as split into a social self and a "deep" self that is somewhat analogous to the Protestants' divine inner light: "Selfhood, and especially the deeper non-social self— Shelley's 'caverns of the spirit'—is the inescapable starting point for a Romantic literature. So much Romantic literature takes the form of an internal dialogue, a communication with the inventive inner spirit" (173). Seeking a basis for the elusive irreducible self, these poets turned to mental processes not under the control of rational consciousness and thus experienced as "other." Therefore, the poetic self that might transcend the boundaries of subjective and objective through its creative activity is constructed as the dialogue of two inner entities—the conscious mind and the unconscious sources of fantasy. If for some, like Wordsworth, that internal otherness was a source of joy inasmuch as it could be integrated into a totalizing creative activity, for others, like Nerval, it represented the self-fragmentation of madness, the impossibility of self-identity.

Indeed, the doubled self of the Romantics leads, in crucial moments of their literary production, to a radical interrogation of the identity of the self—of the identity that would center and order the cosmos. Bloom points out how Shelley's search for the ideal transcendent self (the source, in Bloom's terms, of the imaginative love unifying self and other) falls afoul of the self's multiple identities, which Shelley considers masks:

> [T]he Selfhood's temptations, for Shelley, are subtle and wavering, and mask themselves in the forms of the ideal. So fused do the ideal and these masks become that Shelley, in the last lines he wrote, is in despair of any victory, though it is Shelley's Rousseau and not Shelley himself who actually chants:
>
> > thus on the way
> > Mask after mask fell from the countenance
> > And form of all; and long before the day
> > Was old, the joy which waked like heaven's glance
> > The sleepers in the oblivious valley, died;

And some grew weary of the ghastly dance,
And fell, as I have fallen, by the wayside—

. . . Rousseau speaks here not for himself alone, but for his tradition, and
necessarily for Coleridge, Wordsworth, and the Promethean Shelley as well,
indeed for poetry itself. ("Quest-Romance" 22–23)

Certainly it could be said that the Romantic search of the psyche for
a self that would anchor and center subjectivity led in its ultimate
implications to a "ghastly dance" of masks behind which no identity
emerges. Romantic irony surmounts the failure of the Romantic quest
by making the fictionality of the poetic self into a demystifying knowledge rather than a defeat. For Byron, whose reputation during his
lifetime as the arch-Romantic was in so many ways justified, such
knowledge is a burden to be borne by the Promethean quester, but is
also a liberation: the poet may create and identify with many masks,
make and unmake his own myths, as Byron did.

Thus, we may say that the Romantic construction of the self is
characterized by the unresolved ambivalence in Byron's stance. According to Rajan, "In *Don Juan* he tries to become a modern poet and to
make irony into a modus vivendi. But he succeeds only in raising to a
self-conscious level the cyclical oscillation between the ironic and the
sentimental pervasive in his work" (266). If, on the one hand, the
Romantic self knows itself to be a construct of writing, a verbal sign,
on the other hand, it refuses to become only and purely a sign and insists on its empirical existence as a felt reality. As an element of the
bourgeois cultural revolution, the Romantic movement made a place
within writing for structures of subjectivity that went far beyond the
thinking subject of Cartesian philosophy. The Romantics' poetic self retained the transcendence of the Cartesian subject but libidinized, alienated, and divided it, creating a heterogeneous, expandable construct
that could organize disruptive psychic processes within a fiction of
identity.

Besides providing new images through which personal, poetic, and
historical experience could be assimilated, the Romantic construction
of the self naturalized a basic premise of the new political economy by
taking the autonomous individual as its point of departure. At the same
time, however, as the preceding discussion suggests, other aspects of
Romantic writing had the contrary effect. In pursuing the consequences
of the constituting split of subject from object, many Romantic texts
displayed the inherent paradoxes and contradictions of the concept of

self and thus provided grounds on which the bourgeois subject could be seen as an artificial construct rather than as a natural reality.

Romantic representations of the self also had ambiguous implications with respect to gender. The paradigms of the self that have just been outlined present themselves as incorporating ungendered universal truths of subjective experience—desire's inevitable clash with reality, for example, or imagination's power to transcend limits. The idea that such truths about human experience could be learned through individual introspection rather than from a set of books accessible only to a male elite encouraged women readers to identify with the Romantic enterprise, to identify themselves as active subjects of the quest for the self. However, the forms in which Romantic writing characterized and libidinized the poetic subject strongly conflicted with the dominant feminine norm of domestic womanhood. The Promethean rebel, fired by never-satisfied desire, was almost a polar opposite of the selfless, compliant, passionless feminine ideal, while the Solitary's cultivation of his isolation and difference directly contradicted the domestic angel's commitment to familial interrelationship. Romantic texts themselves tacitly acknowledged the undeniably gendered character of Romantic paradigms of selfhood by identifying them almost exclusively with male figures and coding as feminine those entities that did not represent full, conscious, independent subjects—the beloved, nature, or the poetic creation. The woman writer who responded to the opportunity offered by the Romantic authorization of personal experience and everyday language was thus placed in an untenable position, unable to identify fully with either the masculine poetic and creative subject or with the feminine object. Women writers' solutions to this dilemma both revised the gender exclusivity of the paradigmatic Romantic self, creating a female Romantic tradition, and exposed the inadequacy and the oppressive nature of the domestic angel as the model of feminine subjectivity.

THE FEMALE ROMANTIC TRADITION

That the Romantic canon should be made up almost exclusively of male writers is consistent with the Romantics' own image of the poet, which, as Sandra Gilbert and Susan Gubar point out, incorporates the traditionally close associations among the ideas of "author," "writer," "father," and "universal creator" in our culture:

> Coleridge's Romantic concept of the human "imagination or esemplastic power" is of a virile, generative force which echoes the "eternal act of creation in the infinite I AM." . . . In . . . these aesthetics the poet, like God the Father, is a paternalistic ruler of the fictive world he has created. (5)

If the poetic self the Romantics strove to construct was a godlike orderer of the world, the otherness that he subdued and appropriated through language was identified with women. In her study of nineteenth-century women's struggle for poetic identity in English poetry, Margaret Homans points to the problem posed by this categorization of women:

> In Romantic poetry the self and the imagination are primary. . . . Where the masculine self dominates and internalizes otherness, that other is frequently identified as feminine, whether she is nature, the representation of a human woman, or some phantom of desire. . . . To be so long the other and the object made it difficult for nineteenth-century women to have their own subjectivity. To become a poet, given these conditions, required nothing less than battling a valued and loved literary tradition to forge a self out of the materials of otherness. (12)

It is above all by representing nature as feminine that Romantic poetry equates woman with otherness, with the non-self that confronts the poet's subjectivity in the dialectic of resistance and reconciliation. Taking Wordsworth's treatment of Nature as an example, Homans finds that Mother Nature, as the figure for the feminine, is precisely not the poetic subject, not self-consciousness: "[S]he is valued because she is what the poet is not" (13). Characterized as materiality, diffuseness, unconsciousness, this maternal nature is "prolific biologically, not linguistically" (13). Whereas Wordsworth's poetic self is constituted by the process of separation and differentiation from this all-encompassing maternal body, the female figures in his poetry remain closely linked with nature (20). Northrup Frye indicates just how pervasively nature is identified with the feminine in English Romanticism as a whole:

> We spoke of Wordsworth's Nature as a mother goddess, and her psychological descent from mother-figures is clearly traced in *The Prelude*. The corn-goddess in Keats' *To Autumn,* the parallel figure identified with Ruth in the *Ode to a Nightingale,* the still unravished bride of the Grecian urn, Psyche, even the veiled Melancholy, are all emblems of a revealed Nature. Elusive nymphs or teasing and mocking female figures who refuse to take definite form, like the figure in *Alastor* or Blake's "female will" types; terrible and sinister white goddesses like La Belle Dame sans Merci, or females as-

sociated with something forbidden or demonic, like the sister-lovers of
Byron and Shelley, belong to the concealed aspect [of an ambivalent Na-
ture]. ("Drunken Boat" 21)

Two points may be made about the widespread Romantic use of the
female as a signifier for nature. In the first place, the ambivalence of
the woman/nature sign treated as man's "other" is deeply rooted in
patriarchal culture, as Simone de Beauvoir was perhaps the first to
point out: "In woman man seeks the Other both as Nature and as his
like. But we know what ambivalent feelings Nature inspires in
man. . . . By turns his ally, his enemy, she appears as the dark chaos
from which life springs, as life itself, and as the beyond toward which
it goes" (237). Classing woman with nature in her double aspect, Romantic symbology distances her from the specifically human productiv-
ity of culture. Hence the second point to be noted about Frye's list of
woman/nature symbols—the silence of the female figure, "bride of qui-
etness." Even when a woman figures in the text as a subject, insofar as
she represents the other to whom the poem is addressed, she is silent,
characterized by her receptivity and her absorption in nature, like the
Dorothy of "Lines Composed a Few Miles Above Tinturn Abbey" or
the Sara of Coleridge's "Aeolean Harp." The speaking subjectivity of
Romantic lyricism may respond to woman or to a feminized nature,
but is never hers.

It becomes clear then that the woman writer who situated herself in
any way within Romantic discourse as a writing subject confronted and
challenged a basic premise of that discourse, the premise that located
women outside subjectivity and the production of meaning. Obviously,
some counterdiscourse, some other representation of women in relation
to subjectivity, must have been available to the women who challenged
the gender bias of the Romantic lyrical subject.

One such source of empowerment for women was, as I hinted earlier, the development of a gender system that, in defining women as essentially different from men, endowed them with their own particular
kind of subjectivity, one designed for nurturing children and maintaining the affective ties of the nuclear family. The new domestic image of
woman was, as Nancy Armstrong's study of eighteenth-century English
conduct literature shows, linked with the rejection of aristocratic attitudes that valued women for physical beauty. Comparing passages
from a conduct book describing two competing types of desirable
women, Armstrong calls attention to

the shift in diction that locates power in the mental features of the domestic woman where it was stripped away from the [beautiful] body in the preceding passage. So "compleat," this new woman commands "admiration" as well as "love" where before she deserved only "affection." In this comparison between two desirable women, we are witnessing the fact of cultural change from an earlier form of power based on sumptuary display to a modern form that works through the production of subjectivity. ("Domestic Woman" 119–120)

The power of the new domestic woman, argues Armstrong, was psychological: it was the power to regulate her own and others' desire, producing within the household a space free of conflict, competition, and material concerns, a necessary subjective complement to the marketplace of labor created by the new economic forms of capitalism. The vast number of female ideologists of domesticity, from Maria Edgeworth and Sarah Ellis in England to Mme de Genlis and her ilk in France, attests to the authorization that the new feminine norm extended to women writers as experts in the necessary regulation of a specifically female subjectivity.

The point to be emphasized here is that the new gender scheme allowed women the power of subjectivity only at the cost of curtailing their desire. Laqueur points out that the strains of Enlightenment thought that began to regard women as a civilizing force based this positive female influence on feminine lack of desire: "[W]omen are construed as less passionate and hence morally more adept than men" (23). The link between female passionlessness and women's civilizing or redemptive moral influence reached its apogee throughout Europe in the mid-nineteenth century. Mary Poovey summarizes the strict conditions on which women were granted a small sphere of power:

As embodiments of the pure ideals of the middle classes, [women] were celebrated during the nineteenth century for their superiority to all earthly desires. Depicted as a being completely without sexual desire and delicate to the point of frailty, urged not only to be dependent but to cultivate and display that dependence, the Victorian Angel of the House was to be absolutely free from all corrupting knowledge of the material—and materialistic—world. In her proper sphere, of course, she reigned as queen. (*Proper Lady* 35)

Thus, if the formulation of the domestic feminine ideal provided women writers with a platform of authority from which to challenge the male bias of the Romantic language of subjectivity, that same formulation also decisively foreclosed women's options for assuming the

Promethean aspects of the Romantic self. How to adapt forms of subjectivity constructed upon desire to a female subject authorized by her lack of desire was a crucial problem for every woman writer who situated herself within Romantic discourse. Solutions to this problem constitute a distinct female Romantic tradition.

Nowhere is the contradiction between social norms of femininity and the Romantic modes of selfhood more made more suggestive than in Mary Shelley's *Frankenstein* (1818), which initiates a narrative subgenre and a modern myth. Poovey's reading of the novel shows how Shelley's ambivalence toward female self-assertion structures her rendition of the *Modern Prometheus*. Although in writing the novel Shelley engaged in as daring an act of creation as any of her male contemporaries—who were actively engaged in producing a great many of the canonical English Romantic texts during the same years, 1816–1818—she in fact wrote it against the Romantic cult of the Promethean self, argues Poovey:

> For in the course of her unladylike metaphysical speculations, Shelley explodes the foundations of Romantic optimism by demonstrating that the egotistical energies necessary to self-assertion—energies that appear to her to be at the heart of the Romantic model of the imagination—inevitably imperil the self-denying energies of love. To accommodate this reservation, which implicitly indicts all artistic endeavors as well as more insidious forms of egotism, Shelley essentially feminizes Romantic aesthetics, deriving from her contemporaries' theories strategies that enable her to fulfill her desire for self-expression in an indirect, self-effacing, and therefore acceptable manner. ("Hideous Progeny" 332–333)

Shelley resolves her anxiety about adopting the male persona of creator by demonstrating in her story the destructiveness of departure from the loving domestic web of social relations in which women found their identity. As Poovey's analysis shows, Victor Frankenstein's Promethean desire to transcend human limits, to appropriate the secrets of nature, drives him away from his family and eventually, in the objectified form of the monster, destroys that family, leaving Frankenstein irretrievably isolated and incomplete. Robert Walton, the young explorer who transmits Frankenstein's story, learns its lesson. Although he shares the older scientist's isolating ambition for knowledge and power, "Walton is still capable of redirecting his involuted ambition outward into self-denying love, for Walton has never permitted his desire to escape completely the regulating influence of social relationships" (Poovey, "Hideous Progeny" 340). Thus he accedes to his sailors' wish to abandon the exploration and head south to family and community. The story, then, revises the role of Promethean desire in the configuration of the Romantic self: instead of constituting self-identity, the drive to satisfaction impedes the way to the true, completed sense of self that for Shelley derives from relationship with others.

Furthermore, the form in which Shelley presents herself as a writing subject embodies a relational sense of identity, as Poovey remarks: "The three-part narrative structure enables her to establish her role as an artist through a series of relationships rather than through an act of self-assertion" (339). By avoiding the authorial voice and using the narratives of three of her characters to construct the story, Shelley distances herself from the Romantic tendency toward self-representation within the text as the writing subject, a gesture that seemed to her too assertive for a woman. The function of author or creator in her case is feminized in the sense that it consists of the structuring awareness of the meaningful relationships that tie the three narratives together.

Frankenstein, then, reveals by its radical modifications of the Promethean model the resistant gender-specificity of the supposedly universal Romantic representation of subjectivity. Women writers found it impossible to fit the Procrustean bed laid out by the male Romantic trendsetters; they made adjustments by self-distortion, no doubt, but also, like Mary Shelley, by changing the shape of the bed. If the intricacy of Shelley's strategies contributed to the suggestive power that succeeding generations have found in her innovation, it also exemplifies the torturing difficulty of the enterprise. The destructive marks of that struggle appear even in a more audacious and unrepentant feminization of Romantic Prometheanism—Mme de Staël's *Corinne.* Less constrained than Shelley by English norms of ladylike behavior (which the French author explicitly and negatively portrayed in her novel), de Staël did not hesitate to assert woman's capacity to bring the fires of heaven to humanity in the form of poetic and artistic creation. Created by the writer who explicated German Romanticism to the French public, Corinne stands proudly as the female counterpart of the male genius, of the inspired Romantic poet whose utterances are the spontaneous overflow of an inner self commensurate with the universe in its register of feelings and power of imagination.

The figure of Napoleon is a historical referent for de Staël's Promethean self, just as it is for the male Romantics, but Corinne stands in opposition rather than complementary reverberation to that historical figure. Bonaparte, who became de Staël's archenemy when he banished her from Paris in 1803 as a troublemaker for his regime, is the unnamed referent of many features of her 1807 novel. *Corinne ou l'Italie* crowns its heroine in Italy, *his* Italy by birth and by conquest, and places a whole people at her feet. As Madelyn Gutwirth notes, "[A]gainst the absolute ruler who mocked her pretensions to a place in this world, Mme de Staël raised the figure of the woman of art, peace, love, and a freedom transcending worldly ambition" (182). Corinne, then, and Italy, the cultural context in which she can be fully herself, offer humanity a nonmasculine—that is, neither aggressive nor authoritarian—version of imaginative power. In her, genius is fully feminized. The mythological figure associated with Corinne is the Sibyl (the novel's first description of its heroine compares her to Domenichino's painting of a sibyl). Unlike the Greek prophetess, however, Corinne is inspired not by an external deity but by the depths of her own richly feminine subjectivity. Her unique spontaneity, a refusal to impose an artificial consistency upon the manifestations of her inner being, provides the key to her creative powers: it constitutes a mode of self-discovery through interaction with others rather than solitary introspection. Her specialty as an artist is poetic improvisation, that is, the poetry of her spontaneous response to the mood and expectations of an audience. The other forms in which she manifests her artistic genius—dancing, singing, acting, conversation—also require the presence of and rapport with an audience.

To a dominant model of creative subjectivity that could be said to echo Napoleon's imperialism in its will to rewrite reality according to the self's desire, de Staël opposes an image of artistic creation as a response of the self shaped in interaction with a circle of interlocutors and thus affirms for developing Romanticism the intersubjective values associated with the domestic woman's sphere. At the same time, however, Corinne is a victim of the social norms that exalt the domestic angel as the true, and therefore exclusively desirable, woman. She may exemplify female genius, but her story is tragic because she does not accept the limiting conditions of women's authority: she desires and she creates. Consequently, her lover, Oswald, chooses the passionless and passive Lucile, Corinne's half sister, as his wife. Tormented first by Oswald's indecisiveness and then devastated by his rejection, Corinne finds herself unable to perform or create and wills herself inexorably into death.

Unlike the suffering that ultimately intensifies the subjective powers

of the Promethean rebel or the visionary Solitary, Corinne's anguish
undermines and diminishes her creativity. The difference arises from
the female artist's dependence on response and recognition: Corinne's
muse falters when the gaze of the beloved, the male other, is turned
away from her, first in his physical absence and second in his choice of
a woman who embodies the self-effacing femininity that is the negation
of Corinne's active self-definition. Thus cut off, she feels herself to have
been rendered invisible, and she loses her capacity to create. As Gutwirth perceptively observes:

> The madness with which Corinne is threatened is a terror of invisibility. In
> all the scenes of despair in Mme de Staël's work, it is nonrecognition of the
> heroine as herself by the beloved, and through him by the world, that is the
> cause of the trauma. It is the ultimate lack of seriousness in the quality of
> attention that is accorded woman by man and by society that calls up this
> fear of nothingness, cause of so much genuine, nonfictional madness in
> women. (207)

We see then to what extent de Staël's bold model of female genius was
structured as a compensatory reaction to the fact of her culture's blank
negation of woman as poetic subject: in a cultural field that posits the
nonexistence of feminine artistic creativity, the figure of the female artist defines itself through its capacity to perform—that is, to make itself
visible and to compel recognition. In a feminized Romantic version of
the Promethean myth, Corinne at once asserts the female artist's triumphant coming into existence and acknowledges the baleful negation
with which patriarchy meets her.

Whereas the Prometheanism of the Romantic construction of the
poetic self conflicts strongly with the nineteenth-century social codes of
femininity, the other two related Romantic figures of the self do not at
first glance seem quite so gender-specific. Yet in both the examples of
female appropriation of the Romantic self that we have just examined,
the revision of Prometheanism also entails altering the form and significance of the other two aspects of Romantic subjectivity.

We saw earlier that in the general Romantic paradigm, the image of
the self as solitary, as separated from society by acute self-consciousness and sensitivity, tended, with some ambivalence, to give a positive
valence to alienation, which distanced the poetic self from the degraded
social and historical world. Alienation permitted the Romantic to find
transcendence through the imagination or freedom through irony. Both
Mary Shelley and Mme de Staël, however, present the definition of the
self through alienation as negative and destructive. In *Frankenstein,* ob-

viously, the ultimate figure of the outcast is not an exemplar of rich, transcendent interiority but the pathetic, subhuman monster, who in certain respects seems to represent the consequences of the female subject's exclusion from the full benefits of human culture by male authority.[9] The white, frozen wastes that depict his exile convey the full force of the author's judgment of marginalization as sterile, as well as painful. We have seen, too, how the figure of the genius, Victor Frankenstein, loses its creative potential and becomes destructive when it obeys the impulse to detachment and inwardness.

There is perhaps more ambiguity in de Staël's novel. Corinne's alienation from the English society that obstinately rejects her inner potentiality does conform to the dominant paradigm of the Romantic figure whose marginalization is the mark of the self's superior value, but she never could have become her "self" without the supportive community that she chose as an alternative to England. Furthermore, if Corinne, the triumphant improvisatrice, stands as a feminine alternative to the male Promethean artist, the aspect of Corinne that withdraws from the world after her separation from Oswald represents alienation as a state of declining rather than renewed creative powers. Indeed, in the alienated Corinne can be seen a paradoxical version of the Romantic alienated self as a figure for the subject's incapacity directly to transform the world: in the last part of the novel, Corinne functions as a veiled Demeter. Her grief, her self-separation, cast a blight on all around her—the summery scenario of Rome and Naples is replaced by the wintry Italian Alps and a frigid, somber Florence, and the human beings around her suffer from depression and despair. The withdrawn goddess, then, has the power to punish the world through her death wish, though she cannot artistically manipulate the images of that world according to her desire.

Thus, rather than finding some value in the rupture between self and other as the alienated *enfant du siècle* does, Mary Shelley and Mme de Staël depict marginalization as a crippling experience, one best represented as illness or as a polar waste. The same is true for what is perhaps the paradigmatic female construction of the Romantic *mal du siècle*, George Sand's *Lélia*. The novel's eponymous protagonist suffers from an extreme alienation from others that she cannot elude or mitigate:

> Ennui lays waste to my life, . . . ennui is killing me. . . . I've seen life in almost all its phases, society under all its aspects, nature in all its splendors. What is left for me to see? . . . I withdraw into myself with a quiet, somber

despair and no one knows what I suffer. The unreasoning beasts who make up society wonder what I could possibly lack, who have the wealth to attain all pleasures and the beauty to realize any ambitions. [No one] can understand the terrible unhappiness of not having been able to attach myself to anything and of not being able to desire anything on earth again. (204)

This alienated existence makes Lélia's life worse than sterile, as she is perfectly aware; she brings unhappiness to those who love her. Ultimately, Stenio, the young poet who loves her, commits suicide in despair, and Lélia in turn is murdered by a monk crazed with desire for her.

Published in 1833, toward the end of the French Romantic movement, this novel embodies in its female protagonist the main themes of the French *mal du siècle:* disillusionment with human history and society, radical doubt about religious and moral dogma, and longing for an ideal that can be neither formulated nor realized. In his edition of the novel, Pierre Reboul documents the extent to which Sand adopts the discourse of contemporary French Romanticism, citing Sénancour, Vigny, Nodier, and Balzac as intertexts for *Lélia*. What distinguishes Lélia as a *feminine* subject of this discourse is her relationship to desire. In the first place, as a woman, Lélia is of necessity an object of desire in a way that the male Romantic subject is not. Part of her alienation stems from her refusal to be the object of the men—and women—who desire her, for this refusal leaves her with no place in a patriarchal economy, as Eileen Silvert points out (48–49). "Why," demands Lélia of God, "did you make me a woman if you wanted later to turn me to stone and leave me, useless, outside of communal life?" (99). But Sand herself incorporates the dominant gender ideology in her representation of the Romantic self as female by making the core of Lélia's problematic existence her lack of sexual desire. Her secret affliction, as she confesses only to her sister, Pulchérie, is frigidity. Although capable of metaphysical desire, she is paralyzed by her lack of appetite for the material. "Without my knowing it, a complete divorce had been effected in me between body and mind" (167). In Lélia, Sand demonstrates the debilitating consequences of a gender system that construed women as subjects without bodies.[10] The female form of Romantic alienation was, ultimately, alienation from the body and from pleasure.

Inevitably, then, the feminized Romantic self was a fragmented subject. The contradiction between reductive definitions of feminine identity and the writer's impulse to explore the full range of subjective language produced in all the female-authored texts just mentioned a doubling of the represented self into transgressor and victim. As feminist critics have pointed out, Frankenstein and his monster are doubles of the same subject: Poovey points out that the monster is an objectification of his maker's Romantic desire to harness the forces of nature to imagination ("Hideous Progeny" 334–337), and Gilbert and Gubar observe that both Victor and the monster represent different aspects of the Promethean archetype (229). Indeed, the doubling of characters at every level of the novel—Walton and Frankenstein, William and the monster, to name but two examples—makes it a veritable hall of mirrors.

The protagonists of both *Corinne* and *Lélia* have alter egos who figure the inevitable lack in their female being. Corinne's blond half sister, Lucile, is the self that she has chosen not to be and her successful rival for Oswald's hand. Though divided by a social reality that splits feminine desirability from female creativity, the sisters share a close bond of identification that signals a potential unity. Corinne gives up Oswald because she cannot bear Lucile's suffering, and when Lucile visits Corinne on her deathbed, the latter teaches the rejected young wife how to be more like Corinne in order to win back her husband's love. Thus, though Corinne dies as a consequence of her defeat by her beloved rival, in another sense she lives on through Lucile as Oswald's wife. When, after years of separation, Lélia encounters her sister, Pulchérie, she briefly understands it as an opportunity to recover a lost wholeness, for Pulchérie the courtesan dedicates her existence to what Lélia lacks—sexual pleasure and sensual enjoyment of reality. But Lélia rejects this opportunity, reenacting an earlier moment of division when she refused to identify herself with Pulchérie's desire. In the narrative action, then, these women authors represent self-division as painful but inevitable for the female subject.

At the level of textual or narrative construction, however, the women writers' acceptance of self-division becomes an innovative openness in representing the subject of writing. We observed earlier that Mary Shelley avoids presenting the narrating subject of her novel as a single, unified point of view by dividing up the narrative among three different voices. In this way she rejects the fiction of the artist's self-representation as the single, dominant subjectivity that creates the text. *Lélia* is even more extreme in this regard; in dispensing with the

framing devices employed by Shelley, it has left itself open to attack as
incoherent and contradictory (Silvert 46). Silvert offers an apt description of the "open, loose, plural" nature of Sand's narrative:

> Through letters, poems, songs, speeches, most of Sand's characters slip into
> the role of narrator at one time or another in this text, and each relinquishes
> the place of narration to the next narrator who speaks or writes directly (to
> another character and/or the reader) rather than having his or her story pass
> through the filter of an overall narrator. (64)

The writer of a text so open to intersubjective dialogue did not feel
compelled to construct an image of herself as a coherent, controlling
writing subject. As the cases of Shelley and Sand show, women authors
who used the Romantic discourse of subjectivity tended to explode notions of the self as coherent and self-contained: a writer contending
with her own socialization according to the norms of domestic womanhood confronted the divided nature of subjectivity in every aesthetic act
of self-representation.

A tension between the desire-driven, egocentric self projected in
Romantic discourse and the passionless, other-directed female subject
defined by bourgeois gender ideology runs through and links the diverse productions of Romantic women writers that we have just sur-
veyed. Mme de Staël, Mary Shelley, and George Sand, responding to
both the opportunities and the constraints on female authorship offered
by a cultural revolution that included liberal ideals, the Romantic
movement, and a new ideology of gender difference, became major exponents of a Romantic subtradition. They, and the many other women
who contributed to this tradition, explored the possibilities of the
Romantic language of subjectivity for the female subject. The texts they
produced began to break down the domestic ideal's strict limitation of
the female psyche and challenged certain aspects of the Romantic ideal
of self. In so doing, they anticipated such future developments in the
representation of women and the self as the gradual erosion of the
domestic female norm and the disintegration of the unified subject as
a textual image.

The changes in social and cultural patterns that made participation
in print culture possible to women of the middle and upper ranks occurred later in Spain than they did in England or France. Spanish
women began to write for the press in the 1840s, when the literary
materials and structures available to them included not only the texts
of French and Spanish male Romantic writers (English and German

Romanticism was known directly only to the most erudite of Spaniards—thus, rarely to women) but also seminal works of the female Romantic tradition. Because French literature was the main conduit of European Romanticism into Spain (Byron and Goethe, for example, were generally read in French translation), the models of the female artist and subject offered in the work of Mme de Staël and George Sand were among the important factors that induced pioneering Spanish women writers to use Romantic discourse as their mode of expression.[11] These models helped the Spanish women negotiate the sharp conflict between the egocentric Romantic paradigm of the creative self and the feminine ideal of the domestic angel, which accelerated its ascent as the dominant Spanish norm of feminine identity during the 1840s.

In the next three chapters I will examine the shifts in culture that enabled Spanish women to participate—albeit with distinct limitations—in the production of literature during this period and the literary context that shaped that participation. Going on to look at exemplary texts by Spanish women writers of the 1840s in chapters 4–7, I shall be able to show how pressures comparable to those outlined for earlier, non-Spanish female Romantics produced similar features in their adaptation and revision of Romantic subjectivity. This analysis will show us something new, too, for in rewriting as female the Romantic "I" of lyrical poetry, two of the Spanish women authors—Gertrudis Gómez de Avellaneda and Carolina Coronado—contributed to a European female Romantic tradition that until then had been limited to the narrative genre. But above all, my readings of the narrative as well as poetic texts of three Spanish women will insist on their foundational role in an unacknowledged and unexplored tradition of female writing that played its part in the troubled emergence of a hegemonic bourgeois culture in Spain.

1
Spanish Liberalism and the Romantic Subject

¡*Libertad*! ¿pues no es sarcasmo
el que nos hacen sangriento
con repetir ese grito
delante de nuestros hierros?
                    —*Carolina Coronado*

BOURGEOIS IDEOLOGY AND THE ROMANTIC SUBJECT

In turning from the general picture of European Romanticism to the configuration of Romantic subjectivity in Spain, we must observe from the outset striking peculiarities in the form and the timing of the extended revolution that brought Spain culturally as well as economically into the modern industrial world. In England, an aggressive and thriving bourgeoisie succeeded in establishing the ideological preconditions of Romantic subjectivity—the inviolability of the individual self and the absolute division between the psychological self and the social world—before the end of the eighteenth century. In Spain, however, bourgeois ideas failed to gain cultural hegemony even among the upper classes until well after the turn of the century. Not surprisingly, Romanticism—both as a self-conscious movement and as a pattern of representing self and world—did not emerge in Spain until the 1830s. When it did, it bore the marks of Spain's prolonged, attenuated, and uneven cultural revolution.

The limitations of the Enlightenment in Spain indicate the weakness of the Spanish bourgeoisie going into the nineteenth century. Although Richard Herr, in his study of this period, found some evidence to justify his title—*The Eighteenth-Century Revolution in Spain*—his work makes it clear that even the minority who accepted Enlightenment ideas stopped short of pushing them to their ultimate consequences. In particular, Spaniards were wary of those aspects of Enlightened thought that most directly challenged the tenets of Catholicism: the new science was treated as a technological advance rather than as the basis for a materialist epistemology; reason was regarded as the appropriate use of God-given faculties rather than the means of a radical critique of accepted beliefs. The Church remained the hegemonic force in Spanish culture until the beginning of the nineteenth century, effectively limiting the inroads of a secular, bourgeois mentality that might undermine the traditional worldview. The absence of the Protestant tradition that provided England, Germany, and France with a set of values from which key elements of Romanticism evolved made a significant difference in the configuration of Spanish Romanticism.

Spain's political and economic structures changed during the eighteenth century, of course, but more slowly, less drastically, than in France or England. The impact of the French Revolution on Spain was minimal in comparison to other European countries: it simply threw the crown and the Church into collusion to seal Spain's borders from ideological contamination and frightened the Enlightened minority into even more moderate positions. It was only after the turn of the century that Spain suffered convulsions that shattered the monumental structures of the old regime. The Napoleonic invasion of 1808 had far-reaching consequences: it revealed the weaknesses of the monarchy, drew the whole Spanish population into a struggle conceived alternatively as holy war against the French infidel or as a liberal national revolution, and facilitated the independence movements that soon stripped Spain of her overseas empire. This last effect is arguably the decisive one in giving impetus to the revolutionary process. The government lost with the colonies a crucial source of income and the commercial and industrial bourgeoisie lost its principal market. The monarchy, absolutist as ever in principle, was forced to seek new revenues by appropriating the property of its former ally, the Church, while the bourgeoisie became increasingly aware that its interests—centrally, the creation of an integrated national market—would best be served by a modern liberal state and the replacement of traditional social relations by forms that permitted more individual autonomy and initiative. (See Fontana, *Quiebra* and "Formación.")

Thus the stage was set for the political struggle of which Spanish Romanticism was a concomitant. The tide turned between 1815, when Ferdinand VII, his crown restored by Napoleon's defeat, abrogated the Constitution of 1812 that the liberal parliament of Cádiz had created in his absence, and 1836, when Ferdinand's widow, Maria Cristina, was forced by a powerful liberal faction to swear allegiance to the same constitution; from this point on, the old regime was on its way out in Spain despite frequent reactionary backswings. The diffusion of a new mentality revealed itself in the rising fortunes of Romanticism as a literary school.

The liberal intellectuals of the 1810s, who elaborated their revolutionary program in the Constitution of Cádiz, regarded neoclassicism as the model of cultural values appropriate to their objectives and assumptions: rationality, measure, and objectivity served as instruments of combat against the baroque cultural forms of the old regime. Edmund King has argued that the lateness and relative weakness of Romanticism in Spain is due to the fact that the Age of Reason had still not become firmly established in Spain by the time it was being superceded by Romanticism in the rest of Europe. It is certainly relevant to King's thesis that early liberal leaders, such as Joaquín de Mora, engaged in a fiery polemic against a premature advocate of Romantic aesthetics in Spain. Historical accident played its part in this initial rejection—the early enthusiast of Romanticism was Nicolás Boehl von Faber, a German convert to Catholicism who superimposed his own conservative biases on his translations of the Schlegels. However, the liberals' lack of receptivity to German Romanticism in contrast to their general enthusiasm for neoclassicism also corresponds to the realities of that moment in the cultural revolution. A secular frame of reference for social relations in the here and now had to be constructed in the public mind before liberal ideals could gain common acceptance. To the extent that literary forms signified in this project, the organic structures of Romanticism did not sufficiently contrast with the predominant traditions of Spanish literature.

By the 1830s, however, liberalism as an economic and political program had gained sufficient strength among the governing elite to insure that a decisive portion of the power structure opposed the absolutist, reactionary faction of Don Carlos in the dynastic crisis that followed the death of Ferdinand in 1833. When the Carlists ended their armed rebellion with a truce in 1839, there remained no viable alternative to the transformation of the state and the modernization of the economy upon which the central government had cautiously embarked. Though the persisting premodern structures of Spanish society slowed and attenuated such changes, during this decade the mentality that supported the liberal revolution spread and became more secure. The rise of the

Romantic movement, which reached its apogee between 1836 and 1842, shows that in these conditions the intellectual vanguard found the Romantic elaboration of subjectivity appropriate to the cultural struggle in which they were engaged.

Indeed, Romanticism was central to the cultural agenda of the liberal movement of the 1830s, for the artistic cult of individual subjectivity supplied imaginative and emotional meanings for the new structures that the liberals sought to constitute in Spanish society. This connection was drawn explicitly by Mariano José de Larra, who as a satirist and critic was the most self-conscious of the Spanish Romantics. Surveying the course of Spanish literature in his brilliant and influential essay "Literatura" (1836), he provided what was in essence an analysis of the state of the cultural revolution in Spain. Larra notes the failure of the enlightened vanguard of the previous century to do more than to try to impose foreign tastes on a culture that had developed neither linguistically nor politically to the point of being able to integrate new values and concepts, and declares that the present moment is ripe with new possibilities:

> En el día numerosa juventud se abalanza ansiosa a las fuentes del saber. ¿Y en qué momentos? En momentos en que el progreso intelectual, rompiendo en todas partes antiguas cadenas, desgastando tradiciones caducas y derribando ídolos, proclama en el mundo la libertad moral, a la par de la física, porque la una no puede existir sin la otra. (2: 133)

> Today a numerous young generation rushes anxiously to the sources of knowledge. And at what moment in history? At the moment when intellectual progress, everywhere breaking ancient chains, destroying worn-out traditions and knocking down idols, proclaims in the world moral as well as physical freedom, because the one cannot exist without the other.

We find here the presupposition that grounds the new mentality, or "intellectual progress," as Larra terms it—the construct of the individual self, that physical and moral unit whose a priori autonomy justifies and demands the freedom proclaimed in this paragraph.

Larra's confidence that the new truth would triumph over the old forms of thought was very much a product of the historical moment: Juan Alvarez Mendizábal, the man whom progressive liberals thought of as their champion, had just been named prime minister and was promising miracles of fiscal, land, and legislative reform within months. In Larra's view, "intellectual progress" was on the verge of carrying the day in Spain, of winning acceptance of the premises of liberal ideology as truth.

Cultural and sociopolitical transformation, then, were closely linked in Larra's mind: "[E]speremos que dentro de poco podamos echar los cimientos de una literatura *nueva,* expresión de la sociedad *nueva* que componemos, toda de *verdad* como de *verdad* es nuestra sociedad" 'Let us hope that soon we will be able to lay the foundations of a *new* literature, the expression of the *new* society we compose, a literature entirely *true* just as our society is *true*' (2: 133–134). The anxiety signaled by the writer's emphasis on the two words "true" and "new" reveals the relative insecurity of bourgeois cultural premises in Spain. As a worldview not yet sufficiently integrated with social practices to become unconscious, or at least beyond the need for demonstration, it retains for writer and reader the sense of something new, a replacement of something else, and therefore not uniquely uncontestable. Furthermore, the use of italics suggests that the "new truth" refers to a set of concepts for which the language has not yet been fully elaborated: the writer must rely on a kind of gesture to his audience to supplement his meaning. But this is precisely Larra's message: it is time to create a literary discourse that will embody the new truth of the new society.

Larra defines crucial implications of the "truth" for us in a passage that reveals at once the lucidity and the difficulty produced by his conscious assumption of an ideology:

> En política el hombre no ve más que *intereses* y *derechos,* es decir, *verdades.* En literatura no puede buscar por consiguiente sino *verdades.* . . . Porque las pasiones en el hombre siempre serán *verdades,* porque la imaginación misma, ¿qué es sino una *verdad* más hermosa? (2: 133)

> In politics man finds nothing but *interests* and *rights,* that is to say, *truths.* So it follows that in literature he cannot seek anything but *truths.* . . . Because man's passions will always be *truths,* because imagination itself, what is it if not a more beautiful *truth?*

There is a logical tension here between the syllogistic structure of the argument and the semantic differences among the terms of the syllogism. As the common denominator linking politics and literature, the meaning of "truth" is expanded to include the Romantic values of passion and imagination along with the liberal values of interests and rights. Thus, the new definition of "truth" implies the basic premise of liberal ideology—that the common reality in which society, politics, and literature are grounded is the individual subject. Only by understanding truth to be the locus where interests and passions meet can we make sense of Larra's argument.

With this equation, Larra articulates a connection between the liberal revolutionary program and the literary agenda of Romanticism, for according to this scheme, the model of the individual subject that underlies "truth" is to be propagated and elaborated by both movements at different levels of social activity. Larra succinctly proposes that subjectivity expressed as self-interest, bearing with it inalienable rights, has become the reality that economic and political structures must reflect; that same reality must be represented in art as the inner truth of the subject—passions, fantasies, imagination. Desire stands at the heart of this conceptual scheme as the glue that connects self-interest and passion, the substance of subjectivity. What Larra urges on his generation is simply the project of making space for the individual subject to express its desire in economic, political, and artistic practice—the founding of a new society and a new literature, in other words.

Freedom is the clarion call of such a project, of course: "*Libertad* en literatura, como en las artes, como en la industria, como en el comercio, como en la conciencia. He aquí la divisa de la época, he aquí la nuestra, he aquí la medida con que mediremos" '*Freedom* in literature, as in the arts, as in industry, as in commerce, as in conscience. This is the emblem of our age, our emblem, the gauge by which we will measure' (2: 134). In linking moral with material liberty—"one cannot exist without the other," he remarked earlier in the essay—Larra goes beyond the mere emancipation from established literary convention with which his contemporaries identified the Romantic movement. The function of his essay is to show literature's role in a cultural revolution whose time has come: freedom is necessary so that literature can represent the new truth demanded by a new society. The article's peroration draws together key words now infused with special meaning, as Larra calls upon his generation to produce a new literature that is

> hija de la experiencia y de la Historia . . . , apostólica y de propaganda; enseñando verdades a aquellos a quienes interesa saberlas, y mostrando al hombre, no como debe ser, sino como es, para conocerle; literatura, en fin, expresión toda de la ciencia de la época, del progreso intelectual del siglo. (2: 134)

> born of experience and History . . . , apostolic and disseminative; teaching truths to those interested in knowing them, and showing man not as he should be but as he is, so that he can be known; a literature, finally, that is wholly the expression of the age, of the intellectual progress of our century.

The language of this final statement may seem closer to Enlightenment discourse than to Romanticism. Yet recognizing that the essay has already made it clear that "intellectual progress" corresponds to growing acceptance of the liberal ideological framework and that "truths" refers as much to individual subjectivity as to inalienable rights allows us to see that in "Literatura" Larra has indicated the theoretical space in which literary Romanticism might participate in Spain's cultural revolution.

Larra was not usually so sanguine about the prospects of cultural transformation, and even in this essay the references to the necessity of proselytism reveal to what extent the project of a new literature and a new consciousness involved struggle. In a later essay, "Horas de invierno" (Dec. 1836), he dramatized his sense of frustration about the reception of his message in a well-known passage: "Escribir en Madrid es llorar, es buscar voz sin encontrarla, como en una pesadilla abrumadora y violenta. . . . ¿Quién oye aquí?" 'To write in Madrid is to weep, to seek a voice without finding it, like in an oppressive, violent nightmare. . . . Who listens here?' (2: 290–291). Although the shift in mentality seemed slow from the vantage point of Larra's short life—his suicide at the age of twenty-eight, a few weeks after writing this passage, gives the measure of his frustrated impatience—the longer view reveals that among the literate public, small though it was, certain premises of the new ideology were taken for granted by 1836. With the exception of the soon-to-be-defeated Carlist faction, the principal political tendencies, both conservative and progressive, assumed some inalienable human rights and the necessity of some degree of political and economic expression of self-interest. The major Moderate leaders had been militant liberal revolutionaries in the early 1820s; by the 1830s they had tempered and softened their views but not renounced the underlying principles.

Perhaps the change in mentality that attended the rise of a Romantic movement in Spain can be best illustrated in attitudes about the place and meaning of representations of inner life. The traditional view, maintained and enforced by the Church, regarded depictions of the passional life of the psyche to be significant only insofar as they demonstrated moral and metaphysical absolutes. An early Spanish translation of *Die Leiden des jungen Werther*, for example, was given the title *Cartas morales sobre las pasiones* [*Moral Letters on the Passions*]. But an 1802 censor, describing his expectations as a reader—which the novel failed to meet—shows even more dramatically how little the traditional mentality was prepared to understand Goethe's innovations in representing subjectivity:

> Cuando leí el título de la obra creí, desde luego, que su objeto . . . se dirigía a enseñar a los hombres lo que son estos movimientos del alma que llamamos pasiones, su origen, su naturaleza, su número y efectos, el uso de ellas y los preservativos para contenerlas y sujetarlas a la parte superior y a la ley, y . . . creí que . . . se ordenaba a que el hombre, del conocimiento de sus pasiones pasase a concocerse a sí mismo, y después a Dios, . . . pues estos conocimientos son el cimiento de nuestra verdadera felicidad. (González Palencia 291)

> When I read the title of the book, I believed, of course, that its object . . . would be to teach men about those movements of the soul that we call passions, showing their origin, their nature, their number and effects, their use, and measures for containing them and subjecting them to the higher faculties and the law, and . . . I thought that . . . it was organized so that men would go from understanding their passions to understanding themselves, and then God, . . . for such knowledge is the basis of our true happiness.

The censor's expectations, so irrelevant to the text he encountered, reveal the abyss that separated the Romantic preoccupation with subjectivity from the traditional view in Spain. The literary representation of the inner self, undertaken by the Romantics as an exploration of the self's boundlessness, uniqueness, and potential transcendence, had value for the mentality from which this censor speaks only as a means of measuring and classifying the movements of the psyche according to Scholastic categories, and thereby subjecting them to the law of reason or divine order that transcends and annuls individual emotion and perspective.

Sixteen years later, however, a much more modern set of premises informed a treatise on drama published by Agustín Durán, a conservative literary critic who defended Spain's Golden Age dramatic tradition against the disparagements of criticism based on French neoclassical doctrines (that is, against liberals drawing on Enlightenment values). Durán argued on the basis of a cultural relativism that placed him much closer to European Romantics than to the 1802 censor:

> [L]a diversidad del gusto de las naciones, en materias de teatro, procede de la diferencia de sus necesidades morales, y de sus modos de existir, juzgar y sentir, a cuyas modificaciones tienen los poetas que acomodar la expresión y formas de sus pensamientos, sin que por esto deba creerse que se hallen en diverso estado de ilustración. (70)

> The diversity of taste in theater among nations proceeds from the differences in their moral necessities and in their ways of existing, judging, and feeling, modalities to which poets must accommodate their expression and forms of thinking, without this meaning that some are not as knowledgeable as others.

In addition, Durán drew on modern premises of individualism to defend Spain's literary traditions, which he identifies with the "romantic" literature of Christian Europe as opposed to classical antiquity:

> [E]n la literatura clásica se mira al hombre por sus actos exteriores solamente, y sus virtudes y vicios se consideran en abstracto, prescindiendo siempre del sujeto a quien se aplican. . . . El objeto y fin que se proponen los poetas románticos . . . es . . . el de retratar al hombre individual, dominado con más o menos vehemencia de las pasiones, vicios o virtudes de que es capaz el corazón humano; es, en fin, el de formar la historia del hombre interior considerado como individuo. (84, 85)

> In classical literature man is seen through his external acts alone, and his virtues and vices are considered in the abstract, with no reference to the subject to whom they apply. . . . The object and goal of the romantic poets . . . is . . . to portray the individual man, dominated more or less vehemently by the passions, vices, or virtue of which the human heart is capable; it is, finally, to trace this history of the inner man considered as an individual.

In fact, the individuality and the interiority of the subject become the measure of verisimilitude in Durán's argument against the neoclassical unities, in which he maintains that major shifts in individual feeling cannot believably be restricted to a period of twenty-four hours (86). Durán does not make the value of the individual's inner history contingent upon its demonstration of eternal verities, as the 1802 censor did; instead, "inner individual man" (83) is seen as the basic reality whose representation is truth in literature. Implicit in Durán's statements is something approximating Larra's later formulation concerning the new truth in literature and society, except that for Larra modernity was the present and future, while for Durán it was the Christian past.

Durán's text is marked as transitional, however, by the imposition of a theological framework on the historical and cultural relativism of his argument. Although the historical development that altered the morals, the tastes, and even the truths of ancient society is the cornerstone of Durán's defense of "romantic" literature, he admits no further historical change once Christian society is established. The contradiction is manifested in another way when he justifies the modern depiction of the inner man by reference to divine truth: "[R]epeti-remos, finalmente, que la sublime e ideal belleza de este último género se alimenta y sostiene en los inmensos espacios de la eternidad, en la sumisión del entendimiento humano a la fe divina" 'Let us repeat, in conclusion, that the sublime and ideal beauty of this last genre is fed and sustained by the immense space of eternity, by the submission of human understanding to divine faith' (86). Thus, the continuing force of an older worldview makes itself felt in Durán's *Discurso* as a hesitation between history and theology, between individualism and Catholic doctrine.

What Durán's example shows is that even before the death of Ferdinand VII and the return of the exiled liberals, even under the conditions of strict censorship that prevailed in the late 1820s, the basic premises of European bourgeois ideology were taking hold in Spain. According to Robert Marrast, "the *Discurso* represents an important moment in the development of ideas in Spain, insofar as it constitutes the crystallization of more or less clearly declared tendencies" (257). But, as Marrast also points out, Durán's articulation of the new literary and ideological tendencies was highly conservative: "It was above all . . . a matter of insuring that Spain's traditional moral values not be called into question, nor even rejected under the influence of a romanticism that, in France, was after 1825 identified with liberalism" (257). Indeed, Durán helped to originate the most conservative line of Spanish Romanticism, medievalizing, strongly nationalistic, and resistant to progressive social positions. Yet, as we have seen, even at this least liberal pole of the intellectual elite, individualism and new concern with the interiority of the subject were firmly rooted.

At the other end of the political spectrum, the exiled liberal leader, Antonio Alcalá Galiano, also marked out the ground from which Romanticism was launched in Spain. Sometimes considered to be Spain's Romantic manifesto,[1] his 1834 prologue to Angel Saavedra's *El moro expósito* is not strikingly different in its premises from Durán's *Discurso*, despite Alcalá's more immediate contact with English Romanticism. Alcalá, too, though in different words, asserts that subjectivity is the privileged material of literature:

[S]e ha de observar siempre la regla de que sólo es poético y bueno lo que declaran los hechos de la fantasía y las emociones del ánimo. Todo cuanto hay de vago, indefinible e inexplicable en la mente del hombre, todo lo que nos conmueve, . . . creaciones . . . cuya identidad con los objetos reales y verdaderos sentimos, conocemos y confesamos, en suma, cuanto excita en nosotros recuerdos de emociones fuertes, todo ello, y no otra cosa, es la buena y castiza poesía. (Alcalá 110)

One must always observe the rule that only what derives from the work of fantasy and inner emotion is poetic and good. Everything that is vague, ineffable, and inexplicable in man's mind, everything that moves us, . . . creations . . . whose identity with real, true objects we feel, know, and admit, in sum, everything that excites in us memories of strong emotions, all that, and nothing else, constitutes good, genuine poetry.

Besides using a phraseology that echoes Wordsworth's preface to the *Lyrical Ballads*—"powerful feelings . . . recollected in tranquillity"— Alcalá differs from Durán mainly in asserting the rule of subjectivity almost as an absolute of literature; he claims that poetry's function in ancient Greece as well as the present is the expression "of past memories and present emotions" (125). It is noteworthy that "the real, true objects" of literary creation are inescapably associated in this formulation with movements of the psyche. In Alcalá there is no reference to a transcendent theological reality as the ultimate referent of psychological experience and its literary expression. Instead, the reality of the individual subject is the final test of poetry's truth.

Alcalá Galiano's statements about poetry, then, reveal a more secure and complete integration of bourgeois ideology than can be discovered in Durán. Liberal principles appear explicitly in the surface of Alcalá's text when he explains the artificiality of seventeenth-century Spanish literature as the expression of a society "a quien el poder crecido de sus reyes daba vanidad, mas no felicidad y verdadera grandeza, y para la cual no eran el gobierno, las leyes y la religión materia de examen libre y de atrevida controversia" 'made vain but not happy by the great power of its kings, and for which the government, the laws, and religion were not subject to critical examination and daring controversy' (115). This view contrasts sharply with Durán's positive opinion of seventeenth-century drama and of the established authority of monarchy and Church, which, according to his argument, permitted new heights of creativity (82). The two critics clearly represent opposite ends of the political spectrum—the one a committed liberal, the other conservative in both political and religious terms. Yet beneath their differences we find a common ideological ground—not so firm for Durán as for Alcalá Galiano perhaps—in the basic premise that individual subjectivity constituted a central reality.

In this sense, Larra was correct to affirm in 1836 that the moment had come in which literature could explore new truths sensed by a broadening section of the literate public. From 1835 on the idea that subjective reality is the stuff of artistic expression became a commonplace of Spanish literary criticism. Yet the ideological shift that provided the basis on which the Romantic cult of the self could develop was as tenuous and uneven as the triumph of bourgeois political and economic forms in Spain during the early nineteenth century; consequently, most Spanish Romanticism followed the line set down by Durán: imitative, backward looking, strongly nationalistic. Even the most tradition-centered products of the movement, however, claimed a new freedom of subjective expression and contributed to the elaboration of a vocabulary of the feeling self. Spanish Romanticism thus developed models of the lyrical subject that bore close resemblance to their counterparts in the rest of Europe and that were, like them, distinctly gender-specific.

WOMEN IN THE LIBERAL PROJECT

The liberation of the autonomous individual was in some sense— and with varying degrees of radicalism—the common denominator of the liberal revolution and the Romantic movement in Spain. Larra has shown us the fundamental unity of the political and cultural programs: while political reform must create the social and economic space in which the subject might freely exercise rights and interests, literary innovation must illuminate the inner spaces of that same subject, where desire and fantasy play, as much a part of reality as the actions they generate. The abstract terms in which the theoretical justifications of the liberal Romantic project were stated implied that all individuals, all human subjects, were entitled to such a liberation. Both liberal practice and the more concrete literary manifestations of its ideology revealed, however, that the liberatory ideal was above all a class project, aimed at changing the conditions of existence of a propertied elite but not at freeing the lower classes from economic and political subjection. But it was not class bias alone that excluded certain subjects from the project of liberation. Gender bias was openly and unself-consciously present in the Spanish liberal movement.

Just as even the most radical demands of liberal factions, even the most far-reaching of the several constitutions elaborated between 1812 and 1854, did not conceive of extending suffrage to those without property, so the possibility of granting women the vote remained out of the question. Nor was there any concern, in an age of legal reforms that ensured absolute rights of ownership to property holders, with providing women the same rights to property. Married women, according to the legal code established in the Middle Ages, were only partial juridical subjects: they could commit crimes and testify in court, but a married woman could not make contracts or take legal action without her husband's (or in his absence, a judge's) permission. This in effect gave the husband absolute control over any property to which his wife had title. Instead of rectifying this situation, the legal reforms of the nineteenth century eliminated the marginal areas of property control that feudal law had allowed women: "In the course of the nineteenth century, the husband's prerogatives over his wife, as well as over her property, were increasingly emphasized, so that [by 1868] a woman upon marriage unconditionally surrendered the administration of her own property as well as that of conjugal property" (López-Cordón 89).

Still, considerations about the new premises on which social transformation was based did not leave women out entirely. Even the most timid of moderates believed that woman's lot was improved in modern society. Agustín Durán, who in his *Discurso* fixed the passage from antiquity to the Christian Middle Ages as the constitutive moment of the modern world, remarked on what the more individual-oriented civilization meant for women:

> Prevalecida la mujer de todas cuantas gracias y dulzura la dotó Naturaleza, llegó a ser la piedra fundamental de la felicidad doméstica. . . . Compañera y no esclava del hombre, participaba igualmente que él de los bienes y males, de los placeres y de las penas (81).

> Prevailing with all the graces and sweetness Nature gave her, woman came to be the foundation stone of domestic happiness. . . . The companion rather than the slave of man, she participated equally with him in wealth and misfortune, in pleasure and pain.

Here we find the basic paradigm shared even by Durán's more progressive contemporaries: woman's existence was confined to the private domestic world, within which she shared man's existence. Since she had no place in the public arena, she was attributed no political rights or economic interests of her own; only through a man—father or husband—did she have legal status. Even in her only space of existence, the private circle, she was not seen as an autonomous individual but as man's adjunct, the source of his domestic happiness. In Durán's text it is even questionable whether the woman has her own subjectivity, since she shares in pleasures and pains whose subject is ambiguous—the grammatical structure does not make it clear of whom "los bienes y males," "los placeres y las penas" are to be predicated. Thus, in the liberal scheme, woman could be at best only half that unit—the individual subject—on which the new vision of society was premised; she had only a private side, emotions and imagination, but no interests. At worst, woman was not even a partial subject but simply a function of male subjectivity.

In the 1830s, liberals reiterated as an accepted truism Durán's assertion that Christianity and modern civilization had sufficiently liberated women from their former slavery in the Oriental harem. Juan López Pelegrín, a contributor to the liberal *El Español,* affirmed in 1836 that "[l]a primera conquista de la civilización ha sido de la libertad del bello sexo; respecto del feo quedan todavía sus dificultades que deslindar" 'the first achievement of civilization has been the freedom of the fair sex; with respect to that of the other sex, there remain difficulties to sort out' (3). If it seems puzzling that women's freedom should have been easier to achieve than men's, the reason becomes apparent a few lines further along: "[L]a muger ha conquistado su independencia hasta donde lo han permitido las leyes del pudor y del decoro" 'Woman has conquered as much independence as the laws of modesty and decorum permit.' That is, the laws of nature and society do not permit women the same degree of independence as that sought by men.

López Pelegrín asserts in the next paragraph that women do not desire an active role in public life, which conceals too many dangers to their purity. Such assertions may well have been a response to the ideas about women that disciples of French utopian socialism had begun circulating in Spain. One trace of this contestatory discourse about women can be found in "Congregaciones modernas: Los sansimonianos," an article published in a Madrid review in 1837 that takes issue with the dominant position articulated by López Pelegrín: "El cristianismo ha librado a las mujeres de la servidumbre; empero las ha dejado sujetas a la inferioridad, y todavía las vemos en toda la Europa cristiana condenadas a una inhabilitación religiosa, política y civil" 'Christianity has freed women from servitude; however, it has left them subjected to inferiority, and we still see them in all Christian Europe condemned to religious, political, and civil disqualification' (233). This article maintains that according to the teachings of Saint Simon, granting women full political and civic equality with men will confirm rather than destroy the sacredness of matrimony.

The French socialist notions about women provoked an outburst of ridicule in Spain (although small nuclei of Fourierists took root in Cádiz and Cataluña, according to Antonio Elorza), where the inversion of the idea that political liberties had no relevance to women served as a satirical motif. *El Jorobado,* a notorious satirical paper, printed an article titled "Una sesión en una asamblea de mujeres," which the heading itself was sufficient to set the burlesque tone: "Emancipación de la mujer.—Discusión de los derechos de la mujer.—Reforma de las leyes relativas a la mujer, etc." 'A Session in a Women's Assembly: Women's Emancipation.—Discussion of Women's Rights.—Reform of Laws on Women, etc.' (3). The same motif operates as a sign of satirical intention in the advertisement for a new burlesque journal called *Gobierno Representativo y Constitucional del Bello Sexo Español.* The editors proclaim that "la empresa de esta original publicación mensual . . . ha conseguido . . . que en la portada de cada entrega vaya una viñeta o lámina que represente el grandioso acto de la apertura de las primeras cortes femeninas" 'the publishers of this original monthly . . . have obtained . . . for each issue a vignette or print representing the grandiose act of the opening of the first feminine congress' (*El Eco* 4). These examples make clear that, with the exception of scattered groups of utopians, there was no serious proposal to extend the political and economic benefits of the liberal program to women, whose liberation was figured simply as a release from the harem into Christian marriage.

If the ideological formations through which the bourgeois cultural revolution was carried out in Spain strictly differentiated between individual subjects of one and the other gender, it was no more accidental than was the class bias that characterized that revolution. Indeed, the two biases were related, as can be demonstrated by again turning to the writing of Mariano José de Larra. As a progressive who was exceptionally aware of the contradictions of liberal thought and practice, Larra often articulated with clarity the troubled points in contemporary ideology. His review of Alexandre Dumas's Romantic drama, *Anthony,* which was performed in Madrid in the summer of 1836, shows just how codes of gender difference were incorporated in the newly emerging bourgeois consciousness.

In contrast with "Literatura," written some six months earlier, the review of *Anthony* focuses on a particular Romantic text and, consequently, on a concrete expression of the private, subjective side of the individual. The French drama represents the story of a love-passion that breaks social norms: Anthony convinces Adèle, a married woman with whom he falls in love, that their love is an absolute value above common moral laws; she flees with her lover, abandoning her husband. Thus, *Anthony* poses in concrete terms the question dialectically implied by Larra's own earlier demand for freedom: What is liberty's proper limit? The first part of Larra's review deals with these issues in historical and political terms, leaving the analysis of the drama proper for later. First he takes up the matter of Spain's liberal revolution, which he now views much more negatively than he did in "Literatura." He argues that the French drama, a representation of liberty carried to the extreme, can have a detrimental effect on the Spanish public. Though conceding that Spain must seek the freedoms outlined in his earlier essay, he adds darkly that all it will gain is "libertad para recorrer ese camino que no conduce a ninguna parte" 'freedom to follow the road that goes nowhere' (2: 248). The first part concludes with Larra's promise to analyze next the social implications of *Anthony,* which he says is "la personificación de la desorganización social" (2: 248). The second part of the review begins by identifying as the principal threat to social order Dumas's image of marital and family relations, particularly the implication that the marital bond tyrannically limits women's freedom. It is not surprising that woman should surface in Larra's essay as the crux of the tension between the expression of individual subjectivity and the necessity of social constraint, for women were, after all, the "heart" of private life, and the laws of "modesty and decorum" seemed necessarily to constrain their freedom.

Larra's critique of Dumas's play reveals the essential unity of his conception of public and private, political and literary. In the first paragraph, he deftly intercodes class relations of power with dramatized representations of family relationships:

> En la literatura antigua era principio admitido que todo padre era un tirano de su hija. . . . De aquí pasaba el poeta a pintar la tiranía de la familia, imagen y origen de la del Goberno: cada hijo puesto en escena desde Menandro acá . . . es una viva alusión al pueblo. (2: 249)

> In ancient literature it was an accepted principle that every father was his daughter's tyrant. . . . From there the poet went on to depict the tyranny of the family, image and origin of that of the Government: every son put on stage since Menander on . . . is a living allusion to the people.

The two terms of the power relation designated in this passage—government and people—suggest that Larra has identified the state with the oligarchical aristocracy against whom the "pueblo," or general citizenry (i.e., bourgeoisie), directed its struggle. Since Larra's interpre-

tation of the literary father-son conflict expresses the form in which he
thought of the class struggle, his tone in making this observation is be-
nign, if slightly ironic.

The irony darkens, however, when he asserts that a new configuration has become dominant in modern drama:

> [L]a cuestión en el teatro moderno gira entre iguales, entre matrimonios; es
> principio irrecusable según parece que una mujer casada debe estar mal
> casada, y que no se da mujer que quiera a su marido. El marido es en el día
> el coco, . . . el monstruo opresor a quien hay que engañar. . . . ¡Infelice!
> ¿Hay suerte más desgraciada que la de una mujer casada? (2: 249)

> The dispute in modern theater is between equals, between husband and
> wife; it is an unimpeachable principle, it seems, that a married woman must
> be unhappy and that there are no examples of wives who love their hus-
> bands. Today the husband is the boogeyman, . . . the oppressive monster
> who must be deceived. . . . Oh, woe! Can there be a more unhappy state
> than that of a married woman?

The source of the deepening sarcasm here is the application of the opposition "tyrant" / "victim of oppression"—perfectly acceptable when
referring to government and people—to the pair "man" / "wife." The
text implies that author and reader share the assumption that the liberal demand to free the individual from the constraints of a traditional
hierarchy becomes absurd when made by a woman. Even the Romantic
poet who imagines a female subjectivity that resists constraint by social obligation comes in for attack: "El poeta se pone de parte de la
mujer, . . . porque el corazón . . . no puede amar siempre, y no debe
ligarse con juramentos eternos" 'The poet takes the part of the
wife, . . . because the heart . . . cannot love forever and should not be
tied by eternal vows' (2: 249). The sarcastic clauses that follow show
why, on the contrary, women's freedom must be restricted:

> [L]a perfección a que camina el género humano consiste en que una vez
> llegado el hombre a la edad de multiplicarse, se una a la mujer que más
> le guste, dé nuevos individuos a la sociedad; y separado después de su
> pasajera consorte, uno y otra dejen los frutos de su amor en medio del
> arroyo . . . abandonados a sus propias fuerzas y de los cuales cuide la
> sociedad misma, es decir, nadie. (2: 249)

> The perfection toward which the human species moves will be that once a
> man reaches the age of procreation, he will unite with the woman who
> pleases him most to produce new individuals for society; and then that the
> temporary consorts will separate and leave the fruits of their love in the gut-
> ter . . . abandoned to their own resources and to be taken care of by society
> itself, that is, by no one.

The reasoning is clear: the tendencies dramatized in *Anthony* threaten the very foundation of society by suggesting that such a basic "right of man" as liberty be extended to the only realm of woman's existence—family life, marriage, and reproduction. Women's place marks the boundary at which individual freedom, a positive goal up to that point, becomes a disruptive force in society.

In using a conservative *topos* about women and sexual freedom to support his attack on Dumas's play, Larra underscores the political subtext of the review as a whole, which proposes indirectly that the revolutionary process leads to "desorganización social" (2: 248) in the arena of class relations as well as in domestic life. The passage cited above on the different conflicts figured in ancient and modern drama treats as self-evident the idea that modern society has eliminated the oppression that characterized earlier societies: "[A]penas hay en la sociedad de ahora opresor y oprimido" 'Oppressors and oppressed scarcely exist in today's society' (2: 249). Such an assertion is made more credible to Larra's public—or at least its ironic undertones are attenuated[2]—by the fact that in this context Larra is not alluding to a specific society such as Spain but rather giving the term "la sociedad de ahora" a more abstract sense—"the kind of society we assume exists in France and England." The reader is led to infer that modern society has accomplished the goals of the bourgeois revolution by eliminating the oppression that had characterized previous societies and regarding all citizens as equal before the law.

Marriage becomes the literary metaphor for this social equality when Larra shifts attention to the plot lines of modern drama: "[L]a cuestión en el teatro moderno gira entre iguales, entre matrimonios" 'The dispute in modern theater occurs between equals, between husband and wife' (2: 249). This move allows Larra, as we have seen, to ridicule the application of revolutionary ideas to relations between the sexes. But further, once the parallel between class politics (father vs. son or government vs. people, as Larra reads it) and the sexual politics of marriage has been established, the sarcasm directed at modern drama's claims for women also implies a condemnation of any new demands on the part of the people. In this sense, Larra's chastisement of the way Dumas's drama represents marriage can also be read as a warning to the "pueblo" that it would be as capricious and destructive as a rebellious wife if it sought more freedom or rights. This subterranean message surfaces in the next major portion of the article, which attacks the hero of *Anthony* and Dumas himself for not being satisfied with the status quo.[3]

Larra provides us, then, with a revealing example of how the class and gender biases of early nineteenth-century Spanish liberal ideology buttressed each other. The mechanisms for limiting the radicalizing potential of liberatory ideals represented women as a kind of boundary line: their "natural" function within the family marked the point at which "social" innovation must stop. This location of woman on a border simply reproduces patriarchal culture's age-old tendency. "La femme n'incarne aucun concept figé" 'Woman incarnates no fixed concept,' Simone de Beauvoir tells us; instead she represents the mediator between Self and Other, consciousness and the void, Man and Nature: "L'homme recherche dans la femme l'Autre comme Nature et comme son semblable" 'Man seeks in woman the Other as Nature and as his likeness' (236–237). Representations that function as a frontier are necessarily uneasy and ambivalent. In Spain, liberal and Romantic discourse sometimes acknowledged woman's likeness to man, making her, as Durán affirmed, "la compañera del hombre," a secondary sharer of his subjectivity. At the same time, this discourse relegated the female to the realm of the natural by identifying her with the reproductive function, as Larra's argument does; thus identified with otherness, woman remained the object rather than the subject of consciousness.

FEMALE SUBJECTIVITY

The ambiguity of women's status in the conceptual framework of liberalism is mirrored in the notions of feminine subjectivity that predominated in the Romantic period. When at the end of his article on *Anthony* Larra shifts the focus from the needs of society to the imperative of individual desire, he reveals a typical double-mindedness about women as subjects. At the beginning of the final paragraph, the claims of passion move the author/narrator: "Nosotros reconocemos los primeros el influjo de las pasiones; desgraciadamente no nos es lícito ignorarlo" 'We are the first to recognize the influence of passion; unfortunately, we have not been allowed to be ignorant of it' (2: 252). He grants that women as well as men can be subjects of a passion whose scope, whose value even, dwarfs the limits set by the exterior world of society. Caught up for the moment in the Romantic mode, he posits the case of an extraordinary individual—"el caso excepcional de una mujer que se halla realmente bajo el influjo de una pasión cuyas circunstancias sean tales que . . . la puedan hacer aparecer sublime hasta en el crimen mismo" 'the exceptional case of a woman really under the influence of a passion whose circumstances are such that . . . they can make her appear sublime even in crime' (2: 252). However, having conceded the possibility of a feminine emotion as sublime as that attributed to the male Romantic hero, Larra insists on the exceptionality of such female subjectivity in relation to the majority of women, "cuyos amores no son pasiones, sino devaneos" 'whose love affairs are not passions but frivolous flirtations' (2: 252). That is, in most cases the quality of women's subjective life is sufficiently inferior as to be unable to outweigh society's need to preserve the family. The danger of representing a woman like the heroine of *Anthony,* Larra argues, is that ordinary women will identify with her:

> [D]esde ese momento la mujer más despreciable se creerá autorizada a romper los vínculos sociales, a desatar los nudos de familia, y entonces adiós últimas ilusiones que nos quedan. . . . Y, lo que es peor, adiós socie-dad. (2: 253)

> From that moment on, the most despicable woman will believe herself au-thorized to break social bonds, to undo family ties, and then it's goodbye to the last illusions that remain to us. . . . And, what is worse, goodbye to society.

As Larra waffles through this troubled passage on female passion, he finally places the stress on woman's role in reproduction, denying the autonomous validity of her desires, emotions, and imagination, the very stuff of Romantic poetry.

The contradictions in the liberal conception of woman as at once man's companion and his object began to resolve during the 1840s into the cultural image that would define the feminine ideal for the rest of the century—the angel of the hearth. Pedro Sabater, who later married the poet Gertrudis Gómez de Avellaneda, eloquently synthesized the prevailing ideology of gender in 1842, when he declared that the female of the species was "una especie de ángel descendido del cielo" 'a kind of angel descended from heaven' (115). This image ascribes to women a subjectivity entirely suited to their domestic function:

> El bello sexo, señores, ha sido arrojado a la tierra para personificar al amor; el orgullo, la vanidad y las demás pasiones que dominan en su corazón, están subordinadas a ésta, que es su todo. Cumpliendo con su apacible destino, la mujer ama cuando niña a sus juguetes con mucho más cariño

que nosotros; ama cuando joven a sus amantes con mucha más violencia que nosotros; ama cuando madre a sus hijuelos con fuego más ardiente que nosotros. (Sabater 116)

The fair sex, gentlemen, has been brought down to earth in order to personify love; pride, vanity, and the other passions that rule in her heart are subordinated to love, which is her all. In accord with her gentle destiny, woman as a child loves her playthings with much more affection than we do; as a young woman, she loves her sweethearts with much more violence than we do; as a mother she loves her children with a more ardent flame than we do.

The psyche of woman defined as angel, then, has intensity but little range: it consists only of love. Other forms of desire—ambition, rebelliousness, aspirations for the greater good of humanity—are not even considered in relation to women, and in the final paragraphs of his article Sabater specifically rules out physical desire—"el torpe vicio de la voluptuosidad y el sensualismo" 'the stupid vice of voluptuosity and sensuality'—as a possibility for women. Indeed, the angel-woman's subjectivity contains nothing that is not a function of her role as men's nurturer: thus is her place as object of desire reconciled with her status as a conscious being.

A repeatedly published essay by Fermín Gonzalo Morón from the same period quite blatantly defined female existence in terms of male needs. This essay on women begins, true to the Romantic age's new interest in the psyche, with a bombastic evocation of the heights and depths of man's soul, of the passions and inspirations that move him. Eventually, the theme of woman appears:

Mas entre los sentimientos, que en mayor grado pueden contribuir a hacer tranquila y grata la existencia del hombre, a excitar su mente al culto de lo bello y de lo grande y mantener en su corazón las impresiones más dulces y poéticas, descuella sin duda aquella misteriosa pasión, con que las naciones modernas . . . miraron a la mujer. (476)

But among the sentiments that can most contribute to making man's existence tranquil and pleasant, to exciting his mind to cultivate the beautiful and the great, and to maintaining in his heart the sweetest and most poetic impressions, the most outstanding is doubtless that mysterious passion with which modern nations . . . have regarded woman.

Stimulating man's better feelings and enhancing his inner life, the angel of the hearth implicit in this portrayal of woman has a psychologically and morally redemptive effect on the male rulers of household and so-

ciety.⁴ In fact, her own inner life is predicated here on her disposition
to fulfill this role.

One consequence of this conception of feminine subjectivity as an
angelically loving sensibility is the negation of women's intellectual
faculties. If, as Gonzalo Morón tells us, women is "todo sentimiento,
todo [sic] pasión, todo [sic] imaginación" 'all feeling, all passion, all
imagination' (479), then "en efecto el entendimiento y la razón de la
mujer es [sic] muy débil, porque toda la vitalidad y la fuerza de su
existencia está concentrada en su corazón" 'in fact woman's reason
and understanding are very weak, for all the vitality and energy of
her existence are concentrated in her heart' (479). The angel of Spanish liberal ideology thus inherits a principal element of earlier mi-
sogyny—woman's supposed irrationality. The more modern version,
no less than the traditional one, uses the idea of women's intellectual
deficiency to justify their social subordination.⁵ Accordingly, Gonzalo
Morón's chivalrous language gives way to a slightly contemptuous pa-
ternalism when he draws the practical consequences of his portrayal
of women:

> Esta brevísima idea de la organización de la mujer resuelve la controversia
> sobre la cual debe ser su educación y su destino: el Estado y el padre
> de familias no tienen más que seguir las indicaciones de la naturaleza: así
> pues no deben empeñarse en ejercitar sus fuerzas ni en cultivar mucho su
> entendimiento. (479)

> This very brief idea of woman's constitution resolves the controversy about
> what her education and destiny should be: the State and the father of the
> family need only follow nature's indications: thus they should not insist on
> exercising her physical energies nor on cultivating her understanding very
> much.

As we can see, the State and the father had little to fear from the
ideological representation of women's innate character that emerged
with the rise of bourgeois ideas in Spain; male control of female behavior and destiny found ample justification despite the spread of liberal ideals of freedom and self-determination.

Turning to social history, we can trace a connection between this
preoccupation with circumscribing female mentality within the domestic sphere and the cultural transformations taking place in Spain in the
early nineteenth century. The image of woman as a domestic angel began to be formulated in Spanish writing at a time when the diffusion
of bourgeois social forms in Spain's cities had modified the traditional

Iberian separation of the sexes and cloistering of women. From the Middle Ages onward, Spain had customarily segregated women from men more strictly than had other parts of Europe (Pescatello 20). In public places such as the church and the theater, women were restricted to sections where men were not allowed, and even at home female space was differentiated from male space by furniture as well as partitions, for women sat on cushions, Moorish style, while men had chairs (Domínguez Ortiz 234–235). Only among the lowest classes—landless peasants and urban proletariat—did this rigid segregation ease. By the Romantic period, however, urban customs had relaxed considerably with respect to the social mixing of the sexes. It is difficult to pinpoint just how and when such changes occurred, for Spanish historiography has not yet explored the everyday life of the early nineteenth century in any detail. The historian Antonio Domínguez Ortiz affirms, however, that "by about 1800 the ladies had abandoned the Moorish cushions and mixed with men in the same room, as we see later in Romantic representations of social gatherings" (235). Jean Descola's account of everyday life in Romantic Spain, pieced together from the literature of the time, suggests that urban women enjoyed considerable freedom to move about the city, accompanied by servants, mothers, or male relatives, freely socializing with men in public spaces such as the promenade, the theater,[6] masked balls, or cultural events, as well as in private gatherings at home (116–124).

As the physical gender segregation of traditional Spain dissolved, the emerging ideology of domesticity helped to provide the psychological and moral separation and subordination of women that was more appropriate to bourgeois culture. One symptom of the shift toward the new symbolic forms in Spain was the urban upper class's adoption of the French genitive of possession in married women's last names (López-Cordón 85). Although Spanish law had never required women to change their names upon marrying, the custom of identifying a woman with the possessive plus her husband's last name (Pilar Sinués *de Marco,* for example) became widespread in the nineteenth century, as though the more socially mobile women of bourgeois society required this appellative mark of their domestic subordination.

To the same effect Spain, like other nineteenth-century European societies, developed structures of thought that distinguished the domestic sphere from the arenas of economic and political activity not only as the physical space of the home but also as a distinct emotional ambiance supposed to be identical with feminine subjectivity. Thus it is

precisely in the early 1840s, following a shift in urban customs, that
we see these first formulations of what will become a powerful social
stereotype—woman as the domestic angel.[7] Though upper-class women
were no longer secluded in the house, their behavior was controlled by
an insistent psychological regulation that followed the lines set out by
Sabater and Gonzalo Morón: all their feelings must be dictated by self-
abnegating love for the men to whom they were bound by the family.
Material written for and about women enforced their identification
with this norm by severely castigating any departure from it as contrary
to social well-being and natural law, much along the lines sketched out
by Larra's review of *Anthony*. Alicia Andreu's study of the image of
the feminine ideal documents how the popular press portrayed women
whose desires transgressed the domestic norm as monsters of egotism
and materialism (58–67). As we shall see, women who gave evidence
of "unfeminine" ambitions by taking up the pen ran the risk of being
attacked as unnatural and immoral.

We may conclude, then, that while liberals and Romantics pursued
a cultural revolution that would support and facilitate the transformation of public power and economic structures in Spain, they preserved
traditional gender hierarchy as carefully as they did the hierarchy of
class, developing new ideologies to hide the inherited inequalities. In
the end, identifying female subjectivity with family love amounted to
the same thing as conceiving of woman as the object rather than the
subject of consciousness. The inhibiting consequences of these attitudes
for women who might feel a vocation to write can be guessed from
Gonzalo Morón's assertion that woman "anima la imaginación del
jóven, despierta su numen poético" 'stimulates the young man's imagination, wakens his poetic muse' (478). Thus, when he lists "excitar
sus cualidades poéticas" 'exciting her poetic qualities' (480) among
the goals of female education, his readers could not doubt that he
meant a woman's ability to arouse poetic activity in men, not any
female capacity to create.

Yet, having examined the changing mentality promoted by liberalism and Romanticism, we must acknowledge that the balance sheet
was not entirely negative from the point of view of the female gender.
As "man's companion" woman was necessarily granted a degree of the
inner life that Romanticism began to construct for writer, hero, and
reader. Furthermore, the traditional association of women and emotion, an association emphasized and redefined in the domestic angel
stereotype, was given a more positive meaning by the Romantic cult of

feeling: women could now claim authority as subjects possessing a special sensibility, an expertise in empathy. Thus, despite the persistence of the gender hierarchy that had excluded women from literary production in Spain, the Romantic decades witnessed the emergence of a number of female writers who drew upon the authority of their own subjectivity to produce images of the self.

2

Women Writers in the Romantic Period

Que las cantoras primeras
Que a nuestra España venimos
Por sólo cantar sufrimos,
Penamos por sólo amar.
                —*Carolina Coronado*

At a time when liberal and Romantic ideas of personal autonomy and individual freedom were beginning to make inroads in the cultural structures of traditional Spain, women who were aware of these developments confronted a bitter truth: even the most progressive ideological schemes adopted by the Spanish cultural and political elite denied women the status of autonomous individuals in the public arena and predicated their subjectivity on the domestic and reproductive functions that traditional society had assigned them.

Around 1840 Carolina Coronado, later to become one of Spain's best-known Romantic poets, left a moving account of the frustration and discouragement experienced by women who tried to make space for creative activity beyond the domestic circle to which Spanish society confined them. A collection of letters preserved in Madrid's Biblioteca Nacional shows that some time after beginning a correspondence with Juan Eugenio Hartzenbusch, an influential man of letters who gave her support, advice, and material help in publishing her first book of poetry, she confessed to him that she was on the verge of giving up writing, worn out by the daily struggle against a social medium that frowned on or scoffed at her efforts:

> Mi pueblo opone una vigorosa resistencia a toda innovación en las ocupaciones de las jóvenes, que después de terminar sus labores domésticas deben retirarse a murmurar con las amigas. . . . La capital ha dado un paso más pero tan tímido y vacilante que sólo concede a las mujeres la lectura

de alguna novela *por distracción*. . . . Los hombres mismos a quienes la voz *progreso* entusiasma en política, arrugan el entrecejo si ven a sus hijas dejar un instante la monótona calceta para leer el folletín de un periódico. Calcule V. los enemigos que tendrá la mujer atrevida que se oponga a estas costumbres y si una lucha desigual y sostenida no debe al cabo fatigarla. (Cartas, carta 228)[1]

My home town vigorously resists any innovation in the occupations of its young ladies, who, once their domestic labors are done, are supposed to go off and gossip with their friends. . . . The provincial capital has taken a step up from this but with such timidity and hesitation that it only concedes to women the right to read an occasional novel for *distraction.* . . . The very men who are enthused by the word *progress* in politics frown if they see their daughters drop their monotonous darning to read a newspaper serial. You can imagine the enemies faced by the daring woman who opposes these customs and can guess whether she's likely to be worn out in the end by an unequal and unremitting struggle.

As it turned out, neither her family nor her provincial society were any match for Coronado's powerful will to write, but her letter concretely documents the hostility to female intellectual endeavor that Spanish women of the time perceived in their cultural environment. Even the most progressive men expected their daughters to stick to their darning needles. This observation is particularly poignant coming from Coronado, the daughter of a notoriously liberal family whose menfolk had suffered persecution and prison for their advanced political convictions.

Personal testimony by other women written about the same time—for example, the autobiography of Gertrudis Gómez de Avellaneda, another writer soon to be well known—shows that the frustration expressed by Coronado was widely shared. Yet, paradoxically, the Spanish press of the following decade documents an unprecedented burgeoning of women's writing. The names of a few women had dotted the late eighteenth-century press—the learned Josefa Amar y Borbón, the poet María Gertrudis Hore, the journalist Beatriz de Cienfuegos[2]—but the disruptions of the Napoleonic War and its aftermath were not propitious for female authorship. The 1820s and 1830s show no women writing in the periodical press and only a handful publishing novels or translations. It was only after 1840 that pieces signed by women began appearing with some frequency in papers and journals, and a number of books by women began to receive national attention.

By far the majority of these female productions were of poetry. Josefa Massanés, a Catalan, initiated the trend with her *Poesías,* published in 1841; Gómez de Avellaneda soon followed in the same year, first with a volume of poems and then with her novel, *Sab*. Coronado, who had published poems in the Madrid press since 1839, brought out her first book in 1843. The Valencian poet Amalia Fenollosa began publishing poems in provincial journals in 1841; by 1845 her poetry was appearing in the popular and widely circulated Madrid magazine *El Semanario Pintoresco Español*. Indeed, by mid-decade Spanish periodicals were so actively soliciting work by women that Coronado, for example, complained to Hartzenbusch in 1844 about the "continuas invitaciones de numerosos redactores" (Cartas, carta 213) that she felt obliged to accept. This demand for women writers found a ready supply around the peninsula: besides the writers just mentioned, Dolores Armiño in Asturias, Dolores Cabrera Heredia in Aragon, Manuela Cambronero in Galicia, Vicenta García Miranda in Extremadura, Rogelia León in Andalusia, and Victoria Peña in the Balearic Islands published regularly in the periodical press from about 1845 on; each of them had brought out a volume of poetry by the early 1850s at the latest. They were by no means the only women poets in print, nor was poetry the only genre that women published during this decade. A mid-decade list of contemporary dramatists[3] includes Barcelona's Angela Grassi and Josefa Robirosa de Torrens, as well as Coronado, Gómez de Avellaneda, and Cambronero. At the end of the decade, Cecilia Boehl began her meteoric career as a novelist, outstripping the more modest successes of Coronado and Gómez de Avellaneda in the same genre.

Could such an explosion of women's writing have occurred in a culture entirely hostile to literary activity on the part of its women? Obviously, by the 1840s Spain's traditional taboos against female access to intellectual production were no longer as effective as Coronado felt them to be in the moment of discouragement reflected in her letter to Hartzenbusch. Far from monolithic, the intimidating facade of patriarchal attitudes had developed cracks where female intellectual initiative might push through. The chronology suggests that Spanish women gained a limited access to literary production partly as a consequence of the inroads in traditional upper-class culture made by two related movements—liberalism and Romanticism: the decisive appearance of women as authors in Spain occurred just as liberal reforms and the prestige of literary Romanticism peaked in the early 1840s. New conceptions of the individual and of the importance of interiority were crucial in creating a climate in which women might feel authorized to assert themselves as the subjects rather than the objects of writing. To understand how this could be, we must now examine this climate in greater detail, taking into account the factors that explain the experience of frustration recorded by Carolina Coronado as well as the new possibilities for women that the press of the period makes so evident.

THE EMERGENCE OF WOMEN AS READERS

Women's degree of literacy and their reading habits condition the possibility of their writing. If a woman could not read a novel for distraction, either because she was illiterate or because she was not permitted time for nondomestic activity, she certainly could not write. Thus, we may expect changes in female literacy and education to have had a role in the upsurge in women's writing during the 1840s.

Few definitive figures are available for literacy in early nineteenth-century Spain. A census published in 1860 shows figures indicating that twenty percent of the population could both read and write; of those readers and writers, twenty-three percent were women (Romero Tobar 116). If these proportions held roughly true two decades earlier, then when Donald Shaw (80) calculates that in 1841 only about ten percent of Spaniards were literate, we can assume that literate women made up no more than two and a half percent of the total Spanish population. We can also assume that few of that small number were peasant or working-class women since there is no evidence that such women had any way of learning to read. The first gestures toward setting up a public school system during the liberal reforms of the 1830s mentioned schools for girls only as an afterthought: Article 35 of the Law on Education of 21 July 1838 provided vaguely that "separate schools will be established for girls wherever recourses permit" (qtd. in López-Cordón 99). Private schools for women of the middle and upper classes were scarce. An announcement in an 1822 journal suggests that such establishments were almost nonexistent in the earliest decades of the century:

> Con respeto a las señoritas, es ciertamente vergonzoso el tener que ir a mendigar su educación a Londres o a París. Por esto anunciamos con mucho gusto al público la casa de educación para señoritas bajo la dirección de da. Rafaela Felequia de Miranda. (*Periódico de las Damas* 1: 45)

> In regard to the young ladies it is certainly shameful to have to go beg their education in London or Paris. For this reason we take great pleasure in an-

nouncing the house of education for young ladies under the direction of
doña Rafaela Felequia de Miranda.

Thus, unless they belonged to the extremely wealthy, cosmopolitan
aristocracy that sent its daughters to finishing schools in England or
France, the mothers of the generation of women writers that appeared
in the 1840s probably received no more than a rudimentary tutoring
in their homes.

What they read once they got the basics of literacy seems to have
been very limited. In 1787 a commentator complained that women
tutored at their mothers' sides got lessons only from a book called
"Gritos del purgatorio y del infierno o, cuando más, *Luz de la fe y de
la ley"* 'Screams from Purgatory and Hell, or at best, *The Light of Faith
and Law,*' and there is little evidence that the situation had improved
much by the 1820s (qtd. in Martín Gaite 210). *Periódico de las Damas,*
arguing that it offered educationally beneficial reading to women,
claimed that most women of the day only took up a periodical in order
to study the fashion plate (4: 15).

By the end of the next decade, education for women had improved
somewhat, however. In 1839, *El Buen Tono,* a short-lived paper that
combined fashion reporting with an upbeat survey of new goods and
services offered in Spain, claimed that

> La educación del bello sexo ha mejorado extraordinariamente entre noso-
> tros. . . . En el día son muchos en España las casas de pensión y colegios
> donde a nuestras jóvenes se las enseña e instruye sobre ramos que del todo
> fueron desconocidos a nuestras madres. (2: 6)

> Education of the fair sex has improved extraordinarily in our coun-
> try. . . . In Spain today there are many pensions and boarding schools where
> our young women are taught and instructed in areas that were totally un-
> known to our mothers.

Unfortunately, the article supplies no details about the new branches
of knowledge women were being taught. Schools for upper class
women *did* exist by this time in Madrid and Barcelona, at least. Although Gómez de Avellaneda in Cuba and Coronado in an Extremaduran village were tutored at home, their contemporary Concepción
Arenal was brought from Asturias to Madrid in the mid-thirties so that
she could attend a finishing school. The brilliant young Concha, who
was to become a world-renowned sociologist and prison reformer later
in the century, did not find much intellectual stimulation at her school,

however, according to María Campo de Alange, though she did excel in the main subject taught—sewing. The deficiencies of the women's schools can be gauged by what Arenal had to study on her own: French and Italian (like Carolina Coronado), science, and philosophy (Campo 44–45). The clash of Arenal's desire for higher education with social custom highlights the strict limits placed on female education. Women's attendance at university courses was forbidden, and Arenal's mother refused to allow her daughter to challenge this taboo. Only after the mother died in 1841 did Arenal attend university lectures, dressed as a man—the first female auditor in the history of the Spanish university, according to Campo de Alange.[4] But it was not until the end of the century that women were admitted to the university as regular students.

Arenal's conflict with her mother about intellectual pursuits was not unique. Coronado's complaint to Hartzenbusch about social resistance to women who read made this point about mothers: "[T]odavía las madres, como instigadas por su conciencia, reprenden a las muchachas por entregarse a un ejercicio que a ellas no les fue permitido" 'Mothers still, as if urged by their conscience, scold girls for devoting themselves to an exercise that was forbidden to *them*' (Cartas, carta 228). This and *El Buen Tono*'s remark about "our mothers" provide clues that the generation of women who came of age in the 1830s were better educated than their predecessors, even though the scope of education for women was very limited.

The idea of gender difference that determined the place of women in the liberal program also controlled the educational ideal for women in this period. Articles urging better instruction for women repeated over and over again that women's mission as wives and mothers both justified their education and defined what they should be taught. A concerned liberal paterfamilias who wrote a letter on women's education to *El Español* in 1836 summed up the progressive thinking of the time. Arguing that ignorant women made uncongenial and incompetent wives, he advocated public education for women, but added:

> No se crea por eso que pretendamos formar mujeres sabias, ni que éstas en lo general, olvidando su misión en la tierra, misión en la que vemos algo de celeste, se engolfen en las ciencias físicas o abstractas, o bien en las lenguas muertas. ("Educación de las mujeres")

> Don't think that we therefore seek to form learned women or advocate that women in general, forgetting their mission on earth, a mission in which we

see something of the celestial, should become absorbed in physical or abstract sciences or even in ancient languages.

He then elaborated on the ideal curriculum for women:

> ... un conocimiento algo extenso así de la religión y de la moral, como de la lengua, historia, literatura nacionales y de la aritmética, principios de lógica, álgebra y geometría, alguna lengua o lenguas vivas a elección de los padres con la literatura de la misma (el francés hoy día parece indispensable), y principios de historia general antigua y moderna, geografía y mitología, música, dibujo y baile; sin que por eso se olvidasen las labores propias del sexo, ... el cuidado y gobierno de una casa, asistencia de un enfermo, y hasta nociones de cocina y repostería.

> ... somewhat extensive knowledge of religion and ethics as well as of the national language, history, and literature, and of arithmetic, principles of logic, algebra, and geometry, one or two modern languages to be selected by the parents together with their literature (French today seems indispensable), and the basics of general ancient and modern history, geography, and mythology, music, drawing, and dance; nor should the tasks particular to their sex be forgotten: ... the care and running of a household, the nursing of invalids, and even notions of cooking and pastry making.

Restricted as this scheme was (we can be sure that by "principios" the author had in mind only the barest introduction to mathematics and history), it represents an ideal that Spanish education would not achieve for many decades. According to Coronado, her education consisted of "la lectura de unas cuantas novelas bien escritas y tal cual libro de poesía" 'the reading of a few well-written novels and an occasional book of poetry.' She went forward on her own, she said— "Sin conocer el castellano, aprendí, sola, el francés y el italiano, y subí de un vuelo a leer el Tasso, Petrarca y Lamartine" 'Without knowing Castilian I taught myself French and Italian and went straight to reading Tasso, Petrarch, and Lamartine'—and she begged Hartzenbusch to send her a plan to guide future studies (Cartas, carta 222).

Those girls who went to school fared little better. The Royal Order of April 1816 had designated the function of primary schools for girls: first to teach them *labores,* sewing and household duties, then "to teach the girls to read and even to write, if any of them want to learn it" (qtd. in Scanlon 15). The next decades saw little change in educational philosophy, to judge by a manual for schoolgirls that was first published in the 1840s and became the standard text for public schools in 1855. The first part of *La señorita instruída o sea Manual del bello sexo* is totally devoted to sewing; the second part covers "lo más preciso que debe saber una señorita" 'what is most necessary for a young lady to know' (Cabeza and Cabeza, 1: 7). This second part, only a quarter the size of the section on sewing, includes the Catholic catechism, a set of questions and answers on the Bible (which the students were not apparently expected to read directly), a dry summary of the principles of Castilian grammar, a few pages of arithmetic, a chart of three different calligraphic styles, and a brief section on manners. Parts 3 and 4, which I have been unable to consult, provided "conocimientos de adorno" (Cabeza and Cabeza, 1: 7): synoptic tables of European and Spanish history and geography, and "conversations" about poetry, music, drawing, French, and Italian.

The supposedly better education that mid-century women received, then, emphasized the domestic arts and religious education that were deemed essential to wives and mothers, while allowing as an attractive addition a superficial acquaintance with history, literature, and the fine arts. The real lesson schoolgirls learned from their instruction manual was about the subservient place of women in the social order. The emphasis on sewing made clear that their main business was with the needle, not the pen. The section on manners is entirely concerned with social gestures denoting obedience, modesty, and self-abnegation. Even the description of grammar reiterates the message of gender hierarchy: "Si fueren dos sustantivos, el adjectivo se pondrá en plural con la terminación peculiar del género más noble, esto es, el masculino" 'In the case of two nouns, the adjective should be plural with the ending specific to the more noble gender, that is, the masculine' (Cabeza and Cabeza 2: 87).

Reading the classics of Spanish literature, contemporary poetry, and certain "well-written" novels not likely to affect their morals was, then, in the 1830s, an acceptable, if not enthusiastically encouraged pastime for young ladies. Such reading made it possible for a young woman to discover a vocation for writing poetry and a set of poetic models to follow in trying her own hand at verse, but the superficiality of women's education handicapped the female poet with regard to the technical aspects of verse form and meter. In the process of composing a piece in the Sapphic mode, Coronado described to Hartzenbusch the difficulties caused by her ignorance:

> [E]s el primer ensayo que hago en esta clase de versos cuya estructura comprendo muy confusamente. Una oda de Villegas me guiaba en cuanto al sonido, y el oído, engañado, ha podido extraviar mil veces la colocación oportuna de los acentos que requiere este género de metro. La explicación

de su mecanismo, la precisión de que las pausas estén entre tal y tal sílaba,
me confunde y estoy desalentada por mi torpeza. (Cartas, carta 220)

This is my first attempt at this kind of verse, whose structure I only vaguely
understand. An ode of Villegas's was my guide with respect to the sound,
and my ear, deceived, may have gone wrong a thousand times in the ar-
rangement of accents that this kind of meter requires. I'm confused about
how its mechanism works, the need for a pause between certain syllables,
and I'm discouraged by my blunders.

Vicenta García Miranda, like Coronado brought up in an Extremaduran village, was helped out of similar difficulties by a local male
poet, Juan Leandro Jiménez, who wrote a manual for her. The manuscript's title gives an inkling of what its author felt to be lacking in
his colleague's education: "Carta literaria / o sea / Disertación filosó-
fica / en que se asientan los más esenciales principios de la poesía y
se ponen de manifiesto los vicios más capitales que deben huirse en
este arte divino" 'Literary Letters, or Philosophical Dissertation, setting
forth the most essential principles of poetry and indicating the main
vices that must be avoided in this divine art' (García Miranda, *Notas*
3). Denied the training in classical languages on which poetic theory
was based, even in the Romantic period, women poets were forced to
depend on male mentors to rid their compositions of the telltale signs
of their educational deficiencies.

Despite the lacunae in their education and the pressure at home and
at school to choose domestic rather than intellectual activity, our examples make clear that in the two Romantic decades, many Spanish girls
were permitted to read imaginative literature during their leisure from
domestic duties and religious observances. It was this reading that not
only inspired them to write but also provided them a language of poetic
subjectivity.

WOMEN AND THE EXPANSION OF
THE PRESS

One thing we may be sure of: during the period of liberal reforms,
there was much more in print for women to read than there had been
during the first three decades of the century, or ever before. First the
Napoleonic War and then the repressive policies of Ferdinand VII reversed the expansion of the print industry that had begun in the late
decades of the eighteenth century. Reactionary ecclesiastical censorship

made it very difficult for editors to publish any contemporary literature. This same censorship quickly reduced the multitude of periodicals
that had sprung up during the Constitutional Triennium to only two
or three besides the official government organ in the late 1820s. With
the end of absolutism the situation became much more favorable for
Spanish publishers. They were encouraged to publish more by an 1834
law on the press that provided them with some protection against arbi-
trary prosecution, while the demand for reading matter that had remained unsatisfied during the preceding decade allowed increases in
prices and profits (Llorens 242).

The publication of books grew significantly during the 1830s and
1840s. Novels in translation were popular, profitable, and abundant.
Original novels in Spanish were few and did not seem to sell as well,
but they existed. Drama, both native and foreign, did relatively well,
and after 1840 so did books of poetry, if the fact that authors were
paid much more for poetry than for fiction (Llorens 242) is any indication. Also around 1840, Spanish publishers adopted the procedure developed by British and French entrepreneurs for creating a market
among the less solvent middle classes— the serial publication of books
in small, inexpensive installments (Ferreras; Romero Tobar). The periodical press, for its part, experienced a virtual explosion in the 1830s.
At the beginning of 1834, approximately eighteen papers and magazines were coming out in Madrid, up fourteen from four years before. In this early, unsettled period of expansion papers had very short
lives, some of them lasting no more than a few months, but a few publishers hit upon successful formulas quite quickly. *El Español,* a paper
founded in 1835 and modeled on contemporary papers in London and
Paris, continued into the 1840s, and *El Semanario Pintoresco Español,*
a weekly magazine started in 1836, carried on triumphantly into the
1850s. Most of the periodicals published before 1840 were organs of
a particular political faction, but in addition to aggressively expressing
editorial opinion, they printed poems, foreign news, serialized fiction,
and parliamentary chronicles side by side. In these early days, those
that attempted to specialize, in literature, in political satire, or in fashion, quickly failed. The 1840s, however, saw increasing specialization;
picture magazines and literary and intellectual journals enjoyed a measure of success. In all events, the newspaper with its ranting editorials,
its *folletín,* or serialized fiction section, its theater chronicle, and its society article became a fixture in the daily life of middle-class families.

The expanding press, perhaps more than the gradual changes in education, played a key role in developing a female readership.[5] One of the first journals addressed specifically to women, *Periódico de las Damas* (1822), seemed above all interested in recruiting women for the liberal cause during the highly politicized Triennium. Its contents consisted largely of political education for women trumped out in various forms, such as a long poem narrating the history of government, a dialogue on women's influence on politics, or an essay on women's role as mothers of the new citizen. The editorial voice was explicitly that of a man, patronizing and instructing his female readers. The one concession to lightheartedness—aside from the promise of a fashion plate, conceived as a necessary bait for the female reader—allowed women a carefully circumscribed arena of participation: each issue offered a "charade," that is, a short puzzle in verse, and succeeding issues published solutions, also in verse, signed and sent in by women readers. If these signatures were authentic, it means not only that women did read this journal but also that they looked to it as a medium of displaying their own wit and verbal ability. Such budding possibilities were cut short, however, by the French invasion and the restoration of absolutism in 1823, when *Periódico de las Damas* disappeared.

A decade later, during the rapid expansion of the press that immediately followed Ferdinand's death, another periodical took aim at women readers. *El Correo de las Damas* (1833–1835), however, seemed less interested in political proselytizing than in attracting a profitable number of subscribers. It included a section on fashion and a weekly theater review, written for several months by no less a critic than Mariano José de Larra. The female market was obviously regarded as significant, for the political papers also attempted to draw women readers by making the *folletín* a regular section that printed the types of reading approved for women—sketches of manners, poetry, and increasingly, serialized novels. Some of the more serious-minded papers, like *El Español,* ran essays on the history and the nature of women, a genre that became *de rigueur,* apparently, in the women's journals of the next decade. The journals more oriented toward culture than toward openly partisan politics paid considerable attention to women, interpreting through essays, stories, and poems the ideological reduction of women to "angels of the hearth" that we discussed in the last chapter. These flattering images of women as paragons of love, mercy, and purity were highly manipulative, as Alicia Andreu has pointed out (39–41), not only drawing female readers into the market for pulp literature but also channeling their desires within politically and socially conservative structures. This image, which Andreu terms "la mujer virtuosa," is "firmly rooted in a moral code whose base is composed of a series of social and pseudoreligious virtues and precepts oriented toward submission, obedience, and resignation before God and the status-quo" (69).[6] As we shall see, such images exerted a powerful influence upon women's writing.

Approaches to the woman reader were not yet coherent in the mid-thirties. The illustrated magazines that appeared then offer an instructive contrast in how they treated the female public. *El Observatorio Pintoresco,* born in the spring of 1837, explicitly identified the female reader among its targets but depicted her with almost contemptuous condescension:

> El artículo de modas nos reconcilia con las bellas nayades, cuyo sonrosado rostro, cuyo esbelto talle forman el ornamento del Prado, el orgullo de la Corte; cogen nuestro número, miran la primera página, leen la última, observan las viñetas, juzgan del grabado y se posan ¡o delicia! en el artículo de modas, he aquí mi dominio, he aquí mi imperio. (12: 93)

> The fashion article reconciles us with the lovely naiads whose rosy faces and slender figures ornament the Prado esplanade, the pride of the capital; they pick up our issue, look at the first page, read the last, glance at the pictures, judge the engraving, and settle, oh delight! on the fashion article, which is my dominion, my empire.

This construction of the female reader as interested only in looking at pictures unless the text concerns fashion did not help the *Observatorio* stay afloat—it had disappeared by the end of 1837.

The case of *El Semanario Pintoresco,* which lived to a ripe old age, suggests a rather different profile of the woman reader. Founded by Ramón de Mesonero Romanos, an astute marketer of his own literary product, the sketch of manners, this illustrated magazine identified its intended public in very broad terms:

> Escribimos, pues, para toda clase de lectores y para toda clase de fortunas; pretendemos instruir a los unos, recrear a los otros y ser accesibles a todos. No seguiremos orden metódico en la elección de materias; buscaremos en el estudio de la naturaleza, de las bellas artes, de la literatura, de la industria, de la historia, de la biografía y de las costumbres antiguas y modernas, todos los hechos, todos los adelantos capaces de interesar la curiosidad pública. ("Prospecto" 5)

> We write, then, for all classes of readers and all kinds of fortunes; we seek to instruct some, entertain others, and be accessible to all. We will follow

no systematic order in the choice of material; in the study of nature, fine arts, literature, industry, history, biography, ancient and modern customs, we will try to find all the facts and advances capable of engaging the public's curiosity.

The Prospectus and the first numbers give no indication, aside from an occasional article on fashion, that the *Semanario* counted women as part of its intended audience. Instead, emphasizing cheapness and accessibility, the *Semanario* obviously aimed at social strata that had not yet been fully incorporated into the reading public. Whatever its success—probably small—in attracting the lower classes, this strategy offered middle-class women a new reading opportunity: short, simple articles on historical figures, famous buildings or geographical locations, customs, and sometimes science along with fiction, poetry, fashion reviews, and puzzles and games. The magazine thus supplied women with information on subjects in which their education was deficient and in a form that did not demand any previous knowledge. Women's interest in the *Semanario*'s encyclopedic offerings played its part in expanding the magazine's subscription list, which reached 3,000—an impressive figure by standards of the day—by the end of the decade (Ferrer del Río 143). Certainly when the second series of *El Semanario Pintoresco Español* was launched in 1839, the importance of its women readers was tacitly acknowledged in its new subtitle, *Lectura de las familias*; "la mujer sensible" 'the sensitive woman' (2d. ser. 1 [1839]: 3) was specifically included among those addressed by its introductory remarks.

In 1839, journals directed specifically to women and restricted to traditionally "feminine" subject matter did not do well. Two attempts—*El Buen Tono* and *La Mariposa*—went under in a matter of weeks. Women's magazines had slightly greater success in the 1840s, however, when an expanded market of readers allowed more journals to coexist profitably. *El Semanario Pintoresco Español,* for example, shared the field of the illustrated magazine with a number of other competitors during most of this decade. But the new women's journals did not attempt to compete in this arena; as if in an effort to offer something slightly different to a female audience by this time firmly established as readers of illustrated magazines, fledgling periodicals like *La Psiquis* (Valencia, 1840), *El Defensor del Bello Sexo* (Madrid, 1845), *La Gaceta de las Mujeres* (Madrid, 1845), and *El Pensil del Bello Sexo* (Madrid, 1845–1846) concentrated on essays, fiction, and poetry. One of these journals, *La Moda,* which was founded in Cádiz in 1842 and which billed itself as "A Weekly Review of Literature, Theater, Customs, and Fashion," found a loyal readership and lasted until 1889 (Perinat 18).

The composition of these publications reflects a new nuance in the feminine ideal and in the image of the female reader. An editorial statement in *El Defensor del Bello Sexo* expresses the trend quite well. Having declared that his journal's highest priority is inculcating principles of feminine virtue in his readers, the editor goes on:

> Pero como la virtud no es la única dote, si bien es la mayor, que realza a una joven en la sociedad, procuraremos también ilustrar su entendimiento. . . . Al efecto, les presentaremos en todos los números algunos ejemplos de la literatura que está más a su alcance, y en lindas poesías y escogidas novelas irán formando poco a poco su gusto, para que cuando llegue la ocasión de hablar en público, den pruebas de un talento cultivado y que sabe apreciar el verdadero mérito. (3 Mar. 1846: 134)

> But since virtue is not the only endowment, though certainly the major one, that distinguishes a young woman in society, we will also try to enlighten her understanding. . . . To this effect, we will present our readers in every issue with examples of literature that is within their grasp, and lovely poems and select novels will form their taste little by little so that when the occasion to speak in public arises, they will demonstrate a cultivated talent showing that they can appreciate true merit.

These journals, then, perceived in their public an increased interest in providing its daughters with a degree of urbanity and culture, now that they were expected to mix socially with men. This interest went hand in hand with emerging reading habits and tastes among women. The women's periodicals published a lot of poetry, mostly of the sentimental Romantic type, some undistinguished fiction in translation, and many articles on women—the history of women in antiquity; biographies of famous women, including contemporary writers like Mme de Staël and George Sand; erudite studies of gender and language or the place of women in Genesis; and rhapsodic essays on the nature of women.

If the kind of reading provided by the manual *La señorita instruída*, in its first printing at about this time, constituted the lower end of the scale of what women read, these middle-brow women's journals indicate what might be found near the top. The market did not long sustain the three Madrid women's magazines started in 1845, perhaps because they could not compete with Cádiz's *La Moda*, which had a nationwide circulation. In any case, in the mid-forties less specialized magazines

were making an effort to meet the developing expectations of women
readers by regularly publishing the kinds of poetry and articles that
came out in the women's journals. But by 1851 the female readership
was sufficiently large and stable to support *El Correo de la Moda,*
another woman's journal that ran well into the 1880s.

What was strikingly different about the journals, both general and
specialized, that addressed a female audience in the 1840s is that, unlike the papers of the 1830s, a considerable number of their contributors were women. During the earlier decade, instances of women's
publishing in the periodical press were extremely rare: a short story by
Cecilia Boehl came out in the Romantic journal *El Artista* in 1835, and
Carolina Coronado's first published poem appeared in *El Piloto* in
1839. As we have seen, however, between 1841 and 1843 several
books by women appeared in print, and by the mid-forties women were
regularly publishing in periodicals around the peninsula. If female authorship had been a simple function of the expansion of the press,
which began in 1833, we might expect a gradual rise in the number of
women publishing from that date on. That it took almost a decade
more before women writers were incorporated in the growing press
industry indicates the necessity of building a female readership first.
When women found more to read and began to read more, when their
expectations were perceived by publishers as a market, then women
writers discovered that they had something to say and found outlets
open in the press.

The women's magazines reflected the change. *Periódico de las
Damas* in the 1820s and *El Correo de las Damas* in the 1830s were
explicitly written by men for women to read. But the expectation that
women should stand in a purely receptive, passive position with respect
to these publications was fading in the mid-forties. José de Souza,
editor of *El Defensor del Bello Sexo* (1845), wrote most of the journal's text with a little help from other male contributors, but he let his
readers know that he was eager to print women's contributions by
publishing an exchange of letters with Carolina Coronado. Graciously
thanking him for sending her a copy of the periodical in which her
poem "A Claudia" appeared, Coronado diplomatically suggested that
publishing women writers was a step in the right direction: "Consti-
tuirse en defensor de nuestro sexo es una generosa empresa; hacernos
partícipes de los triunfos que nos conquista, es todavía mayor favor"
'To constitute yourself a defender of our sex is a generous enterprise;

to make us participants in the triumphs you garner us is an even greater favor' (Carta 45). To this Souza replied ecstatically:

> Mi señora: No encuentro palabras para manifestar a V. la satisfacción que he experimentado al leer su muy favorecida a que tengo honra de contestar. Doy a V. un millón de gracias por los elogios (que no merezco) que se digna tributarme. . . . Mi publicación ha tenido una acogida más favorable de la que yo me prometía. Por lo tanto si la fortuna y la bondad de las stas. que, como V., me favorecen con las producciones de su claro ingenio, me conquistan algunos laureles, me tendré por muy dichoso. (46)

> My dear madam: I cannot find words to express my satisfaction on reading your very flattering letter to which I have the honor of replying. A thousand thanks for the praise—undeserved—that you see fit to give me. . . . My publication has had a more favorable response than I had counted on. Therefore if fortune and the kindness of the young ladies who, like yourself, favor me with the productions of their bright genius conquer a few laurels for me, I will consider myself very lucky.

Women responded to this invitation: before six months were up—and with them, the lifetime of the periodical—Amalia Fenollosa and Vicenta García Miranda, as well as Coronado, had contributed poetry to *El Defensor*.

The idea that women might want to take an active role in the publications they read had already occurred to one Madrid entrepreneur who in September 1845 launched *Gaceta de las Mujeres, redactada por ellas mismas* [*Woman's Gazette, edited by women themselves*]. The subtitle apparently indicated an ideal that the journal hoped to live up to rather than a statement of fact. Though the articles were signed only with initials and thus did not reveal the gender of their authors, the subject matter and style did make clear that the writers were male. For example, one contributor displays a degree of erudition—citing Greek and Latin, comparing the Latin version of the Bible with the Hebrew—that was almost unthinkable for a woman of this period; others referred to women as "they" rather than "we." An announcement at the end of October suggests, however, that the editors were sincere in their desire to produce a journal written largely by women:

> Desde el primer domingo del próximo mes de noviembre toma este periódico el nuevo título de *La Ilustración de las Damas* y se reorganiza bajo la dirección de la célebre escritora, Sta. Da. Gertrudis Gómez de Avellaneda. . . . *La Ilustración de las Damas* sin abandonar el objeto que se propuso la *Gaceta de las Mujeres,* aspira a ser el mejor periódico de literatura

que se ha publicado en España; y de ello responden además de la reputación de su directora el ventajoso concepto de las stas. Da. Carolina Coronado, Da. Josefa Moreno Nartos y Da. Dolores Gómez Cádiz de Velasco, cuyas producciones adornarán nuestro periódico. (Gaceta 7: 8)

From the first Sunday of next month this journal will adopt the new name of *The Ladies' Enlightenment* and will be reorganized under the direction of the celebrated writer, doña Gertrudis Gómez de Avellaneda. . . . *The Ladies' Enlightenment,* without abandoning the aims of the *Woman's Gazette,* aspires to be the best literary journal that has been published in Spain; its quality is guaranteed not only by the reputation of the new director but also by the high repute of Carolina Coronado, Josefa Moreno Nartos, and Dolores Gómez Cádiz de Velasco, whose works will adorn our journal.

Whether this blurb was written by the former editor or by Gómez de Avellaneda herself, its bold declaration of the journal's ambition to excel in literature as well as to publish mostly women's work indicates that in 1845 it was at least conceivable to consider women men's equals in the terrain of literature. Unfortunately, only one issue of *La Ilustración de las Damas* was ever published; it carried a poem on war by Coronado and an article by Gómez de Avellaneda titled "Capacidad de las mujeres para el gobierno" that constitutes one of the strongest Spanish statements of this period of women's claim to political rights. But Avellaneda, whose infant daughter fell ill and died a short time later, was in no condition to continue directing the journal, and the paper's financial backers apparently did not consider public response to be sufficiently favorable to try to continue the experiment with another director.

Six years later, in 1851, however, the idea of women's running a publication meant for women seemed more opportune, and *Ellas, Organo oficial del sexo femenino* was born. Although the first two numbers show considerable male collaboration, regular features such as the weekly theater review and the article on fashion were written by women. By the third number, women contributed almost all the articles and most of the poetry and fiction. Many well-known women poets— Amalia Fenollosa, Angela Grassi, Vicenta García Miranda, Robustiana Armiño—contributed to this journal, but what is new is that for several weeks the editorials, the regular features, the obligatory articles on famous women and women's education—the truly journalistic part of the journal, in other words—were all written by women. The various editorial statements and clarifications, most of them defensively claiming not to be feminist, suggest that during December 1851 and January 1852, the periodical was run by two women, Emilia de T. and Alica Pérez de Gascuña.[7] This state of affairs did not last long, for the journal was given a new name (*Album de Señoritas*) and a new male director on January 30, but it did anticipate the rise in the next two decades of women's magazines run by women, some of whom, like Angela Grassi and Robustiana Armiño, had first emerged as writers in the 1840s (Criado 173).

By 1850, then, women readers and women writers had become a firmly established part of a well-developed and growing press industry. The daily newspapers, as well as the illustrated magazines and the specialized women's journals, gave women a place not only as readers of the *folletín* but also as writers. For example, the daily *La Ilustración* published during the course of 1850 an article and a short novel by Gómez de Avellaneda and numerous articles by Coronado. Another daily, *El Heraldo*, serialized Cecilia Boehl's *La gaviota* during the latter half of 1849. The novel came out under a male pseudonym, to be sure, but the newspaper so readily gave up the secret of the author's gender that one suspects that the editors thought it an advantage that the readers should know the novelist was a woman.

FEMALE COUNTERTRADITIONS AND THE LYRICAL SISTERHOOD

About halfway through the Romantic period, Spanish women found and developed a potential readership and access to publication, but to explain how they actually began to write, risking the disapproval of their immediate social circle, we must look for more direct incentives. One powerful form of encouragement to women with a vocation for writing was the example of other women writers. Taking heart from the images of illustrious forerunners like Sappho and Saint Teresa and from the recent examples of Mme de Staël and George Sand, the pioneering female poets of this period in turn provided models that inspired their younger or more timid contemporaries.

Within the cultural matrix of the time, characterizations of certain female literary figures offered a countertradition to the generally negative view of women writers or intellectuals. The prevailing image of Sappho,[8] for example, brought together acknowledged poetic genius with the emotional qualities acceptable, even desirable, in woman, who, as we saw in the last chapter, was supposed to exist for love. A brief anonymous article, "La poetisa Saffo," that offered background for the opera *Saffo,* about to make its debut in Madrid in 1842, provides an attractive portrait of the poet of Lesbos: "[E]l fuego de su alma, origen de sus grandes talentos, sabía pintarse en sus miradas, e imprimir en todas sus facciones un carácter de pasión y de energía superior a la hermosura y gentileza misma" 'The fire of her soul, source of her great talents, expressed itself in her eyes and stamped upon all her features a passion and energy superior to beauty and grace themselves.' This admiring representation of the woman of genius as a charismatic figure whose physical being expresses her passionate soul certainly diverges from the retiring modesty expected of Spanish women according to *La señorita instruída,* but it reverberates with other feminine images familiar to women readers.[9] Indeed, the portrait of Sappho shows the influence of Mme de Staël's *Corinne ou l'Italie,* whose heroine is just such a female poetic genius.[10] First published in Spanish in 1819 (Marco 303), this novel was popularized at the level of oral culture by a ballad that circulated in Spain during the late 1830s.[11]

The network of associations connecting the tenderness and sensibility deemed feminine with literary creation also appears in an article on George Sand published in *El Pensil del Bello Sexo:*

> Apenas habrá una de vosotras, lectoras mías, que no haya tenido ocasión más de una vez, de admirar y entusiasmarse con la lectura de alguna de esas mil novelas que habrán llegado a vuestras manos suscritas con el nombre con que encabezamos este artículo. . . . En efecto, nada hay más apasionado, más tierno, más lleno de poesía y encantos que las obras de Jorge Sand. Ellas son más particularmente escritas para vosotras, que tenéis una alma sensible. ("Jorge Sand" 81)

> Most of you, my dear readers, will have had more than one occasion to be amazed and enthused by reading one of the myriad novels that have come into your hands signed by the name with which we head this article. . . . Indeed, there is nothing more passionate, more tender, more full of poetry and charm than the works of George Sand. They are especially written for you, who have sensitive souls.

Although George Sand was considered scandalously immoral in Spain, this passage suggests that she was widely read. In placing Sand in the category of the "sensitive soul," the author connects her to a term that had become one of the period's most positive epithets for women. *El Semanario Pintoresco Español* used "la mujer sensible" to characterize its female readers in 1839, and the term became ever more widespread in the following decade. The view of women's special sensibility as tender, passionate, and poetic derived from the idea that women's destiny was to love, and dovetailed with the rising vogue of Romantic poetry. As we have seen, women's journals tended to specialize in poetry and fiction, and most of it was on the more lachrymose side of the Romantic spectrum. A fascinating indication that the melancholic, sensitive variety of Romanticism could be read as feminine appears in Carolina Coronado's conviction that Lamartine's work was the expression of a woman's sensibility (Sandoval 54). Thus it was but a small step from the woman reader as *alma sensible* to the woman writer who expressed a feminine sensibility vibrating with Romantic feeling.

The linkage of Sappho, Corinne, and the sensitive soul had, as elements of a tradition that authorized and modeled the female voice in poetry, an important impact on the first women Romantic poets in Spain. Both Coronado and Avellaneda included imitations of Sappho in their first collections of poetry, as if to identify themselves with what the Greek poet stood for in Spain at the time. Sappho seems to have been particularly important to Coronado, who began at an early age to read what she could find on the poet of Lesbos and to develop the theory, later set forth in a pair of articles for *El Semanario Pintoresco*, that Sappho and Saint Teresa of Avila were twin souls, united by their passionate intensity of spirit. Coronado, who put over the table in her study a painting of the Saint of Avila writing (Coronado, *Poesías* 1852 ed., 3), certainly included herself in this line of parentage, whereas Gómez de Avellaneda looked to a more contemporary set of literary mothers—Mme de Staël and George Sand. While she echoed some of Sand's ideas in her work, she had a more profound identification with the image of de Staël's Corinne. As we shall see when we discuss Avellaneda's narrative works, her autobiography shows Corinne to be a model for her construction of her own character, as well as for the construction of female characters in her fiction.

The positive vision of the woman writer embodied in the idea of Sappho and her daughters had another feature that provided an important incentive to the female poets of the 1840s. The 1842 article "La poetisa Saffo" established a difference between men and women poets by referring to the myth that Sappho had been persecuted by an envious male poet:

¿Será posible que su primer perseguidor y acusador fue un hombre, y un hombre grande? ¿Cómo las mujeres que han escrito no han conocido la envidia entre sí al paso que los hombres han convenido constantemente en perseguirse? ¿Consistirá en ser peores éstos según nuestro dictamen, o acaso las mujeres se creerán más obligadas a hacer causa común cuando se trata de la gloria e intereses de su sexo?

Can it be possible that her first persecutor and accuser was a man, and a great one? How is it that women writers have not been envious of one another while men have always persecuted each other? Could the reason be, as is my opinion, that men are morally inferior, or is it perhaps that women feel more obliged to make common cause when it is a matter of the glory and interests of their sex?

The idea that women writers, unlike men, felt solidarity with rather than rivalry for other women became very much a part of the ethos of the women who started writing in this period. For one thing, a stance of self-abnegating supportiveness fit very nicely with the emerging image of femininity as the *mujer virtuosa* or the *ángel del hogar*. In addition, this article's second, more social explanation of female solidarity hit on what seems to have been a widespread feeling among these women that they must join together to defend themselves against the prejudices and prohibitions confronting their sex.

The information available to us on the process through which women incorporated themselves into print culture during the Romantic period shows the importance of the first two or three bold pioneers who crossed the threshold into print in providing not only motivating examples but also direct aid and encouragement to other women who wished to join them. The case of Vicenta García Miranda illustrates this process perfectly. According to Antonio Manzano Garías, who had García Miranda's memoirs and letters in his possession (though they were destroyed in 1936), the latter came across some published verses of Carolina Coronado in 1845. That experience had a powerful impact on the twenty-four-year-old woman, recently bereft of both husband and child: "The verses' incantation made the young widow feel as if her soul, asleep till then, had suddenly awakened, and since she was gifted with a rich fantasy and a natural facility for rhyme, she began to try writing verses of her own" (Manzano, "Década extremeña" 24). Isolated in a tiny village, with little education and nothing in her immediate environment to encourage her to write, García Miranda was sufficiently incited by a publication signed by another woman to begin producing poetry herself. When she had composed two or three viable pieces, she sent them to Coronado. Guessing only too well the oppressive environment in which her Extremaduran compatriot was laboring, the more experienced poet did not disappoint the hope and trust that her work had inspired. Evidence of Coronado's quick and supportive response appeared in *El Defensor del Bello Sexo* in early 1846: on February 8, the journal published García Miranda's poem "Al invicto extremeño, García de Paredes," preceded by a warm letter of introduction from Coronado. Coronado's recommendation obviously had power, for García Miranda published another poem the following month in *El Defensor* and soon was publishing in journals around the peninsula.

The generous encouragement that Coronado offered poets like García Miranda was extended by them to others in turn, creating a circle of solidarity among women writers of this time. Among the papers of García Miranda, for example, Manzano found evidence of abundant mutually supportive correspondence with other poets:

> The chorus of poetesses who in this decade tried their wings in the literary weeklies of Madrid and the provinces formed—as I was able to ascertain in the papers and letters found in the old house of the García Mirandas . . . —a kind of *Lyrical Sisterhood*. Without being personally acquainted, they kept up a copious and effusive correspondence among themselves, greeting each other at the beginning and end of their letters with the sweet title of sister. Every new feminine signature of a poem appearing in a literary magazine intrigued the other poetesses, who started up an epistolary friendship with her. ("Década extremeña" 7)

According to Manzano, García Miranda corresponded with Amalia Fenollosa, Pilar Sinués, Rogelia León, Dolores Cabrera Heredia, Robustiana Armiño, and Angela Grassi. We know also that Amalia Fenollosa and Manuela Cambronero exchanged letters regularly (Manzano, "Fenollosa" 54–55), and that Carolina Coronado, who wrote to many women writers, had a particularly strong epistolary friendship with Robustiana Armiño (Muñoz de San Pedro 22). Another sign of the existence of this "lyrical sisterhood" is the poems that these women dedicated to other women poets. Such exchanges as "A mi amiga la sta. Angela Grassi," by Natalia Boris de Ferrant, and "A mi querida amiga Natalia Boris de Ferrant," by Angela Grassi (1852), or "A la señorita doña Carolina Coronado," by Encarnación Calero de los Ríos, and "A la señorita doña Encarnación Calero de los Ríos," by Coronado (1846), were scattered throughout the journals of the period.[12]

This last-mentioned exchange, published in *El Pensil del Bello Sexo* just about the time that the circle of sister poets was beginning to form, is particularly interesting in regard to what it tells us about the shared consciousness that drew these women together. The first stanza of Ca-

lero de los Ríos's poem suggests that she, like García Miranda, was
moved to write by the feelings Coronado's poetry inspired:

> En armónico acento
> Una voz escuché, que en dulce lira,
> Con tierno sentimiento,
> Sobre el destino femenil suspira,
> Y eleva al firmamento
> Su queja, su canción y su tormento. (67)

I heard the harmonic accents of a voice that sighs on a sweet lyre with tender
feeling about feminine destiny and raises to the firmament its complaint, its
song, and its torment.

It was the sense of oppression evoked by Coronado's poetry, her expression of the anguish caused by feminine destiny, to which other
women responded; and in her answering poem, she sounded the same
chords. Welcoming Calero de los Ríos to the chorus composed of
herself and "[l]a tierna *Massanés,* mi *Robustina,* / La triste *Amalia* y
Angela divina" (85), Coronado confirms that sadness is the dominant
note of female poetry:

> [A]l fin, de las hembras es el llanto,
> Y cantar sin gemir, cantar placeres
> Es propio de varón, no de mujeres.
>
> . . . .
>
> Canta la vida triste, amiga mía,
> Que ellos han de cantar la placentera;
> Y pues que suyos son placer y risa,
> Que dejen el llanto a la poetisa. (85)

Finally, weeping is for women and singing without tears, singing of pleasures, is for men, not women. . . . Sing the sad life, my friend, for they will
sing the pleasant one, and since pleasure and laughter are theirs, let them
leave weeping for the poetess.

The theme of women's painful destiny resounds throughout the
poems published by the lyrical sisterhood, varying from the sighing
melancholy of Fenollosa, who in 1844 concludes her poem "La mujer"
with "¡Pobre infeliz!" 'poor unhappy one' (36), to García Miranda's
stirring 1851 exhortation in "A las españolas":

> ¡Oh, mujeres! luchar a vida o muerte,
> Sin que el ánimo fuerte
> Desmaye en la pelea a que briosas
> Algunas se han lanzado

Del sexo esclavizado
Por romper las cadenas ominosas. (11)

Oh, women! Fight for life or death without letting your strong purpose faint in the struggle into which some of you have boldly thrown yourselves to break the hateful chains of the enslaved sex.

The language that described women's condition in terms of chains and slavery had been circulating since the mid-1830s through the marginal currents of French utopian socialist discourse that can be detected in the Madrid press (see chapter 1) and in Cádiz and Cataluña (Elorza). Gómez de Avellaneda picked up the figure of the female lot as slavery in her 1841 novel, *Sab,* but the injustice and oppressiveness of women's lot did not become a topic of women's poetry until 1844–1845, precisely the years when a self-conscious circle of women poets began to form. The chronology suggests that an interesting feedback process was at work in women's expanding production of poetry for publication. The early books of poetry by Massanés, Gómez de Avellaneda, and Coronado, all published between 1841 and 1843, did not explicitly raise the question of women's destiny, though, as I will argue in later chapters, their construction of a lyrical self was *about* women's place in the world. It would seem, then, that other women read this first female Romantic poetry as the expression of a particularly feminine anguish and were emboldened by it to speak out themselves; and, as the numbers of women poets grew, they all felt more confident about openly discussing their hitherto silent pain and resentment in a language with clear political overtones. Coronado was the leader here: as soon as her 1843 volume was out, she began publishing poems of a feminist cast in many of the journals that solicited her work. But Gómez de Avellaneda, although she remained quite aloof from the lyrical sisterhood and was always distinguished from them by the critics, also polemicized poetically in women's behalf in "El porqué de la inconstancia" (dated 1843 in the 1850 collection) and dedicated a poem on the difficulties of being female and writing poetry to a sister poet ("Despedida a la Señora Da. D. G. C. de V."[13]—also dated 1843 in the 1850 collection).

The focal point of this mid-decade burst of female poetic protest was not specifically political rights but rather the issue at stake in women's entry into print culture during this period: women's right to intellectual activity and literary self-expression. Coronado was particularly vehement on this point, which she developed eloquently in her letter introducing García Miranda to the readers of *El Defensor del Bello Sexo*. She concedes that writing poetry had become a fad among young women—an observation that confirms the other evidence of a sudden burst in female production of poetry—but argues that her protégée, like many others, has a true vocation:

> Las circunstancias de su vida nos conducen a reflexionar sobre lo triste que es la suerte de las mujeres a quienes las preocupaciones no permitían hace poco el desahogo de expresar sus pensamientos. La cuestión de si las jóvenes *deben o no dedicarse a hacer versos* nos parece ridícula. La *poetisa* existe de hecho y necesita cantar, como volar las aves y correr los ríos, si ha de vivir con su índole natural, y no comprimida y violenta. Considérenla sus defensores y sus contrarios como un *bien* o un *mal* para la sociedad, pero es inútil que decidan si debe o no existir porque no depende de la voluntad de los hombres. Estos pueden reformar sus obras, pero no enmendar las de Dios. ("Al Sr. Director" 97)

> The circumstances of her life lead us to reflect upon the sad fate of women, to whom prejudice not long ago denied the freedom to express their thoughts. The issue of whether young women *should or should not write poetry* seems ridiculous to me. The *poetess* exists in fact and must sing, as birds fly and rivers flow, if she is to live according to her innate nature, and not in violent repression. Whether her defenders and their adversaries consider her *good* or *bad* for society, it is useless for them to decide whether she should or shouldn't exist because that doesn't depend on men's will. Men can reform their works, but not amend those of God.

The sense of a vocation shared by other women but not readily recognized by their society emboldens Coronado to appropriate for herself and her sisters an image already claimed for the male Romantic poet. Lamartine, in "Le poéte mourant" (1823), asserted the perfect naturalness of the Romantic poetic voice: "Je chantais, mes amis, comme l'homme respire, / Comme l'oiseau gémit, comme le vent soupire, / Comme l'eau murmure en coulant" 'I sang, my friends, as men breathe, as birds coo, as the wind sighs, as running water murmurs' (147). As Coronado's paragraph shows, this figure was attractive to women as an image of their poetic activity[14] because it represents the woman poet as a fact of divinely created nature, not as the aberration that much of contemporary society declared her to be.

Bolstered by the awareness that her difficulties and aspirations were shared by other women, Coronado led her sisters not only in expressing a female subjectivity that had been suppressed but also in asserting their right to expression in terms adapted from the liberal and Romantic discourses of the period. She echoed her liberal fathers by identifying opposition to women poets with the liberals' enemy, the irrational "preocupaciones," or prejudices, that obstruct the individual right to self-expression. Further, using a Romantic image of the poet to legitimize women's writing, she drew from her ideological milieu a logic that based the female poetic vocation on nothing less than the authority of nature and God.

RESPONSE AND REACTION TO
THE WOMEN WRITERS

If women found something in the cultural dynamics of the period that enabled them to take the difficult step of presenting themselves to the public in print, the response they met also affected, or even shaped, the way they presented themselves and their identity as writers. The above-cited outburst by Carolina Coronado implies the existence of both encouragement and resistance in her audience, which included those who would be interested in reading the work of a new woman writer as well as those who debated whether women *should* write poetry. The press of this period suggests that the reception of the women writers was, indeed, mixed.

The prevailing attitude toward female intellectual endeavor that Coronado complained of in her letters to Hartzenbusch was well represented in the press of the 1830s. In 1836 the conservative editors of the satirical journal El Jorobado launched a series of satires against literary women, women's rights, and women's periodicals,[15] none of which had any perceptible existence in Spain at the time. Perhaps responding to the utopian socialist revindication of women's rights, the series showed that any form of female emancipation was so absurd to the Spanish public that it functioned as a reliable vehicle for satirizing all social change. The writers dished out a stiff dose of ridicule to aspiring literary women in their spoof of the fictitious Safo Cornelia: "Su frente está ceñida de laurel; tiene una lira en la mano izquierda y una pluma de ganso en la derecha" 'Her forehead is circled with laurel; she has a lyre in her left hand and a goose's feather in her right' ("Biografía" 3). Such scornful treatment did not deter some determined young women from taking up the pen a few years later, as we know. The satirical response was felt immediately. In 1841, the year that both Massanés and Gómez de Avellaneda brought out a volume of poetry, a satirical cartoon titled "El mundo al revés" featured a woman writing at a table, who says with satisfaction, "With this sonnet I finish my book of poems," while her unhappy husband sits behind her, embroidering a piece of cloth.

Satire against women writers seems to have become less virulent in the periodical press during most of the forties. As it became necessary to take literary women more seriously, the strategy of the opposition changed. The new tack was even more intimidating to respectable middle-class ladies, for it implied that women who wrote were immoral. For example, in 1842 a diatribe against George Sand came out in *Revista de Madrid,* an intellectual and literary journal that also published poems by Gómez de Avellaneda. The author, José María Quadrado, was provoked by Sand's unflattering picture of Mallorcan society in her accounts of her stay on the island, but his counterattack was *ad feminam,* armed principally by allusions to her private life. He justified Sand's exclusion from the society of Mallorcan ladies, who, he added sarcastically, were "bastante *atrasadas* para preferir la moralidad al talento, y para honrarse con el título de esposas más bien que con el de escritoras" 'sufficiently *backward* to prefer morality to talent and to feel more honored by the title of wife than by that of writer' (201). In case the alternatives were not spelled out clearly enough, he concluded the article with a blast: "Jorge Sand es el más inmoral de los escritores, y Mme Dudevant la más inmunda de las mujeres" 'George Sand is the most immoral of writers, and Mme Dudevant the most indecent of women' (211). The subliminal message here is not only that women win literary fame at the peril of their moral reputations but, further, that the act of writing is in itself contaminating for women, who are better advised to choose virtue and wifely subordination.

This strongest weapon in the arsenal of those who opposed women's participation in print culture, the assumption that female writing and feminine virtue were incompatible, was waved threateningly at the pioneering women writers. It looms large, for example, in Tomás Rodríguez Rubí's review of Massanés's 1841 volume—the only extended review it received in the Madrid press. Although the critic acknowledges the high moral quality of Massanés's poetry, he has reservations about the book's implicit invitation to other women to share in the intellectual life:

[N]os parece que la emancipación intelectual de la mujer ofrece graves inconvenientes sociales. . . . ¿Quién puede asegurar que la multitud de violentas pasiones que abriga el corazón de la mujer, la infinita variedad de sus afectos e inclinaciones, enfrenadas y adormecidas ahora por creencias que luego desaparecerían, no darían un giro diferente del propuesto al prodigarle esos conocimientos? . . . Ejemplos funestos nos suministran esas naciones cuya civilización y cultura tanto se decantan, donde hay mujeres que por su erudición y facultades intelectuales están a igual altura que los primeros talentos de su país y sin embargo no son los mejores apóstoles de esa virtud tan pura que afirma y robustece los vínculos sociales. (24)

It seems to us that the intellectual emancipation of woman has serious social drawbacks. . . . Who can guarantee that the multitude of violent passions that women harbor in their hearts, the infinite variety of their feelings and inclinations, bridled and lulled now by beliefs that would disappear, would not make the proposal to give women knowledge turn out differently than intended? . . . Regrettable examples are offered by nations whose civilization and culture are overestimated, where there are women who in erudition and intellectual faculties are peers of the top talents of their country and yet are not the best apostles of that pure virtue that affirms and strengthens social ties.

These reflections help us to understand the close links between the moralistic arguments against women writing and Larra's concerns in the review of *Anthony* that we examined in the last chapter. Objections to the various forms of women's emancipation hinged on the danger to society of a female subjectivity that might overflow the bounds of loving devotion to family. In his twice-published essay on women's destiny (see previous chapter), Fermín Gonzalo Morón recommended that women be allowed to cultivate art, but within sufficient constraints that "jamás se pierda el sentimiento del pudor y del recogimiento, . . . ni se despierten peligrosas pasiones" 'their sense of modesty and retiring ways never be lost, . . . nor dangerous passions awakened' (480). However benignly stated, such cautions about the moral and social consequences of female self-expression represented the psychic life of women as monstrously different from that of men insofar as women's powers of judgment and intellect were seen as insufficient to hold in check their hypertrophied emotions. Thus, to the voices, like Carolina Coronado's, that claimed for women a natural, even God-given vocation for poetry, a major part of Spanish culture replied that female nature required women's subordination to men in a strictly domestic role.

While Spain's powerful misogynist tradition was producing a predictable reaction against women's writing at all, forces favorable to women's venture into print were channeling their writing into patterns that conformed to female role models. Approbation of these pioneering women was expressed in institutional form by the many literary clubs or societies that celebrated them in one way or another. The relatively humble *liceos* of certain provincial capitals regularly honored the achievements of women writers. Amalia Fenollosa, for example, was named honorary member of the Academia Literaria of Santiago de Compostela, the *liceos* of Valladolid and Valencia, and the Sociedad Filomática in Barcelona and received a letter of appreciation from the Sociedad Económica of Valencia (Espresati 150, 176). In 1846 the Liceo of Badajoz (swayed by the irresistible Coronado) admitted four women at once as honorary members: Encarnación Calero de los Ríos, Vicenta García Miranda, Joaquina Ruiz de Mendoza, and Robustiana Armiño (*El Defensor del Bello Sexo* 22 Feb. 1846, 116).

The great Liceo of Madrid, distinguished from the capital's other intellectual society, the Ateneo, by its emphasis on the creative and performing arts and its admission of women as members, was the scene of heady triumphs by both Gómez de Avellaneda and Coronado. There are many accounts by contemporary witnesses of Avellaneda's presentation at a meeting of the Liceo's literary section in 1841: José Zorrilla read a poem to the assembled audience, and through their applause declared the author to be the buxom, flashing-eyed young Cuban beauty seated in their midst. She caused a great sensation and became one of the literary lions of the season. A few years later Avellaneda triumphed again in the Liceo by winning both prizes in a contest for the best ode on the subject of the Queen's clemency. There were muffled voices of protest that she had, in effect, broken the rules by submitting one of her poems under her brother's name, but nothing could alter the fact that the judges, without knowing the poems were Avellaneda's, deemed them the best of the lot. Toward the end of the decade it was Coronado's turn. When she made her first trip to Madrid in 1848, the Liceo feted her at a special session, and she in turn improvised a poem of gratitude (Coronado, *Poesías*, 1852 ed., 137). The recognition Madrid's Liceo accorded these two women poets, however, was not unmixed with envy and resentment, as Coronado discovered to her chagrin when her entry in the Liceo's poetry competition for 1848 was disqualified on the not quite credible grounds that her sex made anonymity impossible. As she explained in a bitter letter to Hartzenbusch (Fonseca 27), if she had known it was necessary to have a beard to enter the contest, she would have disguised herself. It may be that the male members of the Liceo remembered only too well having been soundly beaten by Gómez de Avellaneda three years before.

The response of these literary institutions was in large measure simply a reflection of the kind of positive reaction that had most impact on women writers—the willingness of many male writers to act as mentors and publicists for young women taking their first hesitant steps in the world of publishing. J. E. Hartzenbusch's support of Carolina Coronado is a classic example: having liked the first sample of poetry she sent him, he found her a publisher for her first volume, wrote its prologue, edited and corrected her early poems, and offered constructive commentary on her later ones. Without Hartzenbusch's active help, it is difficult to see how Coronado could have had the early success she enjoyed. Her letters to him suggest that in any case his faith in her talent helped her through a period of discouragement when she contemplated giving up poetry. The price for this support, however, was a kind of censorship. Among Coronado's letters to Hartzenbusch is the manuscript of a poem that she had sent him for inclusion in her first volume of poetry. Lamenting that "la mujer en su aflicción, / ¡ay!, no tiene ni un acento / para llorar un momento / los hierros de su prisión" 'woman in her affliction has no voice with which to weep a moment over the iron bars of her prison' (Fonseca 180), the poem was an explicit and anguished protest against the silence forced on women. Hartzenbusch recommended against putting it in the collection, and it remained forgotten among his papers.

Enthusiastic support from male writers also helped Gómez de Avellaneda get her start in the highly competitive literary circles of Madrid. Alberto Lista, widely respected as the teacher of the younger generation of poets, admired her work and furnished her with valuable letters of introduction when she moved from Seville to Madrid. As we have seen, in Madrid she received a warm welcome to the profession from a number of established writers. The importance of this response is acknowledged in the biographical notes to her 1850 volume of *Poesías*:

> Los escritores más distinguidos de la capital . . . la rodearon . . . con homenajes de amistad y de entusiasmo. . . . [M]uchos literatos de mayor o menor nombradía, han sido desde entonces, o sus consecuentes amigos, o sus apasionados admiradores. De algunos recibió consejos; de muchos estímulo y aliento: de todos aquella comunicación de pensamientos, de ideas, de impresiones, que necesita el talento para vivir y desarrollarse. (xvi-xvii)

> The capital's most distinguished writers . . . surrounded her . . . with tributes of friendship and enthusiasm. . . . Many literary men of greater or lesser fame have since then been her faithful friends or her passionate admirers. From some she received advice, from many stimulation and encouragement: from all she received that communication of thoughts, ideas, impressions that talent needs if it is to thrive and develop.

But this encouragement also brought pressure on Avellaneda to tailor her work to the taste of her supporters. For example, the review of Avellaneda's first novel, *Sab,* signed "P. D." and probably written by Nicomedes Pastor Díaz, one of Avellaneda's earliest and most loyal supporters, couples high praise of the work to loud hints that the young writer should eliminate social protest from future writing.

Women writers throughout the peninsula were encouraged, aided, and, of course, guided by sympathetic male writers, some of them as obscure as the local poet who wrote a manual on versification for Vicenta García Miranda, others as questionably motivated as Calixto Fernández Camporredondo, the Asturian poet whose voluminous correspondence with various women poets reveals an interest more prurient than professional, according to Manzano ("Fenollosa" 54). Among the most appealing of these mentors is the Catalan poet Victor Balaguer, who actively promoted women's poetry in general, while being especially solicitous in placing the work of Amalia Fenollosa. As a supplement to *El Genio,* the Barcelona weekly he directed, Balaguer published *El Pensil del Bello Sexo* (1845), the first anthology of women's poetry in Spain.[16] Most of the women poets publishing at mid-decade were represented in this collection. In 1844 Balaguer dedicated to Amalia Fenollosa a poem, "Melancolía," that epitomizes one set of cultural attitudes receptive to women poets: "Canta, mujer. Tú comprendes / de las flores la poesía, / de la aurora la armonía / del mundo todo la voz" 'Sing, woman. You understand the poetry of flowers, the harmony of dawn, the voice of the whole world.' Yet, while so expansively declaring women's aptitude for poetry, Balaguer is actually quite prescriptive: it becomes clear as the poem develops that women's song must be loving, innocent, harmonious, and above all, soothing to the tormented Romantic male's psyche. Thus, in case after case, the positive response to women poets applied gentle but firm pressure toward a role in poetic production that was not unlike women's role in the house.

What Spanish culture reflected back to the women writers of the 1840s, when it was not a horrifying picture of themselves as psychological monsters, immoral to boot, was an image highly conditioned by the ideology of female difference. Indeed, the negative and the positive views of female poetic vocation were by no means entirely contradictory. How the gender system and certain modified Romantic assumptions flowed together into a socially acceptable definition of the woman poet and her subjectivity can be seen in an 1844 article that was of compelling interest to the literary ladies of the time because it was about them. In "Influencia de las poetisas españolas en la literatura," Gustave Deville, a French writer who had resided some time in Spain and who was very much in tune with the conservative liberalism prevailing in the mid-1840s, crystallized what was held to be a moderate but enlightened opinion on the subject of women writing.

He begins by arguing for the cultivation of women's talents in order to make them more stimulating companions for men, and he credits women with natural qualities that endow them with a particular aesthetic sensibility. Women are more sensitive than men to the purity and harmony of forms, to the beauty of detail, for their mission consists in "el darnos consuelos, el edificarnos, y el enseñarnos y hacernos apreciar el lado bello de la virtud" 'giving us consolation, edifying and teaching us, making us appreciate the beauty of virtue' (192–193). But in Deville's view, these special aptitudes make it all the more imperative that female creative activity observe gender-determined limits:

> Pero precisamente por lo mismo que contemplo gozoso el desarrollo de sus cualidades creadoras y esenciales, combatiré con todas mis fuerzas el móvil que impulsa a algunas a despojarse de su virginal e inefable sensibilidad, a perder su candor innato. . . . La mujer debe ser mujer, y no traspasar la esfera de los duros e ímprobos destinos reservados al hombre sobre la tierra. Sea enhorabuena poeta, artista; pero nunca sabia. Sea observadora y analice; pero sin tratar por ello de destruir el orden de cosas establecido. (193)

> But precisely because I contemplate with pleasure the development of their creative and essential qualities, I will combat with all my might the motivation that compels some women to divest themselves of their virginal and ineffable sensibility, to lose their innate innocence. . . . A woman should be a woman and not trespass in the sphere of the harsh and arduous roles reserved on earth for men. Let her be observant and analytical; but without trying to destroy the established order of things.

In the scheme Deville articulates, then, women *are* authorized by their nature to be poets, as Coronado asserted, but only to be poets of a certain kind. The character of women in general and Spanish women in particular determines the character of their artistic production: women's genius is "impresionable y versátil," "más expansivo que reflexivo;" women are "accesibles . . . a las pasiones dulces" 'susceptible . . . to the sweet passions' but not equipped to reproduce "las emociones letales de un corazón entregado al desenfreno y a excesos tumultuosos" 'the lethal emotions of a heart given over to wantonness and tumultuous excess' (193). Consequently, women should not at-

tempt to write drama or historical novels, which require knowledge
of a conflict-ridden and harsh public reality; instead, women writers
should attend "tan sólo a las pacíficas investigaciones de la vida íntima,
a las nobles y santas emanaciones del corazón y a la expresión colore-
ada y simpática de los sentimientos tiernos y religiosos" 'only to the
peaceful investigation of intimate life, to the noble and holy effluxes of
the heart and the colorful and sympathetic expression of tender and religious feelings' (194).

Though couched in gallant language, Deville's article applied quite
forcefully to specific women writers the patriarchal code that rigidly restricted their scope even as it granted women a socially approved space
for writing. His praise was pointed. He commended Massanés for her
religious poetry, which showed that she understood the destiny Providence confided to her cultivated talent (195). Coronado was allowed
to be less spiritual; indeed, Deville liked the Romantic qualities of her
poetic persona, "los trozos en que por entre las francas e ingenuas ex-
pansiones de la doncella, resalta el lenguaje sentido y nervioso de la
mujer apasionada y entusiasta" 'passages in which, among the frank
and ingenuous expansions of the maiden, the heartfelt and vigorous
language of the passionate, enthusiastic woman emerges' (196). The
remainder of Deville's essay, however, emphatically sets the bounds
within which Romantic enthusiasm is appropriate for women poets.
Above all, he warns Spain's women poets, they must not succumb to
the temptations of the Byronic mode but leave to men the prideful despair, the lost illusions, the dissatisfaction with the cosmic and social
order, that do not correspond to authentic female subjectivity:

> Cesad, pues, cesad, mujeres jóvenes, de cubrir vuestro hechicero rostro con
> esa máscara lúgubre y prestada. . . . Presentadnos con preferencia el espec-
> táculo de vuestra filial ternura y de vuestros desvelos maternales. . . . A vo-
> sotras pertenece el derramar raudales de sublime poesía sobre las mezquinas
> necesidades del hogar doméstico. . . . Puesto que fuisteis creadas para hacer-
> nos gustar las delicias de la tierra, volved a ella, y ocupad el puesto en donde
> nosotros gozaremos viéndoos y tributándoos un culto que no podríamos re-
> husar nunca a vuestro talento y virtudes. (198–199)

> Cease, then, young women, cease covering your charming faces with that
> lugubrious borrowed mask. . . . Present us instead with the spectacle of your
> filial tenderness and your maternal devotion. . . . The capacity to shed tor-
> rents of sublime poetry upon the petty necessities of the domestic hearth is
> yours. . . . Since you were created to make us enjoy the delights of the earth,
> return to it and occupy the place in which we will enjoy seeing you and hon-
> oring your undeniable talent and virtue.

Deville's article undoubtedly had an impact on the women writers of the mid-1840s, for it was the first full-length essay devoted to Spanish women poets as a new phenomenon and had behind it the prestige accorded to French writers. When Carolina Coronado learned that she was mentioned in the article, she wrote to Hartzenbusch about obtaining a copy of the journal. Her anxiety about Deville's judgment of her is palpable in the letter—which she wrote before reading his review (Cartas, carta 213)—as is her relief and gratitude once she verified that she had been treated very positively (Cartas, carta 218). She and the other women poets mentioned in the article (Josefa Massanés and María de Mendoza) were given a lesson by commendation on their place in the universe of letters. Deville's pointed failure to mention Gómez de Avellaneda, a better-known poet than any of the other three, contained its lesson as well: in lamenting her lost illusions, the Cuban poet had overstepped the bounds of "feminine talent and virtue" and thus deserved neither the recognition nor the praise of the patriarchal arbiters of poetic merit. Even though Deville's article could not have been single-handedly responsible for shaping women's sense of the public judgment of their work, it was an effective statement of a view of woman's place that, as we shall see, did profoundly affect the writing of even the bold Gómez de Avellaneda.

Deville's formulation in effect offers a compendium of the positive terms for the female reader and writer encountered in the press of the 1840s: the emotionally intense and impressionable images of Sappho and Corinne, la mujer sensible, and the pure, consoling female singer of Balaguer's fantasy. Deville, then, helped to articulate in literary terms the cultural revolution's subtle rearrangement of the codes of gender difference. At the very moment when an expanding press required writers for a new female audience, the advance of liberal and Romantic ideas made it seem natural that women as individuals should seek self-expression, that their traditionally close association with emotion should give them poetic authority; thus, women were granted a space previously denied them in literary production. The continuing differentiation of gender roles, however, strictly defined that space as analogous to woman's place in the home. And the mechanism that insured that women's role in literary production should mirror her role in the family was the normative conception of female subjectivity. Sensitive and expressive with regard to the multiple varieties of love, devotion, and piety but incapable of darker emotions, the female subject was seen as equally suited to domestic life and sentimental poetry.

In elaborating a literary discourse of subjectivity, Spanish Romanticism reflected the prevailing view of women. They figured in most Romantic texts as objects of desire or as symbols through which male fears or aspirations were represented. As we shall see in the next chapter, when the male writers who established Spain's Romantic paradigms in the 1830s represented women as subjects, they departed very little from the image of the female psyche developed in the literature promoting the *ángel del hogar*: unlike the Romantic hero, these heroines displayed little individuality,[17] and their emotional range rarely went beyond self-sacrificing love and a sense of honor. This insistent exclusion of the female subject from the fullness of feeling and imagination incorporated in the Romantic self constituted the main textual problem faced by women poets of the 1840s. To break the bounds of the narrow range of sentiment allowed them, they must find in their writing some way of contending with this "masculinization" of passion.

3
Spanish Paradigms of the Romantic Self

In Spain, the years 1834 and 1835 mark the beginning of the Romantic revolution in literature. Before that, the tendencies of European Romanticism had been the topic of discussions about literature and a few productions had been written in the Romantic mode, most of them by liberals in exile in England or France. But it was only after the return of the exiles and amid the crescendo of pressure for liberal reform that the drift toward Romanticism picked up momentum and became a movement.

Romantic dramas written in exile—*La conjuración de Venecia,* by Martínez de la Rosa, and *Don Alvaro, o la fuerza del sino,* by Angel Saavedra, Duke of Rivas—appeared on the Madrid stage in 1834 and 1835 alongside Larra's first original drama, *Macías,* to initiate a new trend in the theater. The same two years saw the publication of *El Artista,* the journal that published poems, short stories, and excerpts from historical novels by young writers—among them José de Espronceda—experimenting with Romantic themes and forms. Other contributors included the artist, Federico de Madrazo, and the pianist-composer, Santiago de Masarnau, both of whom also identified with Romantic premises in art. Historical novels in the tradition of *Ivanhoe* became a fad among these same young writers: Larra's *El doncel de don Enrique el Doliente* and José de Espronceda's *Sancho Saldaña, o el castellano de Cuellar* appeared in 1834, Patricio de la Escosura's *Ni rey ni Roque* in 1835. The movement thus launched continued on into the next de-

cade. Indeed, it was in the early 1840s that Romantic poetry hit its
peak with the publication of two books of poetry by Espronceda, as
well as collections by Rivas, Zorrilla, Gómez de Avellaneda, and Pastor
Díaz. As a movement that to a considerable extent patterned itself on
already established European models, Spanish Romanticism produced
many works that were superficial or imitative. Yet the new trend in
literature toward freedom of expression and emphasis on passion and
imagination corresponded, as we saw in chapter 1, to slow but accelerating changes in Spanish society and above all to a shift in consciousness among the classes that both made up the reading public and
participated in the political process. Certain seminal texts of Spanish
Romanticism, consequently, worked out representations of the self that
explored in fictional and poetic discourse the conjunction between liberal ideology of the autonomous individual subject and the social world
as it was experienced in Spain. Three writers in particular—Larra,
Rivas, and Espronceda—forged images of the self in the modern world
that, while relating to European paradigms of Romantic subjectivity,
also created models of subjectivity that dominated Spanish writing. In
all three cases, these models characterize the subject and the object in
such a way as to make Romantic subjectivity implicitly male.

LARRA AND THE SPANISH *MAL DU SIÈCLE*

Larra did not unequivocally identify himself, either as writer or
critic, with Romanticism, a term that to him signified a school with a
prescribed formula for breaking the classical rules.[1] His drama *Macías*
helped establish the vogue of Romantic theater in Madrid through its
portrayal of a fiery young hero prepared to follow the dictates of his
own heart against the opposition of any authority, but Macías is more
a political emblem than a Romantic hero of any subjective depth. Nor
did Larra's historical novel based on the same medieval figure add anything of substance to the weak development of the novel in Spain during this period. It is through his journalistic essays, particularly those
written in the last year of his life, that Larra definitively contributed to
the development of Spanish Romantic discourse.

The satirical article—political satire when censorship permitted—
was the genre in which Larra displayed his genius and gained success
as a writer. Working within an eighteenth-century tradition of periodical literature that used a narrating persona as a basic device,[2] Larra
very early in his career became adept at creating fictitious alter egos,

ironic representations of the self that served his satirical purposes brilliantly. *El Duende Satírico del Día* and *El Pobrecito Hablador,* the two personae through whom he presented his commentary to the Spanish public before 1833, however, functioned as instruments of satire rather than of self-expression, subordinating subjective individuality to social exemplarity.

Of more relevance to the Romantic discourse of the self is the author's reincarnation as Fígaro in 1833. Playing humorously with the paradoxical relation between author and persona in "Mi nombre y mis propósitos," the first article that he signed with this pseudonym, Larra underlined the ambiguous relation between himself as author and his pseudonymous mask: "[Q]uedábame aún que elegir un nombre muy desconocido que no fuese el mío, por el cual supiese todo el mundo que era yo el que estos artículos escribía" 'I still had to choose a very unknown name that was not my own through which everyone might know that it was I who wrote these articles' (1: 174). Fígaro differs from Larra's previous personae in that his characterization embodies a fissure between inner and outer. As a sign of the author's identity, Fígaro at once represents the self-generated satirical mood—"[S]uelo hallarme en todas partes, tirando siempre de la manta y sacando a la luz del día defectillos leves de ignorantes y maliciosos" 'I'm normally found everywhere, always letting the cat out of the bag and showing up the little defects of the ignorant and the malicious' (1: 174)—and the external expectations produced by the role—"[M]e llaman por todas partes mordaz y satírico" 'Everywhere they say I'm biting and satirical' (1: 174). The tension between subjective being and objective appearance becomes a recurring motif in Fígaro's self-presentations, for he often protests against the difficulty of living up to his reputation for biting wit. Indeed, Larra's choice of Beaumarchais's barber as an alter ego seems to have been influenced by an already established distinction between feeling and appearance. As an epigraph to his article, Larra uses a passage from *Le barbier de Seville* in which Fígaro admits, "[J]e me presse de rire de tout, de peur d'être obligé d'en pleurer" 'I try to laugh at everything for fear of having to cry about it' (1: 173). The implication that beneath the comic mask of Fígaro lies a tormented consciousness projects a new dimension that Larra developed in his later articles, converting the inherited image of the philosopher who seeks detachment in laughter into the more Romantic figure of alienation—the weeping clown.

Larra's ideal as a writer, which had its roots in the eighteenth-century satirical mode that he adopted, involved detachment. In "De la sátira y de los satíricos" he says of the satirist:

> [E]s forzoso . . . que las circunstancias personales lo hayan colocado constantemente en una posición aislada e independiente; porque de otra suerte, y desde el momento en que se interese más en unas cosas que en otras, difícilmente podrá ser observador discreto y juez imparcial de todas ellas. (2: 161)

> It is obligatory . . . that his personal circumstance should have constantly placed him in an isolated and independent position; because otherwise, and from the moment in which he becomes more interested in some things than in others, he will find it difficult to be a discreet observer and impartial judge of all things.

The ideal of detachment for the writer corresponds to the liberal premises of "Literatura," the essay examined in chapter 1: freedom of conscience signifies individual autonomy. But here Larra stretches impartiality into alienation when he declares that, for himself as a satirist, there must exist a strong discrepancy between his subjective state and the images produced in his text: "[C]onfesaríamos que sólo en momentos de tristeza nos es dado aspirar a divertir a los demás" 'We could confess that only in moments of sadness can we aspire to amuse others' (2: 164). This restatement of the structural implications of the Fígaro mask insists on the irrelevance of the author's personal self to the text's representation of truth. Yet in this very article, despite its abstract mode as discourse about satirical discourse, the subjective aspect of the satirist's detachment surfaces as a painful sense of isolation. "[E]l satírico al hacerse enemigos poderosos, no se hace amigo ninguno, no encuentra apoyo ni compensación" 'The satirist, in making powerful enemies, makes no friends for himself at all; he finds no support or compensation' (2: 163), Larra complains. This telling essay on satire ushered in the final year of Larra's life (he killed himself on 13 Feb. 1837), when critical detachment became alienation, ironic distance became *mal du siècle*, and the satirical mask became self-expression.

At once philosophical, political, and personal, Larra's crisis was similar to, though temporally more condensed than, the experience that produced *mal du siècle* as a French manifestation of Romantic subjectivity. Pierre Barbéris's observations about the situation of Balzac's generation are relevant to Larra's view of his historical moment:

> The nineteenth century would be a century of *vouloir-vivre* because it began under the sign of *pouvoir-vivre*. Never had more universal ambitions more

rapidly discovered more innumerable obstacles. Never had the notion of insufficiency and imperfection appeared more clearly linked to the concrete, and therefore changeable, conditions of life. (44)

Although Spain had no equivalent to the French Revolution, the death of Ferdinand VII and then, two years later, the success of the armed revolts that brought Mendizábal to power produced a euphoric sense of new opportunity among liberals.[3] With the liberal prime minister's failure to fulfill his promises and the sordid factional struggles that characterized most of 1836, however, these hopes soon dissolved into frustration and cynicism.

Barbéris argues that in France the second generation of Romantics was particularly disillusioned by the discrepancy between liberalism as an ideal and liberalism in practice:

> Stendhal . . . perceptively underlines the illusions of those who have not yet seen the true nature of established liberalism. The progressive dissociation of the idea people held of liberalism (which corresponded to their needs) from what it objectively was would be one of the determining causes of the new *mal de siècle*. (83)

Larra, whose acute observation of the French scene in 1835 had infected him with the malaise of his French contemporaries, saw all too clearly how this contradiction between liberal ideas and reality operated in the Spanish context. Of Mendizábal he commented in March 1836 that

> lejos de realizar las esperanzas fundadas en sus grandílocuas promesas, ha complicado el laberinto inextricable en que se halla cogida esta mezquina revolución, destinada, según parece, a no dar jamás un paso franco y desembarazado, a no poner jamás un nombre claro y terminante a sus inhábiles operaciones. (2: 215)

> far from fulfilling the hopes founded on his grandiloquent promises, he has complicated the inextricable labyrinth in which this paltry revolution is caught, destined, it seems, never to take a free and unencumbered step, never to give a clear, definitive name to its inept operations.

The anguish of frustration latent in Larra's words bears a close affinity with the French Romantics' sense of the betrayal of their aspirations by contemporary reality: "At the time of Balzac, the *mal du siècle* is at the same time a painful recognition of betrayal by the liberal world and a not-yet-ridiculed need for, a not-yet-destroyed faith in, a future" (Barbéris 111). Larra, in the summer of 1836, however, reached a point where despair about the future exacerbated his disappointment in the present. In the review of Dumas's *Anthony,* which review is impregnated with Larra's gloomy interpretation of what he saw in France, the case he makes for continuing the Spanish revolution rests on a negative premise:

> [N]o seamos nosotros los únicos privados del triste privilegio de la humanidad; libertad para recorrer ese camino que no conduce a ninguna parte; pero consista esa libertad en tener los pies destrabados y en poder andar cuanto nuestras fuerzas nos permitan. (2: 248)

> Let us not be the only ones deprived of humankind's sad privilege; let us have the freedom to travel the road that leads nowhere; but let that freedom consist in having our feet unfettered and in being able to go as far as our strength permits.

By mid-1836, then, Larra's commitment to liberal reform had evolved into a Romantic malaise—alienation from the present realities of liberalism in practice and radical doubt about the future.

Personal traumas that transformed Larra's image of himself magnified and deepened the intellectual crisis that called the satirist's scheme of social and political values into question. Not only did contemporary reality frustrate the journalist's personal ambitions for power—his July election as a representative to the Spanish parliament was nullified by a coup before he could take his seat—but Larra's own actions displayed the inconsistency with principle that he chastised in the political practice of the liberals. The ideal of the writing subject as impartial observer and judge collapsed as Larra discovered his own incapacity to remain disinterested; the articles written after September 1836 abandon the pretense of detachment, and Fígaro becomes the face of the writer rather than the mask of the satirist. For the first time the Romantic assumption that subjectivity is truth insinuates itself into the very construction of Fígaro as the speaking self.

In many respects, the self constructed in Larra's later essays fits the paradigm of the Solitary or the sufferer of *mal du siècle.* Even in the review articles in which Fígaro serves merely as a signature for the relatively objective authorial voice, the subjective experience of alienation colors the authoritative statements of the critic. In reviewing the Spanish translation of a French work, for example, Larra characterized the general alienation of the Spanish writer not through rational argument but through a fantasy that becomes transparently autobiographical in its emotional intensity:

[N]o extrañemos que jóvenes de mérito como el traductor de las *Horas de invierno* rompan su lira y su pluma y su esperanza. ¿Qué harían con crear y con inventar? . . . Dos amigos dirían al verle pasar por el Prado: ¡Tiene chispa! . . . Los más no lo sabrían; las bellas creerían hacerle un gran elogio diciéndole: romántico; algunos exclamarían: ¡Es buen muchacho, pero es poeta! ¡Otra parte, y no la menor, le calumniaría, le llamaría inmoral, y mala cabeza, infernaría su existencia y la llenaría de amargura! (2: 291)

We shouldn't be surprised that talented young men like the translator of *Horas de invierno* should break their lyres and their pens and their hopes. What would creating and inventing get them? . . . Two friends would say as they saw him go by, "He's got wit!" . . . Most wouldn't know it; the ladies would think they were giving him high praise by calling him romantic; some would exclaim, "He's a fine boy, but he's a poet!" Another faction, and not the smallest, would slander him, calling him immoral and wild, would poison his existence and fill it with bitterness.

Although slightly disguised by the use of the third person, the author's subjectivity provides the substance of these observations of social response to the writer.

Earlier in the essay the speaking subject more directly identifies with the Spanish writer's estrangement from his social environment:

Escribir como escribimos en Madrid es tomar una apuntación, es escribir en un libro de memorias, es realizar un monólogo desesperante y triste para uno solo. Escribir en Madrid es llorar, es buscar voz sin encontrarla, como en una pesadilla abrumadora y violenta. (2: 290–291)

To write as we write in Madrid is to take notes, to write in one's diary, to carry on a sad, desperate monologue with oneself. To write in Madrid is to weep, to try to speak without finding a voice, as in an overwhelming and violent nightmare.

Although in "escribimos" the first person is plural, the series of figurative images for writing stress singularity, the isolation of the writing subject from other subjects and from dialogue. We might note that what Barbéris says about the French *mal du siècle*—"The difficulty in being is difficulty in being in the contemporary world, not in the world per se" (111)—is true as well for Larra here: the difficulty of being a writer in Spain has to do specifically with the conditions of Spanish society, not with the activity of constituting oneself as a writer per se. Larra believes that to write in France is different: "Escribir como Chateaubriand y Lamartine en la capital del mundo moderno es escribir para la humanidad, digno y noble fin de la palabra del hombre" 'To write like Chateaubriand and Lamartine in the capital of the modern world is to write for mankind, a noble and worthy objective of the human word' (2: 290). Thus, the alienation of the writing subject figured in this essay is produced as a dialectical response to precisely that surrounding social world from which it is separated. In other words, we see in Larra that complex Romantic configuration of the subject as at once singular and plural, unique and representative.

Locked into a lonely monologue with itself, the writing subject of Fígaro's satirical discourse of late 1836 takes on the shape of the alienated Romantic self. Like the Solitary, "the man alienated from others and himself by excessive self-consciousness," to repeat Harold Bloom's words (*Ringers* 91), the speaking subject of "El día de difuntos de 1836" and "La nochebuena de 1836" produces an image of itself as an intense consciousness radically separated from the surrounding world.

In "El día de difuntos" the awareness produced by Fígaro's preoccupation with his own melancholy leads to the structural opposition on which the satire is based: he is conscious of what no one around him sees. "[C]omencé a ver claro. El cementerio está dentro de Madrid. Madrid es el cementerio" 'I began to see clearly. The cemetery is inside Madrid. Madrid is the cemetery' (2: 280). This consciousness separates him from his fellow *madrileños,* who are hurrying to the cemeteries that lie beyond the city walls: "¡Necios!—decía a los transeúntes—. ¿Os movéis para ver muertos? ¿No tenéis espejos por ventura? . . . ¡Miraos, insensatos, a vosotros mismos, y en vuestra frente veréis vuestro propio epitafio!" 'Fools! I said to the passersby. You're going out to see the dead? Don't you have mirrors by any chance? . . . Look at yourselves, dolts, and on your foreheads you'll find your own epitaphs!' (2: 280). The mirror of self-consciousness, not the illumination of objective judgment, endows Fígaro with superior vision; the central part of the article sets forth the truths that subjective insight reveals about the city, and through it, Spanish society.

For all the brilliant wit of the satirical epitaphs that Fígaro reads on the faces of Madrid's public buildings, the image of the city—the social community—emerges as desolate and lifeless, an alienated landscape. But the most devastating consequence of Fígaro's intensified vision is the inner alienation of self-consciousness:

> Quise salir violentamente del horrible cementerio. Quise refugiarme en mi propio corazón, lleno no ha mucho de vida, de ilusiones, de deseos. ¡Santo cielo! ¡También otro cementerio! Mi corazón no es más que otro sepulcro.

¿Qué dice? Leamos. ¿Quién ha muerto en él? ¡Espantoso letrero! ¡Aquí yace la esperanza! (2: 282)

I wanted to break out of the horrible cemetery. I wanted to take refuge in my own heart, not long ago full of life, illusions, desires. Holy Heaven! Another cemetery! My heart is nothing more than another sepulcher! What does it say? Let us read. Who lies dead here? Frightful epitaph! Here lies hope!

The morbid awareness that allows Fígaro to pierce through the complacent surface of his social environment destroys the illusions of a desiring fantasy when turned upon himself. The self constructed through the processes of introspection, differentiation, and projection is thus doubly alienated: from the surrounding world by a radical separation and from itself by its similarity with the other, with the object.

"La nochebuena de 1836" manifests this basic pattern of Larra's *mal du siècle* with even more clarity. The article is structured around the contrast between Fígaro, who is consumed by insomniac reflection, and his servant, who is unconsciousness personified:

Mi criado tiene de mesa lo cuadrado y el estar en talla al alcance de la mano. Por tanto es un mueble cómodo; su color es el que indica la ausencia completa de aquello con que se piensa. . . . [T]ambién tiene dos ojos en la cara; el cree ver con ellos, ¡qué chasco se lleva! A pesar de esta pintura, todavía sería difícil reconocerle entre la multitud, porque al fin no es sino un ejemplar de la grande edición hecha por la Providencia de la humanidad. (2: 315)

My servant is like a table insofar as he is square and of a size to be reached by the hand. He is therefore a comfortable piece of furniture; his color indicates the complete absence of what one thinks with. . . . He also has two eyes in his head; he thinks he sees with them, what a joke! Despite this description, it would be difficult to pick him out of a crowd, because after all he's just a copy of the great edition Providence made of mankind.

By identifying the servant, to whom any aspect of consciousness is denied, with the general run of human beings, the speaking subject here defines himself as uniquely distinguished from others by subjectivity. The rest of society, like the servant, is able to eat and drink in merry oblivion during the holiday; "Yo/Fígaro" observes them in contemptuous solitude, sustaining himself on the play of his own reflections.

The intensified reflexiveness of the self speaking through Fígaro leads to the self-conscious irony that constitutes the climactic section of the essay when Fígaro is forced to listen to the voice of consciousness coming from the drunken lips of his servant and turned upon himself as its object. The new dimension of awareness obtained by this self-objectification, accentuating the alienation of the subject, defines Fígaro's *mal du siècle*. "¿Por qué ese color pálido, ese rostro deshecho, esas hondas y verdes ojeras que ilumino con mi luz al abrirte todas las noches?" 'Why that pallor, that ravaged face, those sunken, green-encircled eyes that my light reveals when I open the door to you every night?' (2: 316), asks the servant, and then proceeds to give an inventory of the moral, social, political, and metaphysical motives for Fígaro's inner malaise. In some cases he is tormented by guilt shared with the surrounding political and social context: "Te llamas liberal y despreocupado, y el día que te apoderes del látigo azotarás como te han azotado" 'You call yourself liberal and open-minded, and the day you get hold of the lash you will use it as it has been used on you' (2: 316). In others, he suffers from excessive detachment from humanity: "Tú buscas la felicidad en el corazón humano, y para eso le destrozas, hozando en él, como quien remueve la tierra en busca de un tesoro" 'You seek happiness in the human heart, and with that object you shred it to pieces, rooting in it like someone who digs in the earth looking for treasure' (2: 316).

But in the last analysis, it is self-consciousness that destroys the possibility of happiness:

> Concluyo; inventas palabras y haces de ellas sentimientos, ciencias, artes, objetos de existencia. ¡Política, gloria, saber, poder, riqueza, amistad, amor! Y cuando descubres que son palabras, blasfemas y maldices. . . . Tenme lástima, literato. Yo estoy ebrio de vino, es verdad; pero tú lo estás de deseos y de impotencia! (2: 317)

> To conclude: you invent words and of them you make feelings, sciences, arts, objects of existence. Politics, glory, knowledge, power, wealth, friendship, love! And when you discover they are just words, you curse and blaspheme. . . . Pity me, writer. I'm besotted by wine, it's true; but you are besotted by desire and impotence!

We see here to what extent Larra's epistemological framework has become subjectified: this passage presents the subject as the center of being, the creator of its own objects of desire. Yet the self-reflexiveness of consciousness reveals the insufficiency of the solipsistic subject, ever frustrated in its desire to know its object in the non-self, the realm of the other. Thus the paradigm of the alienated self that Larra adopts late in 1836 in his self-representation as Fígaro is closely connected to the other Romantic archetypes. The continual self-division of the alienated subject in its quest for further self-knowledge leads to the consciousness of its own solipsism, a consciousness made painful precisely by the Promethean desire that drives the subject beyond itself in the first place.

For Larra, immersed in a historical circumstance that failed to correspond to liberal hopes and intentions, Romantic introspection revealed the truth of subjectivity to be the agonized conjuncture of desire with impotence. Only words were left as the substance through which the subject could shape the image of its desire, and though the verbal image remained infuriatingly insufficient to the demands of desire, it at least permitted the subject to make itself known. That is, while Larra lacked the confidence of the English Romantics that man could "take existence itself into his mind and rewrite it according to the images of desire" (Rajan 13), his writing at this period of his life shows an overriding compulsion to mirror the self, to give it knowable existence in writing. Fígaro ceases to be the medium through which the author distances his text from his own subjectivity and becomes instead the verbal medium in which that subjectivity is fixed and defined.

The fusion of the public face of the persona and the private face of Larra's interiority leads "La nochebuena" into near solipsism in its conclusion, where enigmatic questions register the despair of a consciousness turned inward upon itself:

> A la mañana, amo y criado yacían, aquél en el lecho, éste en el suelo. El primero tenía todavía abiertos los ojos y los clavaba con delirio y con delicia en una caja amarilla donde se leía *mañana*. ¿Llegaría ese mañana fatídico? ¿Qué encerraba la caja? (2: 317)

> In the morning, master and servant lay, the one in his bed, the other on the floor. The eyes of the first were still open and fixed with delirium and pleasure on a yellow box on which *tomorrow* was written. Would that prophetic tomorrow ever come? What was in the box?

With this purely private reference, Larra's voice sinks to the whisper of monologue, for only he held the key to the box and to the enigma until after 13 February 1837, when the well-publicized details of Larra's suicide revealed that he kept two pistols in the yellow box at his bedside. Larra's use of a totally private reference at the end of "La nochebuena" signals to what extent his despair of transcending the rupture between self and other infected a mode of writing that initially was distinguished by its commitment to comprehensibility and communication. Yet, even if he did not hope to be understood, the compulsion to inscribe within a public statement the key to his most intimate, personal death fantasy corresponded to the need for verbal construction of the elusive and all-too-temporal self.

Larra's suicide—the last interview with his former mistress, the pistol shot that echoed after her as she left his house, the discovery of his corpse by his five-year-old daughter—became a text that together with his late articles established in Spanish culture the prototypical image of the alienated Romantic "I" as a kind of *poète maudit,* a soul too anguished by its sensitivity and hyperlucidity to survive in the humdrum and hostile world of actual social existence.[4] As the cultural model of this version of the Romantic subject, Fígaro/Larra distinctly positioned the female outside subjectivity. Allusions in both "El día de difuntos" and "La nochebuena" class women with those hostile or degraded elements of the world that cause the feeling self to withdraw in pain. In the first essay the list of unfortunates to whom Fígaro compares his melancholy includes "un inexperto que se ha enamorado de una mujer" 'an innocent who has fallen in love with a woman' (2: 279) alongside those who suffer from the sad state of national affairs.

In "La nochebuena" women figure even more prominently among the targets of satire. In the following passage from the first paragraph, subjectivity is masculine; those who believe, suffer, and love are men, while women cause rather than feel pain or joy:

> [I]magino que la mayor desgracia que a un hombre le puede suceder es que una mujer le diga que le quiere. Si no la cree es un tormento, y si la cree—¡Bienaventurado aquél a quien la mujer dice *no quiero,* porque ese a lo menos oye la verdad! (2: 313)

> I imagine the greatest misfortune that can befall a man is for a woman to tell him that she loves him. If he doesn't believe her, he's in torment, and if he believes her—Blessed is he to whom a woman says *I don't love,* for he at least hears the truth!

Here, women seem to have no interiority; whatever they might say, their truth is a lack of feeling, a *no quiero.* Although these opening allusions to women derive from a misogynist satirical tradition, the searingly personal discourse that emerges by the end of the essay reinforces the earlier image of women as incapable of corresponding to male passion and imagination. The servant points out that Fígaro suffers because instead of buying women to meet his physical needs, he foolishly expects emotional reciprocity from them:

> [T]ú echas mano de tu corazón, y vas y lo arrojas a los pies de la primera que pasa, y no quieres que lo pise y lo lastime, y le entregas ese depósito sin

conocerla. Confías tu tesoro a cualquiera por su linda cara, y crees porque quieres; y si mañana tu tesoro desaparece, llamas ladrón al depositario, debiendo llamarte imprudente y necio a ti mismo. (2: 317)

You take your heart in your hand and you go and throw it at the feet of the first woman who goes by, and you want her not to trample and break it, and you give her this deposit without knowing her. You confide your treasure to anyone with a pretty face, and you trust because you love; and if tomorrow your treasure is gone, you call the trustee a thief when you should call yourself an imprudent fool.

Heart, or interiority, is here clearly an attribute of men; women are heartless, or if they do have a subjectivity, it is unknowably hidden behind the faces that constitute them as men's object of desire. Thus, Larra's influential version of the *mal du siècle* as a Spanish form of Romantic subjectivity offered the female writer only the choice of identifying with a male writing subject or with the heartless, soulless feminine figures who epitomized an alienating world.

DON ALVARO: THE DISPERSED SELF

One of the landmarks in the history of Spanish Romantic drama was the performance of *Don Alvaro, o la fuerza del sino* in March 1835 in Madrid's Príncipe Theatre. Its author, Angel Saavedra, Duke of Rivas, had written the work while in exile in France and brought it back to Spain with him when he returned in early 1834. Thus, the play was composed in the context of the author's exile from his homeland and his contact with the French Romantic movement, then at its peak.[5] *Don Alvaro* startled and fascinated its Madrid audience, polarizing the critics but drawing sufficient public to become the drama most frequently performed during 1835.[6] Although Rivas's play did not have the immediate popularity gained by Martínez de la Rosa's *La conjuración de Venecia,* the first of the three dramas that set the trend of Romantic theater for the following decade, *Don Alvaro* went much further in establishing a model of the Romantic hero that corresponded to a very new conception of the subject. Rivas gave a peculiarly Spanish twist to his representation of Romantic subjectivity, however, focusing like Larra on the weakness of the self.

The opening scenes, set in the picturesque streets of Seville, introduce the hero as a handsome, brave, but mysterious being. "Who is he?" wonder the Sevillians, high and low. An initial enigma concerning the protagonist's origins was a commonplace of traditional drama;

what distinguishes don Alvaro as a hero is that the enigma becomes a never fully dissipated mystery in his case. The question mark that hovers over don Alvaro is the sign of an uncertain identity—not only the social identity of name, origins, and rank that traditionally resolved the enigma of the dramatic protagonist but also the self-identity, the subjective possession of one's own being that Romantics sought in the quest for selfhood. Rivas's crucial contribution to the Spanish cultural revolution was to examine in this play the problematic intersection of the two forms of identity, the social and the subjective, displaying in the play's hero the effects of an insubstantial sense of self.

Who is don Alvaro? The question arises in the beginning when he appears in Seville as a stranger who has no known place in the social universe of the Spanish peninsula. Though the protagonist claims to be noble, his antecedents remain unknown and speculations about who he is—a pirate, or the bastard son of a Spanish grandee and a Moorish queen—place him outside the legitimate social community. The protagonist's conflict with society is epitomized in the refusal of the Marquiss of Calatrava to recognize don Alvaro as a suitable match for his daughter, Leonor. While the hero claims aristocratic rank in the traditional social hierarchy on the basis of his own knowledge of his origins and his sense of personal worth, established aristocrats reject him as an outsider. Although this play places an individual protagonist in confrontation with a hostile social hierarchy, it differs significantly from Romantic dramas like Dumas's *Anthony,* in which the hero, standing for the bourgeois individualist, attacks the validity of a social order based on rank. Written by a man who was himself a grandee of Spain, don Alvaro's drama centers on the problem of an individual who finds within himself no alternative to the social value system but whose internal sense of his place in that system conflicts with society's refusal to grant him a place.

The unfolding drama reveals that don Alvaro is the son of a Castilian nobleman and an Inca princess, now in prison for having aspired to set up in Peru a throne independent of Spain. The offspring of two principal forms of Romantic desire—"[A]mor y ambición ardiente / me engendraron de concierto" 'Ardent love and ambition in concert engendered me' (66)—he is no rebel or utopian dreamer. Instead, his mission is reintegration in the social order: he has come to Spain to gain favor with the king by demonstrating his nobility and valor and thus to win a pardon for his parents. The rigid social order he encounters through the Calatravas, however, defines him as a threatening erotic force, as a murderous rebelliousness, and finally, as a racial and cultural other that must be cast out to preserve order. Each of don Alvaro's successive clashes with the men of the Calatrava clan bears out their view of him as a destructive element. The arrogant Calatravas end up dead, either by accident or in duels that they themselves have forced, while don Alvaro, having failed yet again in the attempt to win social confirmation of his identity, finds himself responsible for another crime that widens the abyss separating him from society and his beloved. The autonomous individual's struggle for a social identity, then, leads in Rivas's drama to a frustrated impasse.

Don Alvaro's failure to achieve a place in society commensurate with his concept of himself and to win from the external world the satisfaction of his desire for love has more to do with the insecurity of his self-identity than with the intransigence of the social hierarchy, however. This hero's actions never coincide with the intentions revealed in his speech; like Hamlet, he broods without acting, torn by a guilty sense of inadequacy, and then on hasty impulse, acts contrary to his desires. Midway through the play he reveals that he came to Spain to affirm his name and social status by lifting the onus of treason from his parents. Yet in the course of the drama he does nothing that would further this purpose, from which he is diverted by his passionate love for Leonor and his plan to elope with her. Inadvertently, he creates an insurmountable obstacle to that objective as well, when the loaded pistol he throws at the feet of the old Marquiss goes off, killing the old man and making don Alvaro the murderer of Leonor's father. Next, he seeks forgetfulness and death by serving with the Bourbons in the War of the Spanish Succession, but does not think to use the glory he gains as a soldier to help his parents. In the encounter with Leonor's brother, don Carlos, the protagonist declares that he will never shed the blood of one whom he regards as a friend and relative, but in the end he kills don Carlos in a duel. And finally, when he has abandoned all earthly goals to seek spiritual peace in a monastery, that resolve is broken by the taunts of the next Calatrava brother, don Alfonso, whom don Alvaro kills in the final catastrophe. Don Alvaro never finds a mode of being in which he fully coincides with the identity he projects for himself.

Structurally, *Don Alvaro* breaks not only with the neoclassical rules but also with any notion of unity of character and action. Instead of tracing through a series of actions and their consequences purposes that are eventually achieved or defeated, *Don Alvaro* centers in true

Romantic fashion on the subjective, representing the protagonist's search for an identity as a series of nearly disconnected attempts to define himself in terms of a particular role. In the first act, don Alvaro is a lover, fully surrendered to living out his passion, risking all for his lady, seeking fulfillment of his being in union with her. But that erotic union and fulfillment are not possible: losing Leonor and nearly losing his own life in the confusion following the death of the Marquiss, don Alvaro must find some other possibility of being.

When next presented on the stage (Act III), he has become a soldier, a role that he performs with such bravery and such noble fraternalism with his companions in arms that don Carlos, still unaware of don Alvaro's true name, exclaims, "Nunca vi tanta destreza / en las armas, y jamás / otra persona de más / arrogancia y gentileza" 'Never have I seen such skill in arms, and never a more arrogant and dashing person' (79). Although don Alvaro excels in mirroring the identity of a soldier to the external world, however, it is inwardly hollow to him. Monologues in Acts III and IV reveal that the protagonist's interiority scarcely matches his new self-definition and that a radical gap divides his inner consciousness from the face he presents to the world. Alone with his thoughts in Act III, scene iii, the hero confesses in an important lyrical outburst that those who admire his martial enthusiasm are deceived, for he is motivated not by brave devotion but by a cowardly wish to die. In fact, the monologue that reveals don Alvaro's innermost experience begins with his wish for self-annihilation: "Qué carga tan insufrible / es el ambiente vital / para el mezquino mortal / que nace en sino terrible" 'What an unbearable load life's surroundings are for the wretched mortal born to a terrible fate' (65). The suicidal impulse undercutting his efforts to find an identity is a response to something that he calls fate: something to do with the basic nature of his experience of subjectivity.

Don Alvaro's subjectivity is generated by the desire whose frustration causes his alienation—the desire for union with the other. Whether attempting to unite himself in amorous ecstasy with Leonor or to reconcile his outcast parents with the Spanish establishment, his objective is to cancel the differences that define him as an outsider. Desire in don Alvaro thus lacks the rebelliousness of the Promethean paradigm, although the intensity and utopianism of Romantic desire is very much present on the occasions when the protagonist gives lyrical expression to his imagination:

> ¡Qué porvenir dichoso
> vio mi imaginación por un momento,
> que huyó tan presuroso
> como al soplar de repentino viento
> las torres de oro, y montes argentinos,
> y colosos y fúlgidos follajes
> que forman los celajes
> en otoño a los rayos matutinos! (103–104)

What a happy future my imagination saw for a moment that fled as quickly as do, at the breath of a sudden wind, the golden towers and silver hills and colossal, radiant foliage formed under the morning sun by swift-moving autumn clouds.

But this imagery, even as it connotes a kind of utopian landscape of golden spires and silver mountains, is impregnated with despair: all is a mirage created by the momentary splendor of the autumn sun.

It is this inevitable failure of desire to affect existence that don Alvaro calls fate. Just as it prohibits the coincidence of subject and object in the satisfaction of desire, the implacable destiny that pursues him interposes itself between the subject's attempt to construct a self and the totalization of that self as an objectively (i.e., socially and externally) corroborated identity. While society's resistance plays a part in this fatality, the subject's own weakness, its internal incoherence, is a major factor.

The protagonist's inner reactions to events in his episode as a soldier make clear that his inner being is fragmented and confused. Past selves haunt him with painful memories that he is unable to integrate into present unifying purposes. The monologue in Act III mentions his parents, invoking his identity as loyal son and the obligation it entails: "[E]n la edad de la razón, / a cumplir la obligación / que un hijo tiene acudí" 'When I reached the age of reason, I attended to my obligation as a son' (66). But before he can relate this part of himself to present circumstances or intentions, another memory abruptly surfaces:

> ¡¡Sevilla!! ¡¡Guadalquivir!!
> ¡Cuál atormentáis mi mente!
> ¡Noche en que vi de repente
> mis breves dichas huir!
> ¡Oh, qué carga es el vivir!
> ¡Cielos, saciad el furor—
> Socórreme, mi Leonor. (67)

Seville! Guadalquivir! How you torment my mind! The night I saw my brief happiness suddenly disappear! Oh, what a burden life is! Heavens, sate your fury—Help me, my Leonor.

The two crucial elements of past experience, origins of a potential present identity, here remain disconnected; the evocation of Leonor provides no orientation for the present, except insofar as it leads to don Alvaro's expression of his alienation from his present circumstances and his desire for death.

Don Alvaro's inner fragmentation becomes manifest in Act IV, after he kills don Carlos in a duel that the other insisted on to avenge his father's death. Recollecting that he might have been the dead man's brother-in-law, don Alvaro is assailed by guilt and wonders how the earth can permit him to go on living. Yet when questioned by an investigating captain about the causes of the duel, he sees himself as a nobleman properly defending his honor and justifies his action: "Retóme con razón harta, / y yo también le he matado / con razón" 'He was quite right to challenge me, and I was also right to kill him' (100). As he awaits the decision of the military tribunal that must sentence him for breaking the law against dueling, he muses in another soliloquy about Leonor, about the blood that separates them, and relives briefly the vivid hopes for the future that her love inspired. But this resuscitation of one past self gives way to a succession of other inner voices:

> ¡Mas en qué espacio vago, en qué regiones
> fantásticas! ¿Qué espero?
> ¡Dentro de breves horas,
> lejos de las mundanas afecciones,
> vanas y engañadoras,
> iré de Dios al tribunal severo! *Pausa.*
> ¿Y mis padres?—Mis padres desdichados
> aún yacen encerrados
> en la prisión horrenda de un castillo—
> cuando con mis hazañas y proezas
> pensaba restaurar su nombre y brillo
> y rescatar sus míseras cabezas.
> No me espera más suerte
> que, como criminal, infame muerte. (104)

But my mind is wandering in space, in regions of fantasy! What am I hoping for? In a few hours, far from vain and deceiving worldly affections I will go before God's severe seat of judgment! *Pause.* And my parents? My unhappy parents remain locked up in the hideous dungeon of a castle—when I intended to restore their name and honor and rescue them from their misery

with my deeds and feats. The only lot that awaits me now is an infamous
death as a criminal.

Dreamlike hopes of a future union with Leonor are cut short by the
thought of the present likelihood of death. As we have seen, don Alvaro
desired death when his desire for love was frustrated. Yet the potential
fulfillment of his death wish evokes the still-unfulfilled purpose of one
of his several identities—the vindication of his parents and of his place
in society. Viewed from the perspective of this other component of don
Alvaro's being, death, particularly the dishonorable death of a condemned criminal, now appears as an obstacle to rather than a satisfaction of desire.

Don Alvaro, then, is dogged by a fate that prevents the coordination
of his desires and memories, his past and present projections, into a
coherent whole, a self that might determine its existence in the world.
His final attempt to solve the mazelike puzzle of his identity takes the
form of a negative transcendence through ascetic denial. At the end of
Act IV he declares a course of action intended to resolve his vacillations
between love and duty, death and life: he vows that if he lives through
the enemy attack that has interrupted his trial, he will renounce the
world and live out his life in solitude. And, indeed, don Alvaro reappears in the final act as a monk living far from worldly concerns in a
remote religious community.

In this identity he makes his last effort to define an internally and
externally coherent mode of being—a self whose inner integration is to
be achieved by the eradication of desire and memory through the abandonment of worldly projects and past ties, and whose social validation
is obtained by conformity to the rule of the order. Yet the protagonist
is no more successful in fully assimilating this identity than he was
in previous roles. Though his charity, obedience, and humility are
exemplary, visible ruptures in his being remain. They are perceived by
the clownish and envious Brother Melitón, who reports an incident to
the Father Protector:

> Tiene cosas muy raras. El otro día estaba cavando en la huerta, y tan pálido
> y tan desemejado, que le dije en broma: "Padre, parece un mulato" y me
> echó una mirada, y cerró el puño, y aun lo enarboló de modo que parecía
> que me iba a tragar. Pero se contuvo, se echó la capucha y desapareció;
> digo, se marchó de allí a buen paso. (112)

He does very strange things. The other day he was digging in the garden
and looked so pale and different that I said as a joke, "Father, you look like

a mulatto," and he glared at me, and closed his fist and even raised it—I thought he was going to eat me up. But he contained himself, pulled down his hood, and disappeared—I mean, he walked quickly away.

What Brother Melitón takes to be signs that don Alvaro is the devil in disguise show the spectator that he has not been able to obliterate his past otherness in a present identity nor his awareness of the stigma with which that other self marks him. He has not achieved the peace of a unified self in this new persona as the friar Rafael.

The desperately constructed new identity crumbles in the confrontation with the second Calatrava brother along precisely the fault line revealed in the episode with Brother Melitón. Father Rafael resists his challenger's provocations, aimed at the former don Alvaro, until don Alfonso, who has been to Peru to learn the secret of the protagonist's origins, mentions his mixed blood and calls it impure. Then and only then does an infuriated don Alvaro accept the sword the challenger offers and, tying up the skirts of his habit, follow him out into the mountainous wilderness where the drama concludes.

Don Alvaro's destiny is consummated in the catastrophe that ends the play: as a subject that fails to impose upon its own disparateness a unified identity that also determines its social being, he is finally objectified in self-alienation. Don Alvaro, relinquishing his struggle for self-definition, embraces the role his antagonist—the Calatravas and traditional social hierarchy—assigns him: he becomes society's "other," the principle of its negation and destruction. Don Alfonso brings news that suggests for a moment that the protagonist might yet be what he desires, for his parents have been pardoned, their property restored, and the family is searching for its son and heir, that he might take his rightful place. But when don Alvaro dares to hope that he might change his destiny, his opponent reminds him forcefully that he cannot escape what he has become in society's eyes—a murderer, a deserter from the army, and a monk who has just broken his vows. He is, in other words, a criminal as well as a barbarian, an antagonist of civilized order by action as well as by birth. Don Alvaro surrenders to this definition of his being with the cry "Muerte y exterminio" 'Death and extermination' (130) as he at last raises his sword to join combat with don Alfonso. When the latter falls mortally wounded and requests confession, don Alvaro fully assumes the negative identity in which he has been trapped: "¡No, yo no soy más que un réprobo, presa infeliz del demonio! Mis palabras sacrílegas aumentarían vuestra condenación"

'No, I'm nothing but a reprobate, the devil's wretched prey! My sacrilegious words would only condemn you more' (130).

The final step in the full assimilation of don Alvaro's being within the identity of otherness occurs with the death of Leonor. Brought by don Alvaro's call for religious succor for the dying man to the door of the hermitage where she has lived away from any human contact, Leonor sees her brother and goes to his aid. Don Alvaro recognizes his beloved only in time to see her perish, a victim of the vengeful wrath of don Alfonso, who manages to stab her to death as his dying gesture. Deprived now of his most cherished source of hope, don Alvaro achieves in pure negativity the unity of purpose and being that has so long eluded him. As the community of monks, roused by the cries for help, approaches, the protagonist faces them from the pinnacle of a craggy rock. To the Father Protector's attempt to recognize in this wild-eyed stranger the exemplary monk who had been his protégé, don Alvaro responds:

> Busca, imbécil, al P. Rafael—Yo soy un enviado del infierno, soy el demonio exterminador—Huid, miserables.
> TODOS: ¡Jesús, Jesús!
> DON ALVARO: Infierno, abre tu boca y trágame. Húndase el cielo, perezca la raza humana; exterminio, destruccion—*Sube a lo más alto del monte y se precipita.* (133)

> (Imbecile, try to find Father Rafael—I'm an envoy from hell; I'm the exterminating demon—Flee, wretches.
> ALL: Jesus save us!
> DON ALVARO: Hell, open your mouth and swallow me. Let Heaven sink, let the human race perish; extermination, destruction! *He climbs to the highest peak and throws himself over the edge.*)

The conflicting elements of selfhood have finally been absorbed in an identity that coincides with don Alvaro's destiny: self-annihilation is the only means by which the subject may appropriate, make its own, the alienation it has experienced. Don Alvaro becomes destruction, returning himself to the void from which he has never managed to emerge as a positive self.

In don Alvaro, Rivas produces an image of the Romantic self that is marked by the peculiarities of Spanish culture and history. Don Alvaro's unrepentant and total emotional commitment to his final gesture of defiance against the order of heaven and earth links him to the Promethean figures of English and French Romanticism who stake their

whole existence on the affirmation of their self-generated values. Yet
this Spanish figure of the self, reflecting the lack of a strong religious
or social tradition that affirmed, as Protestantism had, the truth of individual conscience, finds within himself only a death wish to project
upon the world. In creating a version of the modern individual subjectivity that Romanticism promoted, the aristocratic Rivas reproduced
the insecurity of the modern ideology of the self in his own society. The
destiny that dooms don Alvaro is his own inner incoherence: either the
passive creature or the negative other of an immobile society, he has
no individual identity to affirm.

Since, as we noted in the introduction, the aggressive self-assertion
of the Romantic self was implicitly or explicitly identified with masculine gender, we might expect Rivas's less centered version of the individual subject to be more gender-neutral, allowing the possibility of
placing a female in the position of subject. Indeed, the drama provides
the formal space for a speaking feminine subject in the character of
Leonor, who is closely associated with the protagonist. Instead of being either a helper or a hinderer of the protagonist's purposes and thus
tagged as part of the object world confronted by the play's subject,
Leonor is identified with don Alvaro's fate. Unlike the female figures
who epitomize the object's resistance to the realization of desire in
Larra and Espronceda, then, Leonor—both because of the dramatic
form's demand that each character appear as an acting, speaking subject and because of her close association with the subjectivity of the
protagonist—has the attributes of a subject. She in fact has a whole
act—Act II—in which she discharges the function of protagonist. A
closer look at the text reveals, however, that what occupies this subject
position is not properly a self, a subjectivity existing in and for itself,
but rather an awareness of nonbeing, of lack.

The first hint of this lack can be found in Leonor's scenes with don
Alvaro in Act I. Rivas rewrites the traditional female dramatic conflict
between erotic love and the social code of honor in Romantic terms,
presenting it as the clash of deep inward emotions, the paralyzing conflict between Leonor's love for don Alvaro and her attachment to her
father. Having just bid an affectionate goodnight to her father, she confesses her indecision to her maid as she waits for don Alvaro to come
for her on the night planned for their elopement: "[N]o me resuelvo;
imposible— / es imposible" 'I can't make up my mind; it's impossible,
impossible' (18). Yet the development of this scene, in which Leonor's
changes of mind always reflect the emotions of her immediate inter-

locutor, suggests that her vacillations derive not from autonomous movements of her own psyche but from her identification with the subjectivity of the masculine characters who face off as the antagonists of the drama—her father and don Alvaro. Thus, when her father's loving words and tender embrace are fresh in her mind, Leonor identifies with his feelings for her and believes it impossible to leave her family. When don Alvaro, finding her indecisive, expresses the depth of his passion and the intensity of his need for her, she is swayed by its force and resolves to go with him.

The second act shows how Leonor, separated from don Alvaro during the confusion following her father's death and fleeing her brothers' wrath, sets her own course and follows it with determination. Disguised as a boy, she makes her way to a monastery high in the mountains, where she requests permission of the Father Protector to occupy the hermitage where another penitent woman lived and died completely isolated from human contact. The old priest accepts her vow to live the rest of her days sealed away in a cave from all human contact whatsoever. Leonor's success in surmounting all these challenges—remaining incognito, finding the monastery, and convincing the Father Protector of the sincerity of her resolve—is not, however, a true gesture of self-affirmation by an autonomous subject. The difference becomes apparent if we compare the motives for Leonor's retreat from worldly existence with the genesis of don Alvaro's death wish.

As we have seen, don Alvaro turns to ascetic self-denial because the desires that express his inner being have been thwarted as a result of their contradiction of each other or of social norms. Each new resolve he takes is generated by an autonomous will to coordinate the elements of his interiority into a self and an identity. Leonor, in contrast, is driven by shame; since her interiority is modeled on the image others have of her, a negative social definition is for her nonexistence. When she introduces herself to the Father Protector, she displays her sense of what her identity means to the world:

PADRE GUARDIAN: *Sorprendido*
 ¿Sois doña Leonor de Vargas?
 ¿Sois, por dicha—? ¡Dios eterno!
DONA LEONOR: *Abatida*
 ¡Os horroriza el mirarme! (49)

FATHER PROTECTOR: *Surprised.* Are you doña Leonor de Vargas? Are you, perhaps—? Heavenly Father!
LEONOR: *Despondent.* It horrifies you to look at me!

Although the priest hastens to reassure her, Leonor has revealed what compels her to take such drastic measures to make herself invisible: she cannot bear to be what others now regard her. It is not a question of desiring to realize another, inwardly determined mode of being; her interview with the Father Protector nowhere suggests that she aspires to a new spiritual existence in the presence of God alone, for example. Nor is her vow to retire to the hermitage truly motivated by penitence, that is, by a desire to change an aspect of her inner being that she believes to be culpable. What she wants above all is to avoid the gaze of others, as she admits to the priest when explaining why she would not be willing simply to retire to a convent:

> [N]o puedo, tiemblo al decirlo,
> vivir sino donde nadie
> viva y converse conmigo.
> Mi desgracia en toda España
> suena de modo distinto,
> y una alusión, una seña,
> una mirada, suplicios
> pudieran ser que me hundieran
> del despecho en el abismo. (54)

> I cannot—I tremble to say it—live where anyone else lives and could talk to me. My misfortune sounds to all of Spain like something else, and an allusion, a sign, a look, would be a torture that might sink me in the abyss of despair.

Leonor's being seems to be fully circumscribed by her concern with her social identity: in removing doña Leonor de Vargas from the eyes of the world she steps into death. Thus she describes her purpose as entombment: "Vengo resuelta . . . / a sepultarme por siempre / en la tumba de estos riscos" 'I come resolved . . . to bury myself forever in the tomb of these peaks' (51). As she steps behind the doors that will conceal her identity from the world, she is as good as dead. Indeed, when the grotto doors open again in the last act to reveal her identity, she is slain in the act, leaving don Alvaro to exclaim, "¡Te hallé, por fin—sí, te hallé—muerta!" 'I found you at last—yes, I found you—dead!' (132).

Both vengeance, the cause of Leonor's physical death, and shame, the motivation of her self-entombment, derive directly from the code of honor, and therefore reveal the essential determinant of Leonor's characterization and of the form of subjectivity she is granted. In Spain's baroque theater, an influential model both for Rivas's play and for powerful cultural traditions, the obsession with the *pundonor* made of women the repository of male honor rather than characters in their own right or even objects of male desire. In this tradition, insofar as women lived or died as signs of honor, their being was constructed entirely in terms of social opinion. Reputation was synonymous with a woman's identity and, by extension, with the value to which that identity referred—a man's honor, not a female individual. For this reason, in Calderón de la Barca's *El médico de su honra,* doña Mencía must die; even though in terms of her existence as a subject she is innocent of wrongdoing, as a sign of her husband's honor she is tarnished and must be eliminated. Leonor's destiny as a subject is conceived within this same framework. Her autonomy as an individual consciousness and an agent in the drama consists in her identification of her self with honor, in her recognition that as a debased sign (of her family's honor) or a referentless sign (she does not "belong" to don Alvaro), she can have no existence. Thus, her performance of the function of protagonist in Act II demonstrates in its own way that woman cannot be a Romantic subject in quest of autonomous selfhood, as the male protagonist can. Once again we see that while these male writers' representations of masculine subjectivity may be innovative in relation to cultural assumptions, their representation of women draws upon conservative structures of gender hierarchy. Indeed, Rivas's Leonor is a purely baroque creature, as far removed from the subjective qualities attributed to the bourgeois domestic woman as she is from the autonomous passions of the Romantic subject.

ESPRONCEDA AND PROMETHEAN DESIRE

As the most powerful poet of his generation (a fact his contemporaries generally acknowledged),[7] José de Espronceda created the paradigmatic model of the Romantic lyrical self for Spanish poetry. His evolution as a poet shows him in the process of working out an increasingly complex representation of liberal-Romantic subjectivity in relation to the world. The Promethean element is far more pronounced in Espronceda's construction of a poetic self than in the other two writers we have examined, and in this sense the young poet's image of the experiencing subject conforms more closely to the subject-object dialectic codified by Hegel. This being so, woman is cast unequivocally as the object of desire in his poetry, although dialectical reversals on one or two occasions suggest the possibility of female subjectivity.

Espronceda, like all of his generation, was trained in neo-classical literary precepts in his formal education. His schoolmaster and mentor, Alberto Lista, centered his poetic world on Horace (Juretschke 269–270), and anthologized the Castilian poets most influenced by classical literature in order to form the tastes of his students (Marrast 80). So strong was Lista's influence on the young Espronceda that the latter, even in exile in London and Paris, where he was exposed to the new tendencies of Romantic poetry, continued to write in the vein of the eighteenth-century poets dear to his master—Juan Meléndez Valdés and Gaspar Melchor de Jovellanos. But the cumulative impact of Espronceda's experiences abroad, reinforced by the poet's unconventional personal life and radical political convictions, produced a rupture with his previous poetics in the first poems he published after his return to Madrid in 1833. "La canción del pirata," published in *El Artista* in 1835, marked a new line in Espronceda's poetry both formally and thematically. Critical studies of the poem have analyzed its freshness and originality in terms of its metrical variation, its vivid imagery, and its discovery of a kind of democratic poetic diction, based on common language.[8] Since our focus is on the construction of the lyrical subject, however, we shall consider how "La canción del pirata" effects a transformation of the lyrical speaker implied in Espronceda's neoclassical poetry.

In Espronceda's earlier phase, his poetic voice adopted a universalized, poetically conventional emphasis upon the object of its discourse, often an element of nature. For example, in "A la noche," composed about 1827 (Marrast 122), the lyrical subject establishes itself in terms of its position relative to the object it apostrophizes rather than by self-characterization:

> ¡Salve, o tú, noche serena,
> Que el mundo velas augusta,
> Y los pesares de un triste
> Con tu oscuridad endulzas! (*Diablo mundo. Poesías* 25)

Salve, oh you august, serene night that keeps vigil over the world, and sweetens the sorrows of a melancholy man with your darkness.

The self-allusion is attenuated and generalized by the use of the third person—"a melancholy man." Indeed, this single explicit characteristic of the speaking self is carefully depersonalized later in the poem:

> ¡Oh qué silencio! ¡oh qué grata
> Oscuridad y tristura!

> ¡Cómo el alma contemplaros
> En sí recogida gusta! (26)

(Oh, what silence! Oh, what pleasant darkness and melancholy! How the soul in spiritual absorption delights in contemplating you!)

The soul that contemplates the scene described in the poem obviously is to be identified with the speaking subject, but also embraces the generality of any soul in a similar situation. The neoclassical echoes in the poem's themes and images—Marrast mentions Horace, Garcilaso, Meléndez Valdés, and Lista (123–124)—correspond to the representation of the lyrical subject as universal rather than individual.

"La canción del pirata," in contrast, personalizes the speaking subject and locates it in time and space as a pirate captain who speaks from the uniqueness of his adventurous life on the high seas. His discourse, however, epitomized in a refrain, is not so much about his surroundings as about himself:

> Que es mi barco mi tesoro,
> Que es mi Dios la libertad,
> Mi ley la fuerza y el viento,
> Mi única patria la mar. (35)

For my treasure is my ship, my God is liberty, my law is force and the wind, my only fatherland the sea.

Although the poem does not use a language of emotional inwardness, it nevertheless initiates in Spain that "Copernican revolution in poetry"—to use Harold Bloom's words—"marked by the evanescence of any subject but subjectivity" ("Quest-Romance" 8). Indeed, the pirate embodies more than simply his individualized self: he stands as a representation of the new conception of subjectivity in which Romanticism is grounded, a conception whose correlation with liberal ideology is nowhere more clear. As an image of the subject, the pirate emphasizes above all its autonomy, its potential self-sufficiency, and the imperious impulse of its desire: "Y no hay playa, / Sea cualquiera, / Ni bandera / De esplendor, / Que no sienta / Mi derecho / Y dé pecho / A mi valor" 'And there is no beach whatsoever, nor glorious flag, that does not feel my right and face my audacity' (35–36). In later poems the egocentric self-will conveyed by this defiant attitude leads to the dialectic of Promethean desire, the self-defining and destructive conflict with the other, but in this poem there is no other, only the joyous self-affirmation of a subject imagined free of constraint, the idealized figuration of a liberal Romantic self.

The process initiated by this transformation of the lyrical speaker in Espronceda's poetry evolved toward an ever more complex conception of the relations between the self and the surrounding world. Thomas E. Lewis has shown how the subject represented in "La canción del pirata" as entirely free of external social constraints becomes "El mendigo" 'The Beggar' when placed on the underside of a corrupt society, and finally "El verdugo" 'The Hangman' when the mechanisms by which society assigns a function and an identity to the individual subject are taken into account. He comments:

> Once Espronceda socially situates his prototypical speaker, the naiveté of the pirate's comfortable espousal of Enlightened creeds, as well as the ease by which he lives by them, vanishes before a vision of the increasingly problematic relation between liberal ideology and social reality. (12)

By 1838, when Espronceda published two key lyrical poems, "A una estrella" 'To a Star' and "A Jarifa en una orgía" 'To Jarifa During an Orgy,' his model of subjectivity had become far more complex than the abstract love of freedom, the unobstructed pursuit of desire, that characterized his pirate. These two lyrical poems present a version of Romantic subjectivity that opposes the creative forces of the inner self to the power of material reality. The coherent, well-elaborated paradigm that emerges in these poems sets the conceptual framework for the representation of inner life in Espronceda's last, unfinished work, *El diablo mundo.*

Let us take "A Jarifa en una orgía" as an example of how Espronceda articulates the elements of Romantic subjectivity. A dialectic between self and world is set in motion by desire, which generates illusion when projected upon external reality:

> Yo quiero amor, quiero gloria,
> Quiero un deleite divino,
> Como en mi mente imagino,
> Como en el mundo no hay. (52)

I want love, I want glory, I want a divine delight such as I imagine in my mind but that does not exist in the world.

The world's failure to correspond to desire precipitates the mood of bitter frustration with which the poem opens. Since Espronceda conceives subjectivity above all as a temporal process, he shows us the dynamics of his malaise by reviewing his spiritual history. In the first stage, the imaginative powers born of desire propel him out into the world to find the objects of his fantasy:

> Yo me arrojé, cual rápido cometa,
> En alas de mi ardiente fantasía:
> Do quier mi arrebatada mente inquieta
> Dichas y triunfos encontrar creía. (52)

I threw myself like a swift comet on the wings of my glowing fantasy: my impetuous, restless mind expected to find happiness and triumphs everywhere.

The subjective powers of imagination and desire produce the values marked as positive throughout the poem, while the real external world encountered in the subject's search for such values is perceived in negative terms:

> Luego en la tierra la virtud, la gloria,
> Busqué con ansia y delirante amor,
> Y hediondo polvo y deleznable escoria
> Mi fatigado espíritu encontró.
>
> . . . .
>
> Y encontré mi ilusión desvanecida
> Y eterno e insaciable mi deseo:
> Palpé la realidad y odié la vida.
> Sólo en la paz de los sepulcros creo. (53)

Then with eagerness and delirious love I sought virtue and glory on earth, and my weary spirit found stinking dust and crumbly scum. . . . And I found my illusions gone and my desires eternal and insatiable: I touched reality and hated life. I believe only in the peace of the grave.

In Espronceda's paradigm, the gap between subjectively generated positive values and the object world is absolute; as if by definition, reality cannot correspond to desire, illusion must give way to disappointment. Subjectivity, then, is at once the source of positive value and the repeated experience of frustration and pain. Furthermore, desire is unrelenting; only in death does the poet hope to find peace from its insatiable compulsion. It is precisely this dilemma that generates the poem's point of departure, since the poet goes to the brothel to seek a small death in drink and sex. But because desire can neither be stilled nor be satisfied, the poem itself reenacts the ever-repeated process of subjectivity: desire, illusion, disappointment, disgust. Thus the brothel—and I shall explore this further in a moment—provides an apt metaphor for the experience Espronceda wishes to represent.

For Espronceda, man in general is characterized by an insatiable aspiration toward something that finds no correspondence in what exists; this discrepancy causes his fall into despair and rebellion. The presentation of Satan as the voice of man in the introductory canto of *El diablo mundo* fully exemplifies this paradigm. The poet-narrator evokes a series of hallucinatory visions dominated by the gigantic figure of the Fallen Angel, whose lament echoes that of the lyrical subjects of "A una estrella" and "A Jarifa." "Víctima yo de mi fatal deseo, / Que cumplirse jamás mis ansias veo" 'Victim of my fatal desire, I never see my longings fulfilled' (143), he exclaims. Some lines later he makes clear that he represents the Promethean aspect of the human psyche:

> ¿Quién sabe? Acaso yo soy
> El espíritu del hombre
> Cuando remonta su vuelo
> A un mundo que desconoce,
> Cuando osa apartar los rayos
> Que a Dios misterioso esconden,
> Y analizarle atrevido
> Frente a frente se propone. (146)

Who knows? Perhaps I am the spirit of man when he soars up to an unknown world, when he dares to put aside the rays that hide a mysterious God and proposes audaciously to analyze him face to face.

The Romantic Prometheanism of this image of human desire quite overwhelms the negative implications of the traditional Christian view of Satan: the human aspiration to burst the limits of an externally imposed order is here treated as the admirable, even angelic aspect of man, while the inferno associated with Satan is not a punishment for the sin of overreaching so much as it is the psychological consequence of desire's incapacity to affect reality. According to Espronceda's Lucifer, what sinks the human spirit into the abysses of hell is the bitter recognition of the gap between subject (imagination and desire) and object (material reality):

> ¡Ay! Su corazón se seca,
> Y huyen de él sus ilusiones,
> Delirio son engañoso
> Sus placeres, sus amores,
> Es su ciencia vanidad,
> Y mentira son sus goces:

> ¡Sólo verdad su impotencia,
> Su amargura y sus dolores! (146)

Ay! His heart dries up and his illusions flee, his pleasures, his loves are a deceptive delirium, his knowledge is vanity and his enjoyments are a lie: the only truth is his impotence, his bitterness, and his pain!

Here we see that the negative pattern observed in Larra's prose and Rivas's drama reappears in Spanish Romanticism's major poet: as these writers elaborate a Romantic discourse of subjectivity in Spanish, they reenact again and again not the triumph of the aspiring bourgeois self but its defeat.

By representing Satan's voice as the voice of man and recapitulating in it the laments of the speaking self in his lyrical poetry, Espronceda universalizes the poetic subject, extending the elements of his poetic subjectivity to men in general. Yet, like so many of the mental configurations through which Western culture claims to represent universals, Espronceda's image of human interiority is in fact identified with masculine consciousness. Above all, he marks subjectivity as male in the presiding image of "A una estrella," "A Jarifa," and "Canto a Teresa": these poems figure the relationship between self and world as the erotic connection between a masculine subject and a feminine object. In all three poems, the beloved or desired woman stands for the object world that fails to correspond to the values imagined and desired by the lyrical, masculine subject.

The core of "A una estrella," the personal event to which the whole lyrical invocation of the star refers, is the poet's youthful love for a woman:

> Una mujer adoré
> Que imaginara yo un cielo;
> Mi gloria en ella cifré,
> Y de un luminoso velo
> En mi ilusión la adorné. (48)

I adored a woman whom I imagined a heaven; I placed my salvation in her, and in my illusion I adorned her with a luminous veil.

Thus the text represents the intense emotion of this experience in terms that imply that it is all a subjective projection. When the desiring male subject's illusion evaporates, the beloved woman vanishes as well:

> Tan alegres fantasías,
> Deleites tan halagüeños,

> ¿Qué se hicieron?
> Huyeron con mi ilusión
> Para nunca más tornar. (49)

Such happy fantasies, such gratifying delights, what became of them? They
fled with my illusion nevermore to return.

The loss of the beloved woman mourned throughout the poem is in fact
the loss of the values projected in her place. So thoroughly solipsistic
is the male lyrical subject in this poem that the woman has no existence
except as the unstable pretext of desire.

A true dialectic between self and other is, however, established in "A
Jarifa" because in this case, the woman to whom the lyrical subject addresses himself is granted a separate existence. It is precisely the sepa-
rateness of Jarifa, her difference from the poet's limitless desire, that
leads him to push her away in disgust after he has called her to him.
"Huye, mujer: te detesto" 'Leave, woman; I detest you' (51), he tells
her, and then asks:

> ¿Por qué en pos de fantásticas mujeres
> Necio tal vez mi corazón delira,
> Si luego, en vez de prados y de flores,
> Halla desiertos áridos y abrojos? (52)

Why does my perhaps foolish heart run mad after fantastic women, if then
instead of meadows and flowers it finds arid deserts and thistles?

The experience of not finding in the concrete woman, Jarifa, the infinite
object projected by his desire prompts the poet's general reflections on
the inadequacy of reality to imagination. These reflections, in turn, take
woman as a primary exhibit of reality's deficiency:

> Mujeres vi de virginal limpieza
> Entre albas nubes de celeste lumbre;
> Yo las toqué, y en humo su pureza
> Trocarse vi, y en lodo y podredumbre. (53)

I saw women of virginal purity among white clouds of celestial light; I
touched them and saw their purity turn to smoke, to mud and putrefaction.

Woman's status as object, her otherness from the subjectivity that desires her, equates her here with materiality, and justifies the tension between attraction and disgust that structures the movement of the poem.
The germinal figure of this poem—the prostitute in her brothel—be-

comes a privileged metaphor for the object world in which the subject inevitably fails to realize his infinite desires.

The polarized image of woman as split between a positive male projection and a negative material reality is not unique to "A Jarifa." It recurs in Espronceda's work, notably in "Canto a Teresa," where the poet exclaims, "Mas, ¡ay! que es la mujer ángel caído / o mujer nada más y lodo inmundo" 'But, ay! woman is either a fallen angel or merely a woman and filthy mud' (188). Indeed, in the same stanza his reference to the biblical fall of man implies that woman is the source of human unhappiness:

> Sí, que el demonio en el Edén perdido
> Abrasara con fuego del profundo
> La primera mujer, y ¡ay! aquel fuego
> La herencia ha sido de sus hijos luego.

Yes, for in lost Eden the devil burned the first woman with fire from the deep, and ay! that fire has been her children's legacy.

Thus he warns "el corazón ardiente" 'the passionate heart' not to drink at the fountain of love, "[q]ue su raudal lo envenenó el infierno" 'for its torrent was poisoned by hell' (189). The logic of this imagery, then, identifies woman with that impurity in the world which poisons every attempt to slake the thirst of human desire.

As we see, Espronceda's new poetic paradigm for subjectivity tends to represent women not as subjects in their own right but rather as the emblem of a vitiated object world. This should come as no surprise, given the cultural and social context of the period we have been examining. Yet, as the texts discussed in chapter 1 suggest, the written discourse of the 1830s vacillated between treating women as nature and otherness and acknowledging them as sharers of man's subjective experience. This same ambivalence appears in Espronceda's poetry, which does not always relegate women to the status of objects. His poems occasionally postulate the existence of women's subjectivity.

Let us return to "A Jarifa en una orgía," whose conclusion has not yet been taken into account. If, as I have asserted, the poem sets up a dialectic between the lyrical subject and a world that is as alien to its projections as a prostitute to a seeker of love, then the final stanza must be seen as an attempt to transcend the contradiction:

> Ven, Jarifa; tú has sufrido
> Como yo; tú nunca lloras;

> Mas, ¡ay triste!, que no ignoras
> Cuán amarga es mi aflicción.
> Una misma es nuestra pena,
> En vano el llanto contienes . . .
> Tú también, como yo, tienes
> Desgarrado el corazón. (54)

Come, Jarifa; you have suffered like me; you never weep, but—oh, you sad woman—you know how bitter my pain is. Our sorrow is identical, in vain you hold back your tears . . . You, too, like me, have a broken heart.

This shift of perspective, imputing subjectivity to what has been defined as the material object, the other, resolves the dilemma posed in the poem, for it posits a correspondence between the poetic subject and something outside itself—another feeling subject. The world remains stubbornly resistant to the projections of subjectivity, but this grief is mitigated insofar as it is shared with other subjects. Thus, the poem concludes with a recognition that woman, the object whose inadequacy causes the pain and despair expressed by the lyrical subject, also suffers and, by implication, desires. Significantly, however, in granting Jarifa subjectivity, the poet denies her otherness: Jarifa's feelings are presented in the image of the poet's, in reference to his first person—"como yo."

Something similar happens in "Canto a Teresa." In the first part of the poem Teresa's image serves as an adjunct to the poet's evocation of his youthful lost illusions and bliss. She is the screen on which he projects his desires, as Espronceda tells us explicitly:

> Y esa mujer tan cándida y tan bella
> Es mentida ilusión de la esperanza:
> Es el alma que vívida destella
> Su luz al mundo cuando en él se lanza,
> Y el mundo con su magia y galanura,
> Es espejo no más de su hermosura. (186)

And that woman, so innocent and beautiful, is hope's lying illusion: it is the soul that vividly flashes its light on the world into which it throws itself, and the world with its magic and grace is nothing but the mirror of the soul's beauty.

The illusion that the beloved object does indeed correspond to the subject's magical desire gives way to the rage with which the poet blames women—Teresa—for the loss of his happiness: "mujer nada más y lodo inmundo." Yet in the last part of the poem, where the focus shifts from the feelings and memories of the poet to Teresa and her destiny, the figure of this woman acquires a subjective reality of its own.

For the most part, Teresa's subjectivity, like Jarifa's, reflects the poet's own consciousness. At the beginning of the poem he characterizes his state of mind in terms of the "ansiedad" and "agonía" of a "desierto corazón" 'anxiety' and 'agony' of an 'arid heart,' whose bitter pain lies too deep for tears. At the end of the poem, Teresa's interior reality is imagined in parallel terms: "Roída de recuerdos de amargura, / Arido el corazón sin ilusiones" 'Eroded by bitter memories, her heart arid and without illusion' (190). In a series of conditional clauses, the poet elaborates his fantasy of Teresa's final state of mind:

> Si en tu penosa y última agonía
> Volviste a lo pasado el pensamiento;
> Si comparaste a tu existencia un día
> Tu triste soledad y tu aislamiento;
>
> .   .   .   .
>
> Si, en fin, entonces tu llorar quisiste
> Y no brotó una lágrima siquiera . . . (192)

If in your last painful throes of death you turned your thoughts to the past; if you compared your sad and lonely isolation with your former existence; . . . if, finally, you wanted to cry and not even one tear would flow . . .

I find a deep ambiguity in the form in which this poem gives Teresa subjectivity. While on the one hand the poet does include her through suffering in the general paradigm of human subjectivity, on the other hand his image of Teresa on her deathbed, abandoned even by God, borders on the sadistic and suggests a wish to punish her.

Nevertheless, there is a moment in the poem when Teresa gains autonomy. For one brief stanza her destiny is seen as the consequence of her own activity as a subject in the world, her pursuit of her own objectives in a hostile society:

> Espíritu indomable, alma violenta,
> En ti, mezquina sociedad, lanzada
> A romper tus barreras turbulenta;
> Nave contra las rocas quebrantada . . . (190–191)

Untamable spirit, violent soul, launched turbulently against your barriers, petty society; a ship broken on the rocks . . .

Here, the Prometheanism of the Romantic self is attributed to Teresa; she is identified with the liberal-Romantic project of making space for individual subjectivity in a resistant social structure. At the same time her difference as a woman is tacitly recognized: meeting with more resistance from society, she is more likely to be destroyed.

This passage poses an alternative and conflicting version to that earlier image of Teresa which sums up a misogynous Judeo-Christian tradition. When she is seen as Eve's daughter, infecting the very fountains of love with inherited and inherent female corruption, her own downfall and the poet's fall from love's paradise are explained in terms of a myth of feminine nature. When, in contrast, she is presented as an individual struggling against social constraints, her ruin is a consequence of society's imperfection. The traditional image of woman as the daughter of Eve, an irrational, weak, and dangerous other, is not in fact superceded or replaced by the image of woman as a liberal-Romantic subject facing a "petty society." One image alternates with the other, with no confrontation and no resolution, for the poet has not consciously posed the issue of female subjectivity as a problem. Primarily concerned with the poetic expression of personal erotic disillusion as the figure for subjective experience in general, he merely registers various possibilities for representing women that his culture made available to his imagination.[9]

Before such fragmentary images of female subjectivity could be integrated into the new conception of the subject propagated by the Romantic liberals, it was necessary for women writers to appropriate and modify their models of the lyrical subject. As the uncertain process of the cultural revolution in Spain made apertures for female participation in literary production, the women who began to write could not avoid confronting the contradictory assumptions about the place and nature of women that informed liberal and Romantic discourse. In assuming the position of writing subject, a position that had been marked out primarily by and for men, writers like Gertrudis Gómez de Avellaneda, Carolina Coronado, and Cecilia Boehl were forced to deal with the relation of gender to subjectivity as an issue to be resolved in some way by the act of writing.

4

Feminizing the Romantic Subject in Narrative: Gómez de Avellaneda

When in 1841 Gertrudis Gómez de Avellaneda, a pioneering literary woman, staked out her claim in the republic of letters with the publication of a book of poetry and a novel, she boldly entered a territory hostile to women. As we have just seen, not only did society in general disapprove of anything but domestic activity on the part of women, but the prevailing Romantic paradigms gave women little means of imagining themselves as writing subjects. We saw earlier that Larra, the theorist of the connection between liberal ideology and Romantic subjectivity, became quite caustic in his review of Dumas's *Anthony* about the idea that women should claim rights and freedoms that might undermine the institution of marriage. The same attitude constrained the literary imagination of the Duke of Rivas, who denied the possibility of an autonomous female agent defined by her own desire, and of Espronceda, whose poetic image of subjectivity tended to represent women not as subjects in their own right but rather as symbols of a vitiated object world. In producing a new literary language of subjectivity, the trend-setting Spanish Romantics of the 1830s had either foreclosed or stringently limited the possibility of a female subject of desire and experience.

In this literary and ideological context, Gómez de Avellaneda broke new ground by constituting herself as a writing subject whose gender was female. While she used the basic paradigms of the self that had emerged during the Romantic period, she contextualized them in new ways, associating centered consciousness with a position—that of woman—marginalized by social authority. In making this move, she did not tread entirely uncharted territory but confronted the paradigms developed by the Spanish male Romantics in the late 1830s with a non-Spanish tradition of women's writing that also drew on liberal ideology and Romantic values. As it has been identified for us now by feminist critics, this women's tradition includes Mary Wollstonecraft in England and on the Continent Mme de Staël and George Sand (Moers; Kaplan, *Aurora Leigh*; Poovey, *Proper Lady*; and Gutwirth). For Gómez de Avellaneda, who read *Clarissa* and Lord Byron in French translation (Harter 22), the French branch of this tradition was most important. As a girl in Cuba she read three novels that were to have a profound impact on her writing—Mme de Staël's *Corinne ou l'Italie* and George Sand's *Indiana* and *Valentine* (Harter 22, 28). As we shall see in more detail later, in the first novel she found the model of a female genius who is prevented by society from reconciling love with artistic achievement. In Sand's two early novels, Gómez de Avellaneda discovered an exploration of female experience and subjectivity that entailed the critique of marriage as a form of slavery for women. Following these precedents, then, the young Cuban-Spanish woman gave a new dimension—gender specificity—to the existing Spanish paradigms of the Romantic subject that she adapted in creating her first narrative works.

Gómez de Avellaneda's colonial origins also help to explain her willingness and ability to modify and in some respects to challenge the dominant models she found in Spanish Romanticism. Curiously enough, she probably owed her acquaintance with Mme de Staël and George Sand to the fact that she was raised by a Creole family in a provincial Cuban city where slave labor in the household permitted young ladies to spend their time pretty much as they pleased. Her indulgent mother and doting grandfather supplied the precocious young Gertrudis with what she wanted, namely tutors (the Cuban poet José María Heredia among them) and books. (Gómez de Avellaneda, *Autobiografía* 43; Harter 20–21). A young Spanish woman of her class, educated more strictly in domestic duties and religious precepts, would have had neither the leisure nor the permission to read what Gertrudis did, as she discovered when she came to Spain. Besides being better read in French literature than most of her contemporaries, male and female, in Spain, Gómez de Avellaneda was distanced in two ways from the predominant political-cultural discourses of the peninsula. First, she was raised with the fervent Cuban nationalism that characterized a Creole class resentful of Spanish colonial policy. Second, she picked up, probably from tutors like the young lawyer Heredia, a particularly Cuban brand of liberalism that had through bitter historical experience become critical of the hypocrisy of Spain's liberal government toward its colonies.[1] Thus she approached the centers of Spanish cultural and literary life from a doubly marginalized perspective—both as a woman and as a colonial—that gave her a critical consciousness of white, male, metropolitan hegemony.

WRITING THE SELF FOR ANOTHER: THE AUTOBIOGRAPHY

Undaunted by the male bias of Spanish letters, Gómez de Avellaneda began very early in her life to construct herself as a subject in writing. We will examine in another chapter her lyrical self-representation in poetry, which is somewhat different from how she characterized herself as a subject of thought and action in narrative form. It is instructive to recognize that her first attempts in the latter genre are to be found not in her first published novel but in private writing of the sort that women of the educated elite commonly practiced. It was in letters and in diaries that the very young Gómez de Avellaneda, before she had the confidence to enter the man's world of publication, had cultural permission and precedent to construct and represent herself as a woman in writing. None of her very early letters have been preserved, but we do have a travel diary that she wrote from Spain to a cousin in Cuba and an autobiographical sketch in the form of a letter, both of which were written before she ever published anything. The autobiography is of particular interest because it shows her working out in a very personal mode of writing an image of the self that draws on Romantic literary models while registering acute awareness that these models were antithetical to the cultural pattern of feminine existence.

In 1839, at the age of twenty-five, Gómez de Avellaneda wrote an account of her life and personality for Ignacio Cepeda, the man for whom she felt an unrequited passion for many years of her life. The text was written as an extended letter in a small notebook with dated installments. Its personal tone arises from the specificity with which the addressee is designated. Cepeda, who is frequently addressed by name, will be the text's only reader, according to both the opening and closing paragraphs, which command him to burn it once he has read it. This autobiography, then, identifies itself as a private communication ap-

propriate for a woman to write—a letter written in a referential context
shared only with its intended reader.

Indeed, the text reads like one side of an extended dialogue whose
other side we can only infer, for the interlocutors were seeing each
other every day, and each installment begins with a commentary on
some encounter that has occurred—or failed to occur—since the previous writing. As a result, the counterpoint between the present of narration and the narrated past, between narrating subject and narrated self,
a characteristic of all autobiography, reveals with unusual clarity how
the desires and interests of the writing subject shape her self-representations. The *Autobiography*'s first words, in identifying Cepeda as the
text's very reason for being, imply what the writer is after: "Es preciso
ocuparme de usted; se lo he ofrecido; . . . de usted me ocupo al escribir
de mí, pues sólo por usted consentiría en hacerlo" 'I must attend to
you; I have offered to; . . . by writing about myself I attend to you,
since only for you would I agree to do so' (39). In insisting that writing
of herself is a form of thinking of Cepeda, she reveals that her desire
to be seen by him is what prompts her to portray herself in this piece
of writing. As the text unfolds, it shows itself to be essentially an act
of seduction: the writer attempts to produce an image of herself that
will please and capture his desire. At the same time, however, the process of self-representation is governed by the writer's own desires in
the sense that she creates herself in the image of what *she* finds most
attractive. As we shall see, Romantic models of subjectivity exerted a
powerful pull on Gómez de Avellaneda's idea of the self she wished to
characterize for her resistant suitor. Since society's—and presumably
Cepeda's—definition of feminine desirability sharply diverged from the
Romantic contours of the writer's own desired self-image, the characterization of the autobiographical self veers between two nearly irrec-
oncilable poles.

The self-divided nature of the writer's task appears in her first move
to establish the authenticity of her self-portrayal. In the opening paragraph, she asserts the sincerity of her writing:

> La confesión, que la supersticiosa y tímida conciencia arranca a una alma
> arrepentida a los pies de un ministro del cielo, no fue nunca más sincera,
> más franca, que la que yo estoy dispuesta a hacer a usted. Después de leer
> este cuadernillo, me conocerá usted tan bien, o acaso mejor que a sí mismo.
> (39)

> The confession that a timid and superstitious conscience wrings from a re-
> pentant soul at the feet of heaven's minister was never more sincere, more

frank, than the one I am disposed to make to you. After reading this notebook, you will know me as well, or perhaps better, than yourself.

Yet the very terms in which Gómez de Avellaneda wishes to guarantee the unmediated truthfulness of her written self-image alerts us to the shaping presence of literary models. Rousseau's precedent, in the *Confessions,* of equating autobiography with unconventionally direct self-revelation clearly sets the path that Avellaneda intends to follow. Furthermore, the epistolary form of this autobiography, which mentions her reading of Rousseau and comments on the passionate sensibility of Saint-Preux, suggests that Gómez de Avellaneda was hoping to initiate something similar to the soul-baring correspondence between Julie and Saint-Preux.

As the already literary gesture of proclaiming her sincerity implies, Gómez de Avellaneda had of necessity to construct an image of herself from the materials provided by literary precedent. Not surprisingly, Romantic paradigms of the self shaped many aspects of her autobiographical narrative. For example, the narration of her broken engagement to a fiancé chosen by her family follows a familiar pattern. At first Tula, as I shall call the autobiographical character created by the text, uses her power of imagination to idealize her fiancé: "Prodigóle mi fecunda imaginación ideales perfecciones, y vi en él reunidas todas las cualidades de los héroes de mis novelas favoritas" 'My fecund imagination endowed him with ideal perfections, and I saw united in him all the qualities of the heroes of my favorite novels' (45). But as soon as she realizes that he falls short of such perfections, she comes to detest him and rejects the match. Generalizing this trajectory from illusion-filled innocence to alienating experience, she represents her life history in terms that echo the Romantic poets:

> ¡[I]nvocaba al objeto . . . ideal que formé en los primeros sueños de mi entusiasmo! Creía verle en el Sol y en la Luna, en el verde de los campos y en el azul del cielo: las brisas de la noche me traían su aliento, los sonidos de la música el eco de su voz: ¡Yo le veía en todo lo que hay de grande y hermoso en la Naturaleza! . . .
>
> ¡Cepeda! ¡Cuánto me engañaba!—¿Dónde existe el hombre que pueda llenar los votos de esta sensibilidad tan fogosa como delicada? ¡En vano lo he buscado nueve años!; ¡en vano! . . . Yo buscaba un bien que no encontraba y que acaso no existe sobre la tierra. Ahora ya no le busco, no le espero, no le deseo: por eso estoy más tranquila. (49)

> I invoked the ideal . . . object formed in the first dreams of my enthusiasm!
> I thought I saw him in the Sun and the Moon, in the green of the fields and

the blue of the heavens: the night breezes brought me his breath, music the echo of his voice: I saw him in everything that is great and beautiful in Nature! . . .

Cepeda! How deceived I was!—Where is the man who can fulfill the wishes of my sensibility, as fiery as it is delicate? I have sought him in vain for nine years! In vain! . . . I sought something I could not find and which perhaps does not exist on earth. Now I don't seek it, I don't expect it, I don't desire it: therefore I feel more tranquil.

Thus Gómez de Avellaneda appropriates for Tula the transcendent passions, the overweening desires, that constituted the inner selves represented by Rousseau, Espronceda, and even Byron, whom she paraphrases:

> "Cuando navegamos sobre los mares azulados," ha dicho Lord Byron, "nuestros pensamientos son tan libres como el Oceano." Su alma sublime y poética debió sentirlo así: la mía lo experimentó también. (66)

> "When we sail on the azure seas," Lord Byron has said, "our thoughts are as free as the Ocean." His sublime, poetic soul must have felt it thus: my soul experienced this, too.

The self she represents for Cepeda is as passionate, as alienated from a corrupt and inadequate world, as capable of imaginatively outstripping nature as the lyrical "I" of Espronceda or Larra, but with this difference: the object that can never measure up to desire and imagination is not woman but man.

The gesture of constituting herself a subject of Romantic experience, however, was neither as natural nor as unproblematic for Gómez de Avellaneda as her identification with Byron's "sublime, poetic soul" might at first glance appear. The writer herself admitted that female identity—which she must preserve in order to be the object of Cepeda's desire—is socially defined in opposition to the values of the poetic soul. Describing a cousin who is her soul mate and alter ego, she observes, "Como yo, reunía la debilidad de mujer y la frivolidad de niña con la elevación y profundidad de sentimientos, que sólo son propios de los carácteres fuertes y varoniles" 'Like me, she combined a woman's weakness and a girl's frivolity with the elevation and profundity of feeling that are unique to strong, manly characters' (47). Had she worked only with this cultural differentiation between male and female, the author could not have granted a woman—defined as frivolous and weak—the subjective dimensions of the Romantic self. To avoid this contradiction, Avellaneda turned to the non-Spanish female tradition I mentioned earlier, to Mme de Staël and her creation, the sublime poet Corinne.

Among the letters that Gómez de Avellaneda wrote to Cepeda during the same summer that she wrote her autobiography (and which were published together with it after he died) is one that shows how closely she associated the French heroine with the self she constructed for the man she wished to fascinate. Proposing that they read a series of novels together, she suggests Walter Scott first, and

> [s]eguidamente *Corina o Italia* por Madame Staël. . . . [H]an dado algunos amigos en decirme que hay semejanzas entre mí y la protagonista de esta novela, y deseo por eso volver a leerla contigo y buscar la semejanza, que se me atribuye con este bello ideal de un genio como el de la Staël. (116)

> next *Corinne or Italy,* by Madame Staël. . . . Some of my friends have told me that there are similarities between me and the protagonist of this novel, and so I want to read it again with you and look for the similarity I'm supposed to have with such a beautiful ideal of genius as that of Mme Staël.

Given that the ideal represented in Corinne is at once an artistic genius and a seductive, fascinating woman, Gómez de Avellaneda's effort to get Cepeda to look for the similarity is all too transparent. Although no mention is made of Corinne in the autobiography itself, Gómez de Avellaneda's representation of herself includes certain characteristics of Staël's heroine, such as her uncensored spontaneity and emotional intensity. For example, again characterizing herself in a description of her favorite cousin, the writer enumerates a series of Corinne-like contrasts: "[E]ra como yo, una mezcla de profundidad y ligereza, de tristeza y alegría, de entusiasmo y desaliento" 'She was, like me, a mixture of profundity and fickleness, of sadness and happiness, of enthusiasm and discouragement' (47). It is the model of Corinne that makes this range of emotional registers in Tula and her cousin readable as the sign of an interestingly complex female personality, instead of as a monstrous hybrid of "feminine" frivolity and "masculine" profundity.

Mme de Staël's novel, however, demonstrates in its tragic finale precisely the impossibility of reconciling female genius with the social views of femininity that dictate men's choices. Thus, if *Corinne* cannot provide a model for resolving the conflict between what Gómez de Avellaneda wants to be and what she thinks Cepeda desires in a woman, at least it sets out a narrative framework for representing that conflict: the woman who is superior to the social definition of her sex is doomed to unhappiness in love. And, indeed, the autobiographical narrator presents and interprets key episodes precisely in this light. For example, after describing how her relatives attributed her refusal of the arranged marriage to an unladylike willfulness resulting from her "novelesque" (59) education and persuaded her grandfather to disinherit her, she generalizes this as an indication of her destiny:

> ¡Cuántas [veces] envidié la suerte de esas mujeres que no sienten ni piensan; que comen, duermen, vegetan, y a las cuales el mundo llama muchas veces mujeres sensatas! Abrumada por el instinto de mi superioridad, yo sospeché entonces lo que después he conocido muy bien: Que no he nacido para ser dichosa, y que mi vida sobre la tierra será corta y borrascosa. (61)

> How often I envied the lot of those women who neither feel nor think; who eat, sleep, vegetate, and are often called sensible women! Crushed by the instinct of my superiority, I suspected then what afterward I have known very well: that I was not born to be happy and that my life on earth will be short and tempestuous.

Her talent, her imagination, her depth of emotion—the elements of "genius"—make her, like Corinne, "superior" to her feminine identity, since those by cultural definition "are unique to strong, manly characters." But Corinne's dissimilarity to women who conform to their gender roles, "who neither feel nor think," proves fatal, in the end, and so too Gómez de Avellaneda predicts a short and stormy life for herself.

As the autobiographical narrative continues, it shows how the rift between the author's "male" character or subjectivity and her female social identity condemns her to unhappiness in Spain as well as Cuba. In La Coruña, where she stayed with her stepfather's relatives, her interests and behavior were considered scandalously inappropriate to her sex, and she experienced the Spanish equivalent of Corinne's unhappy stay in Scotland:

> Decían que yo era atea, y la prueba que daban era que leía las obras de Rousseau. . . . Las parientas de mi padrastro decían . . . que yo no era buena para nada, porque no sabía planchar, ni cocinar, ni calcetar; porque no lavaba los cristales ni hacía las camas, ni barría mi cuarto. . . . Ridiculizaban también mi afición al estudio y me llamaban la Doctora. (72)

> They said I was an atheist, the proof being that I read the works of Rousseau. . . . The female relatives of my stepfather said . . . that I wasn't good for anything because I didn't know how to iron or cook or darn; because I didn't wash windows or make beds or sweep my room. . . . They also ridiculed my fondness for studying and called me the Lady Doctor.

The French novel, then, provided a narrative language that corresponded to and permitted the expression of the lived difficulty that Avellaneda experienced when the cultural expectations that circumscribed women's existence dogged her efforts to cross gender boundaries in forging an identity as a female Romantic subject.

The dilemma posed by the opposition of femininity and Romantic values surfaces thematically in this autobiography as the author's opposition to marriage. Seeking an all-absorbing passion rather than convenience, she avoided the advantageous match that had been arranged for her, and observing how her beloved cousin's tender suitor became a tyrant once he was a husband (a process she also noted in her stepfather), she concluded that marriage in general was to be avoided: "[M]i horror al matrimonio nació y creció rápidamente" 'My horror of marriage was born and grew rapidly' (63). The reasons for this view of marriage are never fully detailed, but enough is said to indicate that the central issue is the asymmetrical structure of power in that institution: the husband becomes the tyrant, and the wife's only alternative is to suffer in virtuous silence, like the author's cousin (63). What Larra in his review of *Anthony* took to be a political metaphor—husband as tyrant—with dangerous consequences if interpreted literally by women is reversed by Gómez de Avellaneda, who refers to only one form of power as a condition to be dealt with in her concrete life history—the social and legal power of male over female.

Here again the Cuban-Spanish writer draws on a French female tradition to counter a male-oriented Spanish Romanticism, for the legal tyranny of marriage is the thesis of the two George Sand novels that Gómez de Avellaneda had read a few years earlier. In her second preface to *Indiana,* the French novelist stated succinctly the underlying thrust of her first novel:

> Ceux qui m'ont lu sans prévention comprennent que j'ai écrit *Indiana* avec le sentiment non raisonné, il est vrai, mais profond et légitime, de l'injustice et de la barbarie des lois qui régissent encore l'existence de la femme dans le mariage, dans la famille et la société. (20)

> Those who have read me without bias understand that I wrote *Indiana* out of a feeling, not thought through, it's true, but deep and legitimate, about the injustice and the barbarity of the laws that still rule women's existence in marriage, in the family, and in society.

Although mainstream literary and moral critics had reacted with animosity to the series of novels Sand published in the 1830s (*Indiana,*

Valentine, Jacques, Lélia, Lettres à Marci) exploring "le rapport mal établi entre les sexes, par le fait de la société" 'the bad relationship between the sexes established by society' (*Indiana* 14), these popular works provided a contestatory model for other women writers. The process whereby Gómez de Avellaneda translated raw experience into written narrative in her autobiography and expounded her position on love and marriage was possible because Sand's antimarriage novels had established a narrative language and a rationale into which Avellaneda could read her own refusal of her arranged marriage or her cousin's married unhappiness.

Certainly Sand's observations about the unequal relations society sets up between the sexes correspond to the fundamental lesson that Tula learns about a society that permits her grandfather to disinherit her and her stepfather to bully her mother, while denying Tula the right to recover her paternal inheritance without the mediation of a husband. This socially enforced impotence brings the autobiographical protagonist very close to the dreaded state of matrimony in an episode that vividly illustrates the psychological consequence of the contradiction between self-definition and social prescription.

In La Coruña, Tula fell in love with Ricafort, a young military officer whose noble and generous heart was far superior to his intelligence, "unfortunately for me" (68), notes the narrator. "No gustaba de mi afición al estudio y era para él un delito que hiciese versos. Mis ideas sobre muchas cosas le daban pena e inquietud" 'He didn't like my enthusiasm for studying and thought it a crime that I wrote poetry. My ideas about many things pained and worried him' (68). Despite Ricafort's qualms about Tula's intellectual pursuits, he generously offered to marry her when she confided to him her misery and impotence in her stepfather's household. She accepted: "Muchos días vacilé; mi horror al matrimonio era extremado, pero al fin, cedí: mi situación doméstica tan insufrible, mi desamparo, su amor y el mío, todo se unió para determinarme" 'I hesitated for many days; my aversion to marriage was extreme, but in the end I gave in: my insufferable domestic situation, my helplessness, his love and mine, all this came together to decide me' (69).

Though the autobiographical narrator does not deny that she based her decision on a desire to extricate herself from a situation in which as an unmarried woman she felt powerless, she takes pains to establish her womanly capacity for self-abnegation by asserting her resolve to dedicate herself entirely to her future husband: "Talento, placeres, todo se aniquiló para mí: solo deseaba llenar las severas obligaciones que iba a contraer" 'I gave up all idea of talent, pleasures, everything: I only wanted to fulfill the severe obligations I was going to contract' (69–70). But here the rift in a self split between a feminine gender identity and "masculine" ambitions and interests reappears as a discrepancy between intention and act. The statement of resolve to sacrifice her desires to her duties as a wife is followed by a lament: "¡Oh Dios mío! ¡por qué no pude hacerlo!—¡Tú sabes si eran puras mis intenciones y sinceros mis votos! ¿por qué no los escuchaste?" 'Oh, dear God! Why couldn't I do it!—You know that my intentions were pure and my desires sincere! Why didn't You heed them?' (70). She blames her failure to prove her feminine virtue by carrying out her promise to Ricafort on "la funesta debilidad de mi carácter" 'fatal weakness of my character' (70), yet a page later what emerges is not weakness of character but the forceful argument of an opposing identity:

> [P]ensé mucho en las diversidades que existían entre Ricafort y yo, me pregunté a mí misma si aquella superioridad que él me suponía, no sería tarde o temprano un origen de desunión, y reflexionando en las contras del matrimonio y las ventajas de la libertad me di el parabién de ser libre todavía. (71)

> I thought a lot about the differences that existed between Ricafort and me, I asked myself if that superiority he attributed to me would not sooner or later be the source of disagreement, and reflecting on the disadvantages of marriage and the advantages of freedom, I congratulated myself on being free still.

In the narrated action, the question of marriage is settled by Tula's departure from La Coruña with her brother to go to her father's birthplace in Andalusia (the male protection necessary to change her circumstances having been found without the necessity of marriage). The rift in the self is not resolved, however; it continues in the self constructed in the present tense of narration. Anxiety about the implications of the rupture with Ricafort interrupts the narrative in an exclamation directed toward the reader: "[M]ucho necesito ahora de la indulgencia de usted, querido Cepeda, porque me averguenzo todavía de mi ligereza" 'I very much need your indulgence now, dear Cepeda, because I am still ashamed of my fickleness' (71). Here the contradictory desires that shaped Gómez de Avellaneda's self-representation for Cepeda rise to the surface. On the one hand, wishing to identify herself with the ideal feminine capacity for self-sacrificing commitment to loved ones, she anticipates and seeks to mitigate disapproval of her abandonment of Ricafort. On the other hand, she persistently projects the image of herself as the Romantic subject hungering for transcendent satisfaction in a fallen world.

The conclusions proposed by the text about the Ricafort episode are a function of this Romantic version of the self:

> Yo había perdido la esperanza de encontrar un hombre según mi corazón. . . . Sin embargo, . . . sintiendo más que nunca el vacío de mi alma, disgustada de un mundo que no realizaba mis ilusiones, disgustada de mí misma por mi impotencia de ser feliz, en vano era que quisiera aturdirme y sofocar en mí este fecundo germen de sentimientos y dolores. (74)

> I lost hope of finding a man according to my heart's desire. . . . However, . . . feeling the emptiness in my soul more than ever, unhappy with a world that did not realize my illusions, displeased with myself for my incapacity to be happy, it was in vain that I tried to numb myself and suffocate that fertile seed of feeling and pain.

The "I" constructed in this passage coincides strikingly with the lyrical "I" of Espronceda's "A Jarifa en una orgía" in its despair of finding an adequate love object and its unsuccessful effort to deaden desire through superficial sensory experience. But the feminine identity of Gómez de Avellaneda's "I" speaks distinctively in the concluding sentences of this passage: "Hubiera yo querido mudar mi naturaleza. . . . Yo me avergonzaba ya de una sensibilidad que me constituía siempre víctima" 'I would have liked to change my nature. . . . I was thoroughly ashamed of a sensibility that made me always a victim' (74). The impossibility of either fully disavowing or fully identifying with the feminine ideal of self-abnegation or the claims of self-generated desire divides the narrating self, which seeks always to be other than itself, like the Duke of Rivas's Don Alvaro. But unlike the hero of *La fuerza del sino*, Avellaneda's self-alienation derives from a socially specific kind of fatality—the cultural system of gender differentiation that constitutes her the victim of her own sensibility in a way that no male could be.

The complex relationship of the narrating subject of this autobiography to the narrated representation of the self dramatically exemplifies the internal division that marks Gómez de Avellaneda's construction of a self at once feminine and Romantic. The telos of the narration of her life experience is the image of the world-weary soul who no longer seeks happiness in illusory transports of love, who disguises her intimate melancholy by superficial conformity to social expectation. This image, projected as we have seen at various points of the narrative, remains conclusively fixed at the end of the final amatory episode: "Lo confieso: quedé cansada de amor. . . . Por eso me fijé más que nunca en mi sistema de no amar nunca" 'I confess that I became tired of love. . . . Therefore I stuck more firmly than ever to my system of never falling in love' (82). She then announces, "My story is done!" (82) and sums up her final position as parting advice for Cepeda: "Adiós, querido mío. . . . Créame usted: para ser dichoso modere la elevación de su alma y procure nivelar su existencia a la sociedad en que debe vivir" 'Goodbye, my dear. . . . Believe me: in order to be happy, moderate the nobility of your soul and try to suit your existence to the society in which you must live.' But, unable to resist eliciting Cepeda's admiration or remorse, she adds, "Cuando la injusticia y la ignorancia le desconozca y le aflija, entonces dígase usted a sí mismo: Existe un ser sobre la tierra que me comprende y me estima" 'When injustice and ignorance marginalize and afflict you, then tell yourself: There exists a being on earth who understands and esteems me' (83). Thus, the initial projected image of self-possession, transcendence of desire, is undermined by the subtext of the second remark, where the gesture is one of seduction, despite the content of the message.

Indeed, throughout the text similar gestures by the narrating subject belie the narrated self's claim to a self-possession that makes her no longer a victim of her own sensibility—that is, of desires that are neither appropriate to feminine virtue nor able to be fulfilled by reality. The narration of Tula's story is punctuated by a present-time commentary that implies another narrative. These comments about ongoing events in the author's relationship with Cepeda begin or end the dated installments of the autobiography: "25 por la mañana. Hoy no le veré a usted verosímilmente, pues según su sistema, creo no irá a la ópera, a la cual iré yo" 'Morning of the 25th. Today I'm not likely to see you, since according to your system, I don't think you'll go to the opera, which I *am* going to' (44). Although the main episodes and conclusion of this other, meta-narrative lie outside the text in the interaction of the narrator and her unheard addressee, what is said identifies it clearly as the story of the author's obsession with Cepeda and her attempt, in the face of his withdrawal, to seduce and interest him through this writing of herself.

> De anoche acá usted ha decaído tanto en mi opinión, que (¿por qué no he de decirlo todo?) que casi temo aumentar con el nombre de usted la lista de

mis desengaños. Yo perderé, si así fuere, yo perderé una ilusión, una última ilusión que me ha lisonjeado algunos días; pero usted perderá más: sí. Porque ¿dónde hallará usted otra amiga como yo? (54)

After last night my opinion of you has gone down so much that—why not say it all?—that I'm almost afraid that your name will be added to the list of my disillusions. I will lose, if it so turns out, an illusion, a last illusion that gladdened me a few days; but you will lose more: yes. Because where will you find another friend like me?

So with the conclusion of its history the narrating "I" has not solidified itself in self-possession: it still loses itself, still is victimized by its passions:

¡Cepeda!, querido Cepeda! . . . ¿no será usted otra nueva decepción para mí?; ¿quién me asegura que no es usted un hipócrita? ¿quién me garantiza su sinceridad? . . . Sin embargo, ya ve usted que mi imprudencia me arrastra: Este cuaderno es una prueba de ello. Acaso me arrepentiré algún día de haberlo escrito. ¡Qué importa! Será un desengaño más, pero será el último. (62)

Cepeda! Dear Cepeda! . . . are you going to be another disappointment for me? Who can assure me that you aren't a hypocrite? Who can guarantee your sincerity? . . . Nevertheless, as you can see, my imprudence carries the day: This notebook is proof of it. Perhaps one day I'll repent of having written it. What does it matter? It will be another disillusionment, but it will be the last.

Thus, the narrating subject confesses its difference from the self whose liberation from the power of its own conflicting and unattainable desires is always projected beyond the "last disillusionment." The text itself ("este cuaderno") stands as testament to the subject's division insofar as the anguished narrating voice does not correspond to the story whereby the narrated self obtains wisdom and tranquillity. The contradictory forms of selfhood offered by the traditional view of womanhood and the new Romantic individualism could not make an integrated whole of the female subjectivity that the autobiographer experienced as victimization.

THE SELF AS WOMAN AND SLAVE IN *SAB*

As a form of private, very personal writing, Gómez de Avellaneda's autobiography reveals the difficulties that fractured her attempt to construct herself as both a feminine and a Romantic "I." In the non-autobiographical narratives that she wrote for publication we see a related but rather different consequence of her feminization of the Romantic subject. The novel form, in contrast to autobiography's demand for a coherent, centered image of the self, permitted her to distribute the elements of subjectivity among a number of fictional characters. Thus, transgressing the boundaries that confined women to private writing turned out to be as liberating for Avellaneda's writing as it was for her life. The novelist's distance from the expressions of interiority produced by her pen allowed her to explore more freely the permutations generated by contradictions between socially assigned roles and inner consciousness.

In her first novel, *Sab*, which she completed in manuscript around the time she wrote the autobiographical letter to Cepeda, this freedom led to some remarkable innovations. As in the autobiography, Gómez de Avellaneda made woman the subject of Romantic experience in *Sab*, which, developing the fictional possibilities of portraying socially oppressed subjectivity, became the first antislavery novel written in Spanish.[2] Thus adapted to the perspective of a marginalized subject, in Gómez de Avellaneda's novels the Romantic paradigms became instruments of a critique rarely heard before in Spanish culture, where liberalism failed to include the point of view of those subordinated because of their gender or their race. But further, the notes of protest and denunciation sounded in *Sab* add to Avellaneda's representation of female subjectivity an element that was absent or repressed in the autobiography. Let us, then, consider in some detail the patterns of subjectivity exhibited by the novel's main characters.

The novel forms its plot around two interlocking love triangles. Carlota, heiress of a sugar plantation, and Teresa, her orphaned cousin, both love Enrique, the son of an English merchant; Carlota is loved both by Enrique, who eventually marries her, and by Sab, a mulatto slave who is part of her household. The conventional pattern is transformed, however, as the Romantic themes of the novel develop in a plot that primarily traces the impact of a cold, commercial, and unjust society on those characters blessed—or cursed—by a superior capacity for feeling. By the end of the novel, Sab, Teresa, and Carlota form a grouping unified not by rivalry for a love object, as in the conventional triangle, but rather by shared values and a common experience of powerlessness within the social structure. They constitute the novel's subject as a kind of trinity, a fragmented but mysteriously whole entity that at once projects the perception of the Romantic self's division and promotes the values of intersubjectivity. Such a possibility was present in embryonic form in the autobiography, where the narrator's cousin was treated briefly as an alter ego through which she could describe herself, but the genre of the novel offered a wider field for experimentation with this technique.

To illustrate the contrast that differentiates Teresa, Sab, and Carlota from the other characters, let us first consider the case of Enrique Otway. In an interesting reversal of male Romantic narratives, his role is that of object—the a priori object of feminine desire. As if his desirability were a universal given, Carlota and Teresa are already both in love with him when the novel opens. Although the narrative voice enters his feelings and thoughts on occasion, Enrique's subjectivity has no impact on the external world of the novel. Instead, his behavior and indeed his emotions are determined from outside—by his father's demand that he abandon Carlota or by the information that Carlota has won a lottery. Furthermore, he is closely associated with the material world of things, for he primarily concerns himself with business, commerce, and money, values inherently alien to the inner life of the other three main characters. Enrique, then, together with his father, represents the public world of the market. As a subject, he exemplifies the laws and norms of that world. For this reason, though she is finally devastated by Enrique's relentless pursuit of material interests, "Carlota no podía desaprobar con justicia la conducta de su marido, ni debía quejarse de su suerte" 'Carlota could not justly disapprove of the behavior of her husband nor complain about her lot' (213). Enrique is not presented as an evil man; he is simply the human expression of a social structure whose norms the novel challenges.

The three other main characters belong to a different category, explicitly established early on in the novel. The narrator tells us that

> hay almas superiores sobre la tierra, privilegiadas para el sentimiento y desconocidas de las almas vulgares; almas ricas de afectos, ricas de emociones—para las cuales están reservadas las pasiones terribles, las grandes virtudes, los inmensos pesares—y . . . el alma de Enrique no era una de ellas. (74)

> there are superior souls on this earth, privileged with regard to feeling but uncomprehended by ordinary souls; souls rich in affection, rich in emotion, for whom the terrible passions, the great virtues, the immense sorrows are reserved—and . . . Enrique's soul was not one of them.

Carlota, however, is quickly identified as belonging to this privileged category because of her sensibility and the passionate blindness of her love for Enrique. Teresa too, though described as outwardly dry and impassive, has such a soul: "no era incapaz de grandes pasiones, mejor diré, era formada para sentirlas" . . . 'she was not incapable of great passions, indeed, was made to feel them' (55). Sab reveals his own spiritual stature in an internal monologue as he compares himself to his privileged but unemotional rival, reflecting that Enrique has no idea that the slave has the superior soul, "capaz de amar, capaz de aborrecer" 'capable of love, capable of hate' (78). The irony of this inversion of social and spiritual status points up the other trait common to the three exceptional souls: they occupy inferior positions in the social hierarchy. The correspondence between the social destiny of the black slave and that of the two women becomes, as we shall see, the covert message of the novel.

While all three "superior souls" exemplify the basic Romantic paradigm of subjectivity that we have found in Espronceda and Larra—the fall from the illusions of the passionate imagination to the bitter knowledge of alienating reality—it is Carlota's experience that most fully embodies this trajectory. The most startling feature of this representation of a woman as subject of Romantic consciousness is that Carlota's destiny is tragic, like that of Larra's Fígaro or Rivas's Don Alvaro, even though the external world grants her all that is supposed to make a woman happy. As Teresa observes, "Hija adorada, ama querida, esposa futura del amante de tu elección, ¿qué puede afligirte, Carlota?" 'Adored daughter, beloved mistress of the plantation, future wife of the man you have chosen, what could make you unhappy, Carlota?' (51). Yet Carlota does suffer, for the fatal Romantic chasm between desire and its satisfaction yawns inescapably in woman's social destiny. Marriage takes Carlota from the virginal garden created in the text as an externalization of her personality and places her in her husband's sphere, the world of the marketplace, where there is no room for love, beauty, and feeling. Consequently, Carlota languishes after her marriage:

> Carlota era una pobre alma poética arrojada entre mil existencias positivas. Dotada de una imaginación fértil y activa, ignorante de la vida, . . . se veía obligada a vivir de cálculo, de reflexión y de conveniencia. Aquella atmósfera mercantil y especuladora, aquellos cuidados incesantes de los intereses materiales marchitaban las bellas ilusiones de su joven corazón. (213)

> Carlota was a poor poetic soul thrown into the midst of a thousand materialistic existences. Gifted with a fertile, active imagination, ignorant of life, . . . she found herself obliged to live according to calculation, caution, and convenience. That mercenary and speculative atmosphere, that inces-

sant worry about material interests, dried up the beautiful illusions of her young heart.

The culminating experience of Carlota's disillusionment teaches her the truth about her place in the world of social facts and power. She discovers that her father-in-law has falsified her father's will, so that on his death the inheritance goes to her alone instead of being divided with her sisters. Determined to rectify this injustice, she asks Enrique to give her sisters their fair share of the legacy. When he refuses, treating her request as childish nonsense, she tastes the full extent of her powerlessness:

> Carlota luchó inútilmente por espacio de muchos meses, después guardó silencio y pareció resignarse. Para ella todo había acabado. Vio a su marido tal cual era; comenzó a comprender la vida. Sus sueños se disiparon, su amor huyó con su felicidad. Entonces tocó toda la desnudez, toda la pequeñez de las realidades, . . . y su alma . . . se halló sola en medio de aquellos dos hombres pegados a la tierra. (215)

> Carlota struggled uselessly for many months, then she kept silent and seemed to resign herself. For her, all had ended. She saw her husband as he really was; she began to understand life. Her dreams dissolved, her love fled with her happiness. Then she touched in its nakedness all the pettiness of reality, . . . and her soul . . . found itself alone in the company of those two earth-bound men.

The key to Carlota's disillusionment is to be found in the words "struggled uselessly": the gap between her desire and the world cannot be bridged, because women's political subordination enforces the radical separation between feminine feeling and male public world.

We see then how far Gómez de Avellaneda departs from the conventional women's fiction that her novel at first seems to resemble; instead of demonstrating that woman's true happiness is to be found in her socially assigned place, *Sab* exposes that belief as an illusion. At the same time, the Cuban-born novelist infuses the Romantic paradigm of consciousness with a radical new content by attributing it to a female subject. Whereas in Espronceda's lyric poetry, for example, the lack of a social explanation for the subject's alienation and the frustration of his Promethean desire implies a metaphysical determination,[3] Carlota's story, insofar as it reenacts the Romantic syndrome of despair in terms of a woman's experience of what society offers as her optimal destiny, attributes alienation to social injustice. In thus using the Romantic model of subjectivity and the socially prescribed model of femininity to modify each other in the novel, Avellaneda begins to escape the binary opposition between the two in which she was trapped in her autobiography and embarks on an ever-expanding innovatory project.

Further possibilities of the subjectivity of those whom the social structure treats as objects are developed in the characters of Teresa and Sab, both of whom occupy disadvantageous positions in society: Teresa was born out of wedlock and Sab was born a slave. The range of the social critique is in this way extended to include slavery and racism along with marriage and the subjection of women. Furthermore, since Teresa's and Sab's social disadvantages deny them the period of blissful illusion which is granted to Carlota, they can only provide foreshortened versions of the temporal evolution of the Romantic self. They thus readily lend themselves to development as complementary elements of a subjectivity no longer confined by the limits of a single character.

The narrator presents Teresa as a soul capable of passion and feeling; but, "humillada y devorando en silencio su mortificación, había aprendido a disimular, haciéndose cada vez más fría y reservada" 'humiliated and swallowing her mortification in silence, she had learned to dissimulate, appearing ever colder and more reserved' (55). The self-protective repression of her deeply felt emotions becomes a capacity for comprehension in Teresa. The unique lucidity stemming from the detachment she imposes on herself permits her to read Sab's secret love in actions that remain opaque to the other characters. When he reveals to her the extent of his passion and suffering, she is able to grasp the true value of his spirit. It is she who formulates the novel's primary code of ethics by deciding to protect Carlota's illusions about Enrique rather than destroy them with the truth—that he intends to break off their engagement because her dowry is too small:

> ¡Oh, vosotros, los que ya lo habéis visto todo! . . . Respetad esas frentes puras, en las que el desengaño no ha estampado su sello; respetad esas almas . . . ricas de esperanzas y poderosas por su juventud; dejadles sus errores, menos mal les harán que esa fatal previsión que queréis darles. (146–147)

> Oh, you who have seen everything! . . . Respect those pure brows on which disillusionment has not stamped its seal; respect those souls . . . rich in hope and powerful with youth; leave them to their errors, which will do them less harm than the fatal foresight you want to give them.

Teresa prevails upon Sab to accept this code as his own, persuading him to abandon his plan to expose Enrique's materialistic calculations

and instead to use his winning lottery ticket to make Carlota rich and
thus reinforce her fiancé's wavering commitment.

Teresa's sublimated passion, then, becomes compassion, which
stands near the top of the novel's scale of values. In their anguish both
Sab and Carlota turn to her for sympathy and comfort. Sab tells her,
"¡Bendígate Dios! . . . A no ser por vos, yo hubiera pasado por la senda
de la vida como por un desierto, solo con mi amor y mi desventura,
sin encontrar una mirada de simpatía ni una palabra de compasión!"
'God bless you! . . . Except for you, I would have gone through life as
through a desert, alone with my love and my misfortune, without meeting a sympathetic glance or a compassionate word' (174). Romantic
consciousness, as Gómez de Avellaneda has appropriated it both in this
novel and in the autobiography, sees happiness as an illusion, an impossibility in reality. But in the novel she begins explicitly to work out
a compensatory value that is merely implied in the autobiography's gesture toward Cepeda: the sympathy of another feeling soul compensates
for the frustration of desire, confirming the existence of spiritual values
despite the exterior world's hostility. Creating a select fellowship of
"almas superiores" 'superior souls' becomes a way of mitigating the
isolation of the feeling subject in an alien world.

The value of intersubjective relations as a compensation for the failure of the subject-object relation is dramatized in Teresa's final act. As
she lies on her deathbed, Teresa gives Carlota the letter that Sab had
written her when he was dying, pouring out his heart to his only friend.
She offers this testament as a consolation that may help her friend in
the lonely years to come. "Acaso no hallarás nada grande y bello en
que descansar tu corazón fatigado. Entonces tendrás ese papel; ese
papel es toda un alma; es una vida, una muerte. . . . Mientras leas ese
papel creerás como yo en el amor y la virtud" 'You may find nothing
great and beautiful to refresh your weary heart. Then you will have that
paper; that paper is an entire soul—a life and a death. . . . When you
read that paper you will believe as I do in love and virtue' (218).
The lesson that Teresa teaches, then, is that compassion and love, the
shared subjectivity of the oppressed, provide the only consolation in a
hard, mercenary world, the only antidote to solitary despair.

If the sublimation of passion into intelligence, the abstraction of a
philosophy from pain, are processes of the psyche explored in Teresa,
Sab represents the movement of unprocessed emotion. His soul, preserved like a life-giving balm in his letter, has, Teresa tells Carlota, "el
aroma de un corazón que moría sin marchitarse" 'the aroma of a heart

that did not dry up while it was dying' (218). He believes that his love for Carlota fully justifies his life: "¡Mi llama ha sido pura, inmensa, inextinguible! No importa que haya padecido, pues he amado a Carlota" 'My flame has been pure, immense, inextinguishable! It doesn't matter that I have suffered, for I have loved Carlota' (171). And the lucid Teresa agrees: "[E]l corazón que sabe amar así, no es un corazón vulgar" 'The heart that can love thus no ordinary heart' (173). Sab is all heart, all passion. In contrast to Teresa, he cannot sublimate feeling; when he has sacrificed his passion by assuring Carlota's marriage to Enrique, his psychic substance has been spent and he simply dies.

There is more to Sab's emotion than undying love, however, for he supplies what so far has been lacking in Gómez de Avellaneda's representation of female subjectivity as Romantic consciousness—a sense of outrage, the Promethean impulse toward revolt. The fifth chapter links Sab with a rage that, echoed and magnified by nature, escapes the bounds of his character. Accompanying Enrique through the forest as a dangerous thunderstorm approaches, Sab stares somberly at Carlota's fiancé, trying to penetrate his innermost thoughts. Suddenly, as if he has perceived the truth—that Enrique intends to jilt Carlota because her dowry is insufficient—Sab's face changes, crossed by "una sonrisa amarga, desdeñosa, inexplicable" 'a bitter, disdainful, inexplicable smile' (76). At this very moment the storm breaks out in all its fury: "[E]l cielo se abre vomitando fuego por innumerables bocas; el relámpago describe mil ángulos encendidos; el rayo troncha los más corpulentos árboles y la atmósfera encendida semeja una vasta hoguera" 'The sky splits open, vomiting fire through numberless mouths; the lightening describes a thousand burning angles; the bolt fells the sturdiest trees and the burning atmosphere seems a vast bonfire' (76). The object of this violence is Enrique, struck bloody and unconscious from his horse; Sab, standing over him, is identified with the storm: "[S]ombrío y siniestro, como los fuegos de la tempestad, era el brillo que despedían en aquel momento sus pupilas de azabache" 'Gloomy and sinister, like the fires of the storm, was the gleam flashing at that moment from his jetty pupils' (77). Sab does finally subdue the murderous storm in his breast and takes his rival to safety. Still, this episode has revealed in Sab's soul an excess of anger, as if he were the channel for a threatening energy latent in the atmosphere of the island paradise.

Indeed, Sab concretizes the historical threat felt by Cubans during the century following the Haitian revolution insofar as he protests with all his passionate soul against the social order that makes his dream of love an impossible fantasy. In his long conversation with Teresa, he reveals that he harbors vivid fantasies of a slave uprising:

> He pensado también en armar contra nuestros opresores, los brazos encadenados de sus víctimas; arrojar en medio de ellos el terrible grito de libertad y venganza; bañarme en sangre de blancos; hollar con mis pies sus cadáveres y sus leyes y perecer yo mismo entre sus ruinas. (157)

> I have also thought of arming the shackled hands of their victims against our oppressors; of hurling into their midst the terrible war cry of freedom and vengeance; of bathing in the blood of whites; of treading their corpses and their laws under my feet and perishing myself among the ruins.

At another point in the novel he evokes the image of slave revolt, this time reporting the words of Martina, his adoptive mother, who claims to be descended from the now-extinct indigenous population: "[L]os descendientes de los opresores serán oprimidos, y los hombres negros serán los terribles vengadores de los hombres cobrizos" 'The descendents of the oppressors will be oppressed, and black men will be the terrible avengers of the red men' (113).

In this rebellious talk of vengeance, Sab distinguishes himself from the female "superior souls." Although the cases of Teresa and Carlota imply a social critique, exposing the heartlessness of a society ruled by the marketplace and the impotence of women who preserve the human value of love, they conform to the feminine ideal of the domestic angel in that they do not condemn or denounce social injustice, nor do they register the slightest thought of rebellion. Yet the three characters are so closely associated that the anger suppressed in Carlota and Teresa seems to speak in Sab's violent fantasies. And, in the end, the narrative enforces on Sab the submission exemplified by the two women. Just as the violent rage that shakes his soul during the tempest is eventually subdued, so the thoughts of rebellion are carefully constrained. Sab disavows the desire to rebel, though he fully appreciates the logical necessity of revolt. "Tranquilizaros," he tells Teresa, "los esclavos arrastran pacientemente su cadena; acaso sólo necesitan para romperla, oír una voz que les grite: '¡Sois hombres!' pero esa voz no será la mía, podéis creerlo" 'Don't worry, the slaves are patiently dragging their chains; perhaps to break out of them they only need to hear one voice shouting, "You are men!" but that voice will not be mine, believe me' (153). At the conclusion of his letter to Teresa, Sab piously asserts that the oppressed must not act but trust God to raise the throne of justice upon the ruins of the old society. In contrast to the clarity of his indictment of society, Sab's reasons for not acting on his political awareness appear vague, revealing a narrative impulse divided against itself in the attempt both to justify and contain Sab's anger.

Sab's rebellious impulses are implicitly attributed to the female characters at the end of the novel, when Sab's letter to Teresa makes an equation between the destiny of women and that of slaves. Insofar as that letter is passed on to Carlota as a condensation of the secret awareness shared by three souls endowed with superior subjectivity, it also recapitulates Gómez de Avellaneda's identification of the Romantic subject with marginalized gender and race. Through the letter, Carlota discovers Sab's interiority, which harbored a sublime passion that she has come to think impossible. Yet Sab's last words emerge less as a declaration of love than as a powerful attack on the injustice of slavery and a condemnation of society.

Sab begins his letter with a long description of his early reflections on virtue. In his youth he rejected the Church's teaching that "la virtud del esclavo . . . es obedecer y callar, servir con humildad y resignación a sus legítimos dueños, y no juzgarlos nunca" 'the slave's virtue . . . is to obey and stay silent, to serve his legitimate owners with humility and resignation, and never judge them' (220). Virtue must be the same for all men, Sab argues, and he concludes that the God-given harmony of nature has been perverted by human society. Above all, he protests against a social structure that, because he is a slave, prevents him from expressing his superior talents:

> Si el destino me hubiese abierto una senda cualquiera, me habría lanzado en ella. . . . [P]ara todo hallaba en mí la aptitud y la voluntad. ¡Sólo me faltaba el poder! Era mulato y esclavo. ¡Cuántas veces, como el paria, he soñado con las grandes ciudades ricas y populosas, con las ciudades cultas, con esos inmensos talleres de civilización en que el hombre de genio encuentra tantos destinos! (224)

> If destiny had opened one path to me, I would have flung myself into it. . . . I had the aptitude and the motivation to do anything. I lacked only the power! I was a mulatto and a slave. How many times, like the pariah, have I dreamed of the great cities, rich, populous, cultured, of those immense workshops of civilization where the man of genius finds so many functions.

Sab's voice rings with echoes of liberalism; we can detect the tones of an aspiring bourgeoisie that points the finger of blame at those who enforce a system of exclusions to preserve their privileged position: "[S]on los hombres los que me han formado este destino, . . . si ellos han levantado un muro de errores y preocupaciones entre sí y el destino que la providencia me había señalado" 'It is men who have created my destiny, . . . for they have raised a wall of error and prejudice between themselves and the destiny that Providence designed for me' (226).

Significantly enough, when Sab reaches this culminating point of his denunciation, he becomes aware of the shadow of death pressing in, and a hallucinatory vision of Carlota, just at the point of consummating her marriage, interrupts the flow of his argument:

> Es ella, es Carlota, con su anillo nupcial y su corona de virgen—¡Pero la sigue una tropa escuálida y odiosa!—Son el desengaño, el tedio, el arrepentimiento—y más atrás ese monstruo de voz sepulcral y cabeza de hierro—lo irremediable. (227)

> It's she, it's Carlota, with her wedding ring and her virgin's crown—But she's followed by a squalid, hateful crew!—They are disillusionment, loathing, remorse—and behind them comes that monster with the lugubrious voice and the iron head—the irremediable.

The words that immediately follow this accurate prophesy of Carlota's fate suggest that Sab's discourse on slavery has all along been about woman's destiny: "¡Oh! ¡las mujeres! ¡Pobres y ciegas víctimas! Como los esclavos, ellas arrastran pacientemente su cadena y bajan la cabeza bajo el yugo de las leyes humanas" 'Oh, women! Poor, blind victims! Like slaves, they patiently drag their chains and bend their heads beneath the yoke of human laws' (227). He deemphasizes the finality of a slave's fate compared with a married woman's, arguing that slaves at least can buy their freedom:

> [P]ero la mujer, cuando levanta sus manos enflaquecidas y su frente ultrajada para pedir libertad, oye al monstruo de voz sepulcral que le grita: "En la tumba" ¿No oís una voz, Teresa? Es la de los fuertes que dice a los débiles: "Obediencia, humildad, resignación—ésta es la virtud." (227)

> But woman, when she raises her emaciated hands and desecrated brow to ask for freedom, hears the monster of the lugubrious voice shouting to her, "In the grave." Don't you hear a voice, Teresa? It's the voice of the strong saying to the weak: "Obedience, humility, resignation—these are virtue."

With this retroactive reference to his starting point—the "virtues" urged on the underdog—Sab includes women in his entire condemnation of society's oppression of slaves.

Indeed, close attention to the dominant theme of Sab's letter suggests that the issue of slavery was from the start secondary to that of women, even a mask for feminist protest. In general the voice of protest is more concerned with society's blighting of Sab's ambitions and talents than with the oppression of a general class of human beings. Whereas the letter begins with a general argument against slavery that derives from the premise of natural human equality, the extended concrete proof of slavery's iniquity—both in Sab's letter and in the novel as a whole—consists in the denial of an outlet of expression for Sab's innate superiority. The fact that Sab's lament focuses on the frustration of his talent rather than of his love best reveals the true target of the denunciation of oppression. In the imagined expression of a slave's outrage speaks, in fact, the anger of a young colonial woman who aspired to pour out her own subjectivity in writing capable of captivating the great centers of civilization and culture, but who was told to be silent and resign herself to the self-abnegating virtues of the angel of the hearth.

Through the persona of Sab, in fact, speaks the subject of the autobiography. Sab's letter shares the Sandian echoes of the autobiographer's horror of marriage, emphasizing the unnatural finality of the institution and using the rhetorical commonplace equating marriage with slavery. Like the narrator of the autobiography, furthermore, Sab believes in the exalting power of passion and chafes at the social prejudices that thwart his ambition. In the male protagonist these two components were more easily integrated than in the female autobiographical self, since gaining recognition of his superiority would have enhanced Sab's chances of winning the affection of his beloved, whereas the autobiographical narrator felt obliged to disavow her ambition to prove her capacity for love. The advantage of redistributing the attributes of the self among the three fictional protagonists is now clearer: Carlota and Teresa demonstrate the difficulties of the female position without challenging the domestic angel stereotype through unladylike ambitions or resentments. Sab, as a male and as a black slave, can express rage in perfect consistency with his love and his ambition. The cultural injunction against the dangerous emotions of the oppressed sex or race, however, inhibits the consistency with which Sab's justified anger is treated: as we have seen, Sab stops short of the rebellion his arguments justify; his bitter denunciation concludes merely with a recommendation of patience and resignation—not unlike the moral advice he so resented from the priest.

We see, then, in Gómez de Avellaneda's first novel the contradictory effects of the marginal position that, as a woman and a colonial, she occupied in relation to the dominant practices of writing in her time and culture. She was engaged in the struggle to break the socially imposed bounds of that position precisely during the time when, in composing *Sab,* she was constructing herself as a subject of writing. Fresh from the colony, she went to Seville, an important cultural center, where she launched a campaign for admission into the main literary circles. She finished *Sab* in Seville, and its circulation in manuscript helped establish her claim to be a writer. Once that claim was accredited by the performance of a play she wrote and by letters of introduction from Seville's leading literary men, Avellaneda went straight to Madrid, the Mecca of Spanish writers, and there in the same year, 1841, published *Sab.*

Thus, Gómez de Avellaneda's determination to write, to claim her place in the public world and her right to give expression to her inner passions and fancies, led her to assert in this novel that woman, too, can be that liberal and Romantic subject characterized in the writing of contemporaries such as Larra and Espronceda. By constructing the Romantic paradigm of desire and despair in terms of the experience of those excluded from liberal claims to freedom and equality, she gave that paradigm a social specificity that it often lacked in other formulations. Her identification of the subject of Romantic angst with a gender that before had occupied the category of object opened the possibility of doing the same for a race or class that was conventionally objectified in literary representation.

It should be pointed out, however, that in a sense Gómez de Avellaneda also colonized the mulatto slave's subjectivity to suit her own purpose when she represented him as willing to sacrifice both his freedom and his people to his impossible love for a white woman. That a bourgeois white woman's representation of a mulatto was conditioned by the interests of her class and race is hardly surprising. But the fact that she wrote the first Hispanic antislavery novel as a vehicle for an oblique feminist protest points to something less predictable: Gómez de Avellaneda found it easier to express abolitionist sentiments, which were considered so subversive by the Spanish colonial government in Cuba that it would not permit *Sab* to be published there, than to broach directly the issues of sexual inequality implied in its structure. Thus the use of Sab and abolitionist arguments as a mask for self-expression reveals the power of the social injunction against any female subjectivity that remained unsubordinated to love. Gómez de Avellaneda was more fearful of openly representing female ambition and rebelliousness than she was of acknowledging the justice of Sab's anger with her own class and race.

THE FEMALE SUBJECT IN *DOS MUJERES*

Gómez de Avellaneda's assault on the stronghold of Spanish literary culture yielded rapid results. Far from having to struggle on in obscurity like many young writers of her time, she found willing publishers, influential supporters, and a receptive public in Madrid. Within a year of her arrival in the capital, she had published *Sab* and a book of poetry, both of which were favorably reviewed in respectable journals, and had started her second novel, *Dos mujeres,* which began serial publication through subscription in late 1842 and was completed in 1843. Composed in rapid sequence, the autobiography, *Sab,* and *Dos mujeres* not only reverberate with each other but also show the progressive impact of the author's emergence from the private realm of writing into the give-and-take of the public arena and her transition from colony to metropolis.

With the public reception of *Sab,* Gómez de Avellaneda had her first exposure to criticism of her work just as she was beginning to write *Dos mujeres.* The two major reviews of the novel, one published in *El Conservador* in December 1841 and the other in *Revista de Madrid* in February 1842, coincided in praising above all its Romantic depiction of passion and feeling. The *Revista de Madrid* review, written by Gervasio Gironella, a conservative, consists almost in its entirety of a long quotation from the novel taken from Sab's highly poeticized expression of his love for Carlota. The reviewer's comment about the passage signals the characteristics that he believes will appeal most to contemporary readers: "Esta ligera muestra podrá dar una idea del estilo de nuestra apreciable autora, del fuego que comunica a sus expresiones, del interés y vehemencia con que describe una pasión" 'This brief sample gives an idea of our worthy author's style, of the fire she conveys to her expressions, of the interesting intensity with which she describes passion' (211). The other reviewer, who signed with the initials "P. D." (probably Nicomedes Pastor Díaz), was more detailed and more critical in his observations. He agrees that "el carácter y la pasión de Sab que es toda la novela, están descritas con un pincel de fuego" 'the character and passion of Sab, which make the novel, are described with a pen of fire' (14) and praises the author for making character and feeling rather than the intrigues of villains and traitors the motivating components of her story.

Although these critics seem willing to accept a woman writer, their response to *Sab* reflects the prevailing ideology of gender difference: while Gómez de Avellaneda's focus on intensified subjectivity—love, jealousy, grief—receives strong approbation, her protest against the social oppression experienced by her protagonists does not meet with sympathy. Gironella simply ignores the novel's antislavery thesis, treating it as though it did not exist. P. D. chides the author for attempting to deal with social issues in a novel:

> No es la novela la obra más a propósito para luchar con las creencias o con las preocupaciones muy generalizadas, y lo está mucho la que condena a la inferioridad de sentimientos y de inteligencia a la raza negra. (14)

> The novel is not the best genre for disputing widely held beliefs or prejudices, and the one that condemns the black race as inferior in feeling and intelligence is very widely held.

And he adds, as if the novel's covert protest on behalf of women had elicited a subliminal reaction, "Nosotros no sabemos si las almas tienen color, como nos inclinamos a creer que tienen sexo" 'We don't know if souls have color, as we are inclined to believe that they have a sex.' The reviewer's insistence that hierarchical social categories—especially the differentiation of male from female—be maintained in conceptualizing the subject constitutes a clear enough response to Gómez de Avellaneda's revindicatory inversion of the race and gender of the Romantic soul. The evocation of generalized passion in purple prose was welcome from a woman, but impassioned denunciation of social injustice was not.

Despite the critics' praise of *Sab,* they condescend to the author, marking her double marginality with respect to their own central position in Spanish written culture. Gironella limits himself to exclaiming about Avellaneda's sex: "¿Pero qué más pudiéramos decir? ¡Quien esto ha escrito, diríamos sólo, es una mujer!" 'But what more can we say? We would only say that whoever wrote this is a woman!' (211). But *El Conservador*'s reviewer goes further, linking qualities in the novel not only with the author's sex but also with her colonial origins:

> *Sab* tiene algo de la incorrección de la juventud, algo de la amable versatilidad de la mujer, y la desigualdad acaso de aquellos climas tropicales donde fue escrita. Hay en ese libro páginas anubladas y fatigosas como algunos días de aquellas ardientes zonas, pero a poco sale el sol puro,

radiante, abrasador, y se ostenta por él bañada la espléndida y lujosa vegeta-
ción de aquel suelo. (15)

Sab has something of the inexactitude of youth, something of the charming
fickleness of woman, and perhaps the disparities of the tropical climates
where it was written. In this book there are pages as cloudy and tiring
as some days in those burning zones, but a while later the pure, radiant,
scorching sun comes out and bathes the splendid, luxuriant vegetation of
that soil.

Undoubtedly Gómez de Avellaneda, aware of the Romantic vogue of
the exotic in Europe, heightened her tale with references to non-Euro-
pean flora and fauna (whose names she footnoted), to Indian chiefs and
African princesses. But, as she might learn from this review, the ex-
oticism of her colonial origin, like the difference of her gender, was
double-edged: both attracted pleased, not to say titillated, attention,
but at the same time they were regarded as marks of inferiority in relation to the norm. Women's variability might be charming, but was
nevertheless seen as a sign of superficiality, just as tropical brilliance
was suspect as the positive side of an unstable cultural climate.

Dos mujeres maintains the focus on psychological life that was
unanimously praised by critics of Gómez de Avellaneda's first novel,
but it drops the exotic setting that elicited the equivocal comments of
the *Revista de Madrid* reviewer. The action is set in Spain, and its focal
point is primarily Madrid. A brief presentation of the Spanish capital
through the eyes of Carlos de Silva, one of the novel's protagonists,
suggests that Avellaneda could not resist a dig at the condescending
superiority of her metropolitan reviewers: "[La casa de huéspedes]
parecióle a Carlos bien mezquina, acordándose de la elegancia y buen
aspecto que presenta esta clase de establecimientos en Francia, aun en
las ciudades de segunda orden"[4] '[The boarding house] seemed quite
wretched to Carlos, who remembered the elegance and fine appearance
of such establishments' in France, even in second-class cities' (41). The
urban setting, however, is assumed rather than described in this novel.
The plot, like that of *Sab,* is minimal; the main interest derives from
the study of the subjective response of three characters to their triangu-
lar love situation. But what Avellaneda disguised as an antislavery
thesis in *Sab* she brings out as the explicit proposition of *Dos mujeres*:
the moral and psychological critique of the institution of marriage and
of the restricting social codes of feminine behavior. Thus, to the extent
that *Dos mujeres* embodies its author's response to critical reception of
her first novel, its insistence on the women's issue can only be read as

a gesture of defiance against those who would, at the same time that they counsel her against using the novel to combat social prejudice, assert that souls have sexes, that is, that the female subject is limited by its gender.

It is a nice irony that in defying the patriarchal arbiters of Spanish literary taste, this colonial woman drew on an intertextual framework grounded in France, the cultural center to which Madrid saw itself as peripheral.[5] As we have seen, Gómez de Avellaneda knew French literature relatively well, and found in it a female tradition that supplied narrative language for a critique of marriage and the subjection of women. By the 1840s George Sand had become an even more powerful force in European letters than she had been at the time Avellaneda wrote her autobiography. The context provided by her growing prestige was surely a factor permitting Avellaneda to voice explicitly in *Dos mujeres* what had only been implied in *Sab*. In the preface to *Indiana* written for a popular edition in 1842—precisely the year in which *Dos mujeres* was composed—Sand felt sufficiently confident of herself and her public to justify her novel boldly in the face of the angry criticism it had received: "Ainsi, je le répète, j'ai écrit *Indiana,* et j'ai dû l'écrire; j'ai cédé à un instinct puissante de plainte et de reproche que Dieu avait mis en moi" 'I repeat then, I wrote *Indiana,* and I was right to write it; I yielded to a powerful instinct of protest and reproach that God had instilled in me' (19). In Spain, Gómez de Avellaneda, too, felt emboldened to challenge more directly the inequities of women's social destiny.

Thus, the plot of *Dos mujeres* is structured in such a way that it tests the dominant Spanish cultural propositions about marriage. The novel begins with the conventionally ideal courtship and marriage of two young cousins, Carlos and Luisa. The match had been carefully planned by the family and the two youngsters had been educated appropriately: Carlos, though sent abroad to acquire a gentleman's polish, had been raised according to the strictest principles of Catholic morality and filial obedience, while Luisa was taught selfless proficiency in domestic duties, scrupulous religious piety, and nothing whatsoever about the outside world. The two, neither having ever really known another young person of the opposite sex, fall tenderly in love and enjoy perfect bliss as a newly wedded couple. But the narrative voice, commenting on the ideal of happiness embodied in matrimony, casts doubt upon its durability:

¡Qué sublime, qué santa armonía! ¿Por qué la naturaleza en su eterna
mudanza arrebata al hombre este estado divino de ventura? ¿Por qué no nos
es dado hacer estable la concordancia del sentimiento y de la obligación?
¡Oh, imperfección e inconsecuencia de la naturaleza humana! ¡Que el amor
eterno, que es el voto del alma, no pueda ser cumplido por el corazón! (34)

What sublime, heavenly harmony! Why does nature, ever changing, snatch
this divine state of bliss from men? Why isn't it given us to establish a lasting
agreement between feeling and duty? Oh, the imperfection and inconsistency of human nature! That the heart should not be able to achieve the
eternal love that the soul desires!

As the narrator's comment leads us to expect, the marriage is put to
the test when Carlos is sent alone to Madrid to clear up legal problems
connected with a family inheritance.

In the capital, Carlos meets a brilliant and beautiful young widow,
Countess Catalina, and falls passionately, irresistibly in love with her,
despite his continuing devotion to his young bride. The misery and suffering that ensues for the three characters caught in this love triangle
is not presented, as it would have been in the melodramatic fiction of
the time, as the consequence of Carlos's fall from virtue into vice or of
the seductions of an evil temptress.[6] Luisa, Carlos, and Catalina are all
generous, noble, loving individuals, avatars of the "almas superiores"
of Sab. Rather, the protagonists' sufferings are due to the unnatural social law imposed on the human heart in marriage. As Catalina says to
Carlos: "El adulterio, dicen, es un crimen, pero no hay adulterio para
el corazón. El hombre puede ser responsable de sus acciones, mas no
de sus sentimientos" 'They say adultery is a crime, but there is no adultery for the heart. A man can be held responsible for his actions, but
not for his feelings' (127). The irremediable—that aspect of the marriage vow that in Sab was personified so ominously in the mulatto's
hallucination—victimizes both partners, laments Carlos to Luisa:

Pero, ¿puedo hacerte feliz? ¿Puedo serlo yo mismo? Tan imposible es ya,
como el devolverte la libertad perdida. Los hombres nos han encadenado
con vínculos eternos y tú, pobre angel, serás víctima como yo de sus
tiránicas y absurdas instituciones. (157)

But can I make you happy? Can I be happy myself? That's as impossible as
it would be now to give you back your lost liberty. Society has chained us
with eternal ties, and you, poor angel, will be like me a victim of its tyrannical and absurd institutions.

And, indeed, happiness is impossible for all three, although Carlos, benefiting from the male privilege of acting in the public world, is at least able to gratify his ambitions for power through a successful political career. Catalina, pregnant and aware that the future of her relationship with Carlos holds only guilt, social opprobrium, and burdensome dependency, commits suicide as a way of freeing Carlos to enjoy a legitimate conjugal life with Luisa. But neither of the survivors, united by external bonds but not by intimate confidence, can be happy. Several years after the death of Catalina, an old family friend can only describe Luisa as "muy buena y muy infeliz" 'very good and very unhappy' (210) and promises her daughters to tell Luisa's story, from which they may learn a valuable lesson. But, concludes the narrator,

> acaso nada les dijo, nada les reveló, sino que la suerte de la mujer es infeliz de todos modos. Que la indisolubilidad del mismo lazo con el cual pretenden nuestras leyes asegurarlas un porvenir, se convierte no pocas veces, en una cadena tanto más insufrible, cuanto más inquebrantable. (210)

> perhaps it revealed nothing to them except that woman's lot is unhappy no matter what; that the same indissoluble knot with which our laws try to assure our future frequently becomes a chain that is the more intolerable because it cannot be broken.

The author's intentional inversion of the conventional moral lessons concerning love and marriage could not have been made more explicit.

Clearly, Gómez de Avellaneda draws on Romantic paradigms—as did George Sand—for the values she opposes to the traditional view of marriage. *Dos mujeres* represents the individual subject very much in terms of the Promethean and socially alienated aspects of the Romantic "I," as Lucia Guerra Cunningham's observations indicate:

> If the Romantic vision holds that feeling is a spiritual manifestation that defines human essence and gives it transcendence, the conventional rules of marriage that condemn extramarital love are conceived as negative forces that cut down the possibilities of Being. . . . In this sense, . . . the transgression of moral law that leads to marginalization is presented in the novel as the only possible alternative for rising above the imperfections of a corrupt society. (4–5)

This conception of subjectivity as radically other than the social norm and as potentially sublime in its refusal to conform underlies the characterization of all three protagonists, but particularly that of Catalina. In attributing this heroic kind of Romantic subjectivity to a female character, Gómez de Avellaneda follows that other French precedent important to her autobiography—Mme de Staël's *Corinne*.

The plot line of *Dos mujeres* closely follows that of *Corinne*, highlighting the problematic of a female subject that transgresses the social norms. In both novels a dark-haired and unconventional woman shares a sublime passion with a young man who has marital obligations to an angelic blond woman. And at the ends of both novels, the dark woman dies as a consequence of her tragic recognition that social pressures make union with her beloved impossible, while the blond woman becomes aware that she too is a loser in the skewed game of sexual rivalry that society's rules enforce. As we see, then, Mme de Staël had already established a precedent for Gómez de Avellaneda's subversion of the narrative convention governing dark- and light-haired female rivals and its moral injunction that the female reader should model herself on the submissive and innocent blond.[7] Indeed, it is in following Mme de Staël's lead in exploring the subjective possibilities of a female character unbound by social and literary conventions governing women that Avellaneda makes of Catalina the novel's dominant protagonist, the subject with whom the reader's desire aligns itself. In so doing, the author creates Spain's first full-fledged narrative image of the Romantic self as female.

The brilliant countess of *Dos mujeres* is a Corinne who can find no Italy to nourish her genius but instead is condemned to live in a Spanish version of the French novel's England—a world hostile to the exceptional, especially in a woman.[8] That she does possess genius is indicated in a passage that seems directly modeled on Corinne's display of her talents for the bedazzled Oswald:

> Embriágabale [a Carlos] a menudo con la magia de sus talentos; su voz admirable era más dulce y más expresiva cuando cantaba con él o en su presencia. Cuando bailaba era una sílfide que parecía escaparse de la tierra para vagar por los aires. . . . Si Carlos hablaba de pintura, Catalina pintaba ingeniosas alegorías, y bellísimas cabezas que todas se parecían a él. (133)

> [Carlos] was often enraptured by the magic of her talents; her admirable voice was sweeter and more expressive when she sang with him or in his presence. When she danced she was a sylph who seemed to escape the earth and flit through the air. . . . If Carlos spoke of painting, Catalina painted witty allegories and beautiful heads that all looked like him.

But this capacity for artistic expression is, like Corinne's, simply a facet of Catalina's whole, rich personality: "Su conversación era más amena y seductora, cuanto más franca y espontánea. Conocía el secreto de evitar el fastidio poniendo siempre en juego el talento o el corazón" 'The more frank and spontaneous her conversation, the more pleasant and seductive it was. She knew how to avoid boredom by always bringing either her talent or her heart into play' (138). It is through the exploration of the full range of Catalina's subjectivity in its interaction with the external world that Gómez de Avellaneda transforms the French prototype into a feminized version of the late Romantic self. The narrative techniques and the language of character analysis that she used came from an earlier period, from the tradition of the French *récit,* in which action is almost secondary to the narrator's rationalistic explanation of motivation in terms of generalized categories— intelligence, will, passion, amour-propre. But with this somewhat resistant instrument, the Cuban-Spanish writer was able to produce an image of the subject that was thoroughly contemporary, as well as innovative from the perspective of gender.

Catalina's self-characterization places her squarely in the category of the Romantic soul: "En cuanto a mí, sólo sé decir que no quisiera haber tenido por dote al nacer, una imaginación que me devora, y un corazón que va gastándose a sí mismo por no encontrar alimento a su insaciable necesidad" 'With respect to myself, I can only say that I wish I had not been endowed at birth with an imagination that consumes me and a heart that is exhausting itself because it can't find nourishment for its insatiable need' (80). Asked what she could possibly lack—since she possesses beauty, talent, wealth, social position, youth—that would make her happy, she replies simply, "Me falta todo, puesto que no lo soy" 'Everything is lacking since I'm not [happy]' (81). We are reminded immediately of the marquesa portrayed at the beginning of Canto VI of Espronceda's *Diablo mundo,* who has everything, but still feels the emptiness of unsatisfied desire:

> Todo le cansa, en su delirio inventa
> Cuanto el capricho forja a su placer;
> Y ya cumplido, su fastidio aumenta
> Y arroja hoy lo que anhelaba ayer. (305)

Everything fatigues her, in her delirium she invents whatever pleasures caprice can forge; and once she gets them, her ennui increases and she throws away today what she longed for yesterday.

But unlike Espronceda's image of the spirit's eternal dissatisfaction, Catalina's unhappiness is given temporal and spatial dimensions that identify women's historical situation as among its causes. It is true, of course, that the first-person narration of the subject's emotional history had become an essential component in Romantic representations of the self, but in Catalina's case the familiar motifs of the paradigm are modified by the particular constraints to which her sex was subject.

In giving Carlos an account of her spiritual trajectory, Catalina begins with her arranged marriage at the age of sixteen. Never the point of departure for a male Romantic's transition from innocence to experience, marriage was the event through which a young noblewoman was introduced into the world. Once embarked on adult life, Catalina moves through the main stages of Romantic experience. At first enchanted by the glittering social world to which her affectionate but cynical older husband initiates her, she soon discovers inner needs that it cannot meet:

> [N]o me bastó aquella vida aunque tan llena de todo lo que no es amor ni felicidad. Presto mi ardiente imaginación se cansó de aquellas impresiones y mi vanidad saciada dejó hablar al corazón. Entonces concebí que debía existir una felicidad superior a la que el rango y las riquezas pueden darnos. Extremada en todo, pasé en poco tiempo de la más loca disipación al más severo retiro. (87–88)

> Though that life was so full of everything that wasn't love or happiness, it wasn't enough. Soon my ardent imagination tired of those impressions and my vanity, satiated, let my heart speak. Then I conceived the idea that there must exist a higher happiness than what rank and wealth can provide. Extreme in everything, I went in a short time from the maddest dissipation to the strictest withdrawal from society.

In the solitude of her country retreat, she reads the key novels of Romantic youth—*Julie* and *Die Leiden des jungen Werther*—as she engages Nature as the great echo chamber of the mind's desire:

> Muchas veces arrojando el libro con desesperación, salíame como loca por el campo, y me embriagaba de las brisas de las noches suaves como una esperanza de amor, y me prosternaba delante de la luna, que de lo alto del cielo parecía un faro divino allí colocado para alumbrar la ventura misteriosa de los amantes; y escuchaba trémula el silencio de los campos; aquel silencio cuya voz es el susurro de una hoja o la respiración de un pájaro y en él creía distinguir un reclamo mudo del amor que me ofrecía el reposo negado a mi corazón. (88–89)

> Often I threw the book down in despair, ran like a madwoman out through the fields, and became intoxicated by night breezes soft as the hope of love, and went down on my knees before the moon, which, high in the sky,

seemed a divine lantern placed there to light the mysterious happiness of lovers; and, trembling, I listened to the silence of the countryside, that silence whose voice is the whisper of a leaf or the breathing of a bird: in it I thought I could distinguish the mute call of a love that offered me the repose so far denied to my heart.

She recognizes the danger of madness in the solipsism of her self-absorption and returns to society, soon to find herself widowed and free to seek the passion that her marriage had not provided. Now she goes through the familiar process of Romantic disillusionment: "[M]i imaginación inagotable poetizaba todos los objetos, y de ninguno podía juzgar con exactitud, hasta que se disipase el prisma color de rosa al través del cual les miraba" 'My inexhaustible imagination poeticized all its objects, and I could judge none of them accurately until the rose-colored prism through which I looked at them dissolved' (90).

Part of the process of the increasing alienation between self and world is a growing skepticism about the objective reality of religious and moral values:

> Bien pronto se apoderó de mí el desaliento; aquella poderosa imaginación se cansó de engañarme; y sólo conocí la extensión de mi desventura cuando sentí que el manto de hielo de la duda cubría rápidamente todas las nobles creencias de mi juventud. (92)

> Very soon I was seized by discouragement; that powerful imagination tired of deceiving me; and I finally recognized the extent of my misfortune when I felt the icy mantle of doubt rapidly obscuring all the noble beliefs of my youth.

Like so many of the male Romantics before her, she is unable to re-establish an authentic framework of belief through the processes of reason, though she turns to the philosophers from Plato to Rousseau (94). In despair of ever finding reality adequate to the demands of her subjectivity, Catalina ends up seeking diversion in the limited pleasures of Madrid society.

As we see, her trajectory closely parallels that of the lyrical subject of Espronceda's "A Jarifa." Yet the difference in gender is crucial, as Catalina herself points out to Carlos:

> Cuando se llega a este estado, Carlos, en el cual las ilusiones del amor y de la felicidad se nos han desvanecido, el hombre encuentra abierto delante de sí el camino de la ambición. Pero la mujer! ¿qué recurso le queda cuando ha perdido su único bien, su único destino: el amor? Ella tiene que luchar cuerpo a cuerpo indefensa y débil, contra los fantasmas helados del tedio

y la inanición. ¡Oh! cuando se siente todavía fecundo el pensamiento, la
sangre hirviente, el alma sedienta, y el corazón no nos da ya lo que ne-
cesitamos, entonces es muy bella la ambición. Entonces es preciso ser guerrero o político; es preciso crearse un combate, una victoria, una ruina.
. . . Pero ¡la pobre mujer, sin más que un destino en el mundo! ¿qué hará,
qué será cuando no puede ser lo que únicamente le está permitido? (94)

When a man arrives at this state, Carlos, in which the hopes of love and
happiness have faded, he finds the road of ambition open before him. But
a woman! What recourse does she have when she has lost her only good,
her only aim, love? Defenseless and weak, she has to fight hand to hand
against the freezing apparitions of tedium and emptiness. Oh! ambition is
very beautiful when our mind is still fertile, our blood is coursing, our soul
is thirsty, and the heart doesn't give us what we need. Then one must become a warrior or a politician; a fight, a victory, a ruin is necessary. . . . But,
poor women, with only one vocation in the world! What can they do, what
can they be when they can't be the only thing they are allowed to be?

Whereas for Espronceda love is only metaphorically the unique mode
in which desire engages the world's otherness, for Gómez de Avellaneda love is literally the only channel for interaction with the world
available to a subject who is also female. Amid the intertextual echoes
of the dominant Romantic paradigms that resonate throughout Catalina's narration, the jarring image of physical struggle against the
ghosts of nothingness—tedium and vacuity—introduces a raw new
note, the claustrophobic panic produced by the confines of woman's
place. This difference in male and female destiny is dramatized by the
ending of the novel. From the point at which the lovers' affair has no
future, Catalina acts out the possibilities that remain to her by asphyxi-
ating herself. Carlos survives, never again to be happy in love, but able
to engage successfully in the public world of politics.

Catalina's consciousness of the limits binding female experience is
shared by the narrative voice as it generalizes about the particular
character of women's subjectivity. In a passionate outburst motivated
by the anguish of both Catalina and Luisa, the narrator asserts the
unique but unrecognized heroism of women's lives: "[N]o pidáis sino
a la mujer aquella inmolación oscura, y por lo tanto, más sublime;
aquella heroicidad sin ruido que no tiene por premio ninguna gloria del
mundo" 'Don't expect of any but women that obscure and thus more
sublime sacrifice, that noiseless heroism that is awarded no worldly
glory' (160). Women's generosity and goodness, the narrator claims,
make them victims in their associations with men, though men's supe-

rior physical strength also contributes to female disadvantage. A woman's lot, one way or the other, is an unhappy one:

> Pero no vayáis a decírselo a esos reyes por la fuerza, que tan decantada protección aparentan darla; no vayáis a decirles: "el sexo a quien llamáis débil y al que por débil habéis cargado de cadenas, pudiera deciros: ¡sois cobardes! si el valor, mejor entendido, sólo se midiese por el sufrimiento." No se lo digáis, no, porque después de haberle inhabilitado para los altos destinos que exclusivamente se han apropiado, después de cerrarle todas las sendas de una noble ambición, después de anatematizar cualquier lauro que haya arrancado trabajosa y gloriosamente a su orgullo, todavía serían osados a disputarle el triste privilegio de la desventura; todavía querrían despojar a la víctima de su corona de espinas y persuadirla de que era dichosa. (160)

> But don't go to those kings through force, who boast that they protect women, and tell them, "The sex that you call the weaker, and which, as weaker, you have laden with chains, could tell you that you are cowards, if bravery rightly understood is measured by suffering." No, don't tell them that, because after disqualifying women from the high positions that men have appropriated for themselves alone, after closing to women all outlets for noble ambitions, after anathematizing whatever laurels women have painfully and gloriously won, they would still dare to dispute women's sad privilege with regard to misfortune; they would still wish to divest the victim of her crown of thorns and persuade her that she was happy.

The level of anger that seethes in these words is far higher than that of any other passage in *Dos mujeres* dealing with relations between the sexes; the resentment against "esos reyes por la fuerza" appears to correspond to an experience beyond the text, to a struggle in which neither Luisa nor Catalina engaged to break the restrictions on female activity and open the pathways of "noble ambition" to women. The voice of Sab echoes here, but now speaking openly from a woman's perspective. This eruption of the author's emotion provides the key, perhaps, to both novels' fundamental project of contesting dominant ideology: to urge women not to be deprived of their heroism by being persuaded that victimization makes them happy. As we saw in chapter 1, the main arguments addressed to women in the Spanish press of this period held that womanhood's true and only satisfaction was to be found in self-abnegating love.[9] Gómez de Avellaneda concedes that women sacrifice themselves more than men do, but refuses to produce an image of female subjectivity that would suggest that woman's desire is so essentially different from man's that it can find its satisfaction in the narrow space permitted for its exercise. Indeed, her claim for the higher value of female heroism is based on the conception of the female subject as in every way equal in potentiality to the male subject but utterly restricted in its forms of self-realization.

Expressing in narrative terms the consciousness that united Carolina Coronado and the lyrical sisterhood in singing the sad songs of female existence, Avellaneda constructed a plot in which women's heroic but unrecognized suffering creates a common bond of sympathy and understanding among the female characters even when, like Luisa and Catalina, they are set against one another by sexual rivalry. The insistence that we observed in *Sab* on shared subjectivity as source and preserver of value in a degraded world surfaces in this novel as specifically female solidarity. Like so many of the novels written by women in the first half of the nineteenth century, the plot emphasizes an active empathetic connection between individuals as a positive value. Closely following the sisterly rapprochement of Lucile and Corinne in *Corinne*, Gómez de Avellaneda sets up the climactic point of her novel as the encounter between Luisa and Catalina in which the rivalry that has divided them is transcended by generous concern for the plight of the other.[10] The work's original title, *Dos hermanas*,[11] emphasized the idea of sisterly solidarity between the two characters.

Their rivalry for the love of Carlos, however, makes the transcendence of jealousy and suffering a mark of the heroism that, according to the narrator, only women can achieve. A scene that begins as a confrontation between wife and mistress ends with a recognition of each other's merits and misfortunes as the two women embrace and weep together. The narrator comments: "Dos corazones, dos nobles corazones ligados en aquel momento por todos los sentimientos generosos, se confiaron el uno al otro. ¡Y eran dos corazones de mujer, sin embargo!" 'Two hearts, two noble hearts joined at that moment by all the generous emotions, confided in one another. And, nevertheless, they were two female hearts!' (189).

The sarcasm of this last exclamation relates to the earlier outburst concerning the obliviousness of patriarchal culture to female heroism and anticipates the ironic narration of an encounter of Luisa with her father-in-law a few pages later. After Luisa carries out her promise to protect Catalina by persuading Carlos's father that her previous suspicions of an adulterous affair had no basis, the old man responds from the heights of his male complacency:

> [D]espués de declamar largamente contra la ligereza de las mujeres y sus imprudencias, y sus celos, y sus malicias, etc. etc., acabó haciendo mil elogios de sí mismo, de su cordura, de su sensatez en no haber dado entera fe a las acusaciones de Luisa contra su marido. (190)

After expostulating at length about the fickleness of women and their imprudence and their jealousy and their slyness, etc. etc., he ended up praising himself for his wisdom, his good sense in not having entirely believed Luisa's accusations against her husband.

The pointedness with which Gómez de Avellaneda treats masculine assumptions of moral superiority to women suggests that she consciously intended to demonstrate that if souls had sexes, as the critic of *Sab* so firmly believed, the female soul was by no means the inferior one in height, depth, complexity, and moral potentiality.

The treatment of Carlos is revealing in this respect: portrayed with sympathetic interest in the intricacies of his conflicts, he nevertheless fails to match the level of heroism or even of emotional intensity reached by the two women. Despite her innocence and conventional goodness, which in most narratives of the period would have been reliable signs of a lack of subjectivity, Luisa follows a psychologically realistic trajectory through doubt, anguish, and despair until she reaches the moment of sublime compassion for her rival, which Carlos, for all his nobility of sentiment, never attains. Avellaneda's narrator, adopting the conventional imagery of the domestic angel, asserts that "no era ya Luisa una mujer; era un ángel superior a todas las flaquezas humanas" 'Luisa was no longer a woman; she was an angel superior to all human frailties' (188). Yet the novelist endows this stereotypic character with a full subjectivity, including the negative feelings that the angel invented by male domination was not permitted.

If Luisa reveals the angelic heights of which the female soul is capable, Catalina demonstrates that women who are not angels can carry moral awareness even further. There is strong evidence that Catalina views her suicide as a self-sacrifice that will permit Luisa to maintain her spotless innocence. In her last words to Carlos, Catalina reiterates the phrase she used to describe Luisa earlier in their conversation: "[Q]ue el ángel que en la tierra te fue concedido te acompañe por entre los pantanos del mundo, sin manchar la orla de su blanca vestidura" 'May the angel that was given you on earth accompany you through the muddy bogs of the world without staining the hem of her white robes' (200, 192). In the conversation between the two rivals, Luisa expresses her willingness to die in order to permit the happiness of the lovers, but it is Catalina who actually assumes the moral responsibility of suicide, sparing Luisa from any sin in the resolution of the love triangle. Catalina's suicide is intended—in bold disregard of the Catholic morality of the novel's public—to be proof of moral superiority, of the heroic proportions of a woman's self-abnegating love. In her letter to Luisa she writes: "Para fecundar mi corazón, la bondad de Dios me concedió el amor; pero para castigar mi soberbia ese amor bienhechor debió de ser un crimen. . . . El amor salva mi alma, y mi muerte expía mi amor" 'To make my heart fruitful, God in his goodness conceded me love; but to punish my pride, this beneficial love had to be a crime. . . . Love saves my soul, and my death expiates my love' (206). Just as in her final act Catalina in a sense subsumes and preserves the angelic goodness of her rival in a more heroic and complex gesture, so too the author fantasizes through her character the fusion of the alternative identities presented in her autobiography—the feminine, self-denying giver of love and the masculine Romantic seeker of satisfaction.

In several respects *Dos mujeres* represents the endpoint of the evolution of a problematic introduced in the autobiography. What distinguishes Gómez de Avellaneda's cultivation of Romantic subjectivity from that of her leading male contemporaries is her focus on relations between subjects rather than on the relation of subject to object. The autobiography, a narrative intended for consumption by only one reader, consists predominantly of the interaction of the represented self with the "you" addressed and constituted by the text. Here the self is fissured by the conflict between its own desires and those projected as belonging to the male addressee: unity is imagined, but never reached in the text, as the coincidence of image and desire in both subjects. In *Sab* the elements of subjectivity represented in the autobiography are organized in three protagonists. This novel presents the divisiveness of social hierarchy as responsible for the frustration, repression, and isolation of the characters. *Sab* also contains within itself the image of happiness, of a plenitude of the subject in which there exists barriers neither to communication nor to satisfaction. Speaking with her betrothed, Carlota imagines a possibility of existence outside history and society in which community, equality, and happiness are simply the conditions of the natural paradise that she believed Cuba to be before the European invasion. The closest the novel's characters come to that dream of utopia is in the sharing of Sab's letter. The island utopia of *Sab* is replaced by a European city in *Dos mujeres*; here the possibility of communion and completeness is glimpsed only momentarily, in the brief emergence of solidarity between the two rivals. The death of Catalina and the unhappiness of the two survivors, however, emphasize the isolation and incompleteness that is the lot of the subject in modern society.

5

Modulating the Lyre: Gómez de Avellaneda's Poetry

Although Gertrudis Gómez de Avellaneda's early fiction received, as we have seen, generally positive reviews, it was her poetry that won her acclaim during her first years in Madrid. Madrid's Liceo opened its heart to her in response to Zorrilla's reading of one of her poems, and poems constituted her first publications in Madrid's periodical press. Poetry was the dominant literary mode during the opening years of the decade of the 1840s; among the many books of poetry published then were the Duke of Rivas's *Romances históricos* and Espronceda's *El diablo mundo*. In this context, the first products of women poets were greeted with interest, though with definite reservations, as the critic reviewing Josefa Massanés's 1841 volume (review cited in chapter 1) revealed. The concern with a supposed antithesis between feminine innocence and poetic production voiced by Massanés's critic was not openly articulated in print with respect to Gómez de Avellaneda, but its pressure was inscribed in her writing. In the genre of lyrical poetry Avellaneda could not question the social and historical consequences of the norms of femininity as directly as she did in her narratives. Thus, the impact of the dominant models of feminine identity on her voice as a poet is less obvious and less explicit. Yet analysis of her poetic voice shows that gender was a crucial issue in her construction of a lyrical subjectivity.

The general uneasiness about the relation of Gómez de Avellaneda's gender to her poetry cropped up in the critical reception of her *Poesías,*

published in 1841. The most extensive review of the book, written by
Avellaneda's friend Nicomedes Pastor Díaz, pointedly compared her
work with contemporary publications by "poetas masculinos":

> Ninguno de ellos le excede en imaginación, en talento, en genio. Ninguno
> en la grandeza, elevación y originalidad de los pensamientos; ninguno en la
> robustez y valentía de la expresión, ... y muy pocos y contados en la
> filosofía y profundidad de sus conceptos, en la extensión y trascendencia de
> sus ideas. ("*Poesías*" 16)

> None of them surpass her in imagination, talent, or genius. None in gran-
> deur, elevation, and originality of thought; none in strength and boldness
> of expression, ... and very few in depth of philosophical concept or in
> breadth and transcendence of ideas.

The critic follows up these sweeping claims for Avellaneda's poetic
excellence by identifying the public reaction to the poet's gender as the
source of adverse criticism: "Han tachado algunos los versos de que
nos ocupamos de que falta en ellos aquella suavidad y ternura que
parecía debía ser el carácter distintivo de la poesía del bello sexo"
'Some have accused the verses in question of lacking the mildness and
tenderness that apparently should be the distinctive character of poetry
written by the fair sex' (17). Pastor Díaz had anticipated the special
burden that his culture's gender ideology would place on the woman
poet in the opening paragraphs of his review essay, where, enumerating
the indignities endured by poets in contemporary society, he added,
"Pero sobre todo, sed poeta mujer, y a todas las desgracias y miserias
de vuestro sexo, y a todas las agitaciones y tristezas de vuestro corazón
añadid una más grande todavía" 'But, above all, be a woman poet, and
to all the misfortunes and miseries of your sex and to all the agitations
and sorrows of your heart, add still another, greater one' (15). In thus
asserting that her gender was a major problem for the female poet,
Avellaneda's supportive male colleague enunciated a theme that would
echo through the writing of the lyrical sisterhood of the mid-1840s.[1]
Pastor Díaz's defensiveness about Avellaneda's sex throughout his
essay reveals that it was the inevitable issue to be addressed in a review.

The expectation of Gómez de Avellaneda's readers that gender
should determine the essential character of a woman's poetic voice
made the issue of gender a necessarily central problem in the process
of producing her poetry. The texts themselves bear witness to her struggle against the constraints of female identity in the various strategies
she used to represent the poetic "I," marking it as feminine while

assuming the authority of the poet's experience and perception. The burden of establishing the lyrical voice falls particularly heavily on the volume's initial poem, in which the poet first presents herself to her readers. So let us begin by considering "Al partir," the poem that opened all three of Gómez de Avellaneda's editions of her *Poesías*.[2]

By virtue of its position as first poem, the sonnet in which the poet bids farewell to her native Cuba as her ship sails toward new horizons connotes another kind of departure—the embarcation on the poetic adventure represented by the book. In an ardent invocation of Cuba, the first quatrain establishes the poet's love for her motherland—"¡Perla del mar! ¡Estrella de Occidente! / ¡Hermosa Cuba!" 'Pearl of the sea! Western star! Lovely Cuba!' (1841 ed., 7)—and expresses her regret at the rupture of this tie—"cubre el dolor mi triste frente" 'pain covers my sorrowing brow.' This sentiment, the only one explicitly attributed to the "I" constructed by the poem, resolves the potential discrepancy between the speaker as poet and the speaker as woman since it satisfies the conventions governing both identities. The tie to Cuba is equally appropriate as a poet's attachment to the source of inspiration and as a familial bond especially strong in the domestic woman.

In the second quatrain a rupture occurs: the ship detaches itself from the land when its sails catch the outward breeze. To maintain the lyrical self's conformity to cultural codes, this separation is figured as the effect of powers external to the poet's will: "La chusma diligente / Para arrancarme del nativo suelo, / Las velas iza" 'The crew, diligent in tearing me away from my native soil, hoists the sails.' The text insists upon the idea of the speaker's lack of agency in the separation from Cuba, reiterating it in the first tercet: "¡Do quier que el hado en su furor me impela / Tu dulce nombre [h]alagará mi oído!" 'Wherever fate in its fury may impel me, your sweet name will be a pleasure to my ear!' Thus, at the level of explicit content, that is, what would come through in a paraphrase of what the poem says, the lyrical voice expresses only regret at leaving the motherland and the ties that bind, a position that allows the feminine aspect of the lyrical self to remain within the conventions of domestic womanhood.

If we look at the connotative play of images and rhythms, however, we find a suggestive countercurrent to the grief of separation. Consider the last tercet:

> ¡Ay! ¡que ya cruje la turgente vela,
> El ancla se alza, el buque estremecido,
> Las olas corta y silencioso vuela!

Ay! the turgid sails are already rustling, the anchor is raised, with a jolt the ship cuts the waves and noiselessly flies!

For Raimundo Lazo this conclusion creates "a happy impression of almost airborne movement in the fleeting instant of departure, insuperably captured and reproduced" (19). In his opinion the rhythm and the phonetic values of the verse contribute to making the sonnet

the synthesis of the author's inner drama as she is torn emotionally by the pull of contrary forces, the intimate pain of abandoning her native land, . . . and the fear of a future that at once attracts her and deeply disturbs her with its mysterious uncertainties and question marks. (19)

A sensitive reader can speak of the inner drama captured in this sonnet precisely because the text constructs a tacit aspect of the lyrical "I" that strains along with the wind and sails toward unknown horizons. If the poem opens with an invocation of what is to be left behind, it closes in breathless expectation of what is to come. The poetic adventurer who speaks in this poem powerfully feels the lure of the unknown, even though she conforms to the conventions of feminine domesticity by externalizing what propels her as the fury of fate rather than her own will. Rather than inveigh against fate as the obstacle to self-determination, like Rivas's don Alvaro, Avellaneda's lyrical persona disguises as fate an inner drive too strong to be compatible with the norms of femininity.

Just as the departure from Cuba opened the way for Gómez de Avellaneda's unorthodox ventures in the metropolitan literary world, so this sonnet introduces the reader to the journey of exploration and discovery embarked upon by the female lyrical self of Avellaneda's poetry. In this densely packed poem we observe a tension that is re-staged in some form or another in succeeding poems: on the one hand, the poet adheres to the social and literary codes of gender difference; on the other, she attempts to break free of the constraints inherent in these codes. The effect of the contradictory impulses embodied in the process of producing these texts frequently shows up as a division of the speaking subject, a splitting of the self into heterogeneous parts. Here, too, "Al partir" anticipates the poems that follow by revealing some of the social and cultural polarities that fracture the speaking self of Gómez de Avellaneda's poetry.

One such fault line concerns national identity. In an era when Cuba was still part of the Spanish empire, Avellaneda could—and did—consider herself both Cuban and Spanish (her father was Spanish, her mother Creole), but strong political tensions between metropolis and colony troubled the issue of national identity. We saw that in her early narrative works, Avellaneda vacillated between presenting herself as the Cuban author of *Sab* and as the cosmopolitan, Spanish author of *Dos mujeres*. The sonnet, written earlier—1836—and in a different genre, expresses this tension as a constitutive aspect of the lyrical subject, caught between the explicit nostalgic pull of the island and the implicit attraction of the unknown metropolis. Designating her receding birthplace as an "Edén querido" 'beloved Eden,' the poet anticipates her later poetry, where, as in the novel she wrote soon after her arrival in Spain, Cuba became the image of the lost Eden that so haunted the Romantic imagination.[3] This configuration of the self as a lyrical voice combines Sab's desire to conquer the centers of civilization with Carlota's prophetic dread of leaving Cuba: the speaking subject is split between an irretrievable past, a childhood concretely and materially associated with the unspoiled nature of the New World, and the present, lonely exile in the European centers of civilization.

The second source of tension in Avellaneda's construction of a poetic identity is the culturally defined difference between the domestic feminine ideal and the Romantic image of the poet. In "Al partir" this tension merges suggestively with the polarity of colony and metropolis to expand the meaning of the poem's central ambiguity—the pain of separation versus the eagerness for new experience. The lyrical subject explicitly avows an identity based on feelings appropriate to femininity—a deep attachment to the colonial birthplace, to the maternal, to the past—but projects on external forces a masculine desire that pulls toward the metropolis, source of the father's authority, toward a possibility of power and independence not conventionally open to a woman. Although the tensions in both national identity and gender identity work together in Avellaneda's poetic production as well as in her early narrative, the omnipresence of binary gender oppositions in poetic language and meanings gives predominance to the issue of gender in the splitting of the lyrical "I" that characterizes her poetry.

THE AUTHORITY OF THE
FEMALE LYRICAL SUBJECT

The ambivalence noted in "Al partir" becomes contradiction when it manifests itself in the strategies through which the "I" of Gómez de Avellaneda's poetry claims authority as poetic voice. Identification with the masculine was an option that she exercised in various ways. Although Avellaneda never represented her own poetic voice as masculine, she included in the 1841 *Poesías* a considerable number of translations of famous male poets, most of them English or French Romantics. By this gesture she offered proof of her own poetic credentials by assuming the voice of poets authorized not only by their gender but further by a worldwide prestige unmatched by any of her male Spanish contemporaries. In the translations of Byron, Hugo, and Lamartine she demonstrated her undeniable mastery of fluent, correct Castilian versification. And indeed, virtuosity in the craft of poetry making was one form of authority she asserted with no concession to the proprieties of feminine modesty. Having devoted considerable energy to the mastery of technically difficult verse forms, she did not hesitate to call her successes to the attention of critics.[4] The same urge to insist on her own prowess as a poet complicated the strategy she followed in translating prestigious poets: some of these pieces are designated "imitations" as opposed to "translations," indicating that the Spanish poet shaped the translated material according to her own criteria. Thus she compromised between identifying with the authority of Lamartine or Hugo and demonstrating her independence as a poet in her own right.

Such is the force of Gómez de Avellaneda's feminine identity that it asserts itself even as she assumes masculine authority via translation. In some cases this produces no contradictions. For example, in "Los duendes, imitación de Victor Hugo," she departs from the original ("Les Djinns," from *Les Orientales*) by representing herself as the speaking subject in references to insomnia, a recurrent theme in Avellaneda's poetry,[5] but this change in no way conflicts with the spirit of Hugo's poem. However, when she translates or imitates a poem whose objective is to represent the interiority of the speaking self, the result is quite different. Her version of Byron's stanzas "To Inez" in *Childe Harold's Pilgrimage* is a valuable case in point because the original illustrates so well the problem posed for the woman poet by the Romantic model of the self.

"Imitación de las estrofas a Inés, del Child Harold, de Byron, dedicada a mi amiga C***" 'Imitation of the stanzas to Inez from Byron's Child Harold, dedicated to my friend C***' is one of two parts of a piece in the 1850 collection with the title "Conserva tu risa," the other part being "Versos que acompañaron a los anteriores cuando fueron enviados a la persona a quien están dedicados" 'Verses that accompanied the preceding when they were sent to the person to whom they are dedicated.' Avellaneda's version of the Byronic song is in effect framed by the verses that follow it, providing the context in which it is to be understood: the poet explains that the smiling innocence of a friend who tried to cheer her up produced the same kind of gloomy despair in her that Childe Harold had expressed in response to Inez's attempts to lighten his melancholy. The lyrical persona of these explanatory verses is closely identified with the Byronic persona. The poet insists that the English bard wrote his poem "[m]irando igual cariño / En otros bellos ojos; / Mirando igual sonrisa / En otro labio hermoso" 'seeing the same affection in other lovely eyes; seeing the same smile on another pretty lip' (1850 ed., 240). Here the lyrical subject appears to position itself in the same erotic relationship to the female addressee as the one that exists between Childe Harold and Inez. However, both the title of this poem and the anecdote of daily life to which the text refers induce the reader to interpret it as the utterance of Gertrudis Gómez de Avellaneda, who would be unlikely to have exactly the same relationship to C*** that Childe Harold had to Inez. Consequently, when toward the end of these accompanying verses the speaker announces, "Del bardo los acentos / Sin vacilar me apropio" 'Without hesitation I appropriate the accents of the bard' (241), we cannot know whether the gender as well as the words of the English poet will be appropriated. Indeed, the sexual indeterminacy of the speaker of these explanatory verses creates an uneasy awareness of gender as an issue of poetic voice.

A close look at the Byron poem shows that in fact the female appropriator of his accents could not evade the issue of gender. The stanzas "To Inez" encapsulate the essential features of the Byronic "I," so influential in the configuration of the Romantic self throughout Europe. Byron's protagonist, aspiring to something beyond what reality has to offer, is marked by the guilt of his Promethean desire to transgress man's given boundaries. Thus, he "had buried long his hopes no more to rise," and "life-abhorring gloom / Wrote on his faded brow curst Cain's unresting doom" (1.825–827). His inner pain drives him restlessly on, allowing him no pleasure in life's beauties, Inez among them. He describes his suffering in part as the inner alienation of self-consciousness, the relentless awareness of his human condition:

> What Exile from himself can flee?
> To zones, though more and more remote,

> Still, still pursues where-e'er I be
> The blight of life—the demon Thought. (1.857–860)

But the innermost level of the poet's subjectivity, the guilt and knowledge produced by his overreaching desire, cannot be communicated to the female addressee, whose smiling innocence, the sign of her true femininity, also betokens her ignorance of the truth learned through experience, and consequently her lack of inner depth. Pressed by Inez about the source of his bitter pain, he replies:

> What is that worst? Nay, do not ask—
> In pity from the search forbear:
> Smile on, nor venture to unmask
> Man's heart, and view the Hell that's there. (1.869–872)

The words "man's heart" have an abstract sense—the human heart—but their intersection with internal context and cultural reference makes the phrase gender-specific: Inez, a woman, is denied access to "man's heart" because cultural convention requires women to remain pure, uncontaminated by the desire that brings experience and knowledge. Implicitly, then, woman's subjectivity is limiting: she cannot share in the depth of self-knowledge that is at once the Byronic persona's burden and his pride.

We can see Gómez de Avellaneda's dilemma in appropriating Byron's poem. If she retained the gender of the speaker, she divested her own female voice of the authority of experience that speaks in Byron's poem as masculine knowledge. But changing the gender of the speaker to match her own would create dissonance with the gendered terms in which the original poem constructs self and other, knowledge and ignorance. Her solution to this problem was to identify the speaking subject with her own gender grammatically—in "Huir de mí misma necesito" 'I must flee from myself' (239), "misma" 'myself' is feminine—and, through slight modifications of wording and imagery, to alter the implications of the subjectivity expressed.

In Gómez de Avellaneda's version, the speaker does not insinuate that it is the knowledge of man's fate in general that torments her; her sadness stems rather from past misfortunes that are beyond repair. Byron's "And wilt thou vainly seek to know / A pang, ev'n thou must fail to soothe?" (1.843–844) becomes:

> ¡Ay! ¿de qué sirve conocer los males
> Que no tienen remedio?

> Los que yo sufro, amiga, no se templan
> Ni con tu dulce afecto. (238)

Ay, what good does it do to understand misfortunes that have no rem-
edy? The ones I suffer, friend, could not be tempered by even your sweet
affection.

The female speaker's troubles seem concrete, external, part of her lot
in life. "¡Me ensangrienta el azote de la vida!" 'I am bloodied by the
lash of life!' (239), she declares in a line that has no counterpart in the
original. In keeping with the particularization of the corrosive grief suffered by the lyrical "I" in her version, Gómez de Avellaneda slightly
but significantly alters Byron's ending, "Smile on, nor venture to un-
mask / Man's heart, and view the Hell that's there." Where the English
poet claims for his subjectivity the universal status of "man's heart,"
the Spanish version speaks only for the poet's own particular soul:

> No inquieras por qué causa misteriosa
> Tan infeliz me encuentro.
> Al cielo mira y a la luz sonríe,
>   Yo en verte me recreo;
> ¡Mas nunca intentes penetrar en mi alma
>   Que en ella está el infierno! (239)

Don't ask what mysterious cause makes me so unhappy. Look at the sky
and smile at the light, I take pleasure in seeing you; but never try to penetrate my soul, for in it is hell!

What inhibits communication in this version is not the addressee's difference in sex but the uniqueness of the source of suffering—by implication it cannot or should not be shared. Displaying a depth of feeling
and perception that the original denied to its representation of woman,
this female version of Childe Harold makes no claim to subsume the
farthest reach of human subjectivity within her own, though she conveys a tinge of Byronic pride.

    The emergence of a distinct female identity even in Gómez de Avella-
neda's translations of male poets indicates the insistent operation of a
second strategy for establishing poetic authority, a strategy that reversed the tendency to identify with the male voice. A good example
of how self-assertion superceded appeal to male authority is found in
"A la poesía," the second poem of the 1841 volume. Directly broaching
the issue of her position as poet, Gómez de Avellaneda here uses a conventionally humble attitude toward the power of poetry as a screen for

anything but humble claims about the relation of the female to poetry. She devotes over three-quarters of the poem to exalting—and reifying—the art itself as a transcendent entity in which the processes of making are erased. Thus, poetry, "del alto cielo / Precioso don al hombre concedido" 'the precious gift conceded by heaven to man' (1841 ed., 8), has divine powers. It creates—"Hablas: todo renace. / Tu creadora voz los yermos puebla" 'You speak: all is reborn. Your creative voice populates wastelands' (11)—and it reveals truth—"Tu genio independiente / Rompa las nieblas del error grosero, / La verdad preconice" 'May your independent genius disperse the mists of common error, proposing the truth' (11). Yet this godlike force is presented with distinctly feminine attributes. It celebrates peace and harmony rather than war, conquest, or ambition (stanzas 6–9) and embodies the higher power of beauty: "Tu sublime misión ¡oh poesía! / Ni acero ha menester ni tiranía" 'Your sublime mission, oh poetry, needs neither steel nor tyranny' (10). The lyrical speaker praises the poets of gentleness and love, sweet Garcilaso, tender Meléndez Valdés, Spanish poets who, instead of celebrating raging, arrogant heroes, sing of love, lacing myrtle with roses in their poetry (stanza 18).

It is this muse, for whom she claims poetry's sublimest power, that the poet invokes as she begins: "Deja que pueda mi dorada lira / Cantar la gloria que tu fuego inspira" 'Make it possible for my golden lyre to sing the glory your flame inspires' (8). The authority to which the poet appeals in speaking—the authority she assumes—is closely related, then, to the authority of feminine virtue in promoting love, harmony, beauty, and gentleness (see introduction). And just as poetry has no need of heroic male power—"No envidies sus blasones / Ni del poder la efímera grandeza" 'Don't envy his escutcheons nor the ephemeral grandeur of power' (10)—neither does the female poet aspire to "el lauro refulgente . . . / De Homero o Taso en la radiosa frente" 'the gleaming laurel . . . on Homer's or Tasso's radiant brow' (15). In the context of the female poet's identification with the spirit of poetry she celebrates, this trope of feminine modesty implies quite the reverse of modesty. Feminine poetic power does not need to rely on the monumental accoutrements of glory. "Ardiente poesía / Alma del Universo" 'Flaming poetry, soul of the universe' (8) is the abstracted version of the woman poet's sensibility; she supplies a quality of consciousness and emotion that is lacking in the world: "sin ti templo vacío / . . . cadáver frío" 'without you an empty temple, . . . a cold corpse' (14).

Thus, the poet's final request of her female muse can be understood as the aspiration to something higher than the signs of masculine poetic glory:

> Dame que pueda entonces,
> ¡Virgen de paz! ¡Sublime poesía!
> No transmitir en mármoles y bronces
> De un siglo en otro la memoria mía;
> Sólo arrullar, cantando, mis dolores,
> La sien ceñida de modestas flores. (16)

Virgin of peace, sublime poetry, grant that I may then, instead of transmitting my memory from one century to another in marbles and bronzes, cooingly sing my troubles to sleep, my brow circled by modest flowers.

Instead of enduring as an image engraved on the hard materiality of bronze and marble, she wants her poetry to be perceived as existing in the mode of being of inner life, with the temporality of sound, the intimate emotionality of song. The codes of gender difference operating in this contrast complete the implicit message: the poet's feminine qualities are closely associated with her poetic power as the soul of the world.

To counter the predominant identification of the poet as male, Gómez de Avellaneda asserts in other poems as well that the lyrical is closely associated with the feminine voice. "Romance contestando a otro de una señorita" 'Ballad in response to one by a young lady,' a poem published in the 1850 edition, affirms women's capacity to pursue the good and the beautiful:

> En mí pretendo probarte
> Que hay en almas femeninas
> Para lo hermoso entusiasmo,
> Para lo bueno justicia.
>
> . . . .
> No son las fuerzas corpóreas
> De las del alma medida;
> No se encumbra el pensamiento
> Por el vigor de las fibras. (1850 ed., 243–244)

By my example I hope to prove to you that there exist in women's souls enthusiasm for the beautiful and justice for the good. . . . Bodily strength does not measure that of the soul; thought is not uplifted by muscular vigor.

And then she goes on to offer herself as an example of the innate lyricism of which women are capable:

> Canto como canta el ave,
> Como las ramas se agitan,
> Como las fuentes murmuran,
> Como las auras suspiran.
>
> . . . .
>
> Canto porque hay en mi pecho
> Secretas cuerdas que vibran
> A cada afecto del alma,
> A cada azar de la vida.
>
> . . . .
>
> Que yo al cantar sólo cumplo
> La condición de mi vida. (244–245)

I sing as the bird sings, as the branches stir, as the fountains murmur, as the breezes sigh. . . . I sing because in my breast there are secret strings that vibrate to every emotion of the soul, to every hazard of life. . . . For in singing, I simply fulfill the condition of my life.

The vibrations of the world produce song in her own, female soul, she argues here, using the Romantic authority of nature to justify her "unfeminine" practice of writing.

The difficulties that undermined any simple view of women's relation to the poetic muse are, however, well illustrated by this poem. The stanza in which Avellaneda presents the naturalness of her poetic activity is almost a direct quotation from one of the male authorities whose prestige she borrowed on other occasions in avowed translations. Lamartine's "Le poète mourant" (*Nouvelles méditations poétiques,* 1823) had asserted his spontaneous lyricism in the same terms:

> Je chantais, mes amis, comme l'homme respire,
> Comme l'oiseau gémit, comme le vent soupire,
> Comme l'eau murmure en coulant. (147)

I sang, my friends, as a man breathes, as a bird laments, as the wind sighs, as running water murmurs.

The Romantic *topos* about the inherent naturalness of poetic activity was reiterated by other Spanish women poets of this same decade in defense of their unorthodox vocation, as we saw in chapter 2.

In some poems Gómez de Avellaneda adopted the strategy of explicitly addressing the social norms that problematized the female vocation for poetry. "Despedida a la Señora Da. D. G. C. de V.," written in 1843 after the first *Poesías* had been published, compares the choices made by the poet and by "Lola," to whom the poem is addressed.[6] The latter is leaving Madrid, where, the poet assures her, cultivation of her talent would have brought her glory and made her "a tu sexo admiración y ejemplo" 'the admiration and model of your sex' (1850 ed., 177). But in comparing her friend with that foremother so often invoked by Spanish women writers, Sappho, the poet acknowledges the suffering that accompanies genius and advises Lola to leave Madrid: "¡Huye y no tornes más! Tu hogar tranquilo / Ama, cual ama el náufrago la tabla" 'Flee and never return! Love your tranquil hearth as the shipwrecked man loves his plank' (180). Clearly, the choice of conventional domesticity is presented here not as inherently positive but only so in relation to the disastrous consequences of the unconventional alternative, which the speaking subject of the poem represents as her own experience. Her friend rests safely in the harbor of home and family, but the lot of the poet is very different, as she shows at the conclusion: "[D]el puerto distante, / Sin brújula, piloto ni camino, / Navego con los vientos del destino" 'far from the port, without compass, pilot, or route, I travel according to the winds of destiny' (181). Once again, as in "Al partir," the force behind Avellaneda's literary quest is represented as external to her own will.

If in "Despedida" Gómez de Avellaneda suggests that women who choose to cultivate their artistic vocation must sacrifice the security and comfort available to women who adopt the traditional feminine role, in another poem she addresses the assumption of female inferiority that supports a cultural system in which women are denied fully satisfying options. "El porqué de la inconstancia," a polemical poem written in the mid-1840s, counters the traditional misogynist view that women are incapable of constancy. The poet argues that there is no essential difference between women and men in the question of "el vago ardor del deseo" 'the vague burning of desire':

> Que son las hijas de Eva
> Como los hijos de Adán.
>   A entrambos el daño vino
> De la funesta manzana. (1850 ed., 182)

For the daughters of Eve are like the sons of Adam. Both were damaged by the ill-fated apple.

It is, of course, inevitable that, having represented women as subjects of poetic song and of feeling, Gómez de Avellaneda should assert that women are no different from men as subjects of desire. By insisting on this parity, her poem challenges the implicit gender positioning of the dominant Romantic paradigm, which identifies woman as the object of desire, without questioning the basic structure of the paradigm. The poem simply includes women specifically as subjects when it reiterates a major Romantic doctrine of subjectivity and its meaning:

> Unas y otros nos quedamos
> De lo infinito a distancia,
> Y en todos es la inconstancia
> Constante anhelo del bien.
>
> . . . .
>
> Y aquí, do todo nos habla
> De pequeñez y mudanza,
> Sólo es grande la esperanza
> Y perenne el desear. (184)

Both sexes remain distanced from the infinite, and in both inconstancy is constant yearning for the good. . . . And here on earth, where everything speaks of pettiness and change, only hope is great and only desire is eternal.

In this thematic, rational argument on behalf of her sex, then, Gómez de Avellaneda would open to women the same structure of subjectivity that Romanticism postulated for an implicitly male self. Insisting on the equivalence of the male and the female subject was a valid tactic in the debate, necessarily governed by liberal axioms, about women's right or authority to speak as poets. But establishing a simple symmetry was impossible in practice. We already have seen how the asymmetries of women's relation to the practice of writing affected Gómez de Avellaneda's self-presentation as a poet, forcing her either to borrow the prestige of a male voice or to insinuate, within the restrictive framework of the ideology of domestic femininity, the unique authority of a woman's voice. Now we will see how the texture of the poems themselves reflects the unsettling effect of feminizing the subject.

THE METAPHORICAL CONSTRUCTION OF THE SELF

In Gómez de Avellaneda's poetry we find the standard Romantic metaphors for the self and its relation to the world. Examination of the metaphorical universe of this poet, however, soon reveals that her assimilation of the Romantic paradigms was not so simple as a substitution of Eve's daughters for Adam's sons.

Gómez de Avellaneda joins a long list of Romantic poets who used birds—nature's lyricists—as externalized, objectified images of the self or some of its qualities; Shelley's skylark, Keats's nightingale, Musset's pelican, all permit the lyrical self to discover and represent its inner being through processes of projection, empathy, and differentiation. Avian images as counterparts of the self are especially frequent in Gómez de Avellaneda, but in her poetry they are closely associated with the subject's feminine aspects. In "El insomnio" the poet, isolated by insomnia from a sleeping world, finds her sorrows echoed in the coo of an early-rising turtledove: "Amores llorando del bien que perdiste, / Al cielo en la noche le cuentas tu afán" 'Weeping the loves of a lost happiness, you tell heaven at night of your passion' (1841 ed., 116). The idea that the dove shares her experience mitigates the solitude of the lyrical subject: "Tú sola la confidente / De mis pesares serás" 'In you alone will I confide my sorrows' (117). Thus far, we have a familiar Romantic pattern, but it is altered in the lines that follow: "Tu pecho abrasado . . . / Del mío el secreto merece guardar. / Mas no digas a los vientos / Mi tierna pena jamás" 'Your burning breast . . . deserves to hold the secret of mine. But never ever tell the winds my tender anguish' (117). Just as the bird complies with this request, so does the poem, never revealing the content of the subjectivity shared by dove and poet. A throwback perhaps to a more neoclassical mode, this reticence departs from Romantic poetic practice in which the objective is self-discovery and revelation. In Carolina Coronado, too, we shall see that silence surrounding the intimate core of the self is the mark of the feminine.

That the dangers to which a woman who desires is subject might be a cause of her secretiveness is suggested in "El cazador" 'The Hunter,' a very early poem that links an amorous dove and a woman as victims of a dangerous male. In a natural setting representing idealized beauty and harmony, the dove's song attracts the fatal attention of the hunter: "Mas, ¡ay! que cuando gime / Y al dulce amor convida, / Vacila y cae herida / Del bello cazador" 'But, ay, when she moans and invites sweet love, she falters and falls wounded by the handsome hunter' (1841 ed., 28). The shepherdess Elmira, who comforts the dying bird, points out their identical position in relation to the hunter: "De su mano tirana / Recibes honda herida, / Y devoró mi vida / La llama de su amor" 'You receive a deep wound from his tyrannical hand, and my life was devoured by the flame of his love' (30). The poem's concluding lines stress the metaphor linking woman, hunter's game, and feminine desire: when the hunter comes to retrieve his game, he finds the dove and Elmira expiring together.[7]

Another poem that focuses on the vulnerability of a winged creature
provides a good opportunity to see how Gómez de Avellaneda fem-
inizes common Romantic metaphors of subjectivity. While there is no
intertextual link between Gómez de Avellaneda's birds and those of
Keats and Shelley, whose poetry she did not know, the Spanish poet's
"A una mariposa" has a significant relationship to "Le papillon," by
Lamartine, a poet whose work she knew well and translated more than
once. In Lamartine's little poem from the *Nouvelles méditations
poètiques* (1823), the butterfly, pictured in a world of intoxicating sensual delight, is explicitly equated with desire:

> Il ressemble au désir, que jamais ne se pose,
> Et sans se satisfaire, effleurant toute chose,
> Retourne enfin au ciel chercher la volupté. (128)

It resembles desire, which never settles, and without being satisfied, skim-
ming over everything, goes back finally to heaven to seek pleasure.

This is a standard Romantic argument, one that Avellaneda herself
used in the poem on inconstancy: that never-satisfied desire is the sign
of the human spirit's need for transcendence. Seen thus as an attribute
of mankind, desire is universalized, considered abstractly in relation to
man's fate and purpose. But when Gómez de Avellaneda associates the
metaphor for desire with a specific female subject, the lyrical "I," she
concretizes.

What Lamartine subsumes in the line "Balancé sur le sein des fleurs
à peine écloses" 'Poised on the bosom of scarcely opened flowers,'
Avellaneda spells out, devoting well over half her poem on the butterfly
to the enumeration of the flowers, their colors, and their perfumes. Despite the multitude of choices, her butterfly, too, refuses to be satisfied:
"Mas ¡ay! cuán en vano / Mil flores y mil / Por fijar se afanan / Tu
vuelo sin fin!" 'But, ay, how vainly thousands of flowers strive to fix
your endless flight!' (1841 ed., 18–19). Yet having thus characterized
the butterfly as a metaphor for desire, Gómez de Avellaneda's poem
moves not toward the question of the ultimate ends of desire but toward the projection of consequences that reveal this as a specifically
female desire. As the butterfly moves toward the red rose, the lyrical
persona warns it, "¡Temeraria, tente! / . . . ¿No ves las espinas / Pun-
zantes salir?" 'Stop, reckless one! . . . Don't you see the sharp thorns
sticking out?' (19). Unlike the male Romantic's problem with desire—
that it cannot find satisfaction—the problem for the female subject is

the danger inherent in certain satisfactions, such as the sexual pleasure that the rose traditionally symbolizes, a danger evoked by the final two verses of the poem: "No quieras, incauta, / Clavada morir" 'Don't want, imprudent one, to die impaled' (19).

From this network of metaphors, then, emerges a rather different relationship of subject, desire, and object than the one we observed in Espronceda's poetry. Desire, for Espronceda, though painful in its consequences, is an affirmation of the self insofar as it is the inexhaustible going-out of the subject toward a world that can never match its values. This is the same scheme that Gómez de Avellaneda adopts in "El porqué de la inconstancia," when she is arguing for the symmetry of male and female subjectivity. The metaphors associated with the specific, feminized lyrical self, however, represent desire as threatening the female subject with annihilation instead of as affirming it.

This second pattern reappears in the sonnet "Imitando una oda de Safo," from the 1850 collection. Shielded by its status as the semitranslation of a classic (albeit one of the few female-authored classics), the poem permits itself to express in physical terms the female sexual passion that was judged so dangerous for the butterfly:

> Ante mis ojos desaparece el mundo,
> Y por mis venas circular ligero
> El fuego siento del amor profundo.
>
> Trémula, en vano resistirte quiero—
> De ardiente llanto mi mejilla inundo.
> ¡Deliro, gozo, te bendigo y muero! (1850 ed., 163)

The world before my eyes disappears and I feel circulating swiftly through my veins the fire of deep love. Atremble, I try in vain to resist you—Burning tears flood my cheek. I grow delirious, take pleasure, bless you, and die.

In the circumspect guise of a translation, this sonnet represents the experience of erotic ecstasy for a female subject. It is comparable in some respects to Canto IV of El diablo mundo, where Espronceda evokes in vividly sensual terms the discovery of sexual pleasure by his hero. For Adán there is only appetite for and delight in the object, the female body: "Al corazón la aprieta, el juicio pierde, / La besa hambriento y con placer la muerde" 'He presses her to his heart, loses his head, hungrily kisses her, and bites her with pleasure'; "Donde quiera él gusta, toca y mira, / Dicha, hermosura e ilusión respira" 'Whatever he tastes, touches, and sees breathes happiness, beauty, and illusion' (256).

The only trouble with sexual pleasure, the remaining cantos will show, is that it does not suffice for the ever-questing subject embodied in Adán. The beloved in Avellaneda's sonnet, in contrast, is not treated as an object to be tasted or bitten; he or she is indirectly invoked only as a presence whose impact on the lyrical subject becomes the sonnet's focus. And the poem's elaboration of the overwhelming effects of erotic ecstasy on the female "I" culminates not in the urge to go on to new pleasures but in surrender to annihilation.

Such a trajectory for female sexual passion was the only possible one in the context of the broad cultural redistribution of aspects of human experience between the sexes that we discussed in the introduction. Erotic desire and gratification meant the death of a female social identity defined by the absence of sexual pleasure; this ideological imperative is evident in the writing of all Spanish women of the time.

THE STRUCTURE OF THE FEMINIZED SELF

If in picking up a lyre (to use the imagery of Avellaneda's own era) tuned for the male voice the Cuban poet adopted some of the stances and melodies of the male Romantic poets, she also, as we have just observed, found a female lyrical voice that modified prevailing figures of the relation between the self and the world. Such transformations necessarily affected the configuration of the self's internal structure: Gómez de Avellaneda's elaboration of the lyrical "I" is not simply a female equivalent of Espronceda's or Lamartine's. Its alienation has a special internalized character, and its fragmentation becomes a constitutive characteristic.

The destructive character of desire as it emerges in Gómez de Avellaneda's poetic logic has consequences for the inner structure of the lyrical subject. Let us take as an example "Amor y orgullo," one of her most often cited poems from the 1841 collection. Its distinctive formal feature, the framing of a central lyrical section by introductory and concluding narrative sections, symptomatizes the inner division indicated by the title. María, who speaks in the middle section, is torn by the contradictory impulses of love and pride. In the past, pride prevented her from falling in love; now her heart has betrayed her by succumbing to love's illusions. The ensuing battle between head and heart is never resolved. At the end, although love seems to have won, for María's resistance vanishes in the presence of her beloved, the narrator

suggests that María is unlikely to be so lucky that love's victory will
last: "¡Feliz si de su orgullo la memoria / No turba más su pecho sojuz-
gado!" 'How fortunate if the memory of her pride never again troubles
her subjugated heart!' (1841 ed., 195).

The source of María's irreparable self-division is the character of
female desire. Before the fall into love, her intact and integrated self
conformed to the patterns of the male Romantic subject:

> Mi pensamiento en temerario vuelo
> Ardiente osaba demandar al cielo
>   Objeto a mis amores;
> Y si a la tierra con desdén volvía
> Triste mirada, mi soberbia impía
>   Marchitaba sus flores.
>
> Tal vez por un momento caprichosa
> Entre ellas revolé, cual mariposa,
>   Sin fijarme en ninguna;
> De un misterioso bien siempre anhelante,
> Clamaba en vano, como tierno infante
>   Quiere abrazar la luna. (188–189)

In reckless flight my burning thought dared demand of heaven an object for
my love: and if I cast a gloomy look with disdain at the earth, my pitiless
pride withered its flowers. From time to time I flew among them, capricious
as a butterfly, without settling on any; always yearning for a mysterious
happiness, I clamored in vain like a tender child who wants to embrace the
moon.

Here the butterfly of desire is akin to Lamartine's, never fully capti-
vated by an earthly object, looking always beyond the confines of the
human condition. References to María's pride as "soberbia impía" indicate, however, that we are to read the Promethean aspect of her autonomous self as a form of hubris that must be punished by a fall to
erotic passion according to a venerable literary tradition. In making
María's longing for transcendence a form of hubris, Avellaneda reveals
the gender bias of this supposedly universal attribute of Romantic subjectivity: the male Promethean self is heroic, but its female version is
capricious and willful, deserving punishment rather than admiration.
The form of desire that brings María low—a self-dispossessing passion
of the sort associated with the Sappho translation or the feminized
butterfly—illustrates the difference between the male and the female
subject. Unlike the forms of desire we have discovered in the male
Spanish Romantics, this passion brings a disastrous loss of autonomy,

figured in "Amor y orgullo" as captivity. Though she borrows this image from the poetic tradition of courtly love, Avellaneda elaborates it in an insistently negative way. María's captivity is in no sense bliss: her heart, "mísero esclavo de tirano dueño" 'wretched slave of a tyrannical master' (189), is oppressed by a chain "que a servidumbre eterna te condena" 'that condemns you to eternal servitude' (190). Unlike the courtly tradition's golden chains of love, María's chains are forged of "eslabones de pesado acero" 'heavy steel links' (191). Threatened with the annihilation of its sovereignty, the self struggles against its own impulse, splitting into opposing elements that correspond, as we have seen, to the different paradigms of desire identified as male and female.

The fracture manifests itself formally in the two "I"s who speak in the poem. A narrating voice identifies the position from which it speaks in the first and third sections as that of observer—"Ya la victoria del orgullo miro" 'Now I am seeing the victory of her pride' (194)—and source of the narration—"Guardó mi memoria / Su canto fugaz" 'I kept in my memory her fleeting song' (188). The second voice, quoted by the narrator, is that of María in the lyrical middle section. María's fission in turn into "pride" and "love" creates the effect of an infinite regression: at whatever remove the self is represented, it cannot be seen as whole.

If the division of the speaking subject into a narrating "I" and a quoted lyricist serves as a distancing device to give the poet greater control over her textual self-representation, the splitting of the self represented as María's in the lyrical middle section demonstrates the other side of the coin, the loss of control that accompanies fragmentation. The "I" who speaks in María's song identifies itself as the head, addressing the heart as the second-person "tú," and claiming to speak for reason as it analyzes the heart's errors. As the song develops, however, we see how the speaking voice is gradually taken over by the "other," the element that the head has tried to repress. Analysis gives way to hallucination, as the speaker sees the name of her beloved, which she has refused to pronounce, written everywhere—"¿Escrito no le ves en las estrellas?" 'Don't you see it written in the stars?' (192)—and hears it in every murmur—"¿No le pronuncia en gemidor arrullo / La tórtola amorosa? / ¿No resuena en los arboles?" 'Doesn't the amorous dove pronounce it in moaning coos? Doesn't it resound in the trees?" (192). The infiltration of the head by the heart is reflected in the speaker's growing obsession with the name of the beloved in the final stanzas of the middle part. The reasoning element of this split consciousness has been taken over by the emotional element it initially resisted, yet the two can never exist in integrated harmony, as the vacillations recorded by the final narrative section show. Unable to achieve a stable coherence through voice, María resorts to silence:

> Con un gemido enmudeció María,
> Y dando de rubor visible muestra,
> Su rostro que el amor enardecía
> Cubrió un momento con su blanca diestra. (194)

With a moan María fell silent, and blushing visibly, for a moment covered her face, which burned with love, with her white hand.

But through her silence her body acts out the contrary impulses that divide her being. The poem that presents María's plight, then, turns the Romantic construction of the sovereign self inside out, representing desire, as experienced by the female subject, not as the driving power of imperious consciousness but as an internally devisive, destabilizing force.

The fracture of the subject in Gómez de Avellaneda's poetry often manifests itself in relation to the lyrical object, that is, the entity the poem addresses or evokes. But these images are not true objects or heterogeneous others; instead they act as mirrors of the self, products of self-alienation. Gómez de Avellaneda's conversion of the lyrical object into a mirror is dramatically illustrated in "En el álbum de una señorita cubana" 'For the album of a Cuban señorita,' a poem that follows the Romantic practice (discussed in the introduction) of drawing a parallel between woman and nature, in this case between the young Cuban woman addressed by the poem and the natural environment of Cuba. Despite its use of a formula that almost always linked nature and woman as objects of the lyrical subject's feeling and interpretation, however, this poem identifies woman and nature with self. The poem's first line, "Naciste en la tierra virgen" 'You were born in the virgin land' (1850 ed., 274), establishes the figurative identity of the young addressee with her native land. There follows a description of Cuba as beautiful, harmonious ("No se albergan crudas fieras, / Ni viles sierpes se arrastran" 'No cruel beasts lodge there, nor vile serpents crawl' [274]), and fertile ("Florece el útil cacao, / Se mece la dulce caña" 'Useful cacao flourishes, and sweet sugarcane sways' [275]). Never touched by snow or ice, the island is warm and receptive, but it is also sublimely tempestuous, shaken by earthquakes and hurricanes (stanzas 11–12). Then, at the center of the poem, as the hinge that turns from Cuban nature to Cuban woman, a single verse equates nature, addressee, and poetic self: "Allá, como yo, naciste" 'There, like me, you were born' (276). The text then goes on to infer explicitly the qualities of the young woman from the description of Cuba:

> ¿Qué mucho que en ti se vean
> Combinaciones tan raras
> De pasión y de dulzura,
> De languidez y pujanza?
>
> . . . .
>
> ¿Qué mucho que en ecos lances
> De tu armoniosa garganta
> Esos cantos que sorprenden,
> Que electrizan y avasallan? (276)

Why should it be surprising to find in you such rare combinations of passion and sweetness, languor and vigor? . . . Why should it surprise that you send forth in echoes from your harmonious throat those songs that astonish, electrify, and subjugate?

Indeed, so close is the connection that the girl's value for the lyrical speaker is her function as a signifier; she is the image through which the distant island is made present:

> ¡Digna imagen de tu patria!
>
> . . . .
>
> ¡En ti la gozan mis ojos,
> En ti mi pecho la ama,
> En ti la admira mi mente,
> Y en ti mi lira la canta! (277)

Worthy image of your homeland! . . . In you my eyes take delight in it, in you my heart loves it, in you my mind admires it, and in you my lyre sings it.

This, the conclusion of the poem, does in fact make the girl and Cuba objects of the subjective activity of the lyrical "I." But there is ambiguity here, a doubleness that returns in the final line's reference to singing: the addressee is also a singer—two stanzas are devoted to her talents and achievements—as well as a daughter of Cuba like the poet. If she is an image of Cuba, is this singer of songs that electrify and subjugate not equally an image of the poet's own constructed self? And is that self not also mirrored in the more removed image of Cuba? Thus, the objects of the lyrical self in the final stanza are in fact objectifications of the self, mirror images.

The poetic subject in Gómez de Avellaneda's work tends to direct itself to mirror images even when apparently addressing a true object. "A mi jilguero," from the 1841 collection, provides a good example. On its surface, the poem reproduces the structure of Romantic poetry that we have seen in Espronceda's "A una estrella," in which the poet, directing himself to an object in nature, delineates the self through an alternating process of projection and differentiation. "A mi jilguero," in which the poet addresses her finch, seems at first to follow that pattern. At the beginning of the poem, the "I" who speaks finds the little animal to whom she directs her attention mysteriously alien. Puzzled by the singing bird's "silencio triste" 'sad silence,' she asks innocently:

> En tu jaula preciosa
> ¿Qué falta a tu recreo?
> Mi mano cariñosa
> Previene tu deseo. (1841 ed., 89)

In your precious cage, what more does your enjoyment require? My affectionate hand anticipates your desire.

Later she discovers a similarity between the bird's plight and her own and asserts, "Cuando tu pena lloro, / También lloro la mía" 'When I grieve for your sorrow, I also grieve for my own' (91). Assuming that the bird's sadness is caused by nostalgia for its native meadows, the poet expresses her own longing for the lost Cuba of her childhood and invites the bird to share its sorrows by singing along with her, "[p]ues somos en desventura, / pájaro infeliz, iguales" 'since, unhappy bird, we are equals in misfortune' (92).

Thus far the poem follows the Romantic model in which self and other remain differentiated, though empathy discovers that they share common ground. But now an unexpected twist reveals the poem's ironic architecture, for the bird refuses to sing and looks reproachfully at his captor:

> Mas tu mirar angustiado
> En mí fijas con tristura
> Y tal parece que osado
> Me atribuyes tu amargura. (93)

But you fix your anguished gaze on me with melancholy, and it seems that you dare to attribute your grief to me.

The finch's mute, accusatory gaze signals a deeper identity than the lyrical speaker has been willing to acknowledge, for he reflects back to her her female condition. In his subjection and his silence, the caged

bird is analogous to woman, while through an ironic gender reversal
the text places the female lyrical persona in the position of man, for
whose pleasure woman has been confined to the domestic. Interpreting
the finch's silence, the poet puts these accusing words in its mouth:

> "Eres libre, eres amada,
> ¡Yo, solitario, cautivo—
> Preso en mi jaula dorada,
> Para divertirte vivo!" (93)

"You are free, you are loved, but I, alone and captive, live imprisoned in
my golden cage to entertain you!"

In a further undermining of the conventional model, the finch rejects
the false equality implied by the poet's earlier condescending projection
of her emotions upon her own captive. "'Tu compasión me maltrata, /
Y tu cariño maldigo'" "'Your compassion mistreats me, and I curse
your affection'" (94), says the finch, as Espronceda's Jarifa might have,
had the poet been able to imagine the female perspective.

With the veils of facile sentiment cleared away, the lyrical "I" recognizes the essential identity between herself and the finch and performs
a symbolic self-liberation:

> Libertad y amor te falta:
> ¡Libertad y amor te doy!
> Salta, pajarillo, salta,
> Que no tu tirana soy! (94)

Freedom and love are what you lack: freedom and love I give you! Spring
out, little bird, spring out, for I will not be your tyrant!

Setting the bird free will end his silence, the poet assumes; she hopes
only that for a moment she might hear his sweet song.

Thus, the finch allegorically figures the female lyrical subject who is
imprisoned and silenced by the cultural practices that make her an object of desire and interpretation by men, but who sings when made free
to act as a subject of desire. However, this allegorical projection of the
female lyrical self, liberated in an act of imagination, is free of the constraints of a woman's real existence and takes flight, leaving the poet
behind: "[Y]a se lanza / Donde mi vista no alcanza / Donde no llega mi
voz" 'Now he darts beyond the limits of my sight, where my voice cannot reach' (95). In this poem's final ironic inversion of the relation
between the self and its mirrors, then, the lyrical self remains in the

position of captivity and exile—the feminine condition—that the bird initially occupied.

As we have seen, insofar as the particular constraints on female desire and the asymmetrical position of the feminine in literary convention produce the internal division and alienation of the subject in Avellaneda's poetry, her texts alter familiar Romantic patterns. In poems in which she addresses a male beloved it becomes clear that the difference is more radical than a mere switch of the customary genders of subject and object. The intertextual resonances that link the first of Avellaneda's two poems titled "A él" to Espronceda's "Canto a Teresa"[8] reveal that in placing a woman in the position of the lyrical subject of this kind of Romantic love poem, the female poet constructs the self in a very different manner.

"A él" begins, as does Espronceda's "Canto," by recapitulating an earlier moment in the subject's personal history, evoking the self in a state of innocence and expectation: "Era la aurora hechicera / De mi juventud florida" 'It was the enchanting dawn of my flowering youth' (1841 ed., 49). Gómez de Avellaneda's poem focuses on a single episode, whereas Espronceda's longer one covers a longer *durée,* but the objective is still the same—to evoke the awakening of desire that anticipates its future object in surrounding nature. For Espronceda, this awakening is a demonstration of the imaginative power of the subject. The woman that the young poet glimpses "[s]obre las cumbres que florece el mayo" 'over the summits that bloom in May' or "por entre el bosque umbrío" 'within the shady wood' (*Diablo mundo. Poesías* 185) is a creature of the mind:

> Es el alma que vívida destella
> Su luz al mundo cuando en él se lanza,
> Y el mundo con su magia y galanura,
> Es espejo no más de su hermosura. (186)

It is the soul that flashes its vivid light on the world into which it throws itself, and the world with its magic and grace is nothing but the mirror of the soul's beauty.

In Avellaneda's poem, however, the lyrical subject is not so certain of its projective power. The source of the vision that entranced the poet's younger self during a moment of communion with nature remains very ambiguous in the text:

> Y trémula, palpitante,
> En mi delirio extasiada,

> Miré una visión brillante,
> Como el aire perfumada,
> Como las nubes flotante. (1841 ed., 50)

And, tremulous, throbbing, in delirious rapture, I saw a brilliant vision, perfumed like the air, floating like the clouds.

Lee Fontanella has argued that Gómez de Avellaneda draws on the poetic tradition of Spanish mysticism in representing the relation between the self and the beloved. Certainly the paradox elaborated in this poem presents itself as analogous to mystical experience insofar as the beloved other is at once autonomously external and intimately interior to the self. Unlike the vaporous female figure imagined by the youthful poet of "Canto a Teresa," Gómez de Avellaneda's "él" is not simply the creature of the poetic mind's magical power. He is an "imagen divina" 'divine image' that "ilumina / La vida futura" 'illuminates future life' (51) and holds sway over the lyrical subject in a way that Espronceda's vision does not: he is the speaker's "ignoto señor" 'unknown lord' (51).

Where "A él" sharply departs from the pattern exemplified in "Canto a Teresa" is in the relationship between the poet's vision of the beloved and the beloved's real existence. In Espronceda's poem the mind's movement from dreamed-of woman to the real Teresa prompts a lament: "¡Oh Teresa! ¡Oh dolor! Lágrimas mías" 'Oh, Teresa! Oh, pain! Oh my tears' (186). And the source of pain is, inevitably, the gap between the mind's projection and the reality:

> ¿Quién pensara jamás llegase un día
> En que, perdido el celestial encanto
> Y caída la venda de los ojos,
> Cuanto diera placer causara enojos? (187)

Who would have thought that a day would ever arrive in which, the celestial charm lost and the bandage fallen from the eyes, what once gave pleasure should cause animosity?

For Gómez de Avellaneda, in contrast, there is exact correspondence between the anticipated image of the beloved and his real being, a correspondence the poet immediately perceives when she meets him. But the identity of the object with the female subject's image of desire hardly results in a positive unity of subject and object; instead it seems to threaten the self's ruin:

> Que tú eres no hay duda mi sueño adorado
> El ser que vagando mi mente buscó,

> Mas, ¡ay! que mil veces el hombre, arrastrado
> Por fuerza enemiga, su mal anheló. (52)

There is no doubt that you are my adored dream, the being sought by my wandering mind, but, ay! a thousand times man, moved by a hostile force, yearned for what would do him harm.

With this dark intimation, Avellaneda's poem abruptly shifts to a figurative rather than a narrative mode. Instead of continuing the narrative of her life's trajectory, she suggests her loss of control over its direction by elaborating two images: the moth, drawn to the flame "hasta que la luz ingrata / Devora su frágil ser" 'until the ungrateful light devours its fragile being' (52), and the squirrel that runs to its death, attracted by a legendary Cuban serpent. Again in this poem, a feminized desire leads not, as in Espronceda, to disappointment or frustration but to annihilation.

Indeed, Gómez de Avellaneda's poetry constitutes the self by a very different process than we discerned in Espronceda. As that process is represented in "A él," the subject initially creates a mental image of the object of desire and then invests it with an autonomous power capable of turning against the self that generated it. Its own alienated desire now represented as an overwhelming external force, the self is figured in terms of vulnerability and weakness—as the fragile moth, for example. The final step in the poem is to equate the self with objects that represent lack of control:

> ¿Dónde van, dónde, esas nubes
> Por el viento compelidas?
> ¿Dónde esas hojas perdidas
> Que del árbol arrancó?
>
> ¡Vuelan, vuelan resignadas,
> Y no saben donde van,
> Pero siguen el camino
> Que les traza el huracán! (53)

Where, where do the clouds driven by the wind go? Where do the lost leaves torn from the tree go? Resigned, they fly, they fly and know not where they go, but they follow the path the hurricane marks out for them!

In this poem the female subject's erotic passion, initiated with a phantasm of projected desire, is represented as a process of radical self-alienation that leads finally to the self's loss of autonomous direction. The force of its own desire is experienced as an external power, unknowable as well as uncontrollable. Such a self has little in common with Espronceda's poetically created self, which, though embittered and suffering, is never estranged from its striving, directed desire.

The wind-blown leaf is a predominant metaphor for the self in Gómez de Avellaneda's poetry. It appears, for instance, in "Amor y orgullo" as one of the images through which María describes her present, fallen mode of being: "Cual hoja seca al raudo torbellino, / Cedo al poder del áspero destino" 'As the dry leaf to the swift whirlwind, I cede to harsh destiny's power' (1841 ed., 189). Here "harsh destiny" refers to the action of that feminine form of desire which I identified earlier. In the light of this emerging pattern of images of the self, we might consider again the reference to fate in the opening sonnet, "Al partir": "Do quier que el hado en su furor me impela" (7). Insofar as the buried metaphor here closely parallels the other images in which the winds of destiny blow the speaking self before them, it confirms our initial suspicion that the wind that carries the ship toward Europe and new possibilities in "Al partir" is a disavowed projection of the self's own desire. Thus, this specific pattern of self-alienation in the female lyrical subject is already inherent in the first poem of the *Poesías*.

The connection between the feminization of the lyrical subject and its constitution as self-dispossessed produces ironic, even parodic overtones when it comes to the surface in the short poem "Al destino," dated 1844 in the 1850 edition of *Poesías*. The first stanza, in which the gender of the speaking subject remains unspecified, presents the self in bitter struggle with an ironclad destiny: "[S]e rompe en vano / Una vez y otra la fatal cadena, / Y mi vigor por recobrar me afano" 'In vain the fatal chain is broken time after time, and I strive to recover my strength' (1850 ed., 202). But when in the second and final stanza the lyrical subject reveals itself as feminine, it also treats as inevitable the construction of the self as without agency, as the windblown leaf, in fact:

> ¡Heme aquí! ¡Tuya soy! ¡Dispón, destino,
> De tu víctima dócil! Yo me entrego
> Cual hoja seca al raudo torbellino
> Que la arrebata ciego.

Here I am! I'm yours! Destiny, dispose of your docile victim! I surrender myself like a dry leaf to the swift whirlwind that blindly seizes it.

In contrast to earlier examples, the leaf image here is treated with a certain critical distance. A verse like the following seems self-consciously to duplicate in its feminine endings and exclamatory style the language of the feminine victim of melodrama: "¡Tuya soy! ¡Heme aquí! ¡Todo lo puedes!" 'I am yours! Here I am! You can do anything!' The poem's conclusion capitalizes on this parodic allusion through an implicit image that figures destiny as a wily seducer: "Pero sabe, ¡oh cruel!, que no me engaña / La sonrisa falaz que hoy me concedes" 'But know, cruel one, that I am not misled by the deceptive smile you concede me today.'

"Al destino," then, can be read as a comment on the connection between cultural determinism of gender and the autonomy of the self. Indeed, the construction of the "I" in Avellaneda's poetry as a whole demonstrates that woman's destiny—defined for upper-class women during this period as either the lot of the passionless domestic angel or defilement, ruin, loss of identity—ineluctably shapes the female lyrical subject.

THE LIMITS OF THE ROMANTIC SELF

Pressured by cultural definitions of the feminine to disown desire in both its sexual and its Promethean versions, Gómez de Avellaneda represents herself as a lyrical subject in ways that exhibit different and more extreme forms of alienation than do the lyrical selves of her male Romantic colleagues. Split off from and disavowing its own impulses of desire, Avellaneda's lyrical "I" lacks the integrity that allows the Esproncedan self to distinguish itself from a degraded world. Avellaneda's alienation is internal, the estrangement of self from self rather than the isolation from the social world observed in Larra. Her representation of the self is perhaps closest to the Duke of Rivas's image of the individual subject in don Alvaro, insofar as both writers depict in quite different genres the ultimate consequences of internal division—the very disappearance of the self as an autonomous agent. But, whereas don Alvaro embodies his author's aristocratic intuition of the emptiness of the bourgeois ideology of individualism in Spain, the fragmented speaking subject of Avellaneda's poetry reveals the stresses exerted on the female subject by new cultural formations.

At its best, Gómez de Avellaneda's sense of the impossibility of an autonomous, unified self produces poems that, like "Amor y orgullo," represent with a certain irony the infinitely regressive fracturing of the self and the inevitable subversion of the rational "I" by the rejected emotional elements of the splintered psyche. "A * * * " (titled "A él" in the 1869 edition), dated 1845 in the 1850 edition, also expresses awareness and even acceptance of the self's divided condition. A poem about the external rupture of a relationship that is echoed by internal ambivalence, it begins, "No existe lazo ya: todo está roto" 'No tie exists now: all is broken' (1850 ed., 233), but ends, "Sabe que aún tienes en el alma mía / Generoso perdón, cariño tierno" 'Know that you still have in my soul a generous pardon, tender affection' (234). The denial of feeling and the experience of feeling that coexist in the text are integrated as a consciousness of the self's interest in disavowing desire: "Te amé, no te amo ya; piénsolo al menos. / ¡Nunca, si fuere error, la verdad mire!" 'I loved you, I don't love you now; at least I think not. If that's not the case, may I never see the truth!' (233). The lyrical "I" does, however, confront the truth of its own contradictions. If, on the one hand, she celebrates her freedom from a subjugating passion, on the other hand she recognizes the solitude in which the lack of an object leaves her:

> Mas, ¡ay!, ¡Cuán triste libertad respiro!
> Hice un mundo de ti, que hoy se anonada,
> Y en honda y vasta soledad me miro. (234)

But, ay! what sad freedom I breathe! I made a world of you that today is destroyed, and I find myself in deep, vast solitude.

The ambivalence is transcended by awareness of the fundamental solipsism of her passion, that with or without it, she exists in solitude.

The painfully honest self-examination conducted in this poem disrupts the poet's ordinarily euphonious and fluent style. The abrupt, broken rhythm of the verses ("Te amé, no te amo ya; piénsolo al menos") and sound combinations that produce emphasis rather than musicality ("No existe lazo ya: todo está roto") give the poem a dry, almost harsh quality that is unusual not only in Gómez de Avellaneda's own work but among her Romantic contemporaries as well.

Much more frequently, however, the instability and internal division of the self in Gómez de Avellaneda's poetry produces not a questioning of the Romantic concept of self but an anxiety that seeks an external guarantee of identity and order. Two very different voices reflect the breakdown of the coherent, controlling subject in her lyrical poems. One, like don Alvaro in his final moment, vents a terrifying rage at the order of things and gives itself entirely to imagining the disintegration into chaos of existing structures. In "En una tarde tempestuosa: Soneto" ("Deseo de venganza" in the 1850 edition) the poet invokes "[d]el huracán espíritu potente" 'the powerful spirit of the hurricane' (1841 ed., 180), inviting it to come and "con el tuyo mi furor excita" 'excite my fury with yours.' The storm's fury, reverberating with the subject's own wrath, selects as one of its objects the oak, an image of patriarchal strength and stability:

> ¡Deja que el rayo con fragor reviente,
> Mientras cual hoja seca o flor marchita,
> Tu fuerte soplo al roble precipita
> Roto y deshecho al bramador torrente! (180)

> Let the lightning bolt explode with uproar while, as if it were a dry leaf or withered flower, your strong gusts precipitate the oak, broken and torn, into the roaring torrent!

The imagery suggests that this rage is associated with the inequities of gender: the subject fantasizes the reduction of the firm, rooted oak to the status of the dried leaf through which Avellaneda tends to represent the female subject's vulnerability and lack of power over its own destiny. Indeed, in the concluding tercet, the speaker begs the hurricane to lend her its power:

> Ven, y al inerte pecho que te implora
> Da tu poder y tu iracunda saña,
> Y el llanto seca que cobarde llora.

> Come and give your power and angry rage to the inert breast that implores you, and dry the cowardly tears that it weeps.

Rage is seen, then, as the antidote to feminine weakness.

A similar fury of anger breaks out in another poem, or rather, a fragment of a poem whose full text Avellaneda never published. Her ambivalence about the poem[9] is explicable when we consider the violence of the imagery. Titled "La venganza," the poem invokes the spirits of the night:

> ¡Venid, venid! del enemigo bárbaro
> Beber anhelo la abundante hiel—
>
> . . . .
>
> ¡Dadle a mis labios, que se agitan ávidos,
> Sangre humeante sin cesar, corred!
>
> . . . .
>
> ¡Hagan mis dientes con crujidos ásperos
> Pedazos mil su corazón infiel
> Y dormiré, cual en suntuoso tálamo,
> En su caliente, ensangrentada piel! (1850 ed., 165–166)

Come, come, I yearn to drink the bile of my barbarous enemy. . . . Run, bring to my lips, which avidly stir, ceaseless steaming blood! . . . May my teeth with harsh crunches make a thousand pieces of his unfaithful heart, and I will sleep, as if in a sumptuous wedding bed, in his warm, bloody skin!

Though the exaggeration and unusual dactylic meter tinge these verses with humor, the fantasy that determines the imagery is of angry revenge.

That same voice and fantasy speaks with utter seriousness in "El día final" 'The Final Day,' where the respectable biblical topic of the final judgment allows it full range. Here the "I" positions itself as observer rather than agent and describes the dissolution of order in the universe:

> Rota la ley que ordena el movimiento
> De innumerables mundos
>
> . . . .
> Se escapan de sus órbitas, y errantes,
>
> . . . .
> Vagan entre tinieblas confundidos,
> Sin rumbo ni compás. (1850 ed., 186–187)

The law that orders the movement of innumerable worlds broken, . . . they escape from their orbits, and off course, . . . wander confused in darkness, without route or compass.

The psychological correlative of this image is soon made clear: "¡No hay amor! ¡No hay piedad! Del furor ciego, / Del profundo pesar, del negro espanto, / Los afectos suaves / Huyendo van" 'There is no love! No pity! The tender emotions run fleeing from the blind fury, the deep sorrow, the black fear' (187). This is the disturbing deeper implication of this torrent of rage: it is not really an antidote to the weakness of the divided self, but is part of the dissolution of the self, the scattering of the affects, the descent into a chaos that envelopes the world.

The lyrical subject of Avellaneda's work cannot tolerate such a possibility for long. In "El día final" she imagines the loss of the self as an apocalyptic cataclysm that must imply salvation. But where is that salvation to come from? Not from the poetic project, where male Romantic poets from Shelley to Nerval had found the means to counteract the disintegrating temporality of the self, for the feminized self as it emerged in Avellaneda's poetry was split and undermined in the very process of finding a voice. The poet of "El día final" looks outside self and world for salvation to a deity that transcends all the elements in play. The poem is brought to a close by the appearance of God:

upon the chaotic ruin of creation "[e]l almo trono del Señor se asienta: / . . . / ¡Y el tiempo inmóvil a su lado duerme!" 'the white throne of the Lord establishes itself . . . and time sleeps immobile at his side!' (188). With this verse, the poem ends along with all mutation in God's eternal stability: facing this salvation, the poetic voice falls silent.

The pattern of "El día final," in which belief in divine order is the only guarantee—an ambiguous one—against the processes of disintegration that operate in the self, recurs again and again in Gómez de Avellaneda's poetry. This is her explicit argument in a number of poems belonging to a genre then called "philosophical": for example, "La juventud," "A la felicidad," and "Contemplación" from the 1841 collection and "A la muerte de José de Espronceda" from the 1850 edition. This anxiety to find stability in a transcendent guarantor explains the increasing frequency with which she wrote religious poetry, particularly in periods of personal turmoil.

One of the poems that expresses most poignantly the self's impulse to look beyond for a coherence it does not find within is addressed not to God but to the Virgin. Images of exile, solitude, disorientation characterize the female speaker:

> En tempestuoso océano
> Mi bajel navega incierto,
> Sin que un fanal en el puerto
> Encienda piadosa mano:
> Entre escollos gira roto,
> Sin piloto;
> Y sin brújula ni vela. (1841 ed., 203)

In a tempestuous ocean my vessel sails uncertainly, with no beacon lit in the port by a compassionate hand: it veers broken among the reefs, without a pilot and without compass or sail.

In directing herself to the maternal figure of the Virgin, "Madre amada," who is "[d]e los débiles amparo, / De los tristes alegría" 'refuge for the weak, joy for the sad' (203), the lyrical subject seems to be regressing to a fantasy associated with a time before the construction of the individualized, autonomous Romantic ego—a time of infantile dependency in her own personal history and a time of premodern religious tradition in Spanish cultural history. Such a wish is, ultimately, the negation of the poetic voyage of self-discovery on which she embarked in "Al partir."

As the consequences of Gómez de Avellaneda's refusal to conform to the restrictive norms of middle-class femininity accumulated in her life, her poetry reflected a growing anxiety for the security of religious belief. After the terrible crisis in which she bore a child out of wedlock, watched her baby die, fled into a precipitate marriage with the cancer-stricken Pedro Sabater, and nursed him through his painful last days, all in the span of little more than a year in 1845–1846, she retired to a convent for several months and there wrote nothing but a book of prayers and some religious poetry. If we can trust the dates she assigned to her poems in the 1850 *Poesías*—and I see no reason to doubt them— we can conclude that her poetic inspiration ended with this conversion. After 1845 she continued to write prolifically, turning out excellent theater in particular, but she wrote no more significant lyrical poetry, only occasional verse and some religious poems. Her exploration of the female lyrical voice had, it seems, led her to a point of no return.

6
Waterflower

Carolina Coronado's Lyrical Self-Representation

Tú, poetisa, flor del lago
Por amante, por cantora,
Has venido en mala hora
Con tu amor y tu cantar.
              —*Carolina Coronado*

Whereas Gertrudis Gómez de Avellaneda elected to scale Madrid's literary Parnassus in person, her younger contemporary Carolina Coronado made her voice heard in the capital from a remote hamlet of Extremadura. "A la palma," a poem Coronado wrote at the age of fourteen, made its way to publication in a Madrid newspaper through the young poet's family connections with Madrid liberals. The poem captured the imagination of no less a Romantic and liberal figure than Espronceda, who acclaimed Coronado's advent as a poet in verse that, while it celebrated the harmonious purity of her lyrical voice, also insinuated an erotic interest in his young compatriot (Espronceda was born in a house not far from Coronado's family home). With the help of the Madrid dramatist Juan Eugenio Hartzenbusch, to whom she first wrote in 1840 (Fonseca 174), Coronado continued to place her poems in periodicals in the provinces and in the capital in 1841 and 1842. Encouraged by these successes—and, no doubt, by the examples of Josefa Massanés and Gertrudis Gómez de Avellaneda—to publish a book of her poetry, she enlisted Hartzenbusch's aid in editing the collection and finding a publisher. The book appeared in 1843. With this first volume of poetry, Coronado became a recognized literary figure in Madrid, even though she had not yet set foot in the capital; in 1844 her name began to appear on lists of contemporary writers and of contributors and editors for literary journals.[1]

While Coronado and Gómez de Avellaneda gained public recogni-

tion at almost the same time, sometimes publishing poems in the same
issue of a journal, there is an immediately apparent difference between
them: Coronado's lyrical voice is coded much more explicitly as feminine according to cultural gender conventions. Whereas the Cuban poet's first book of poetry came under attack for its lack of feminine
tenderness,[2] Coronado's first volume won Hartzenbusch's praise, in his
introduction to the work, for precisely the features that would identify
the poet to her readers as a well-brought-up young girl:

> [S]us versos pintan su corazón, su gusto, su edad, su estado, su posición
> social y hasta la noble compostura de su semblante: sus versos son ella
> misma. . . . [S]iempre los ecos de su voz llevan entre los rasgos del ingenio
> el encanto de la bondad, del candor y de la ternura. . . . [S]e echa de ver en
> la templada vehemencia de sus quejas y en el manso correr de sus lágrimas
> la natural timidez y encantadora modestia de una joven de 22 anos. (ix–x)

> Her verses portray her heart, her taste, her age, her marital status, her social
> position, and even the noble composition of her face: her verses are the poet
> herself. . . . Along with the signs of wit, the echoes of her voice always carry
> the charm of goodness, innocence, and tenderness. . . . In the controlled ve-
> hemence of her complaints and the gentle flow of her tears can be seen the
> natural timidity and the charming modesty of a young woman of twenty-
> two.

These words, echoed by Gustave Deville a year later in his review of
Spain's women poets (see chapter 2 above) reflect the emerging de-
sideratum for the woman poet in the Romantic period: that she be a
domestic angel who sings. Although Hartzenbusch concedes that occasional "acentos vigorosos y enérgicos" 'vigorous and energetic accents'
(x) show that Coronado has forgotten her sex momentarily and become exclusively a poet, he concludes by underlining the relationship
between the poems and the gender of their author: "[S]on versos de
una hermosa y les alcanza el privilegio de la hermosura" 'They are the
verses of a beautiful woman, and they come under beauty's privilege'
(xii).

The damning gallantry of Hartzenbusch's reference to Coronado's
physical appearance reflects the paradoxical tendency of the male literary establishment to eroticize her even as it insisted on her virginal purity. The poem with which Espronceda greeted her poetic debut set the
paradigm. At the conclusion of the poem, after inviting the young poet
to join him in the woods to sing in the shade of her innocent palm tree
(a reference to the title of Coronado's poem), he adds:

Mas, ¡ay, perdona! Virginal capullo,
Cierra tu cáliz a mi loco amor:
Que nacimos de un aura al mismo arrullo,
Para ser, yo el insecto; tú, la flor. (Coronado, *Poesías,* 1852 ed., 2)

But, oh, forgive me! Virginal bud, close your calyx to my mad love: for we
were born to the same breeze's lullaby to be, I, the insect, you, the flower.

The pointedly sexual innuendo of the poem's emphatic last line
snatches back from the addressee what the preceding stanza had
seemed to grant her—parity with the speaker as the subject of poetic
discourse.

In drawing on a venerable tradition that identifies the woman with
the flower as a pleasure-producing object, Espronceda repeated the
timeworn gesture that puts a woman in her place by an expression of
sexual desire for which she is supposed to be grateful. Gómez de Avellaneda repelled such covertly hostile advances by degendering, at least
in conventional terms, her poetic self-presentation; Coronado did not.
In fact, she was fascinated, even captured, by Espronceda's poem,
which she included in the introduction to her 1852 *Poesías.* Therefore,
in writing herself as a poet who was also a woman, she was obliged to
engage in an elaborate, sometimes self-contradictory fencing match
with that dual image of herself as at once virginal angel and erotic object reflected back to her by male readers, poets, and critics.

ADAPTING A TRADITION TO
THE FEMININE PERSONA

In the 1843 volume, Carolina Coronado did not attempt, as Gómez
de Avellaneda did in her first book, to identify herself with leading male
Romantic poets, either by translating their work or writing on "philosophical" themes. Instead, she looked back to a tradition that went
from Horace through Renaissance and neoclassical poetry in order to
find lyrical models that combined modest retirement (easily translated
into the *recato,* or discreet modesty, Spanish culture demanded of
women) with introspective contemplation of the harmony between nature and self.

The first poem of the collection, "A la soledad," follows Horace,
Fray Luis de León, and Juan Meléndez Valdés in presenting a lyrical
"I" that retreats from society to find calm and consolation in the natu-
ral world.[3] "Danme, sí, tierno alivio / La soledad del campo y su be-

lleza" 'The solitude of the country and its beauty do give me tender relief' (2), she informs us. In enumerating the pleasures through which nature soothes her pain, she echoes the motifs inscribed in the Spanish tradition by Fray Luis's famous sixteenth-century poem "Canción de la vida solitaria": the fountains, the river, the hills, the scattered flowers, the birdsongs. Coronado also uses the verse form of Fray Luis's poem, the Renaissance *lira* (a five-line stanza combining heptasyllabic and endecasyllabic verses), but her diction shows the influence of Meléndez Valdés's more sentimentalized late eighteenth-century version of the same theme ("Mi vuelta al campo") in references to weeping, to sonorous turtledoves, to softly accented laments (Meléndez, lines 11, 32, 39–40).

Meléndez's status as a model is even more evident in Coronado's "Una despedida," in which the poet bids goodbye to her favorite spot near a spring. Although in this poem Coronado reverses Meléndez's happy greeting of nature in "El mediodía," she echoes many of the images through which the poet concretizes his participation in nature's pleasures: reposing and dreaming on the shady grass, looking at the sun through the branches of a tree, listening to the songbirds, feeling the breeze in his hair. At a climactic point, Meléndez exclaims:

> ¡[O]h sagrado
> retiro delicioso!
> En ti solo mi espíritu aquejado
> halla calma y reposo. (335; lines 69–72)

Oh, sacred, delicious retreat! In you alone my afflicted spirit finds calm and repose.

In much the same vein, Coronado too declares:

> ¡Ah! si mi vida entera,
> Mi cara soledad, recinto amado,
> Consagraros pudiera
> El mundo huyendo y su falaz cuidado! (24)

Ah, my dear solitude, beloved nook, if only I could consecrate my whole life to you, fleeing the world and its deceitful cares!

In following the model of the neoclassical poet, Coronado thus inscribed her early poems in the Horatian tradition that he cultivated— the retreat from the city to a poetically constructed nature whose simplicity and modesty represented a fusion of aesthetic and moral values.

Meléndez's "El mediodía" gives us the key to Coronado's choice of this tradition instead of the more grandiose subjectivism of the Romantic mode. In the concluding stanzas of his poem, the lyricist characterizes himself directly: "Mi alma sensible y dulce en ver se goza / una flor, una planta" 'My sweet and sensitive soul delights in seeing a flower, a plant' (lines 77–78). The end of the next stanza echoes this with "el tierno pecho mío" 'my tender heart' (line 84). Such a version of the lyrical self was plainly more compatible with predominant conceptions of female subjectivity than the aggressively egocentric paradigms of the Romantic poetic subject. Coronado perceived this particular strand of Renaissance and neoclassical poetry as a tradition in which a woman might insert herself without significant disruption of the codes of gender difference. Indeed, many of the less well known women poets of the 1840s shared her perception, for the conventions of diction and imagery that characterized their writing derived from Meléndez's "tiernos acentos," "liras de marfil," "sonoros plectros," "lágrimas encendidas," and "númenes divinos" rather than from Espronceda's more heterogeneous poetic language.

In the 1843 collection, Coronado makes clear that she does not wish to challenge contemporary standards of femininity in presenting herself as a writer of poetry. In a sonnet to her uncle Pedro Romero, who was involved in national politics, she openly acknowledges the limits that maintaining femininity—that is, the innocent purity and modest self-abnegation mandated by the cultural stereotype of the *ángel del hogar*—imposed on her writing. The poet says she would sing of the fatherland and its troubles, of genius, of virtue, of vice; "pero mi voz de niña desmayara, / Y desmayara endeble el harpa mía" 'but my girl's voice might fail, and my weak harp be too faint' (57). She casts the idea of feminine weakness or insufficiency with respect to "high" masculine topics in terms of natural images in the second half of the sonnet:

> Más quiero, humilde abeja, aquí en el suelo
> Vagar de flor en flor siempre ignorada,
> Que al águila siguiendo arrebatada
> Con alas cortas, remontar mi vuelo. (58)

A humble bee, I would rather fly unnoted from flower to flower here on the earth than, following the eagle, impetuously aim higher with my short wings.

The imagery justifies as a natural given her self-restriction as a poet: the feminine bee must stay close to the earth and its flowers because her wings are not made for the altitudes in which the eagle flies. Thus, the domestic angel is recast as nature's humble, hive-centered laborer, the bee.

However, the bee figure's intertextual relations with certain male-authored texts provide a slightly different meaning to this apparently self-effacing sonnet. In the first place, we might note how deftly Coronado reverses the terms of the insect-flower metaphor that Espronceda used to assert sexual difference in the poem dedicated to the young Carolina at her poetic debut. There the woman is figured as the passive flower, object of the buzzing activity of the male poet. A sonnet by Meléndez Valdés, "El pensamiento," elaborates the same metaphor, specifically identifying as a bee the poetic fancy of the male poet that hovers around the flower of female beauty. Here in Coronado's sonnet, however, the female escapes from the objectified image of the flower to identify herself with the poetic activity of the honey-making bee, a figure whose traditional connotations of domestic industriousness make it a ready metaphor for female creativity.

Furthermore, by employing a trope that seems to emphasize the modesty of her poetic aspirations, Coronado simultaneously conforms to the norms of femininity and draws upon the authority of Horace himself to bolster her claims as a poet. Her contrast between two types of poets, the high-mounting eagle and the earthbound bee, rewrites the central metaphor of Horace's Ode iv.2, in which the poet claims that he cannot follow Pindar, "the swan of Dirce," in the "cloudy heights." Instead, he says, "[m]y methods are those of the bee on Matinus, working hard to gather the sweet-tasting thyme . . . a painstaking minor poet, shaping my lyrics" (161).[4] Just as Horace's modesty served as a becoming pose through which he could intimate pride in his poetic craftsmanship, so too Coronado's use of the bee image identifies her with an illustrious precursor even as it disclaims any intention to compete with male poets.

Indeed, Coronado was able to adapt the Horatian tradition of retreat to the countryside to her purposes as a female lyrical subject, for that tradition's emphasis on nature, simplicity, and modesty allowed her to mark out a poetic space that went beyond the household concerns and maternal tenderness prescribed by Deville for the woman poet without directly challenging contemporary standards of femininity. Like the chapter in *Sab* in which Carlota's expansive, sensitive, and imaginative soul can be fully seen and represented when she shakes off the oppressive social and historical world by stepping into her garden, this early poetry of Coronado's constructs the lyrical subject in the realm of nature, outside the contaminating world of politics and economics, on the one hand, and the confines of domestic space, on the other. To seek pleasure in exterior space without calling her purity and innocence into question required that Coronado represent nature not as the sublime and contradictory realm of the Romantics but as the pastoral nature she found in Meléndez and Fray Luis de León—all rosy morning light, flowers, laughing hills, and crystalline springs, as it is portrayed in "A la soledad," stanza 5. It was necessary to rework that tradition in certain ways, of course, to adapt the signs and tropes established by masculine authority to the needs of the female lyricist. As we shall see, in identifying the feminine subject with a reworked poetic nature, Coronado implemented a strategy that subtly exalted the values attached to the "feminine."

A primary element of Coronado's strategy was to stress innocence as a constitutive quality of the lyrical self constructed in relation to nature. Thus she was concerned that her rustic retreat be not only "consuelo del dolor" 'solace of pain' (22), as it was for Meléndez and Fray Luis, but also "asilo de inocencia" 'asylum of innocence' (22). To this end, she altered the convention according to which the Horatian ode directs itself to a male peer, a friend or fellow poet. Instead, Coronado's poems typically address their object in nature; when they are directed to a human interlocutor, it is a child—Emilio, the poet's brother—whose innocent pleasure in nature becomes associated with the lyrical subject. In "Melancolía," for example, although a contrast is drawn between the frolicking child addressed and the melancholic "I," the lyricist's empathetic representation of the child suggests an identity between the two, an identity that the poet acknowledges: "De niña, el riachuelo / Y las aves también me divertían" 'As a child, I also took delight in the stream and the birds' (6). In this Wordsworthian touch, we see another effect of Coronado's revision of the Horatian tradition: not only does she transform the seasoned wisdom of the neoclassical poet into the virginal naïveté that Hartzenbusch describes as candor, but she endows the lyrical speaker with something of the temporal subjectivity of the Romantics. The child's Edenic experience is remembered by, but inaccessible to, the lyricist: "Mas ya, ¿dónde el hechizo / De esas llanuras para mí se encierra?" 'But now, where does the magic of those fields hide itself from me?'(7).

Another alteration that Coronado makes in the Horatian tradition tends in the direction of Romantic subjectivity. In Horace, Fray Luis

de León, and Meléndez Valdés, the poet retreats to the country from
the political turbulence and moral corruption of city life; but that alternative is not open to the female lyricist, who must maintain her innocence of the political and economic world. Coronado resolves this
problem by making the innocent, peaceful nature she describes her retreat from unfeminine emotions. In "A la soledad" it is from the pain
of a passion she cannot openly avow that she seeks solace:

> Al fin en tu sosiego,
> Amiga soledad, tan suspirado,
> El encendido fuego
> De un pecho enamorado
> Resplandece más dulce y más templado. (1)

At last in your longed-for repose, my solitary retreat, the burning fire of an
enamoured breast glows more sweetly and temperately.

In "A las nubes" nature stands in a more ambiguous relation to the
lyrical subject, for which it is at once a source of recreation and a disturbing symbolic mirror. The poet finds pleasure and poetic stimulation
in the clouds when they form fanciful shapes (9) or tepid veils (10) appropriate to feminine fantasy, but not when they become boiling, raging stormclouds:

> ¡Ay! que medrosa entonces se ahuyentara
> La inspiración sublime:
>
> . . . .
>
> Muda contemplo de pavor cercada
> La turba misteriosa
> Que en pos del huracán revuela osada. (10–11)

Ay, because then, fearful, sublime inspiration might flee: . . . Mute, besieged
by fear, I contemplate the mysterious mob that daringly swirls in the hurricane's wake.

The key to the lyricist's tongue-tying panic appears in the next
stanza: "Allá en la inmensidad os mueven guerra / Furiosos aquilones: /
. . . Así de las pasiones / Es juguete infeliz la vida humana" 'Beyond in
the immensity furious winds move you in war: . . . likewise, human life
is an unhappy plaything of the passions' (11). The disruptive fantasies
and emotions that the stormy sky reflects back to the poet are unacceptable as the poetic expression of female subjectivity; they can only be
acknowledged by an explicit rejection of them as a source of inspiration. That source, the lyricist claims in her conclusion, is found primar-

ily in the clouds that float "tranquilamente / Con nevada blancura" 'peacefully, with snowy whiteness' (12). That Coronado correctly used the codes of gender that her readers assumed is evident in Hartzenbusch's comment on this poem in his introduction: "A un hombre no se le hubiera ocurrido o no hubiera sabido decir tan poéticamente que le asustaban las nubes amenazando tempestad" 'It would not have occurred to a man, or he wouldn't know how to say so poetically, that he was frightened by clouds threatening a storm' (x).

As we can see, Coronado's femininization of the Horatian relation to nature involves the lyrical subject in the more Romantic stance of the self who reads the secrets of its own being in nature. Coronado's construction of self and nature is, however, akin to that of Gómez de Avellaneda, for whom the stress is on nature's likeness to the lyrical "I," rather than to that of the male Romantic poets, who sought the self in nature's otherness according to the Hegelian dialectical logic. This peculiar construction of the lyrical subject in relation to the natural phenomenon it takes as the object of its discourse is a significant feature of the series of flower poems placed toward the end of Coronado's 1843 collection.

In one sense, these poems about flowers—"El girasol" 'The Sunflower,' "A la amapola" 'To the Poppy,' "La rosa blanca" 'The White Rose,' and so forth— unmistakably signal the poet's gender and status: focusing on objects equally appropriate for needlepoint or watercolors, these poems seem rather like a verbal analogy of the embroidery designs commonly used by young ladies of the period. Read in terms of their intertextual relations with a poetic tradition that goes from the Spanish Golden Age through the neoclassical period, however, the flower poems can be seen as complex transformations of the significance of the flower as a poetic figure. Writing poems to flowers was a favorite device of the Baroque poet Francisco de Rioja. In his early seventeenth-century poems, the flower served as the basis for extended metaphorical elaboration of the hazards of erotic desire. Although the play of conceits sometimes makes the flower a figure for desire itself,[5] more commonly it is figuratively identified with the female object of desire.

Rioja's "Al clavel," for instance, in addressing the carnation worn by the beloved, reifies the provocative features of both flower and woman through the standard Petrarchan procedures:

> Cuantas veces te miro
> entre los admirables lazos de oro
> por quien lloro y suspiro,

> por quien suspiro y lloro,
> en invidia y amor junto me enciendo. (Blecua 249)

Every time I see you among the admirable golden knots for which I weep
and sigh, for which I sigh and weep, I burn with envy and love together.

The double meaning of "lazos"—braids of hair and snares—conveys
the negative connotations that this poetry of the Counter-Reformation
gave the sign constituted by flower/carnal feminine beauty. The concluding verses of the same poet's "A la rosa" indicate the final term of
the chain of associations that linked the rose with the eroticized female
body:

> Tan cerca, tan unida
> está al morir tu vida,
> que dudo si en sus lágrimas la Aurora
> mustia, tu nacimiento o muerte llora. (Blecua 251)

So close, so joined is your life to death, that I don't know whether with her
tears sad Dawn weeps over your birth or death.

The baroque elaboration of the flower-as-woman figure, then, connected with the misogynist Christian tradition that equated women
with the deathly trap of the flesh.

Between Carolina Coronado and the baroque vision incarnated in
Rioja's treatment of the subgenre of poems to flowers, however, stood
the neoclassical humanism of Meléndez Valdés. In his poem "A las
flores," he showed himself more interested in the metonymical play
suggested by the flowers' natural history than in reifying metaphorical conceits. Thus "A las flores" characterizes various flower species
through details drawn from common horticultural knowledge: characteristic shapes, colors, fragrances, positions on the plant (high on a
stalk or hidden under leaves), and typical habitats supply the imagery
from which the poet fashions a feminine personification of each flower.
For example, the proud, showy tulip is odorless, but

> [n]o tú, azucena virginal, vestida
> del manto de inocencia en nieve pura,
> y el cáliz de oro fino recamado;
> no tú, que en el aroma más preciado
> bañando afortunada tu hermosura,
> a par los ojos y el sentido encantas. (324)

not you, virginal lily, wearing the snow-white mantle of innocence, your
chalice embroidered with fine gold; not you, for bathing your happy beauty
in the most treasured aroma, you enchant the nose as well as the eyes.

In this treatment the flower is still very much the sensual object of the male poet's erotic fancy, yet its personification provided a potential subjectivity that Coronado was able to develop as she followed Meléndez in poetically exploring the individual characteristics of a number of flowers.

Although Coronado dispenses with the mythological apparatus—Flora and Cupid—employed by Meléndez and with the verbal and conceptual play of the baroque poets, she uses much of the flower tradition's figurative language in her own poems. Coronado's flowers attract bees, butterflies, and the lyricist's fancy with their rare beauty, their jewel-like color, their sweet perfume, their graceful stalks, their short-lived brilliance. However, she revises the relation between the lyrical subject and the flower-object even in poems whose imagery is rather clichéd.

"Al jazmín," for example, expands and elaborates the motifs presented in Meléndez's five lines on this flower in "A las flores"—its brief bloom, its scent, its whiteness against the green leafy vines (323). Yet Coronado develops these motifs in such a way as to suggest the identity of lyricist and flower, rather than the poet's erotic perception of the flower's otherness. The poem's first stanza conveys a hint of this revision in the selection of features for which the jasmine is valued:

> Orgullo de la enramada,
> Blanca y leve florecilla,
> Más que todas delicada,
> Y más que todas sencilla. (66)

Pride of the arbor, brief white flower, the most delicate of all, and the simplest of all.

Simplicity, delicacy, purity—these are qualities associated with feminine virtue rather than erotic appeal; as values, they correspond to a desire on the part of the lyrical subject to construct a positive—that is, appropriately gender coded—image of herself. The reiteration of these image motifs as values halfway through the poem reads like a conduct book's assurance to girls that they will be better rewarded for modesty than for ostentation:

> Por sencilla y delicada,
> En el jardín entre ciento
> Fijas tú, flor, la mirada,
> Y fijas el pensamiento. (67)

Because of your simplicity and delicacy, flower, looks and thoughts fasten on you among a hundred in the garden.

When the poem closes with a repetition of this stanza, however, a slight variation in the last two verses reduces the distance between the lyricist and her object by characterizing the speaking self specifically in its relation to the flower: "Se fija en ti, florecilla, / Mi vista y mi pensamiento" 'My sight and my thoughts fasten on you, little flower' (68). The intimacy of tone produced by the diminutive and the change from the impersonal article to the possessive creates a close association between woman poet and jasmine flower by suggesting the sympathy of like natures. Unlike the male poets, who associated the flower with the female body as an erotic object (either by abstracting the qualities of short-lived sensory attractiveness or using the proximity of the flower to the woman's body as its adornment), Coronado establishes the figurative bond of woman and flower as a pathetic fallacy, the projection of subjectivity.

Thus, although Coronado's flower poems do not challenge the dominant ideology of gender—indeed, they utilize the values coded as feminine as positive materials for the construction of the lyrical subject—they transform the value of the feminine in the poetic tradition into which they are inserted by producing the image of the woman as subject. The intimacy between poetic subject and object established in "Al jazmín" characterizes all the flower poems. Presenting themselves as a special insight about the flowers' quality of existence, these poems imply a kind of shared subjectivity between the speaking "I" and the object it addresses: reading the flowers' secret language, the poet discloses her own emotional life. The lyricist empathizes, for example, with the lonely poppy:

> Yo te vi, triste amapola,
> De las flores retirada
> Mecer la roja corola
> Entre la espiga dorada. (62)

I saw you, sad poppy, far away from the flowers swaying your red corolla among the golden spikes of wheat.

The last stanzas provide the key to the poppy's sadness: not only is its life brief, but "tu aureola / Pura luciente / Desconocida / Muere también" 'your pure, shining halo dies unknown as well' (64). The same theme surfaces in "Al lirio," when the poet questions the wild iris:

¿Qué te vale ese prendido
De celeste brillantez,
Si ignorado y escondido,
En los desiertos perdido
Ha de hallarte la vejez? (75)

What good does that celestial blue adornment do you, if old age must find
you unknown and hidden, lost in the desert?

As the lyricist's projective empathy reveals the configurations of her
subjectivity, we see the outlines of a tension between identity and desire. If, on the one hand, the self is identified with the retiring delicacy
of the jasmine, the shy modesty of wildflowers—both floral analogies
of the angel-woman of contemporary ideology—then, on the other
hand, the self is also tinged with a unladylike ambition through the
irises' painful regret for the obscurity of their destiny.

The most original and dramatic of the flower poems, "El girasol,"
elaborates precisely this tension between desire and female identity.
Enumerating the beauties of the night, the lyricist identifies herself with
most of the flowers in the garden, who are glad for the dark coolness
after a hot day. But the sunflower languishes in this obscurity, waiting
for dawn and the sun, "coronado / De abrasadoras llamas" 'crowned
with burning flames' (70). Though this lover inflames the earth around
the flower, "[m]írasle fija; y de su rayo apuras / El encendido fuego que
derrama" 'you look at him fixedly; and drink to the last drop the burning fire he sheds' (71). The lyricist, firmly ensconced in her identification with the ladylike flowers who retire from the sun, admonishes the
flower that her passion is self-destructive: "¡Ay triste flor! que su reflejo
abrasa / Voraz, y extingue tu preciosa vida. . . . / Presto sin vida, seca
y deshojada / Caerás deshecha, en polvo convertida" 'Oh, sad flower!
Its reflection voraciously consumes and extinguishes your precious life.
. . . Soon, lifeless, you will disintegrate, dry and defoliated, turned to
dust' (71). This representation of desire inverts the terms of the baroque poems of Rioja; here it is the flower/woman who is destroyed
by her attraction to the male, figured according to traditional patriarchal codes as spirit and energy, not as flesh.

In the conclusion of the poem, however, ambition displaces sexual desire as the connoted referent of the sunflower's death-dealing
passion:

¿Qué valió tu ambición, por más que el vuelo
Del altanero orgullo remontaste?

Tu mísera raíz murió en el suelo,
Y ese sol tan hermoso que adoraste,

Sobre tus tristes fúnebres despojos
Mañana pasará desde la cumbre.—
Ni a contemplar se detendrán sus ojos
Que te abrasaste por amor su lumbre. (72)

However high you mounted on the wing of your arrogant pride, what good
did your ambition do you? Your wretched root died in the earth, and tomorrow that beautiful sun you adored will pass on high over your sad, funereal
remains. His eyes will not even pause to consider that you consumed yourself for love of his light.

Though the sun can still with some effort be construed as the flaming
consummation of sexual desire—in which case the poem would seem
to reiterate the conventional warning to women against the seducer
who ruins and abandons—the language here invites us to reinterpret
the sun as an Apollo-like figure of poetic glory. In this case, "El girasol" reverberates with the sonnet on the eagle and the bee, providing
a veiled explanation of the female poet's choice not to attempt to follow the eagle's flight: no matter how high her ambition takes her, glory
eludes the woman; rooted in her feminine condition, she is bound to
die in obscurity.

It is hardly surprising that Coronado should conflate erotic desire
with ambition as destructive to women, given the contemporary association of female writing with immorality that I examined in chapter 2.
"El girasol" allows us to see, however, how Coronado converts the culturally demanded repression of feminine desire into the constitutive
tension of her expression of female subjectivity. The strain of root
against wing that consumes the sunflower (at one point in the poem,
leaves are figuratively transformed into wings) later became Coronado's predilect image of the female poet's mode of being. Its analogue
at the level of the organization of lyrical discourse is the simultaneous
separation and identity of the lyrical voice and the object addressed.
The self speaks to the flower from a position grounded in the ideology
of feminine identity, though it comprehends only too readily the flower's passion, which reflects the desires the self must repress to preserve
its secure identity.

In rewriting earlier masculine versions of this genre, then, Coronado
charged the lyrical relation of poet and flower with new meaning, discovering the means of constructing the female self as a subjectivity

at odds with itself. While accepting predominant definitions of femininity—and for this reason rejecting certain self-aggrandizing models of the Romantic poet—she developed a poetic discourse based on the strains and contradictions that the female position in her culture generated in the female subject. We will see that as she set her poetic aspiration, her sense of the value of expressing female experience, against the requisite feminine modesty, her poetry exhibited the drama of a conflict between voice and silence, between the authority of women's experience and the social subordination and consequent devaluation of the female.

BEYOND THE CODES: THE OTHER SELF

The conventionally feminine modesty and innocence adopted by the "I" speaking in the 1843 *Poesías* created expectations of unproblematic humility and gentleness that the collection did not always meet. Hartzenbusch's introductory comments on this volume acknowledged an occasional note of unfeminine energy, though Coronado's mentor generally characterized the lyrical subjectivity expressed in her work as "templada vehemencia" 'temperate complaint' (ix) and "manso correr de sus lagrimas" 'docile flowing of tears' (x).

In "A la palma," the very early poem that won Espronceda's homage, the lyricist reveals the obverse side of the humility she professes in the sonnet on the eagle and the bee. Referring to the use of the palm fronds as an emblem of honor, she confesses to a fantasy that links her with the aspiring sunflower:

> Si una hoja solamente
> Ciñera yo a mi frente
> Que acallara el afán del alma mía;
> . . . .
> Allí en el trono que el Señor levanta
> Te viera yo a mi planta. (16)

If I could circle my brow with just one leaf that would satisfy my soul's desire, . . . from the throne that the Lord raises high, I would see you at my feet.

The modest self-deprecation through which the lyrical "I" affirms its adherence to the codes of femininity quickly masks this fantasy of rising high above the rest, however, declaring it "[d]elirio nada más" 'merely delirium.' As the poet matured and mastered the strategies through which so many women writers tailored their self-representations to social convention, she never again quite so transparently revealed the desire that propelled her writing. She did, however, later find new ways of modifying that unladylike desire for preeminence by extending it to all of her sister poets, as we shall see when we discuss her second book.

Suppressed ambition is not the only unladylike emotion to make itself felt in the poetic voice of the 1843 *Poesías*. A white-hot, accusing rage burns in "El marido verdugo," a poem on the physical brutality of husbands toward wives. Though the violence of this poem's thematic material and the scathing sarcasm of its tone mark a shocking departure from the pastoral tradition in which most of the volume is written, the opening of the poem refers back to the *topos* that contrasts the savagery of human society with the harmony of nature. Some may fear the animals of the wild, the poet asserts, but "¡[m]ás feroces dañinas alimañas / La madre sociedad nutre en su seno!" 'mother society nourishes in her breast more ferocious, harmful beasts!' (45). And in condemning violence toward women as her specific topic, she does not mince words. Abandoning the refined imagery culled from neoclassical poetry, the poet designates wife beaters as society's brutes, "[q]ue ceban el placer de sus sentidos / En el llanto infeliz de las mujeres" 'who excite the pleasure of their senses with the unhappy weeping of women' (45). She scornfully points out that these men do not test their bravery on the field of battle: their "glorious deeds" are executed on their trembling wives. The indignant poet calls attention to the physical evidence of male brutality, describing the contusions of the beaten wife in a language that scarcely concedes to poetic diction:

> Que a veces sobre el seno transparente
> Cárdenas huellas de sus dedos halla;
> Que a veces brotan de su blanca frente
> Sangre las venas que su esposo estalla. (46)

For sometimes the purple marks of his fingers remain on her transparent breast; for sometimes the veins her husband has broken ooze blood on her white brow.

Although a remote literary precedent for this poem can be found in George Sand's *Indiana,* which describes with only slightly periphrastic language the injuries Colonel Delmare inflicts on his wife, these verses read like an outburst of indignation and horror that is only with difficulty fit into poetic form. The emotion seems to spring from a sense of common female experience that lies beyond conventional literary discourse, and whose powerfully felt reality demands expression. What causes Coronado to break out of the modest docility through which she usually signaled her femininity is a consciousness of a victimization shared by women. Here we see the possibility of a female identity that was more compelling to Coronado than defensive conformity to socially dictated codes.

The poem that Hartzenbusch declined to include in the 1843 volume (see chapter 2) provides explicit evidence of Coronado's early sense of identity with women's experience of oppression. In a letter dated 31 December 1842 (196), Coronado sent Hartzenbusch an untitled poem that had mistakenly been left out of the manuscript whose publication he was arranging. The first stanza announces the main theme: the female poet cannot express her inner pain for fear of being laughed at in a society that devalues and disparages female experience. As she states a few stanza's later, "Si llora joven doncella / es necia peurilidad" 'If a young maiden weeps, it is foolish childishness' (Fonseca 179). The poem goes on to argue that only emotions and griefs having to do with money, power, and related male enterprises are taken seriously. Figuring men as "libres azores" 'free falcons,' she accuses them of egotistical blindness to "la estrecha jaula" 'the narrow cage' that encloses the sighing doves (180).

A second theme of the poem ironically subverts men's claims to greatness by considering male enterprise from a woman's perspective:

> Diocesillos imprudentes
> que alzando grandes ciudades,
> fuertes muros, arcos, puentes
> legan a sus descendientes
> miseria y calamidades. (180)

Imprudent little gods, who in raising great cities, strong walls, arches, bridges, bequeath poverty and calamity to their descendents.

This irreverent questioning of the values produced by male domination of society leads her back to the impact of this domination on female self-expression. Observing that despite their failures, men have wings and air (the wing image again as a figure for the capacity to transcend limitation), the poet points out that "la mujer en su aflicción, / ¡ay!, no tiene ni un acento / para llorar un momento / los hierros de su prisión" 'woman in her affliction has not one accent with which to grieve a moment over the bars of her prison' (180). The final stanza sums up the repression of the female voice in personal terms:

> Que el temor de ver reído
> por otros mi mal llorado
> en el corazón herido
> tiene el dolor comprimido,
> tiene el llanto sofocado. (181)

The fear of seeing the expression of my malady laughed at by others keeps pain compressed in my wounded heart, suffocates my weeping.

Thus this poem, at once a protest against male power and an account of the difficult situation of the woman poet, explicitly links male domination of society to cultural and psychological controls that inhibit women's self-expression.[6] The fate of the poem itself dramatically exemplifies Coronado's complaint: her male mentor, Hartzenbusch, suppressed this open protest at the silence enjoined on women by deciding not to publish it in the 1843 collection.

Hartzenbusch very likely would have defended his decision by claiming that it was based on the formal quality of the poem, not on its theme, for the suppressed poem is less graceful, less unified and balanced, than the poems that met with Hartzenbusch's approbation in the *Poesías*. The poem's two main themes—the silencing of women's pain and the disastrous consequences of masculine values and power—remain rather unintegrated; their connection is not fully worked out either logically or figuratively. The mode of lyrical lament associated with the first theme contrasts sharply with the satirical, almost scornful tone of the critique of male values. The poem thus conveys an uneasiness, a sense of conflicting perspectives, that is absent from the smoothly coherent poems that adapt conventional pastoral models to the feminine voice. The suppressed poem conveys formally as well as thematically the woman poet's difficulty in finding a poetic language adequate to the female experience of subordination, an experience in which, the poem suggests, fear, pain, anger, self-esteem, and self-doubt mix and alternate unevenly. The speaking subject moves jerkily between three modes—a self-deprecating confession of her fear of scorn, a protestation at the pain produced by repressing emotion, and a self-justifying anger that ridicules masculine power—as if trying and abandoning a series of never entirely suitable poetic forms and modes.

In at least one poem of the 1843 collection Coronado did find a way to suggest obliquely, through an oracular juxtaposition of conventional figures, the quality and structures of silenced female subjectivity. "Rosa Bianca" (or "Rosa Blanca," as it is spelled in the 1852 edition)[7] reverses the terms of the basic figure in the flower poems: here the object of poetic meditation is a woman, not a flower, and the poem dramatizes her objectification by figuratively associating her with the flower (in contrast to the other poems' personification of the flower). This is one of the few poems in the volume—indeed, in Coronado's entire opus— that does not directly incorporate the speaking subject as a first person within the text. The poem is a sort of narration: the first seven stanzas describe and speculate about the distracted wanderings of Rosa Bianca under the poplars; the next four stanzas narrate what may or may not be her history; and two concluding stanzas present her again, mute and distracted, in the grove. The impersonality of the lyrical voice accentuates its distance from Rosa Bianca, who, like the flower her name invokes, can be seen only from the outside because she is mute.

In the first part of the poem, the speaker closely observes the woman's movements. She has not slowed her step, "indiferente y errante" 'indifferent and erratic' (100), to watch the sunset,

> [n]i de la noche llegada
> A las tinieblas atiende,
> Ni objeto alguno suspende
> Su turbia incierta mirada. (100)

nor does she pay attention to night's darkness when it comes, nor does any object arrest her opaque, uncertain glance.

But there are few external indications of what might be going on in Rosa Bianca's consciousness, for no tears, no words, not even "un suspiro mal ahogado" 'a badly suppressed sigh' (100) reveals what she might be suffering. The observing subject can only speculate that Rosa Bianca has no form of expression (tears, sobs) commensurate with her inner pain: "¡Tal vez sus ojos rendidos / Están, de mal tan llorado!" 'Perhaps her eyes are exhausted by a sorrow so long wept over!' (100). Or perhaps her very consciousness, her subjectivity, has been blasted:

> Tal vez no hay un pensamiento
> En su cabeza marchita,
> Y en brazos del desaliento
> Ni oye, ni ve, ni medita. (100–101)

Perhaps there is no thought in her weakened head, and in the arms of depression [spiritlessness] she cannot hear, or see, or reflect.

Rosa Bianca, then, at present exists in a state not unlike that of the flowers the poet addressed earlier in the volume: mute, giving no sign that other objects exist for her or even that she exists for herself. Her subjectivity is simply a figurative construction of external poetic observation.

The poetic narrative shifts abruptly at this point, moving from present to past tense and changing the scene to suggest a kind of explanatory flashback. The text gives us no cues about the source of the narrative fragments that follow in an eerily uncontextualized sequence of images:

> El poeta "suave rosa"
> Llamóla, muerto de amores....
> ¡El poeta es mariposa
> Que adula todas las flores!
>   ¡Bella es la azucena pura!
> ¡Dulce la aroma olorosa!
> Y la postrera hermosura
> Es siempre la más hermosa.
>   En sus amantes desvelos
> La envidiaron las doncellas:
> Mas, ¡ay! son para los celos
> Todas las rivales bellas.
>   Vióse en transparente espejo
> Linda la joven cabeza;
> Mas tal vez dio en su reflejo
> Su vanidad la belleza. (101; lines 29–44)

The poet, dying of love, called her "soft rose"—The poet is a butterfly who adores all the flowers! Lovely is the pure lily, sweet its fragrant aroma! And the last beauty is always the most beautiful. The maidens envied her amorous troubles: but, oh! all rivals seem beautiful to the jealous. She saw her young head as lovely in the transparent mirror; but perhaps vanity supplied the beauty in her reflection.

Whether we take this as the poetic narrator's projection or as the "true" history of Rosa Bianca's malady, the outlines of a conventional love story are present: Rosa Bianca's anxious insecurity about a fickle lover has brought her to the pass described in the first part of the poem. Yet the reverberations among the dominant images through which the story is sketched suggest that under the narrative cliché of feminine vulnerability lies a rather different story, giving the poem the palimpsestic structure that Gilbert and Gubar find in many English women writers.[8] The relationships between male poet and flower, mirror and silence, provide the key to this second story, an allegory about Coronado's difficulty with the dominant poetic language. Women's own reality is covered over, suppressed by the poetic language that names them as flowers. Even Rosa Bianca's given name, so close to "suave rosa," the epithet that "el poeta" uses for her, covers her identity with a metaphor. The language of lines 31–34 almost parodically echoes that of two male-authored poems that Coronado knew well—the sonnet in which Espronceda designated her the flower and himself the insect, and the passage on the lily, cited above, from Meléndez Valdés's poem on flowers—as if to evoke within the text, but from a certain distance, the verbal conventions that identified women as beautiful, and interchangeable, objects, even to themselves. No wonder Rosa Bianca is tormented by anguished uncertainty about her status, for if she looks into the mirror of the poets' language to find and to know herself, she can only see herself reflected as some other object.

Rosa Bianca's response is to reject the mirror of language, to remain mute herself and to shun the image reflected by others:

> ¿Y qué importa si es hermosa?
> Sola, muda y abismada
> Sólo busca la apartada
> Arboleda silenciosa. (102; lines 45–48)

And what does it matter if she is beautiful? Alone, silent, and sunk in pain she only seeks out the remote, silent grove.

The price Rosa Bianca pays for her refusal of language, however, is not only her suppressed pain but also her self-alienation, which the concluding verse emphasizes through reiteration: "Ni oye, ni ve, ni medita" 'She cannot hear, or see, or reflect' (102). In telling us of Rosa Bianca's plight, the lyrical subject, whose use of the word and whose projective consciousness differentiate her from the poetic protagonist, indicates that though she recognizes the objectifying dangers poetic language poses for the woman, she will not renounce language as a means of communicating the female experience concealed by established literary convention. Indeed, "Rosa Bianca" is one of Coronado's most successful attempts to convey the alienating effects of cultural objectification of women, perhaps because in this poem she found a way to use conventional poetic language against itself.

Such evidence of Carolina Coronado's perception that male-authored poetic conventions suppressed female subjectivity just as women's subordinate status inhibited their self-expression helps to explain the significance of female precursors in her poetic project. Although

there is no sign that Coronado found an existing female poetic tradition on which she could draw (if Gómez de Avellaneda, in contrast, did
inscribe herself within a female tradition, we must remember that it
was a *narrative* tradition), she did give considerable weight to the example of a woman creator of poetic tradition and language, Sappho.
While she despaired of being able to write in the tradition of Sapphic
verse, accessible only to those possessed of the classical education reserved for men (see her letter to Hartzenbusch cited in chapter 2), Coronado did find vital inspiration in the myth of Sappho,[9] the story of a
universally acclaimed poetess whose songs gave language to female experience. In the 1843 collection, "Los cantos de Safo" stand at the
center of the volume. In these four songs, plus a companion piece titled
"El salto de Leucades," the lyrical voice assumes the persona of Sappho
and is thus able to speak as a woman from a position of poetic authority outside the modest innocence that Spanish culture designated the
only valid ground of feminine subjectivity.

Speaking as Sappho, Coronado can openly avow ambition and pride
in her talent as attributes of the female subject:

> Y citara en mis manos peregrina
> Las hermanas de Febo colocaron,
> Y de entusiasmo el corazón llenaron,
> De amor ardiente e inspiración divina.
>
> . . . .
>
> Yo a esa Grecia opulenta, sabia, y justa
> Arrancaré un aplauso duradero;
> Una corona como el grande Homero
> A mis sienes tal vez ceñiré augusta. (50–52)

And the sisters of Phoebus placed a rare citara in my hands, and filled my
heart with ardent love and divine inspiration. . . . From that rich, wise, and
just Greece I will win lasting applause; perhaps I will encircle my temples
with an august crown like that of great Homer.

And, like Gómez de Avellaneda when she adopted the persona of Sappho, Coronado can also speak the erotic passion forbidden to the middle-class nineteenth-century Spanish woman. A good part of the songs
of Coronado's Sappho are devoted to the pleasures and pains of her
love for a man, Phaon, whose fickleness fans the flame of her longing
and leads to her suicidal leap from the rock into the sea. In the guise
of Sappho, then, Coronado lays claim for the female subject to a wide
gamut of the feelings expressed by the male Romantic poet: the erotic
desire for the sexual other (Coronado is following a tradition that sup-

poses Sappho's love object to be a man, Phaon), the aspiration to transcendent poetic power, the refusal to accept reality's negation of desire.

The experiences that structure the poetic subjectivity of the "Cantos" correspond, however, to those of Mme de Staël's feminized model of the Romantic poet, Corinne, even though Coronado's lyrical subject and protagonist names herself Sappho. The implied story that gives "Los cantos de Safo" its dramatic shape is not so much based on the tradition of legends surrounding the figure of Sappho, whose poetry expressed the erotic passion of a woman for other women, as it is on the myth crystallized in *Corinne ou l'Italie,* the myth of the female genius and the excision of love from creative fulfillment. The trajectory of Coronado's Sappho closely follows that of Corinne. The first song, like the first part of *Corinne,* shows the protagonist secure in her recognized creative powers while enjoying reciprocated passion for a male lover. But in the succeeding songs, as in the novel, the woman poet loses her lover to a woman who plays the passive female role of object, and her suffering from this abandonment eclipses her poetic powers and leads to her death. Coronado slightly alters the terms of the bind that captures the woman poet; instead of posing the opposition as that between the dark and brilliant Corinne and the blond, conventionally ladylike Lucile, Coronado's lyricist presents it as the binary of talent and beauty. Sappho confesses that she is not beautiful, but counts her genius as an even higher value, one that cannot perish, as physical beauty does. But talent loses its value for her when she discovers that Phaon prefers beauty. She begs Venus:

> Dame atractivos, dame esa ilusoria
> Forma y hechizos con tu luz tocados;
> ¡Y quítenme los Dioses irritados
> Mi citara, mis cantos y mi gloria! (53)

Give me attractions, give me that illusory form and charms touched by your light; and let the irritated Gods take away my citara, my songs, and my glory!

Although Coronado couches Sappho's dilemma in terms inherited from a convention that has its roots in antiquity—the contrast between mortal flesh and immortal fame—the context of the lyricist's reactions gives it new meaning. Both Mme de Staël and Carolina Coronado construct female subjectivity upon the need for recognition by the male other. It is annihilated when the woman is not corroborated and desired as subject—that is, as the active, creating, speaking subject of poetry—but as an object, the beautiful body preferred by Phaon, or the selfless robot chosen by Oswald.

Faced with this sort of negation, the female poetic subject created by Coronado in the image of Sappho responds, as Corrine does, with self-obliteration. In contrast to the "Cantos," "El salto de Leucades" is narrated in the third person. Sappho's voice first becomes incomprehensible, then disappears as she throws herself, "misteriosas palabras murmurando" 'murmuring mysterious words' (56), into the void: "Giró un punto en el éter vacilante; / Luego en las aguas se desploma y hunde" 'She rotates a moment in the unfirm ether, then collapses and sinks under the waters' (56). Thus, even when Coronado empowers herself, by adopting the persona of a glorious though remote woman poet, to speak the poetic ambitions forbidden to women, she ultimately represents the drowning of the female voice in a culture that negates self-generating feminine subjectivity.

The 1843 *Poesías,* then, represents the emergence of a female identity that does not strictly correspond to the culturally approved "feminine" attributes behind which Coronado's lyrical persona often took shelter. In fact, as we have seen, many of these early poems enact a kind of drama in which a repressed female experience is trying to speak through, or past, a poetic mask constructed in conformity to ideological models of femininity. This struggle against the suffocation of a female voice in these poems struck chords of response in women readers like Vicenta García Miranda and Encarnación Calero de los Ríos (see chapter 2). After the successful publication of her book and its positive reception, Coronado more clearly defined her poetic project as that of giving voice to the pain and dissatisfaction that women experienced in the role society had assigned them.

REWRITING WOMEN'S EXPERIENCE

Carolina Coronado never published the poem that Hartzenbusch decided not to include in the 1843 collection of her poetry. Yet a major share of the poems she wrote in the next few years closely followed the model of that suppressed poem, explicitly characterizing women's experience as one of suffering and repression. The ambiguous, double-voiced discourse of the flower poems was replaced by a more direct and even discursive poetry that expressed conflict and duality in explicit images for female experience.

Between 1844 and 1847, years in which Coronado was in contact with a number of other women poets who had just begun to publish (the lyrical sisterhood discussed in chapter 2), many of the poems she contributed to periodicals were very outspoken on the theme of women's oppression. Although the revisions of these poems for the 1852 *Poesías*[10] eliminated topical allusions, impassioned laments about women's subordinate position remained. For example, "A Lidia," dated 1845 in the 1852 edition, begins:

> Error, mísero error, Lidia, si dicen
> Los hombres que son justos, nos mintieron,
> No hay leyes que sus yugos autoricen.
>
> ¿Es justa esclavitud la que nos dieron,
> Justo el olvido ingrato en que nos tienen? (100)

It is an error, a wretched error, Lydia, if they say men are just, they lied to us; there are no laws that authorize their yoke. Is the slavery they have given us just? Is their ungrateful forgetfulness of our needs just?

Less explicit references to this social oppression are interwoven in the imagery and intertextual resonances even of poems not addressed to women's journals and other women poets.

A particularly forceful elaboration of a figure central to Coronado's expression of women's experience is found in the poem that concludes a section of superficially tender but tacitly resentful songs addressed to the poet's younger brother, Emilio. Titled "Ultimo canto," the poem uses an image associated with the boy's play to figure the constraints that smother the lyricist's poetic voice:

> Cuando aspira todo el viento
> Que circula en su fanal,
>   El insecto que aprisionas
> En su cóncavo perece
> Si aire nuevo no aparece
> Bajo el cerrado cristal. (30)

When it has breathed all the air that circulates in its bell jar, the insect that you imprison in its concavity will perish if new air does not appear under the glass enclosure.

The rhyme *fanal-cristal* and the idea of enclosure in glass create an intertextual echo with a key passage in Espronceda's *El diablo mundo*, published in 1842, some four years before the date given for Coronado's poem. Espronceda's protagonist, Adán, compares his situation—desiring what is beyond his reach—with that of a goldfish in a bowl. "¿Vistes aquel pez dorado / Que en tu casa en un fanal, / Breve lago de cristal, / Da vueltas aprisionado?" 'Did you see that goldfish in your house that in a glass jar, small crystal lake, swims round and round imprisoned?' (266), Adán asks La Salada, his lover, adding that just as the goldfish seems to want to break past the glass to enjoy the world it sees on the other side, so he longs to do things that he does not know how to make possible. Later, La Salada, apparently representing a constraining female reality principle, tells Adán that if he escaped from his own element, he, like the fish, would die. In rewriting Espronceda's figure of Romantic Promethean desire for the female lyrical subject, Coronado makes some significant modifications. In her poem the feminine voice does not warn of death as a result of overstepping boundaries but instead announces the suffocating consequences of the enclosure imposed on women. For Espronceda the bell jar represents the metaphysical limits of man's condition; for Coronado it represents the socially dictated constraints that smother women's spiritual life.

What is particularly interesting about "Ultimo canto" is that it rewrites Coronado's earlier poetry by including within the figure of female enclaustration the natural *locus amoenus* that had provided the lyricist of the 1843 *Poesías* with an escape from the domestic circle. In this poem, the outdoor haunts of 1843 are made expressly analogous to the bell jar:

> Celebré de mis campiñas
> Las flores que allí brotaron
> Y las aves que pasaron
> Y los arroyos que hallé,
>   Mas de arroyos, flores y aves
> Fatigado el pensamiento
> En mi prisión sin aliento
> Como el insecto quedé. (30–31)

I celebrated my countryside, the flowers that budded there, and the birds that passed by and the streams that I found, but my thought exhausted by streams, flowers, and birds, I've remained in my airless prison like the insect.

Unable to explore the larger world—"Mar, ciudades, campos bellos" 'Sea, cities, beautiful fields' (31)—the poet finds the limited circle of her previous "feminine" poetic inspiration to be claustrophobic. Metonymically associating the insect in the glass jar with the bee that earlier had figured the limits of the female poetic project, the lyricist declares,

"Agoté como la abeja / De estos campos los primores" 'I exhausted like the bee the beauties of these fields' (31).

Now she is unwilling to concede high-flying poetic power to men exclusively, but sees herself as an eagle:

> Tal ansiedad me consume,
> Tal condición me quebranta,
> Roca inmóvil es mi planta,
> Aguila rauda mi ser. . . .
>   ¡Muera el águila a la roca
> Por ambas alas sujeta;
> Mi espíritu de poeta
> A mis plantas de mujer!—
>   Pues tras de nuevos perfumes
> No puede volar mi mente. (31)

Such anxiety consumes me, such a condition splits me: my feet form an immobile rock, my being is a swift eagle. . . . Let the eagle die bound to the rock by both wings, my poet's spirit to my woman's feet, since my mind cannot fly in search of new perfumes.

The opposition between the winged and the earthbound that had represented a gender distinction in the earlier poetry is here transformed into the internal tension that constitutes female lyrical subjectivity in Coronado's poetry from 1844 on. The female self is split between its creative powers and aspirations and its social condition as woman.

While "Ultimo canto" provides a key image of the female subject, its resolution of the tension between desire and constraint through the death of the eagle, the suffocation of the poet, does not reflect the predominant trend of the 1852 *Poesías*. Poems that deal explicitly with female subjectivity far more frequently stress the necessity of self-expression, even against social opposition. In "Cantad, hermosas," one of the 1845 poems addressed to other women poets, Coronado associates the silence that had been enforced on women with suffocation:

> Aquellas mudas turbas de mujeres,
> Que penas y placeres
> En silencioso tedio consumían,
> Ahogando en su existencia
> Su viva inteligencia,
> Su ardiente genio, ¡cuánto sufrirían! (97)

Those mute crowds of women who consumed their pains and pleasures in silent tedium, smothering in their daily life their lively intelligence, their ardent genius, how they must have suffered!

She acknowledges gratefully that writing and publishing poetry has allowed her to break out of that claustrophobic circle:

> ¡Oh, cuánto es más dichosa el alma mía,
> Desde que al arpa fía
> Sus hondos concentrados sentimientos!
> ¡Oh, cuánto alivio alcanzo,
> Desde que al aire lanzo,
> Con expansión cumplida, mis acentos! (98)

Oh, how much happier my soul is since I've confided to my harp its deep, concentrated feelings! Oh, how much relief I feel since in fulfilled expansiveness I've launched my accents upon the wind!

One image of expanding possibilities, then, opposes all the images of constriction or confinement that Coronado associates with female experience: "expansión cumplida" refers not just to writing but to publication, to communication, and to public, recognized self-creation. "Hondos concentrados sentimientos" repressed within do not constitute a subject in Coronado's poetic discourse; instead they stagnate ("los pensamientos oprimidos / . . . ulceran los sentidos" 'oppressed thoughts . . . ulcerate the senses' [98]), alienating the subject from herself, as in the case of the mute Rosa Bianca. The anxiety produced by her culture's hostility to women writers, however, does not allow Coronado to end this poem, which invites women to write and publish, with this bold declaration of the necessity of women's creative agency. In her last stanzas she concedes to paternalistic concerns about feminine "purity" by warning women "sin inocencia y sin virtudes" 'without innocence and without virtues' against writing.

In acknowledging that women of Coronado's day had the option of publishing, while women of previous ages did not, "Cantad, hermosas" suggests that the tension between creative impulse and female condition is mediated by history. Indeed, the poetry written after 1843 shows Coronado's growing preoccupation with historical developments (in a series of poems dated 1848, for example, she reflects on the revolutionary turbulence of that year in most of Europe) and how they affected women. The male members of the Coronado family were protagonists of the struggle for liberal reform that had recently achieved significant changes in Spanish political and legal structures; Carolina's own sympathies were strongly liberal (Muñoz de San Pedro 21). Yet in her writing, when she confronted the historical gains of liberalism with the oppression and suppression of women that she had been protesting, the result was on occasion a feminist critique of liberalism that had much in common with Gómez de Avellaneda's *Sab.*

A remarkable poem, written in a satirical mode that no doubt surprised those who associated her poetry with flowers and birds, puts this critique in sharp focus by asking women to consider just what the liberal revolution has done for them. "Libertad" begins with a skeptical look at the rejoicing men:

> Risueños están los mozos,
> gozosos están los viejos
> porque dicen, compañeras,
> que hay libertad para el pueblo. (71–72)

The young men are smiling, the old ones are happy, because they say, *compañeras,* that there is freedom for the people.

She then goes on to give the woman's perspective on the political triumph of the liberal cause:

> ¡*Libertad*! ¿qué nos importa?
> ¿qué ganamos, qué tendremos?
> ¿un encierro por *tribuna*
> y una aguja por *derecho*?
>   ¡*Libertad*! ¿de qué nos vale
> si son los tiranos nuestros
> no el yugo de los monarcas,
> el yugo de nuestro sexo?
>   .   .   .   .
>   ¡*Libertad*! ¡ay! para el llanto
> tuvímosla en todos tiempos;
> con los déspotas lloramos,
> con tribunos lloraremos. (72)

Freedom! What does it matter to us? What do we win, what will we have? A sequesterment for our speaking platform and a needle for our right? *Freedom!* What good will it do us, if we are tyrannized not by the monarch's yoke but the yoke of our sex? ... *Freedom!* Oh, we've always had it for weeping; under the despots we wept, under the tribunes we'll weep.

The irony created by opposing women's experience of unalleviated oppression to the rhetoric of progress undermines complacent liberal assertions. To the insistence that "igualdad hay en la patria, / libertad hay en el reino" 'there is equality in the fatherland, there is freedom in our country,' the poet replies:

> Pero os digo, compañeras,
> que la ley es sola de ellos,
> que las hembras no se cuentan
> ni hay Nación para este sexo. (72)

But I tell you, *compañeras,* that the law is theirs alone, that females aren't taken into account, nor is there a Nation for this sex.

This last line deftly recapitulates the rhetorical procedure that throughout the poem debunks the claim of liberal terminology to universal meaning: national sovereignty, a concept fundamental to liberal political programs, has no existence for the sex that is given no rights or representation in the political arena. Lightened by the swift-moving rhythms and subtle assonances of the ballad verse-form, the *romance,* Coronado's irony points with fine precision to the marginalization of women in the historical advance of Spanish liberalism.

In a later poem, "En el castillo de Salvatierra," Coronado returned to the question of women's relation to history. This poem claims for the woman poet the scene from which Romantic poets from Wordsworth ("Tinturn Abbey") to Hugo ("À Louis B.") launched their meditations on the universe, history, and the self, a scene that includes historic ruins and a height from which to survey the world. "¿Por qué vengo a estas torres olvidadas?" 'Why do I come to these forgotten towers?' (64) asks the woman lyricist in the first verse of her poem. For the old castle does not arouse in her reflections on Spain's imperial past and a renewed patriotism as it might for a man; instead, she queries the spirits of ancient Visigothic kings that may still inhabit the ruins about the women, slaves of both Moorish and feudal lords, who watered the towers with their tears. Is it not true, she asks,

> ¿que tras tantos siglos de combate
> Que empedraron de fósiles la tierra
> Subo a la misma torre de la Sierra
> Aún a pedir también nuestro rescate?
>   ¡Ay! Que desde aquellas hembras que cantaron
> Gimiendo, como yo, sobre esta almena,
> Ni un eslabón los siglos quebrantaron
> A nuestra anciana y bárbara cadena. (64)

that after so many centuries of combat that paved the earth with fossils, I climb to the same mountain tower to ask still again for our deliverance? Oh, since those women sang weeping like me from this turret, the centuries have not broken even one link of our ancient and barbaric chain.

Seeing the ruined castle and the ancient town beneath it as a grim re-
minder that history has made no change in "la eterna condición de
nuestras vidas" 'the eternal condition of our lives' (in context, the referent of "nuestras" is unmistakably "we women"), the lyricist looks
away from history, toward a personal transcendence figured in the
tower's lofty proximity to the sky.

Identifying with the doves that inhabit the tower, the lyricist claims
that "[n]o pudo el mundo sujetar mis alas, / He roto con mi pico
mis prisiones. / . . . Yo libre y sola . . . / Vengo a juntarme al campesino
bando / Para vivir con vuestra libre enseña" 'the world could not tie
down my wings; I have broken imprisoning bonds with my beak. . . . I,
alone and free, . . . come to join your rural band, to live under your free
emblem' (64). Taken at face value, this affirmation reads like a defiant
reversal of the image of the eagle in "Ultimo canto," its doomed poetic
spirit bound to the rock of women's inescapable historical condition.
The hubristic desire to break free of social bonds and rise far above the
rest, however, cannot be unequivocally assumed by the female subject.
The move from contemplation of a painful historical reality to a fantasy of spiritual freedom produces a distinct change of tone: the lyricist's anguished identification with women's suffering through the ages
gives way to whimsicality and growing self-directed irony as she elaborates the fantasy of escape. Her identification with the birds' soaring
freedom becomes ever more pointedly grandiose until it culminates in
the following stanzas:

> Por cima de las nubes nos hallamos,
> ¡Libertad en el cielo proclamemos!
> Las mismas nubes con los pies hollamos,
> Las alas en los cielos extendemos.
>   ¡Bajen hasta el profundo mis cadenas,
> Circule en el espacio el genio mio,
> Y haga sonar mi voz con alto brío
> La libertad triunfante en mis almenas! (64)

We find ourselves above the clouds; let us proclaim liberty in the sky!
Our feet tread on clouds themselves, our wings extend into the heavens. Let
my chains fall down to the depths, let my genius circle round in space
and let my voice make triumphant freedom resound vigorously from my
battlements!

This vision of the female poetic self breaking free from history and
becoming the voice of the very liberty history has denied her is immediately debunked. The very next verse indicates that an approaching

storm has driven the speaker from the tower toward nearby shelter. As the thunderstorm bursts around her, she appeals to God to rescue her from the heights, "porque ya creo / Que le falta a mi orgullo fortaleza! . . . Porque estoy aquí sola y—¡tengo miedo!" 'because now I see that my pride lacks fortitude! . . . because I'm alone here—and I'm afraid!' (64). Thus, the second part of the poem, which describes how the hubristic fantasy of transcendence is succeeded by the desire for secure mediocrity, tells the story of the woman poet's desires with a comic irony that clashes disconcertingly with the mood of feminist vindication that begins the poem. Coronado adopts the perspective of paternalistic critics like Hartzenbusch and Deville in treating the aspiration to a sublime freedom of the imagination and creative spirit—regarded as admirable in the male Romantic self—as untenable for the feminine self.

"En el castillo de Salvatierra" does not leave us with the bare contradictions of Coronado's ambivalence about women's liberation, however, for the lyricist's representation of the thunderstorm obliges us to place the source of her self-diminishing fear in the internalization of a patriarchal history. As the storm swirls around her, the lyricist's narrative becomes hallucinatory; the tower detaches itself from the earth and becomes a symbolic representation of phallic anger:

> La torre estalla desprendida al trueno—
> La sierra desaparece de su planta—
> La torre entre las nubes se levanta
> Llevando el rayo en su tonante seno.
>   El terrible fantasma hacia mí gira—
> Tronando me amenaza con su boca—
> Con ojos de relámpago me mira—
> Y su luz me deslumbra y me sofoca.
>   El rayo está a mis pies y en mi cabeza;
> Ya me ciega su lumbre, ya no veo. (64)

The clap of the thunder breaks the tower loose—The mountains at its foot disappear—The tower rises among the clouds, carrying the lightning bolt in its resounding cavity. The terrifying apparition turns toward me—Roaring, it threatens me with its mouth—It looks at me with eyes of lightning—and its light dazzles and suffocates me. The lightning bolt is at my feet and in my head; its glare blinds me, now I see nothing.

With its towers and its blinding lightning bolts, this dramatic, breathless passage mobilizes fundamental cultural images of the phallus and of castration. Masculine authority and power take, in the lyricist's perception, the aspect of an angry god who strikes down her self-assertive

pride, reenacting the castration that she had dared to disregard by seeking the sublime poetic power reserved for men. No wonder she is afraid
and backs down: the patriarchal lightning bolts strike in her head, in
her concept of herself, as well as at her feet.

The poem on Salvatierra Castle, then, provides some context for
Coronado's recurrent image of the strain between root and wing that
characterizes the subjectivity of the female poet. The poet's aspirations
to flight, freedom, poetic transcendence are held back by the dead
weight of her historical and social condition as woman, a condition
that is as integral to her psyche as the upward yearning. Although in
poems like "Libertad" and "En el castillo de Salvatierra" Coronado
implied that women's position of subordination had changed very little
despite the supposed progress of Western civilization, other poems
explore how the tide of history affected the forms in which the woman
poet experienced her existence. In "La flor del agua" she returns to
the flower/woman metaphor to elaborate a vision of the agonizing tensions to which her own century subjected women poets. In its first published version (*El Genio,* February 1845), this poem was dedicated
to Robustiana Armiño, a woman poet who had just appeared on the
literary scene: the water lily figures a collective experience, a shared
subjectivity.

The poem begins like Coronado's early flower poems; the first five
stanzas give an empathetic account of the water lily's mode of existence, its head pulled by the water's current against the roots anchored
in the riverbed:

> Ni el agua que sus pies ata
> Sostiene a la débil flor,
> Ni deja, en sus olas presa,
> Que vaya libre flotando,
> Quiere que viva luchando
> Siempre en continuo temblor. ("La flor" 194)[11]

Not even the water that binds her feet sustains the frail flower, nor does it
let her, taken by its waves, float free; it wants her to live in struggle, always,
continuously atremble.

Unlike the earlier poems, however, "La flor del agua" quickly supplies
the metaphorical link between flower and woman: "*Robustina,* flor
del Lago, / . . . / Has venido en mala hora / Con tu lira y tu pasión"
'*Robustina,* water lily, . . . you've come at a bad time with your lyre

and your passion' (194). Then the poet spells out why the contemporary woman poet must live like the water lily:

> Que las cantoras primeras
> Que a nuestra España venimos
> Por sólo cantar sufrimos,
> Penamos por sólo amar.
> Porque en la mente quimeras
> De un bello siglo traemos
> Y cuando este siglo vemos
> No sabemos dó bogar. (194)

For as the first women singers who come to our Spain, we suffer just for singing, we feel pain just for loving. Because in our minds we bring fantasies of a beautiful world, when we see this century's world, we don't know which way to sail.

Like butterflies hatched too early, she argues in the next stanzas, today's women poets struggle to survive in an unpropitious climate that future generations will be spared. The visions of a better world that pull the female poet against her roots, the poem seems to imply, have some prospects of realization. The problem for the poet and her sisters is that they are suspended in unavoidable tension between two worlds.

The individual poetic subject caught in this bind cannot withstand the tension. As we have seen in the previously examined poems, when the lyricist represents herself as a singular subject, one of the poles gives way, succumbing to the pull of the other; it is usually the eagle who dies bound to the stone, the timorous woman who suppresses her hubristic poetic spirit. "La flor del agua," however, constructs the lyrical subject as plural, a "we" rather than an "I." The poem's conclusion finds the antidote to the water lily's perpetual anxiety in the awareness of sharing a historical predicament that cannot yet be resolved:

> Mas escucha, no estás sola,
> Flor del agua en el riachuelo:
> Contigo en igual desvelo
> Hay florecillas también,
> Que reluchan contra el ola,
> Que vacilan, que se anegan,
> Que nunca libres navegan
> Ni en salvo su barca ven.
>   Pero enlazan sus raíces
> A la planta compañera,
> Y viven en la ribera

Sosteniéndose entre sí,
Y cual ellas más felices
Desde hoy serán nuestras vidas
Si las pasamos unidas,
Hermana, las dos así. (195)

But listen, you aren't alone, water lily in the stream: with you in equal
anxiety there are other little flowers that struggle against the wave, that
wobble, that go under, that never sail free or see their barks safe. But they
interlace their roots with those of their companion plant and live near the
bank supporting each other, and like theirs, our lives will be happier from
now on if we spend them, sister, united thus.

This poem works out in lyrical form the ethos of mutual support
exemplified in the lyrical sisterhood of the 1840s, the group of fledgling
women poets who encouraged each other by corresponding privately
and acknowledging each other's work in print. The guiding spirit of
this group, Coronado made her sense of the value of women's solidarity in suffering an integral part of her poetic construction of the female
subject.

The poetry written after 1843, then, makes manifest what was only
latent, semiconcealed, in the earlier writing: the female lyrical speaker
of Coronado's poems is both eagle *and* bee. Despite the renunciatory
gesture of the early sonnet "A mi tío Pedro Romero," the female poet
is no more willing to cede the whole poetic territory of the sublime, of
history, politics, and ethics to her male colleagues than she is able to
excise the corresponding scope of desire from the subjectivity that is
both motive and construct of her poetic activity. Ambition, aggressive
self-affirmation, awareness of injustice, adventurousness, scorn, anger:
all these emotions that the ideology of the *ángel del hogar* rejected as
unnatural and inappropriate in women were incorporated in one form
or another in the poetic self created in Coronado's poetry. But far from
simply ignoring the cultural and historical pressures to which women
were subject—that shaped women *as* subjects—she duplicated them
in the fundamental structuring of her poetic voice and textual image.
The pressure of the contemporary feminine ideal can be seen in Coronado's feminization of the poetic models of a male-dominated tradition, on the one hand, and in the recurrent image of the inhibiting
force of the female condition, on the other. The strain between the two
forces, between the pull of a poetic lust for experience, knowledge,
and achievement and the restraint of feminine socialization, became the

constitutive figure of the poet's subjectivity. In this sense, Coronado's poetic self is, like that of Gómez de Avellaneda, a divided self, a victim of the contradictions between the Romantic concept of the sovereign individual subject and the nineteenth-century ideology of gender.

7
Denying the Self

Cecilia Boehl and La gaviota

The powerful commitment of Gertrudis Gómez de Avellaneda and Carolina Coronado to make a space in the literary world for the woman writer was not necessarily shared by all women with similar interests and talents. Whereas these pioneering women contested in one form or another the emerging ideal of the domestic woman, albeit without rejecting it entirely, another option for women was to attempt to write from the position assigned them by gender ideology. Constructing a female subject of writing within the boundaries prescribed for the domestic angel was, however, inevitably a self-contradictory project, as the case of Cecilia Boehl, known to her public as Fernán Caballero, demonstrates.

The paradoxes of Boehl's position are evident in the barest facts of her relation to writing. Although she was the very first woman writer to be published in the Romantic press, she resolutely opposed women's participation in literary production. Having written privately for the entertainment of family and friends since an early age,[1] she protested when she saw one of her stories, "La madre, o el combate de Trafalgar," published in an 1835 issue of the Romantic journal *El Artista*. In a letter to the editors insisting that they publish no more of her work, she claimed that her mother had sent them the manuscript without consulting her and explained that her own convictions prohibited the publication of her writing:

[T]engo por íntimo convencimiento que el círculo que forma la esfera de una mujer, mientras más estrecho, más adecuado a su felicidad y a la de las personas que la rodean, y así jamás trataré de ensancharlo. . . . [N]o sólo no he pensado jamás en escribir para el público, sino que es mi sistema, tanto en teoría como en práctica, que más adorna la débil mano de una señora la aguja que no la pluma. (Valencina 45)

It is my deep conviction that the narrower the circle that forms a woman's sphere, the better suited to her happiness and that of those around her, and I will never attempt to widen it. . . . Not only have I never intended to write for the public, but further it is my system, as much in theory as in practice, that the fragile hand of a lady is better adorned by the needle than by the pen.

Although Boehl's belief in an ideology that consigned women to a strictly domestic sphere seems here to be based on an idea of "natural" sexual difference, the next paragraph of her letter offers the contradicting explanation that the separation of male and female spheres is a consequence of male social practices: "La severidad e intolerancia del *sexo fuerte* es la que ha creado la opinión general de ser incompatibles las calidades domésticas y las inclinaciones literarias" 'The severity and intolerance of the strong sex is what has created the general opinion that domestic capacities and literary inclinations are incompatible' (Valencina 45). Concluding that in such a situation no sensible woman would risk her domestic peace for the equivocal benefits of literary fame, Boehl suggests that her position on women's writing is perhaps more a matter of expedience rather than of absolute principle.

The fact that in 1849 Cecilia Boehl reversed her position, at least in practice, and began to publish with a vengeance—four novels in one year—attests then to the change in public opinion that Gómez de Avellaneda and the lyrical sisterhood had wrought in less than a decade. Male intolerance and severity toward women writers was no longer so formidable as in 1835. While the celebrity of Carolina Coronado had eliminated any doubt that a woman could publish literature and remain eminently respectable, the examples of Gertrudis Gómez de Avellaneda and Angela Grassi proved also that women could earn an income from their writing. For Cecilia Boehl, recently bankrupted by her third husband and always timorous about public opinion, the demonstrated acceptability and economic benefits of women's writing swung the balance in her decision to publish the manuscripts that she had accumulated over the years. This shift in her practice, however, did not entail a corresponding adjustment in the theory of gender difference that informed her work, which preached in flagrant contradiction to her own example the doctrine of feminine subordination and restriction to the domestic sphere.

Cecila Boehl's identification with the values embodied in the *ángel del hogar* as the image of feminine self-fulfillment placed her in direct opposition to the Romantic constructs of the self that Gómez de Avellaneda and Coronado adopted and modified. Indeed, the novels that Boehl published in 1849 can all be read as attempts to discredit Romantic ideas of self and the cultural revolution of which they were a function. Yet the enemy she combated reinsinuated itself at the very heart of her writing, contradicting and subverting her most cherished doctrines. This process is most pronounced in *La gaviota,* the first of the novels published in 1849 and the most ambitious as a representation and condemnation of the cultural revolution.

SOCIAL BOUNDARIES AS DOUBLE BINDS

Even after she had published many novels and was an established literary figure, acclaimed even beyond Spain's borders, Cecilia Boehl continued to insist that writing should be reserved for men. "La pluma, como la espada, se hizo para la fuerte mano del hombre" 'The pen, like the sword, was made for the strong hand of a man' (Montesinos, *Caballero* 109), she wrote in 1857 to Juan Eugenio Hartzenbusch, who, remaining unconvinced that writing was an exclusively male prerogative, acted as Boehl's mentor and agent in much the same way he had for Carolina Coronado. Despite this persistent view, Boehl not only used the pen but also flourished it aggressively in the war of political ideologies, for her militantly antiliberal novels were read by many contemporaries as right-wing provocations.[2] In order symbolically to uphold the law of gender difference, Boehl adopted the pen name Fernán Caballero with the intention of maintaining a radical distinction between this male personification of her writing activity and Cecilia Boehl, the woman. "Yo daría mi vida," she wrote ten years after publishing her first novel, "por haber podido lograr el que mis escritos y mi persona quedasen tan separados como la noche y el día!" 'I would give my life to have been able to keep my writing and my person as separate as day and night!' (Montesinos, *Caballero* 111). Although the secret of her personal identity proved impossible to keep, she insisted that correspondence about her work be addressed to

Fernán and refused interviews and public appearances in the name of Cecilia Boehl. The private letters that she signed as Cecilia criticize and mock Fernán as if he were an autonomous, other-gendered person.[3] This refusal to drop the fiction of the otherness of her identity as a writer signals the depth of Cecilia Boehl's anxiety about transgressing the boundaries that her culture imposed on feminine activity. Unable to give up her vocation as a writer despite her fear of social disapproval, she resorted to self-estrangement: to deny having stepped over the gender boundary, she severed herself in two.

The circumstances of Boehl's life help to explain why conflict about gender-determined roles might have been even more acute for her than it was for other women writers of her time. Disagreement concerning the rights of women was for her a family problem manifested in the simmering strife between her father, who detested female intellectuals, and her mother, whose vocation as an intellectual seemed irrepressible. Before they were married, Juan Nicolás Boehl tried to discourage his fiancée's penchant for study and debate by making the standard argument that intellectual endeavor corroded women's moral fiber: "I have never yet encountered a woman in whom the slightest intellectual superiority did not produce some more deficiency. The day that you burn [Mary Wollstonecraft's] *Rights of Women* will be a great day for me" (Herrero 39). Once they were married, Francisca Larrea seemed no more inclined to conform to her husband's expectations. Boehl complained to his mother-in-law of her independence of mind: "When she makes a conversion, when she becomes humble, docile, obedient, eager to please and economical, she will be received by me with open arms." In another letter he moaned, "if only she could go against her temperament and burn Mad. Wollstonecraft" (Carnero 80–81).

The unresolved situation surely confused young Cecilia: by all accounts her parents were bound together by strong loyalties and affection despite emphatic differences, and their separation for many years of their marriage was due not so much to a decision to live apart as to a failure to agree about where to live. Cecilia remained with her father during the separation and consciously adopted his point of view on women and on her mother, with whom she tended to have somewhat hostile relations. Nevertheless, we can infer a repressed identification with her mother's intellectual ambitions from Boehl's decision late in life to publish her work, which completed the agenda that Francisca had set for her daughter by sending the latter's short story out for publication in 1835.

Cecilia Boehl's circumstances placed her on both sides of social dividing lines other than gender. Not only was she half German, through her father, she also spent a good number of her formative years in a French girls' school in Germany. As a consequence, her cultural formation was more European than Spanish. Though her emotional identification with Spain remained passionate, she never became as comfortable in Castilian as she was in French; in fact she wrote most of her novels in French, and they had to be translated to be published in Spain. Boehl's class affiliation was as ambiguous as her nationality. Her father, whom she idolized, was a respected import-export merchant in Cádiz, a city whose commercial middle class was one of the more progressive political and economic forces in Spain at the time. Boehl von Faber, a man of solid bourgeois stock, dreamed of living like a landed aristocrat; his attempt to do so on an estate he purchased near Hamburg accounts for Cecilia's residence in Germany during her early years.[4] As an adolescent, Cecilia returned to Spain and moved in the social milieu of the commercial middle class of Cádiz until her second marriage (the first ended in widowhood after only a few months), to a rich Andalusian landowner whose title of nobility, though respectable, was of fairly recent vintage. By the time she began to publish her work, she was once again widowed and remarried, living in genteel poverty on the margin of the aristocratic circles in which she had earlier figured prominently.

Because she crossed in several ways the borders of nationality and class as well as of gender, the definition of her place in those categories became troublesome. Her pseudonym shows that in addition to inventing a fictional sexual identity, she sought to define herself in terms of class and nationality. Fernán (associated with Castilian kings and epics) Caballero (at once "knight" and "gentleman") covered her own name, marked as feminine and German, with one that was nostalgic, aristocratic, and Spanish as well as self-consciously masculine.

If Cecilia Boehl's position in Spanish society—marginal with regard to gender, nationality, and language, ambiguous with regard to class— helps to account for her anxiety about transgressing gender codes by writing, it also offers a key to her compulsion to continue writing. Whereas Avellaneda and Coronado wrote in some measure to expand in language their possibilities of existence, Boehl used her writing, as well as her pseudonym, as a means of symbolically fixing her unstable relation to the categories that organized Spanish society. Though her narratives, in contrast to the lyrical poetry of the other two women,

seem to focus on society and nature at the expense of self, these images
of the world of social meanings and practices define the writing subject's place in that world as the position from which it interprets and
communicates meaning.

FINDING A PLACE IN THE
WORLD OF WRITING

Because of Cecilia Boehl's deep conflicts about writing and publishing, her work has a peculiar gestational history that complicates the
task of determining how she situated herself as a writer with respect to
the universe of literature. As Javier Herrero reconstructs this history
(333–334), she began to write brief descriptions of local customs and
landscape around 1822, at the beginning of her marriage to the Marquiss of Arco-Hermoso, and by 1835, when he died, she had worked
these shorter pieces together into at least two novel-length narratives
that aimed at representing contemporary Spanish life. If these novels—
La familia de Alvarado and Elia—had been published when they were
written, not only would they have constituted an innovation in Spain,
but, according to José Montesinos, they would also have made her "a
great figure in the incipient European novel" (Prólogo 13). However,
only her family and a few friends knew of these works, which Boehl
put aside during the difficult years after 1835, when her parents' deaths
followed that of her husband.

Around 1842 she began earnestly to apply herself to writing again,
fashioning several of her best novels—including La gaviota—from the
materials she had accumulated during the previous decades. During
these years, as she began to conceive the option of publishing her
work, she thought of her novels in terms of a more ambitious framework, the Romantic realism of Balzac. Her creative vein more or less
exhausted by the end of the decade, when her novels started appearing
in print, Boehl formulated the defensive aesthetic position that characterized what she had to say about her own work. This history means
that Boehl's published texts were actually composed in contexts that
sometimes were quite different from the context in which they were
published. Such superimposition of context must be borne in mind as
we examine how this writer situates herself in the panorama of contemporary literature.

The primary gesture of Boehl's self-presentation as a writer is the
standard one for nineteenth-century women authors—modesty. The

first words with which she presented herself to the public, in the prologue of the serial edition of *La gaviota* in *El Heraldo,* are self-effacing:
"Apenas puede aspirar esta obrilla a los honores de la novela. . . . Para
escribirla no ha sido preciso más que recopilar y copiar" 'This little
work can scarcely aspire to the honor of being called a novel. . . . In
order to write it, it has not been necessary to do more than compile
and copy' (Caballero, *Gaviota* 63).[5] Yet these words do more than
make a conventional gesture of feminine modesty; they subtly indicate
her affiliation with a literary tradition that for her was first and fore-
most represented by her parents.

   Juan Nicolás Boehl had gained notoriety in the 1810s as the
polemicizing advocate of a conservative brand of German Romanticism
that found aesthetic and moral value united in whatever reflected the
traditional, organic *volkgeist* of Catholic Spain. A fervent convert to
Catholicism, Juan Nicolás believed liberal Spanish intellectuals and
writers had lost contact with a national culture that could be found
in its pure form in the traditional beliefs, customs, legends, and sayings
of the Andalusian peasants. Cecilia Boehl's mother shared these views
and, acting on her theoretical convictions, began to record scraps of
information—customs, remarks, tales, oral histories—that she gleaned
from contact with villagers and rural workers in her area. When Cecilia, newly married to Arco-Hermoso, went to live on his country
estate in an Andalusian village, she adopted her mother's practice, jot-
ting down stories and legends she heard from local peasants or descriptions of local scenes while her immediate impressions were still fresh
(Herrero 306, 309). These writings were presented to and preserved
by her parents,[6] a token of their common commitment to "genuine"
Spanish culture and reality. Thus, in claiming that her work was produced by collecting and copying, Boehl completes her display of feminine modesty with a reference that makes her literary filiation literally
an act of daughterly devotion.

   By inscribing herself within a family-defined tradition that translated
German Romanticism into a practice of textualizing certain aspects of
the everyday life of rural Spain, Cecilia Boehl set her writing in opposition to the narrative genres and conventions identified with Romantic
Prometheanism and the *mal du siècle* that frequently accompanied it.
In other words, she sought to represent alternatives to the extreme individualism of Romantic representations of subjectivity, and in this she
set herself against the mainstream of the Spanish Romantic movement,
as Montesinos points out:

> Hers is that German Romanticism whose patriarch is Herder, that does not devote itself to the cult of the Satanic self or exalt rebellion of any sort. To the contrary, its guiding principle is the spirit of nationalism, the communion of all the members of the nation in one single ideal. This spirit . . . is nourished by a desire for unanimity in which life becomes poetic as it becomes virtuous. . . . The rebel that breaks the chain not only destroys the miracle of tradition and what tradition has been creating but also condemns himself to dissatisfaction and sterility. (Prólogo 10)

Whereas Avellaneda and Coronado, though they did not openly identify themselves with Promethean rebellion, clearly found in that strain of Romanticism nourishment for their desire to break the bonds of women's condition, Boehl found justification for her writing in opposing the manifestations of Romantic individualism. Boehl's father had tried but failed to implant in Spain the other, traditionalist and nationalist Romanticism; writing to defend it was thus for her not rebellion but a filial mission.

In Cecilia Boehl's writing about her work, she underlines its difference from the kind of literature she terms "romancesco," by which she means "bad Romanticism" (Herrero 328–329).[7] In the preface to *Elia* she forewarns her readers that the heroine is not the passionate type now in vogue:

> Puede que una mujer que no ama con furor no sea el tipo que llena el ideal que muchos se creían; pero puede también que sea el que prefieran almas menos romancescas y más poéticas; es decir, las que simpaticen más con la verdad y la sencillez, que no con la elevación y energía, a veces ficticia y forzada en las producciones literarias, como en la vida real. (Caballero, *Elia* 30)

> Perhaps a woman who doesn't love with a fury of passion is not a type that fulfills the ideal in which many believe; but it is also possible that this is the type preferred by less "romantic" and more poetic souls, that is, souls that find truth and simplicity more sympathetic than elevation and energy, which are sometimes, as in real life, fictitious and forced in literary productions.

This assertion scarcely bothers to make a bow to modesty in signaling the writer's claim to superiority to the exaggerated portrayals of human emotion in contemporary "romantic" literature. Her repeated attacks on the exaltation of unrestrained passion in contemporary novels were clearly directed at the melodramatic fiction derived from Romanticism that had invaded Spain as well as Europe with the new serialized marketing of literature. While much of this fiction was male authored, Boehl's strictures apply so accurately to the novels of two of her most famous female contemporaries—Gómez de Avellaneda and George Sand—that it is difficult not to see these statements as an effort to distance herself radically from a female tradition that included *Sab* and *Dos mujeres* in Spain and *Indiana* and *Lélia* in France, a tradition that she considered rebellious and impious.

In contrast to such forced and "poisonous"[8] fictions, her work offers truth and simplicity—the truth and simplicity of genuine Spanish ways of life—Boehl insists, not only in the prologue to *Elia* but also in the previously cited statement that *La gaviota* had been produced by simply collecting and copying. In the prologue to *La gaviota,* the author adds, "Al trazar este bosquejo, sólo hemos procurado dar a conocer lo natural y lo exacto, que son a nuestro parecer, las condiciones más esenciales de una novela de costumbres" 'In tracing this sketch, we have tried to make known only what is natural and exact, which are in our opinion the essential characteristics of the novel of contemporary customs' (63–64). With this affirmation, Boehl transforms her stance of filial piety into something more assertive and self-generated. By suggesting that she has produced an exact mimesis of Spanish life through what she claims to be "la verdad de los pormenores" 'truth of detail,' Boehl has gone beyond her parents and distinguished herself from the Romantic women novelists by affiliating her work with the contemporary European narrative vanguard, the realist novel.

Boehl articulated these larger ambitions when she was trying to find a publisher for *La gaviota* in 1848. An unfinished draft of a letter she wrote to Joaquín de Mora, the well-known writer who eventually both translated and published the work, describes the gap in Spanish letters that she thinks her novel will fill: "[A]nuestra literatura moderna . . . le falta un género que en otros países tanto aprecian y a tanta perfección han llevado. Esto es, la novela de costumbres" 'Our modern literature . . . lacks a genre that is greatly appreciated in other countries, where it has been developed to perfection' (Caballero, *Gaviota* 454). Her novel, which "está llena de actualidad . . . y creo pinta la sociedad del día con exactitud" 'is highly current . . . and paints today's society with exactitude, I think' (455), will supply Spain with a "novel of customs," a term Boehl translated from the French *roman de moeurs*. As Montesinos has shown, her conception of this genre was based on Balzac, whom she cited repeatedly (*Caballero* 16–21, 31–35) and admiringly called "el gran padrote Balzac" 'great papa Balzac' (17). To signal her devotion to this new paternal authority, she even inserted within the text of *La gaviota* a self-referential dialogue that proposes a narrative project modeled on the *Comédie humaine*. As the kind of novel most appropriate for Spain, a likable young aristocrat proposes a series of "novelas de costumbres":

> Escritas con exactitud y con verdadero espíritu de observación, ayudarían mucho para el estudio de la humanidad, de la historia, de la moral práctica, para el conocimiento de las localidades y de las épocas. Si yo fuera la Reina mandaría escribir una novela de costumbres en cada provincia, sin dejar nada por referir y analizar. (306)

> Written with accuracy and a real spirit of observation, they would be very helpful for the study of humanity, of history, of moral practices, for knowledge of different places and periods. If I were the Queen, I would order that a *novela de costumbres* be written for each province, leaving nothing further to be reported or analyzed.

By the time she wrote *La gaviota*, then, Boehl's parentally inspired project of documenting folk manifestations of essential Spanish spirit had expanded under the influence of Balzac into a mapping of the main features of Spanish society as a whole. Both versions were based on an anti-individualistic notion of the writer's activity; Boehl was true to her parents' attitudes in rejecting the products of creative fantasy and imagination as elements of her project. No doubt Balzac's explicitly conservative moral and political theses persuaded her to overlook the crucial role of larger-than-life passions and figures in his novels. But, just as she grasped the underlying claim of Balzac's novel to disclose the real and the true, she also adopted as her own another of his narrative messages that was compatible with her conservatism.

In 1845 while she was composing the original French version of *La gaviota*, Boehl wrote in her peculiar German to Dr. Julius, an old friend of her father's in Frankfurt, "[J]etz schreibe ich immer in franzosischen, ein roman um die heutige Lage der société zu schildern—diese transicions's époque, wo das Alte, von einem unreifes Neues mit Spott verbant wird" 'I am now writing, still in French, a novel in order to describe the present state of society—this period of transition in which the old is being expelled with ridicule by something new that is not yet ripe' (Pitollet 288). The Balzacian model provided her, then, with the idea of historical change as an overarching narrative form, a story that might explain, order, and take in the multiplicity of phenomena that made up the changing "present state of society." To the extent that she was able to realize this goal—and we shall see shortly the impact of her inhibiting anxieties—she could indeed lay claim to a more original contribution to Spanish letters than any of her female contemporaries had conceived. For what Fernán Caballero offered to the Spanish novel that was new was not the treatment of contemporary life as a novelistic subject[9] but the possibility of a narrative of everyday Spanish life informed by acute consciousness of larger processes of historical change.

Cecilia Boehl's comment to Mora that her novels might fill a gap in Spanish literature was by no means an innocent observation. She was well aware that for over a decade Spanish critics had been lamenting the absence of an indigenous novel of Spanish life. In "*Panorama Matritense*" (1836), Larra himself had praised Balzac as the genius of *costumbrista* writing, implying his brand of realist novel as the culmination to which Spanish sketches of types and customs should aspire (2: 240). Preoccupation with the failure of such a novel to emerge was reflected in P. D.'s 1841 review of Avellaneda's *Sab*; titling his article "De las novelas en España," the critic argued that this first novel announced a writer capable of remedying Spain's generic lack (14). However, in 1848, the year in which Cecilia Boehl wrote to Mora, the well-known critic Antonio Neira de Mosquera still found it necessary to exhort Spanish novelists to depict the conflicts arising from historical change in Spain. In such a context, Boehl's feminine modesty in presenting herself to the readers of *La gaviota* as the mere copyist of Spanish reality can be read inversely as a covert declaration of her immodest ambition: she was conscious of attempting to bring into Spanish letters a realist narrative discourse that had gained prestige throughout Europe as an accurate representation of contemporary reality.

It is totally consistent with Boehl's anxiety about being a good daughter to the patriarchal order that she should have believed an insistent didactic moralism to be compatible with the aims of realist observation. Defending herself in an open letter against the attacks of a critic in 1853, she presented her claims to originality in terms of her moral objective: she wished to introduce in Spain "una clase de literatura amena que se propone por objeto inculcar buenas ideas en la juventud contemporánea. . . . Esto es hacer una innovación, dando un giro nuevo a la apasionada novela, trayéndola a la sencilla senda del deber y de la naturalidad" 'a type of entertaining literature that proposes as its goal the inculcation of moral ideas in contemporary youth. . . . This is to make an innovation, giving a new twist to the novel of passion, bringing it back to the simple path of duty and naturalness' (Mon-

tesinos, *Caballero* 35). She thus refuses to admit of any discrepancy between moral law and actual human experience. As we shall see, this
will to repress whatever might offend paternal and patriarchal law at
once undermined her representational project and failed to prevent the
incursion of the rejected self into her writing.

It should be clear from this examination of Cecilia Boehl's statements about her work that when called upon explicitly to present herself as a writer to the public or to her male epistolary correspondents,
she constructed a self-justifying image of her place in the literary world,
an image whose intricacies reveal the peculiarities and stresses of her
position in the social world. Rejecting the Romantic and strongly male-
gendered idea of the artist as creator and genius, she drew on her
extensive knowledge of European literature to lay claim to the accu-
racy of representation that was beginning to confer literary prestige.
Lest such cosmopolitanism cast doubts upon her commitment to Spain,
she pointed to her faithfulness to the details revelatory of the national way of life. This gesture, too, identified her with the values of
her conservative father, values that her tacit personal literary ambitions
nevertheless betrayed. Her doctrinaire insistence on traditional morality seemed designed to compensate for her violation of the paternal
injunction against women's intellectual activity—a violation that involved both publishing her work and expanding the scope of her aesthetic ambitions.

The gestures of self-representation through which Boehl justified her
writing after the fact, however, had already been worked out in the
texts of several novels. Certain of Boehl's female protagonists stand as
imaginary representations of a self split and truncated by the double
binds of which she, as a woman and as an artist, was a victim.

ELIA: THE ANGELIC FANTASY
OF SELF-REFUSAL

Elia, a novel written very early in the course of Cecilia Boehl's evolution as a novelist,[10] although it was not published until after *La gaviota*
in 1849, offers a compelling characterization of the angelic feminine
ideal as a subject of novelistic experience. In her prologue the author,
perfectly well aware that the required traits of this model scarcely corresponded to the paradigms of subjectivity that Romanticism had led
readers to expect, lectured her male readers about the inconsistency

between their social and literary expectations as she defended her protagonist's resistence to passion:

> Esta falta de pasión cuando nace de la mansedumbre del alma, del poder de la razón, de la fuerza e influencia de la religión, de esa delicada modestia femenina que se extiende hasta sobre los sentimientos, es una cosa que, lejos de vituperarla y hallarla poco interesante, deberían los hombres apreciar, teniendo para ellos el atractivo que tienen todos los puntos de contraste con la mujer, y que son justamente los que le dan todo su encanto femenino. (Caballero, *Elia* 30)

> When this lack of passion stems from mildness of soul, from the power of reason, from the force and influence of religion, from that delicate feminine modesty that affects all the feelings, it is something that men should appreciate rather than censure and declare uninteresting, for it has for men the attraction of all their points of contrast with women, which are rightly those that give women all their feminine charm.

Here Boehl offers a theory of characterization based on the binary logic of the dominant gender system: feminine character is defined as passive by contrast with masculine passion and energy. According to this concept, woman's very desirability, whether as a textual construction or a personal attribute, is dependent on her difference from the masculine forms of subjectivity incorporated in the Romantic self.

For Cecilia Boehl, the patriarchal law that defines Elia's subjectivity posits a fundamental difference between men and women: women must lack the desire that drives men to pursue knowledge and power. Elia is thus characterized as possessing a prelapsarian innocence that makes her incapable of even conceiving the possibility of sexual or self-interested motivations. She has, in fact, the unself-conscious transparency that Romanticism attributed to the child. Neither a prude nor a colorless cipher, she delights in nature, in family affection, in the religious culture taught at the convent where she is educated. Her childlike naïveté confronts the world when her adoptive mother, doña Isabel, brings her home from the convent and she is reunited with the cousins—Clara, Fernando, Carlos—who had been her playmates. Her response to the attentions of Carlos, who soon falls passionately in love with her, bears no trace of sexuality. In fact, the narrator takes pains to establish that the passion in Carlos's declaration of love repels Elia: she looks away and steps back with a "primer e instintivo movimiento de desvío" 'first, instinctive movement of aversion' (109). Unable to imagine that her former playmate could feel or express anything deserving of distrust, however, Elia accepts Carlos's proposal of marriage with perfect simplicity as the natural extension of their childhood affection. The narrative further underlines the difference between Carlos's sexually contaminated passion and Elia's pure, almost sisterly love in a scene designed to show that while Carlos is tormented by jealousy, she cannot comprehend the existence of such an emotion.

Elia is as incapable of worldly ambition as she is of sexual passion. When news of Carlos's intention to marry Elia leaks out, the townspeople consider Elia to be "presumida" 'presumptuous' (128), aspiring beyond her station—though adopted by the wealthy Isabel, she is an orphan of unknown parentage—to marry into the bluest-blooded family of Seville, the Orreas. When her son informs her that he will not renounce his commitment to marry Elia, Carlos's mother, the imperious doña Inés, leaps to the same conclusion: "Voy . . . a desengañar a la osada que se ha atrevido a admitir juramentos insensatos . . . ; voy a disipar sus ilusiones locas" 'I am going to open the eyes of the upstart who has dared to allow foolish vows . . . ; I'm going to dispel her mad hopes,' (134) declares the enraged marquise as she rushes off to confront Elia. But the supposed schemer is innocent of the kind of worldly self-interest that others attribute to her; she is not aware of the importance society attaches to differences in rank. Thus, she cannot understand why Carlos should be apprehensive about his mother's reaction and wish to keep their engagement secret for a time, nor can Carlos bear to explain it to her honestly. When Carlos's mother does make clear to Elia the social significance of the vast discrepancy between Elia's birth—she is the daughter of a bandit—and that of Carlos, the girl gives up without question the thought of marrying Carlos.

If Elia represents an ideal of feminine purity, however, she also reflects an aspect of her author that transgressed the norm incarnated in the *ángel del hogar*: Elia, like her author, is a writing subject, the author of a poem that she presents to her adoptive mother. In an attempt to resolve the conflict between her vocation as a writer and the feminine ideal with which she identifies, Boehl constructs an episode that legitimates Elia's creative activity as the product not of self-aggrandizing desire but of unself-conscious filial love. On the occasion of doña Isabel's name day, Elia astonishes all present by offering to her mother, along with a basket of flowers, a short poem of gratitude based on a religious model. The company that was prepared to mock her verses finds them charming, agreeing with doña Isabel that "son tan sencillos, tan ingenuos y tan dulces como tú" 'they are as simple, as ingenuous and as sweet as you are' (77). Thus, the narrative implies, writing that reflects the true selfless spirit of the domestic angel cannot violate the norms of feminine modesty. Indeed—and here we see a symptom of Boehl's own repressed ambitions—the aesthetic value of Elia's verses, as spontaneous and natural as "un ramito de florecitas del campo" 'a bouquet of little wild flowers' (78), is deemed by several of those present as superior to the ode presented by the Francophile intellectual don Narciso Delgado, a target of the author's running satire on followers of French fashion. The narrative, in fact, endows Elia's feminine innocence with an authority of which she is not aware, as she replies shyly but with unshaken faith to don Narciso's attacks on Catholicism.

The law of novelistic structure, based on temporal process and accumulating experience, cannot permit a protagonist like Elia to retain the pristine innocence she demonstrates at the beginning. Although Elia's childlike purity successfully resists contamination by the eroticism that tinges Carlos's passion, she tastes the fruit of the tree of knowledge when the secret of her origin is forcibly revealed to her by the marquise, Carlos's mother. The original sin of Elia's family history is the crime of her bandit father and his paramour, who gave birth to her out of wedlock and then died. For Elia to recognize herself as the product of sin is to be aware of the existence of destructive erotic desire and its taint in her own flesh. Her reaction to this knowledge is violent self-revilement. She throws herself at her adoptive mother's feet, berating herself:

¡Soy la despreciable hija de un bandolero—, de un padre que me abandonó! ¡Yo no soy digna de que me deis el dulce nombre de hija! ¡Llamadme esclava, señora! ¡Yo serviré a vuestros criados si no desdeñan mis servicios! (140)

I am the despicable daughter of a bandit—, of a father who abandoned me! I don't deserve for you to give me the sweet name of daughter! Call me your slave, madam! I will serve your servants if they don't disdain my services!

She then falls unconscious and sinks into a brain fever that almost takes her life. She comes out of her delirium with the firm resolve to renounce Carlos: no longer innocent, in the sense that she is now aware of sin, she determines to be virtuous. This self-abnegating and generous virtue is tested and confirmed by a chance encounter with her bandit father, wounded and dying in an inn where he has been taken prisoner. Instead of fleeing from this bloody embodiment of depravity, she brings comfort and forgiveness to his dying moments, accepting in this way her identity and her duty as his offspring.

When the dying bandit confirms that Elia *is* his daughter, it becomes evident that Boehl has invoked the narrative paradigm of the Cinderella story only to make her readers aware that she rejects it. And even though the story offers no final anagnorisis that reveals the nobility of the pure maiden and permits her to marry her prince,[11] a later development of the plot still teases us with this possibility. Disheartened to the core by the suffering of her beloved child, Elia's adoptive mother falls into a decline and dies, leaving Elia as her universal heir, disinheriting her nieces and nephews, the marquise's children. All assume that Elia will now marry Carlos, at once satisfying the laws of true love and economic succession. Elia, however, now in firm control of her destiny, disposes otherwise: she takes vows in the convent where she had gone to school and leaves her fortune in a trust, to pass to the Orrea family on her death. In subverting the norms of popular fiction to give this outcome to the story of the *ángel del hogar,* Boehl in fact takes her out of the hearth and away from the domestic circle of the patriarchal family. It appears that the novelistic characterization of the patriarchal feminine ideal has taken a strange, potentially subversive turn.

The surface thematics of the novel indicate that we are to read Elia's response to the knowledge of her origins as proof of her properly feminine humility, her willingness to subordinate her wishes to the authority of a correct social hierarchy. She defends the marquise against the vituperations of doña Isabel for having disclosed the secret of Elia's paternity, calling her "la digna madre que vela sobre la honra de su casa y de su estirpe" 'the worthy mother who watches over the honor of her house and her lineage' (162). Nor does doña Isabel, though enraged by the marquise's cruel behavior to Elia, ever criticize the marquise's goal of preventing the marriage of Carlos and Elia. A clear-cut system of values within the novel, then, defines a match between Carlos Orrea and a bandit's daughter as impossible. On another level, however, the narrative makes it clear that Elia's decision to renounce marriage and enter the convent is the conscious rejection of a state of affairs to which she does not wish to submit. In her final interview with Carlos, just before taking her final vows, she tells him: "Carlos, ¡rápida fue la ojeada que eché al mundo! pero fue lúcida; ¡y la repercusión la he sentido en el corazón! La sensatez, a falta del dedo de Dios, me trazaría la senda que debo seguir" 'Carlos, the glimpse I had of the world was rapid, but it was lucid; and I felt its repercussions in my heart! Good sense, if not the finger of God, would show me the path I must follow' (206). Having learned of the existence of desire and

its destructive effects, she never hesitates in her decision to withdraw
from the possibility of being contaminated by it, not merely as a subject
but as an object of desire as well.

What on the surface appears to be docility to patriarchal structure
is on another level a refusal to submit to the law that makes women
the object of male desire. As an image of the female subject, Elia en-
acts the only form of self-definition permissible within the constraints
Boehl's ideology imposes on feminine desire: she cancels herself as an
object of the male gaze by disappearing within the convent. In fact,
Elia's choice echoes that of a well-known fictional predecessor, Mme
de Clèves, insofar as her withdrawal from the world, while not openly
contesting patriarchal structures of desire, implicitly signals a desire for
something else. Nancy K. Miller argues that the decision of Mme de
Lafayette's heroine not to marry Nemours, the man she loves, and to
retire from the life of the court represents a feminine victory, "a by-
passing of the dialectics of desire," " a rewriting of eroticism" (39). For
this reason, Miller regards *La Princesse de Clèves* to be an example of
women's writing that conceals an impulse to power in its treatment
of the question of the erotic: "a fantasy of power that would revise
the social grammar in which women are never defined as subjects; a
fantasy of power that disdains a sexual exchange in which women can
participate only as objects of circulation" (41). The venerable Spanish
tradition that Boehl draws on, the tradition of feminine cloistering,
provided women in Spain with the means to enact such a fantasy at
least partially. As Electa Arenal points out, in the "semiautonomous
culture" of the convent, "nuns found a way of being important in the
world by choosing to live outside it" (149).

Elia's gesture of renunciation is just such a disguised expression of
ambition: considered by the world as too low to be the bride of an
Orrea, she demonstrates that by a different set of standards she is too
high—in purity and spirituality—for marriage. The gist of her final
statements to Carlos is that the world is not good enough for her, that
in giving it up, she is not renouncing happiness but assuring it. The
end of the narrative underscores Elia's superiority through a kind of
apotheosis:

> Elia, inspirada, llenos de santas lágrimas sus ojos, se presentó a la vista de
> Carlos divina como una aparición bajada de altas regiones y pronta a volver
> a subir a ellas. . . . Carlos se postró y apoyando su inclinada cabeza sobre
> los hierros de la reja, exclamó:—¡Comprendo, por mi desgracia, demasiado
> tarde, . . . que hay seres, cuyas almas arden como divinas antorchas en las

tinieblas, como faros en la noche, que están tan elevados que los profana una pasión, y que sólo se deben amar sobre la tierra como se aman los ángeles en el cielo! (208)

Elia, inspired, her eyes filled with holy tears, appeared to Carlos's eyes as divine as an apparition descended from higher regions and about to return to them. . . . Carlos prostrated himself and, leaning his bowed head against the iron bars of the grill, exclaimed: "I understand, unfortunately for me, too late, . . . that there are beings whose souls burn like divine torches, like beacons in the night, who are so high that passion profanes them, who should only be loved on earth in the way that heavenly angels love each other!"

In constructing an image of the ideal female self, then, Cecilia Boehl relentlessly pushes the *ángel del hogar* toward a pure identification with one of its models, the Virgin Mary. Transcending the legacy of original sin, the carnality of the body, Elia becomes a purely spiritualized being who, like the Virgin, escapes the sexual and reproductive economy that the domestic angel stereotype was meant to serve by being pure and self-sacrificing, but not bodiless. Thus Elia finds a mode of conforming to a patriarchal ideal that in fact represents a triumph over male desire.

But is Elia's alternative, the "other" world for which she refuses patriarchal love and marriage, as devoid of libidinous charge as the analogy with the Virgin might imply? Though certainly a rejection of male-defined forms of sexuality, Elia's choice of the wholly feminine world of the convent corresponds to the desire for a conflict-free maternal love that motivates her actions and strongest emotions throughout the novel. In view of the contention of recent feminist criticism that the fantasy of the girl-child's preoedipal, symbiotic relation with her mother plays a crucial role in much of modern Western women's writing,[12] it is interesting to note that *Elia* turns out to be a novel predominantly concerned with maternal relationships. Only three narrated encounters involve Elia and Carlos; the rest center around Elia's interactions with three mother figures who substitute for the real mother Elia lost at birth: doña Isabel, her adoptive mother; María, her wet nurse; and the marquise, her adoptive aunt and potential mother-in-law. The latter plays the role of an angry and reproving mother. Nevertheless, her story of Elia's origins tells not only of male crime and destructive sexuality but also of a nurturing maternal love that transcends social and natural frontiers—the story of how Isabel took in an abandoned baby and raised it as her own. The ties that bind Elia and her adoptive mother and Elia and her former wet nurse are as powerful

as any imaginable between a biological mother and daughter; many
scenes in the novel show the intense maternal tenderness of the older
women and Elia's joyful and deep love for them.

Elia's grief after the death of doña Isabel is movingly expressed as a
rejection of the pious platitudes that we might have expected a meek
domestic angel to mouth. When a visitor offers the conventional conso-
lations—"¡Cuántas penas y males le ha quitado Dios llevándosela para
sí!" 'How much suffering God has spared her by taking her unto himself!'—Elia replies, "¡Y cuántas felicidades y dulzuras a mí!" 'And how
much happiness and sweetness He has taken from me!' The visitor,
astonished by Elia's undisguised difficulty in accepting her mother's
death, exclaims:

> —¡Pero, hija, si ya no tiene remedio!
> —¡Pues, ese, ese es el dolor que parte mi corazón!—exclamó Elia, hun-
> diendo su cara en el cojín del sofá, mojado de lágrimas. (177)

> "But, my child, nothing can be done about it!"
> "That's just what breaks my heart with pain!" exclaimed Elia, burying
> her face in the tear-soaked sofa cushion.

Elia's uncomplaining resignation to separation from Carlos has nothing
in common with the acute and concrete sense of loss with which she
reacts to her mother's death. Only the convent where Elia was educated, another woman-centered maternal world, had ever competed
with her desire to be with her mother and María. Arriving home from
the convent early in the novel, she reassures doña Isabel that though
she is weeping, "no quiero separarme de usted nunca, nunca. Pero—iré
a ver a las madres a menudo, ¿no es cierto?" 'I don't want ever, ever,
to be separated from you. But—I can go often to see the mothers
[nuns], can't I?' (61). Thus, it is perfectly consistent within this emotional orientation that when death does separate Elia from her beloved
adoptive mother, she should return, taking María with her, to her other
mothers in the convent.

The language with which Elia describes that elsewhere for which she
is abandoning the world is taken from religious discourse. It is a height,
she says, far from earth but close to heaven, "en donde se reunirán
todos los corazones amantes en el amor celestial y perfecto, que es la
bienaventuranza" 'where all loving hearts will be reunited in the perfect
and celestial love that is beatitude' (208). Yet the terms in which Elia
represents her vision of beatific happiness seem equally applicable to
an image of union of mother and child, a return to the enveloping,

conflictless perfection of the womb. In Elia, then, Cecilia Boehl, while conforming to the limitations of female desire demanded by the patriarchal model of the *ángel del hogar,* constructs a positive image of the woman as the subject of a desire that, like Mme de Clèves's, simply bypasses the dialectics of gendered sexuality, aiming at a beyond or a before of undifferentiated symbiosis with the maternal.

As the creation of an image of the self in the symbolic space of writing, Boehl's characterization of Elia resolved a number of her own conflicts. Satisfying her unavowed ambitions in Elia's spiritual transcendence of all around her, she also signaled her conformity to patriarchal law in her heroine's modesty and purity. On a deeper level, Elia's irreproachable filial and religious piety served Boehl as an effective disguise for her perhaps unconscious dissatisfaction with the paternal order and her dream of a maternal alternative. Nevertheless, Elia could not function as an image of the female writing subject, for she represented the female subject's withdrawal from the world of political and communicative practices with which Boehl was engaged by the very fact of her writing, even if she did not intend it at first for publication. That is, as a symbolic construct Elia represented an impossible solution to Boehl's double binds as a female subject; ultimately Elia defines herself through her refusal of the male gaze, whereas her author remains captured, in the very act of writing, by her concern about masculine judgment.

Furthermore, Elia proved to be a paradoxical protagonist of a kind of narrative that justified itself—as Cecilia Boehl's attempted to do—as a copy of the real historical world. From its beginning, the novel is painstakingly grounded in contemporary Spanish history and close observation of Seville society. The first chapter introduces the reader to Seville and to the two grand ladies, doña Isabel and the marquise, during the city's celebration of Ferdinand VII's return to the Spanish throne after the defeat of Napoleon. The end of the Napoleonic War sets the plot in motion, for the homecoming of Carlos and his brother, who have served as soldiers in the Spanish army, determines doña Isabel's decision to take Elia out of the convent. Historical events fade from view as Elia's story begins to develop, but a good part of the narrative is devoted to closely observed accounts of manners, customs, and speech in the interior of Seville's great houses as well as in the surrounding fields and villages. The values and attitudes of Seville's conservative aristocracy are noted with special precision; they explain a crucial twist of the plot—the marquise's unbreakable opposition to the marriage of Carlos and Elia—and are validated by Elia's willingness to respect them.

Once Elia undergoes her symbolic apotheosis in the penultimate chapter, however, her spiritual scheme of values supercedes the values of the social and historical world that heretofore have played an important role in the story. The last chapter, recounting the subsequent fortunes of the Orrea clan, plays out the process of discrediting the social values transcended by Elia's spiritual vision: the Orreas' history, closely intertwined with Spain's history of civil strife and crisis in the 1820s and 1830s, shows the family's rapid decline to the point of extinction. The grieving mother of the last two scions, killed fighting on opposite sides of the civil war of the late 1830s, finds only in Elia's convent a vision of the world that does not lead to madness. Thus, history and society, experience in the world, evaporate as meaningful referents in a narrative that is finally dominated by Elia's idealized transcendence.

Elia brought her author up against a dead end. Driven by the complex impulses that made writing her vocation, Cecilia Boehl was forced to find an alternative mode of representing the female subject in writing if she was to continue her novelistic project. The most remarkable product of this necessity was the protagonist of *La gaviota,* like her author a transgressor of the feminine ideal represented in *Elia.* Whereas Elia was only accidentally a writer—she composed a poem to express her love for her mother—María Santaló, the central character of *La gaviota,* is defined by her vocation as an artist, as a singer in this case. Like other artist-heroines of the nineteenth century, such as Aurora Leigh and Corinne, María embodies the gender-vocation conflict of her author. Unlike these more positive projections, however, she bears a strong resemblance to the monster characters that Gilbert and Gubar find obsessively cropping up in Englishwomen's fiction of the same century not as heroines but as negative images of feminine rebelliousness through which "female authors dramatize their own self-division, their desire both to accept the strictures of patriarchal society and to reject them" (78). Since the contradictions of the novelist's symbolic self-representation converge in such a protagonist, the problematic figure of María Santaló stands at the center of the correlations that the text as a whole established among a number of fictional conventions and social myths. And these correlations, in turn, condition the success of Cecilia Boehl's own artistic ambitions—her desire to pioneer a form of the realistic novel in Spain.

THE CONSTRUCTION OF AN ANTISELF:
MARISALADA

The central female character of *La gaviota* becomes a successful and famous artist—as the author herself did upon the novel's publication. The sea gull of the title is the daughter of a fisherman in a tiny Andalusian village. She marries Stein, the gentle German doctor who, when curing her childhood illness, had discovered her musical talent and trained her to sing. The Duke of Almansa, impressed by her voice, acts as her patron in Seville and Madrid, where she rapidly rises to stardom in the opera. But all her glory comes to an end as the consequence of her love affair with a famous *torero*. Ultimately, having lost voice, husband, lover, and patron, she returns to her village. Thus, the same concerns that compelled Cecilia Boehl to use a male pseudonym are expressed as disapproval for the unwomanly ambition and egoism that lead María Santaló to pursue her musical career. Boehl's characteristic strategy of simultaneous transgression, disavowal, and appeasement produces a peculiar fictional character, a protagonist constructed of heterogeneous and often dissonant literary types.

The novel's plot line, then, makes María's story above all a didactic fable about women's proper place. In adopting this moralizing pattern for her novel, Boehl follows the example of many women writers of her time,[13] who, as Gilbert and Gubar observe, justified their own venture into the forbidden territory of writing "by inspiring other women with respect for the moral and social responsibilities of their domestic duties" (153). The most obvious aspects of María's characterization derive from her function as the transgressor whose experience will demonstrate the force of the moral laws she breaks. From the outset the narrative presents her character as defective in femininity, flawed by the cold, prideful unresponsiveness evident in her first reaction to the doctor's suggestions for the cure of her childhood disease: "La muchacha . . . lanzó una mirada díscola a Stein, diciendo con voz áspera—¿Quién me gobierna a mí?" 'The girl . . . shot a rebellious glance at Stein, saying with a harsh voice, "No one can tell *me* what to do"' (Caballero, *Gaviota* 166). This, the germinal idea from which her characterization unfolds, stands in opposition to the positive ideal incarnated in the Duchess of Almansa, who, unlike the other-worldly Elia, is a truly domestic angel:

Hija afectuosa y sumisa, amiga generosa y segura, madre tierna y abnegada, esposa exclusivamente consagrada a su marido, la Duquesa de Almansa era

el tipo de la mujer que Dios ama, que la poesía dibuja en sus cantos, que la
sociedad venera y admira, y en cuyo lugar se quieren hoy ensalzar *esas
amazonas,* que han perdido el bello y suave instinto feminino. (362–363)

Affectionate and submissive daughter, generous and reliable friend, tender
and selfless mother, a wife exclusively consecrated to her husband, the
Duchess of Almansa was the type of woman whom God loves, whom poetry
venerates and admires, and whose exalted place is now sought by *those
Amazons* who have lost the soft, beautiful feminine instinct.

The rules of this value system, a succinct condensation of the dominant
gender ideology I examined in chapter 1, have all been broken by
María at the end of the novel: like those Amazons condemned by the
narrator, she seeks the pleasures and glories of the public world, abandoning her home and her duties to father and husband.

The point is heavily underscored in a sequence alternating descriptions of María's highest triumphs in Madrid with an account of her
dying father calling for her in vain. María's implied responsibility for
her father's death is further established by the old man's falling ill with
grief on the day she leaves her native village. In Boehl's intensely over-
determined scheme, the unwomanly female is not merely unfilial; she
is necessarily an Amazon, a patricide. María's refusal to subordinate
herself to the males to whom she is socially bound brings them, symbolically, death in place of nurturance: her father, her husband, and her
lover all die as a more or less direct consequence of her behavior.

In a moral fable, the transgressor must be punished. Accordingly,
María is put in her place, quite literally as it turns out. The cautionary
reversals are worked out in highly revealing terms. It is María's sexuality, ineluctably masochistic despite her proud, willful stance toward the
world, that brings about her downfall. Here the obsessive negative
vision of sexuality that was only hinted in the story of Elia's birth—in
the vignette of her helpless, moribund mother and her crime-bloodied
father—receives a fuller elaboration.[14] Pepe Vera, the bullfighter, is the
only man who evokes a sexual response in María. Although he first
excites her interest by his fearless performance in the ring (288), Pepe
succeeds in breaking through the armor of her coldness by insulting her
(359). María's affair with the matador is represented as a savage struggle of wills, for the Amazon can only conceive of love as combat. Angry
and humiliated after a display of pride, María accedes for no clear
reason to a series of demands through which Pepe seeks to demonstrate
his domination. He insists that she sing for his friends at a tavern even

though she is ill. Disaster comes as a direct consequence of her submission, for her husband and her patron-admirer discover her adultery and abandon her while she is delirious from the fever that ruins her voice. Pepe of course is killed in the ring.

This moral lesson has a nasty aftertaste: since María does not freely choose to subordinate her will to the loving and protective men to whom she is bound by duty, she suffers the consequences of her own sexuality, which is treated as a masochistic response to the bullfighter's brutal insistence on male prerogative. In response to the cultural taboo against female desire, Carolina Coronado and Gertrudis Gómez de Avellaneda, too, represent feminine sexuality as self-destructive but not as essentially a desire for humiliation. Thus Cecilia Boehl's more intractable conflicts in relation to female identity mark her representation of women with a very particular quality of self-disgust.

María's downfall implies the necessity of forcing women to accept the feminine role so "venerated and admired" by society, and in this sense undercuts the narrator's exaltation of woman's place. The final reversal María suffers, though it is formally a satisfying example of poetic justice, also implies in its specific content further doubt about the desirability of woman's assigned role. Retributive justice in this novel does not allow María to die of her illness but instead decrees that she end up where she belongs—in her native village, married to the barber she once scorned, keeping house, bearing and raising children as she should have done all along. Thus denying her protagonist the stature a tragic death might have bestowed upon her, Boehl purposefully dismantles the Romantic paradigm that glorifies the overreacher even in his defeat. In contrast to the tragic dignity of a Romantic death, María's destiny is pictured as a comic hell; thin, pale, unkempt, surrounded by wailing children, she is condemned to listen to the false notes of her second husband, who fancies himself a tenor in the grand style. But the moral thus achieved undermines itself: if woman's "exalted" place is not accepted willingly, then it is imposed anyway as a penalty.

The ironic structure of the plot, then, projects the shadow of ambivalence on the straightforward code of sexual difference propounded by the narrative voice. Cecilia Boehl may have set out to propitiate the patriarchy by condemning her protagonist's venture into male territory, but a tinge of positive identification colors María's characterization as an artist, revealing her to be the image of a self that Boehl could neither fully accept nor successfully deny. One telling feature is that the narrator never suggests that María's talents do not match her aspirations. From the beginning, when the idealized German, Stein, is first enraptured by María's unschooled trills, to the end, when her musical judgment is treated as authoritative, the reader is meant to believe in the superiority of her musical talent and achievement. In this novel's ideological system, one cannot be both a good woman and a good artist. María remains childless while she pursues a career, as if her art drained the energies that should be directed toward the function of motherhood. The undenied validity of María's vocation as a singer, however, introduces a disturbing element into the novel's value system, creating an aperture through which a contradictory set of values asserts itself.

The points at which a positive evaluation of María surfaces in this novel reveal that her characterization as a talented artist is fueled by the same Romantic myths of the self, expressions of cultural revolution, that Cecilia Boehl so explicitly set herself against in upholding traditional social hierarchy and gender ideals. Boehl represents in María the individualistic fantasy that had spread from Romanticism to the novel as a dominant myth of the time—the story of an individual of genius whose superiority succeeds in gaining confirmation from a reluctant society. Instead of revising this Promethean figure to adapt it to a feminine subject, as Gómez de Avellaneda did, Boehl casts her protagonist in its image as a bad example that validates the traditional and anti-individualistic code of feminine conduct. Yet the myth of genius operates as a positive norm in the episodes dealing with María's talent. For example, in her response to the music of Stein's flute, María reveals a passionate intensity that belies her cold, hostile demeanor and that evokes the extraordinary devotion and admiration of positive characters like Stein and the Duke of Almansa. Thus the duke, who embodies the double nobility of class and of soul (91), categorizes her as also superior: "Sus ojos son de aquellos que sólo puede mirar frente a frente un águila. . . . En cuanto a su voz, . . . es demasiado buena para perderse en estas soledades" 'Her eyes are such that only an eagle could look her in the face. . . . As for her voice, it is too good to be lost out here in these lonely parts' (244). Although María's instantaneous agreement with the latter judgment becomes further evidence of her prideful egotism, it also identifies her with the Lucien de Rubemprés of early nineteenth-century fiction, those characteristic provincial youths who set out to win fame in the metropolis. María's climb to stardom from this point in the story leaves no doubt that she is a literary incarnation of that bourgeois aspiration for upward mobility and competitive success to which the Romantic myth corresponds.

We might also note here the influence of the female version of the Promethean myth on María Santaló's characterization as an artist. As an acclaimed and charismatic opera star, María is an antipathetic version of Mme de Staël's archetype of the female genius. But whereas Corinne can only realize her triumph in Italy, the idealized utopia of artistic value, María Santaló sets off on her quest for glory in a fictional context that explicitly refers to changing political hegemony in a slowly modernizing society. Boehl, of course, treats that defiant quest negatively from the standpoint of both sexual and class politics. By representing María as a case not only of female insubordination but also of the disruptive middle-class ambition to impose talent over blood rank, the author doubly justifies feudal and patriarchal order through the singer's downfall. The narrative structure provided by the moral fable of transgression and punishment ensures that in María the conjunction of genius and ambition with female gender makes the desire for social mobility appear more absurd than it might have seemed in a male protagonist.

Even so, the linking of types—ambitious artist and woman—in María's character was potentially as subversive of gender ideology as Avellaneda's and Coronado's more positive conflation of the two types in their images of the female self. Indeed, Cecilia Boehl's own unavowed ambivalence about the patriarchal feminine ideal prevented her from closing off in a purely negative sense the meaning of this conjunction of elements in the construction of her central character. While in general she castigates the liberal tendencies embodied in her protagonist, María's climb to preeminence appears at times to exert an irresistibly positive pull on the narrative presentation. The village girl's decisive first performance before an aristocratic audience in a Seville drawing room is a case in point. The narration highlights María's awareness of the malicious murmurs with which the elegant company remark her dark complexion and inappropriate dress and describes with grudging admiration the protagonist's presence of mind in this painful situation. The detachment previously attributed to lack of feeling becomes "inalterable calma y aplomo" 'unshakable composure and aplomb' (396). With the sangfroid of a male Romantic hero, she refuses to be intimidated by her supposed superiors and takes their measure in an instant. They, misled by appearances, do not yet have hers. As María prepares to perform, the narrative's emphatic one-sentence paragraphs single out the different postures of disdain, indifference, and skepticism among the audience and thus heighten the following climactic passage:

> Pero apenas se alzó la voz de María, pura, tranquila, suave y poderosa, cuando pareció que la vara de un conjurador había tocado a todos los concurrentes. En todos los rostros se pintó y se fijó una expresión de admiración y de sorpresa. (338)

> But scarcely had María's pure, tranquil, smooth, and powerful voice resounded, when it seemed that a magic wand had touched all those present. On every face there appeared and stayed an expression of admiration and of surprise.

The author herself in this episode appears unable to break the spell of the Corinne myth, as channeled through the work of another Romantic woman writer, George Sand. This passage distinctly echoes—perhaps unconsciously—a parallel episode in the French novelist's *Consuelo,* another story of a Spanish opera star. Consuelo, too, surprises her audience with the charismatic signs of genius when she rises to sing: "But what a miraculous transformation had taken place in this young girl, a moment before so pale and worn! . . . [H]er calm glance spoke of none of those trivial passions which aim at ordinary success. There was instead something grave, mysterious and profound . . . which commanded respect" (qtd. in Moers 189). Although *La gaviota*'s insistence on condemning and belittling rather than glorifying its prima donna makes it an anti-*Consuelo,* Boehl obviously cannot maintain her disapproving distance from the fantasy of the female artist's triumph.[15] In the light of Boehl's explicitly conservative thesis, it is equally astonishing that part of the emotional charge of this episode results from the humbling of an arrogant aristocracy and the triumph of a commoner's talent and sense of equal worth. Although the novelist ostensibly attacked the perspective of both "Amazons" and bourgeois upstarts, she could not exclude them from her text any more than she could fully exterminate them in herself.

The use of the magic wand simile to indicate the compelling power of María's voice correlates exceptionality and masculinity (through the phallic image) with supernatural power and, in so doing, signals the presence of another fictional mode. The formulas of melodrama, adapted from the discourse of Romanticism by way of the satanic hero, had clearly won the day in popular fiction as well as in drama.[16] They counted for effect on oppositions often motivated simply by allusion to a supernatural scheme of energies in conflict—good and evil. Traces of melodramatic devices emerge in the portrayal of María as endowed with a charisma that is not wholly explained by her artistic talent—for example, in the contrast between her detached demeanor and flashes of passionate intensity that leads the duke to equate her glance with that of an eagle. The connection between María and the force of will and repressed energy of the melodramatized Romantic self is made when María and the bullfighter exchange looks at a *corrida* and discover that they are kindred souls. A shift of narrative perspective occurs here; the narrator who throughout the episode has presented the bull-fight as barbarous now acknowledges that

> en verdad, Pepe Vera había estado admirable. Todo lo que había hecho en una situación que le colocaba entre la muerte y la vida, había sido ejecutado con una destreza, una soltura, una calma y una gracia, que no se habían desmentido ni un solo instante. (288)

> in truth, Pepe Vera had been admirable. In a situation that placed him between life and death, everything he did had been executed with a dexterity, a freedom of movement, a serenity and grace that had not faltered for a single instant.

Pepe Vera thus steps into the novel trailing the glamour attached to the serial novel's elaboration of popular fantasy, and the narration of María's relations with him frequently employs the sensationalist clichés of such fiction: "[L]as miradas terribles de Pepe Vera la fascinaban, como fascinan al ave las de la serpiente" 'The terrible gaze of Pepe Vera fascinated her, as that of the serpent fascinates the bird'; "A todo me atrevo yo por vengarme!" 'I will dare anything to have my revenge!' (391, 393).

As a means of controlling and subordinating the melodramatic mode, the narrator self-consciously debunks the images used to describe María's passion: "Aquellos amores parecían más bien de tigres que de seres humanos. ¡Y tales son, sin embargo, los que la literatura moderna suele atribuir a distinguidos caballeros y a damas elegantes!" 'Their love was more like that of tigers than of human beings. And yet it is this kind of love that modern literature habitually attributes to distinguished gentlemen and elegant ladies!' (393).

Boehl proposed through such devices "to combat the novelesque, a subtle poison" (see chap. 7 n. 8). Despite these decorous intentions, however, the emotive energy of melodramatic language sometimes asserts itself over the other meanings.[17] The description of María as she watches Pepe meet the fateful bull slips into the idiom of the serial novel:

> María amaba a aquel hombre joven y hermoso, a quien veía tan sereno delante de la muerte. Se complacía en un amor que la subyugaba, que la hacía temblar, que le arrancaba lágrimas; porque ese amor brutal y tiránico, ese cambio de afectos profundos, apasionados y exclusivos, era el amor que ella necesitaba. (418)

> María loved that young and handsome man whom she saw facing death so serenely. She took pleasure in a love that subjugated her, that made her tremble, that wrung tears from her, because that brutal and tyrannical love, that exchange of deep, passionate, and exclusive affection was the love she needed.

This passage projects an uneasy, almost dissonant ambivalence toward María's passion: despite the rather derogatory allusions to María's masochistic penchant, the first sentence and the reference to "deep, passionate, and exclusive" affections seem to enlist our sympathy for an ill-starred, potentially heroic "true love." This is a momentary lapse, however. Only a couple of chapters later, in the novel's conclusion, the author regains control of her narrative by aggressively puncturing the expectations raised by the melodramatic mode. María does not die of a broken heart; she is recaptured by another genre in her humdrum life as a village housewife, so that adultery, ambition, and serial fiction may be simultaneously disavowed.

The pattern of characterization that we have observed shows a María who is almost a split personality—dry, unfeeling, taciturn on the one hand and talented, charismatic, passionate on the other. Indeed, her characterization unfolds as a battle between two perspectives on her story, each embodied in sets of narrative norms. The opposing sides of María, like the opposing value systems implied in the conventions that characterize her, reflect the unresolved conflict between Cecilia Boehl's socially defined identity and the desires or ambitions it proscribed. Indeed, insofar as the figure of María Santaló fails to present the image of an integrated, coherent self, it duplicates the divided subjectivity of its female author. This "schizophrenia of authorship"[18] accounts for the author's self-confessed aversion to her main character: "[E]sa horrible *Gaviota* y el ordinario Pepe Vera los he trazado de mala gana y con coraje y porque era preciso" 'I portrayed that horrible *Sea Gull* and the vulgar Pepe Vera unwillingly and angrily and because I had to' (Caballero, *Gaviota* 462), she wrote to her editor-translator. This repugnance was so pronounced that the 1849 text included no courtship scene between María and Stein, her husband-to-be. When, at the insistence of friends and critics, Boehl wrote such a scene for the 1856 edition, she declared it to have been nearly impossible because María's subjectivity consisted of little more than "instintos brutales" and "mezquinos cálculos de egoismo" 'petty self-interested calculations' (Letter to Núñez de Arenas, *Gaviota* 470). This stubborn relegation of María to the category of "other" is so insistent that Rodríguez-Luis interprets the author's antipathy to her protagonist as the result of "some obscure antagonism between Fernán Caballero and someone whom she identifies with *la gaviota*" (130). Yet, as we have seen, María embodies those sexual and artistic desires that Boehl cannot, must not, recognize as her own.

As the sign of the author's radical self-division, the starkly contradictory figure of María would disturb a narrative based on conventional ideas of character consistency if it was not for the mediating effect of a third component of her character. Derived from the myth of nationalism as embodied in *costumbrismo,* the popular contemporary sketch of local manners and customs, this third element tended to subordinate the oppositions between genders and classes that produced the contradictory characterization of María. Both Boehl and her critics regarded *costumbrismo* as the dominant generic influence on her writing. It is the starting point of *La gaviota,* whose first volume consists mostly of a series of *costumbrista* scenes describing an Andalusian village and discovering the marks of Spanish national temperament in its inhabitants.

This framework, too, provides a third view of Marisalada, as the protagonist is known in her village, for she displays some of the traits presented as the "essence" of the Spanish people. Her musical talent is closely associated with the popular songs that the author exalts as the very soul of Andalusia: "María, además de su hermosa voz y de su excelente método, tenía, como hija del pueblo, la ciencia infusa de los cantos andaluces" 'María, besides her beautiful voice and excellent technique, possessed, as a daughter of the people, the inherent knowledge of Andalusian song' (341). She first attracted Stein's admiration with these songs, and with them made the most favorable impression on her Seville audience. This spirited, improvisational folk music, we are told, corresponds to the Spanish character: "Un español puede ser insolente; pero rara vez grosero, porque es contra su natural. Vive siempre a sus anchas, siguiendo su inspiración, que suele ser acertada y fina" 'A Spaniard can be insolent; but he is rarely vulgar, because that is against his nature. He always lives freely, following his inspiration, which is normally appropriate and elegant' (342). This kind of spirit is attributed to Marisalada by her nickname; "salada" connotes wit, grace, and verve. In effect, the arrogant assurance, the flashing dark eyes, and the musical grace that mark María's rise to the peak of operatic fame come to her because she is a daughter of the people. True to the nationalistic spirit of her conception, she refuses to go to Paris, preferring the applause of her countrymen to that of the French, and inspires the worship of her Madrid fans, who idolize her as a diva of purely Spanish blood.

The elements drawn from the code of nationalist *costumbrismo* function as an alternative explanation for María's attractiveness and success and, at the same time, for her final destiny. If her independence and self-contained bearing demonstrate stubborn insubordination and lack of feeling in a woman, they nevertheless appear appropriate in a member of the Spanish *pueblo*. But Boehl's image of Spain's rural lower classes grants them such pride of bearing only to the extent that it reflects their unquestioning acceptance of their place in society. Stein observes of the national character that "el español pobre, que se contenta con un pedazo de pan, una naranja y un rayo de sol, está en armonía con el patricio que se contenta casi siempre con su destino" 'the poor Spaniard, who is happy with a piece of bread, an orange, and a ray of sunlight, is in harmony with the patrician, who is almost always content with his destiny' (301). The inhabitants of María's native village—not to mention the novel's contented aristocracy—corroborate Stein's statement. They have no other aspirations than to be what they are, and they lament only the changes a liberal government has made in their traditional way of life. By pursuing her ambition for a higher place in the world, María departs from—indeed, betrays—the national character in which her talent is rooted and thereby justifies the nemesis that brings her back to the village of her origin.

The idea of national character, then, provides María an identity that mediates or covers the schizophrenia of her function as both antiself and denied self. Undeniably Spanish, the protagonist compensates for the ambiguity of her author's nationality. By the same token, María's association with the Andalusian *pueblo* allows self-assertive female talent to be coded for brief moments as positive. At the same time, however, by suggesting that it is as "unnatural" for one of the people to abandon social geographical roots as it is for a woman to seek public success, the novel's image of Hispanic nature counteracts the Romantic individualism represented in María's will to triumph. By using the myth of national identity to control the Romantic myth of the self, to whose power she was susceptible despite herself, Boehl succeeded in defusing the explosive implications of her protagonist's identity as both female and the subject of bourgeois and Romantic aspiration.

The measure of her success can be seen in the fact that she is and must be read as antifeminist and antiliberal, even though she was the only one of the Spanish women writers of her time who cast a woman in the Romantic role of the artist-hero who struggles to overcome his or her social obscurity. Sab, for example, was a male, while Coronado's lyrical subject spent more time deploring her constraints than trying her wings. Boehl's paradoxical success in closing off the subversive elements of her complexly self-contradictory writing, however, caused the ultimate failure of an artistic ambition she could not disavow—the desire to justify her novel as an image of historical reality.

ON THE THRESHOLD OF A NEW ERA

As I noted at the beginning of this chapter, Cecilia Boehl claimed for her writing not the Romantic status of poetic creation but the apparently more modest mode of existence of a copy of reality. What she meant by this at first was that she transcribed local legends, stories, or events or that she wrote *costumbrista* descriptions of scenes and customs; but by the time she was engaged in composing *La gaviota* her conception of the reality she wished to convey had, under the influence of Balzac's *Comédie humaine,* been redefined to include the underlying changes in contemporary society. According to the previously cited letter to Dr. Julius, written while she was composing *La gaviota,* her objective was to depict present-day society as a period of transition in which the old ways were being replaced by something still in formation. She understood perfectly well the claim to capture a total historical dynamic that was giving the modern realist novel prestige and authority throughout Europe, and she intended to be the first to apply that model of novelistic truth to Spain. Focusing on the social signs and consequences of the dissolution of tradition, she could vaunt the "truth" of her narrative while avoiding the Romantic fascination with individual subjectivity that would have forced her to look more deeply at the emotions and motivations of her characters. However, the self-inhibitions that marked Boehl's treatment of her protagonist also affected her depiction of temporal process, producing narrative techniques that worked against the representation of change.

By privileging *costumbrismo,* the genre whose close semantic association with nationalism contained the disturbing contradictions of Marisalada's characterization, Boehl follows formal conventions that counteract the temporal expansiveness of the novel form. The main narrative units of *La gaviota* are cast in the mold of the *cuadro de costumbres* and associated forms such as the folktale and the short story—short, self-contained, focused on a point in time rather than on temporal process. Several chapters follow the shorter genres so closely that they form individual set pieces that actively work against any novelistic flow of time or action. Because the author conceived the main narrative units as static moments whose sequence forms a plot line, time as *durée,* the continuum of subjective experience that links these moments, is excluded from the narration itself and relegated to the silent spaces between the chapters. Many chapters begin with references to these gaps in time: "Un mes después de las escenas que acabamos de referir" 'One month after the scenes we have just narrated'; "Tres años había que Stein permanecía en aquel tranquilo rincón" 'For three years Stein had remained in that tranquil spot'; "Tres años habían transcurrido" 'Three years had gone by' (170, 203, 237). What becomes clear as the chapters accumulate is that the interstices between the narrative episodes, far from containing empty time, are the location of psychological change and development in the novel.

The problem can be illustrated by an example related to the characterization of Marisalada. The protagonist is presented to the reader first as a tubercular, willful, wild girl in an episode in which Stein, the doctor, prescribes that she be moved from her father's primitive hut by the sea to the more nurturing environment of a family home. Here begins the process by which her health and vitality are restored while she is transformed from a kind of savage into a socialized, attractive young woman. This transformation takes place, however, entirely outside the text, which occupies itself in the relevant chapters with the description of village types, with the telling of folktales around the fireside, and with the transcription of traditional songs. Only at the end of this series of chapters do we read that Stein

> habíase dedicado a la educación de la niña enferma, que le debía la vida, y aunque cultivaba un suelo ingrato y estéril, había conseguido a fuerza de paciencia hacer germinar en él los rudimentos de la primera enseñanza. Pero lo que excedió sus esperanzas, fue el partido que sacó de las extraordinarias facultades filarmónicas, con que la Naturaleza había dotado a la hija del pescador. (205)

had devoted himself to the education of the sick girl, who owed him her life, and although he cultivated ungrateful and sterile soil, he had managed by dint of patience to germinate in it the rudiments of an elementary education. But what exceeded his hopes was the profit to be reaped from the extraordinary philharmonic faculties with which nature had endowed the fisherman's daughter.

A paragraph later we learn, in addition, that the teacher has fallen in love with his pupil, although we do not know the process that produced a subjective change of such import to the plot line.

María's affair with Pepe, a development decisive to the destinies of all the main characters, is treated equally schematically. Its narration consists of an initiating anecdote, a climactic episode some chapters later, and then Pepe's death. Only a couple of summary statements refer to the intermediate psychological processes that might explain the cool and self-possessed María's fall into adulterous passion. A narrative procedure that thus refuses to explore the unfolding of subjective experience works against the image of temporal continuity implied by the sequential reference to actions, and, in fact, undercuts the author's objective of representing historical change.

The decisive innovation of the nineteenth-century novel, an innovation facilitated by Romanticism's elaboration of a discourse of subjectivity, was to use the narration of the flow of experience, of subjective process in time, as a signifier of larger historical and social processes. Cecilia Boehl, though she intuited the vaster ambitions of the new novelistic models, could not allow herself to adopt narrative techniques designed to incorporate subjective *durée* for the very same reasons that she could not allow herself to empathize with her protagonist. She refused to abandon the static, disarticulated format of *costumbrismo* in order to disavow and close off the dangerous, forbidden meanings that threatened to emerge as she grappled with the conflicting values of her culture and her time. She straddled the major boundaries that cut through Spanish society—the lines that marked off male from female, liberal from conservative, city from country, middle-class professionals from old-style aristocrats, foreign vogues from Spanish traditions, fledgling industry from established agricultural interests. But she could not seize the artistic advantages that this unusual perspective might have offered her, for she could not permit herself to see—in herself or in the world—those ambiguities of historical process that defied the coded oppositions defining social place. And thus her ambivalence about her feminine identity thwarted her prospects for pioneering the Spanish realist novel.

The ultimate paradox of the literary production of Cecilia Boehl is that although she tried to make her writing a point of resistance to the cultural revolution in which Romantic individualism, liberal political forms, and the beginnings of a critique of female subordination played a part, her novels reproduced the contradictory nature of her resistance to the forces of history. The psychological dynamics of her personal history compelled her to write in defense of traditional codes of feminine behavior that she herself violated by writing. Even her portrayal of the feminine ideal in Elia exposed inconsistencies in the domestic angel stereotype and implicitly rejected the patriarchal order of worldly society; nor could she prevent the negative image represented by María Santaló from acquiring the positive charisma of the successful artist. As if to compensate for these unacknowledged transgressions, Boehl's insistence on feminine subservience to patriarchal authority was inseparably tied to the hierarchies of an old Spain organized around altar and throne. Although she thus expressly opposed the modernization of Spain, of necessity that great historical transition constituted her frame of reference: she found the "old" meaningful precisely because it was being superseded by the "new." And, indeed, the language, forms, and myths she had at her disposal as a novelist formed part of the transition. To engage with her public, she mobilized—in order to debunk them—Romantic ideas of the self. Even the genre of costumbrismo, which she had adopted in order to subordinate a new bourgeois individualism to images of a traditional national character, had been generated by a new mode of literary production in which the periodical press sought an expanded and more avid consuming public (see Kirkpatrick).

And, finally, in direct contradiction to the defense of tradition through which she was determined to justify her writing, her work further contributed to the modernization of Spanish literary institutions by pointing the way toward a Spanish version of the realist novel, that dominant form of bourgeois literary expression to which she aspired even as she resisted its implications.

8
Conclusion

THE SHAPING OF A SPANISH WOMEN'S LITERARY TRADITION

In 1839 Spanish Romanticism was an exclusively male affair, as, indeed, was Spanish print culture as a whole. A short story, a poem or two by women had appeared in the press, but there was nothing to indicate that within a few short years women poets would be counted among the major literary figures of the day and that women would have a palpable presence in the press in general. By 1849 the acclaimed publication of four novels by Fernán Caballero, the critical success of Gómez de Avellaneda's *Saúl* in the theater, and the continued rise of Carolina Coronado's literary prestige, along with the active collaboration of numbers of less well known women in the periodical press, made it incontrovertibly clear that women had established a significant place in literary production. In preceding chapters I have examined in detail how a few key texts produced during this period of unprecedented feminine literary activity defined the character, the scope, and the limits of female authorship. Let us conclude our study by considering the ambiguous legacy that the pioneering women writers of the 1840s thus passed on to later Spanish women writers.

The polar extremes of the legacy in question appear in the sharp contrast between Concepción Arenal and Angela Grassi, two members of Coronado and Avellaneda's generation who have been mentioned only briefly in this study because their work is tangential to Romanticism. Yet their evolution in the 1840s responds to the same pressures as the women Romantics and defines two contrary lines of development that became strongly marked after 1850.

On the one hand, the highly intellectual, independent-minded Arenal had broken protofeminist ground in her own life choices by 1850. She had defied the laws excluding women from the university by attending classes in disguise, and she had rejected contemporary definitions of marital roles by entering into a marriage in which she and her husband considered themselves equal partners, contributing the earnings from their writing to support the family. Her concern with social justice was already perceptible in the 1840s, although her definitive works on prison reform and on the condition of the working class and of women would not be written until later in the century. During Arenal's maturity, her critique of the inequities of nineteenth-century Spanish society led her to attack the juridical and economic inequality of women and to call into question the ideal of the domestic angel. In *La mujer de su casa* (1881) she argued forcefully that "*[l]a mujer de su casa es un ideal erróneo; . . . corresponde a un concepto equivocado de la perfección, que es para todos progreso, y que se pretende sea para ella inmovilidad*" "the 'woman of the house' is an erroneous ideal; . . . it corresponds to a mistaken concept of perfection as immobility for women, rather than progress" (Arenal 202). Though Arenal, like many nineteenth-century women writers, opposed women's suffrage as entanglement in a morally degrading and corrupt system, she became an important model for early twentieth-century Spanish feminists who carried on her struggle for women's equality in both writing and political action.

Angela Grassi's career, on the other hand, describes quite a different—and more common—trajectory. One of the first and most prolific of the women poets who appeared in the 1840s, Grassi, in her early poems, lamented the lot of her sex along with her lyrical sisters. She succeeded in establishing herself as a professional writer, particularly for the women's press that emerged in the second half of the century. From 1867 until her death in 1883 she directed the women's journal *El Correo de la Moda*. Her writing after 1850, however, increasingly served the ideology of the domestic angel. Her essays and her didactic stories and novelettes condemned any interests or aspirations that would distract women from the selfless duties of motherhood and exalted the redemptive mission of the angelic but entirely passive Virtuous Woman (Andreu 66, 88, 170). Her conservatism on the question of gender roles, like that of Cecilia Boehl, also involved a strong conservatism with respect to class.

The unrelenting social pressures exerted on the women who began to write in the 1840s made Grassi's route the one most frequently traveled. The earliest document in which a member of this generation justified her intellectual and creative activity reveals the molding force of the sexually conservative attitudes with which the author knew she must contend. In the "Discurso preliminar" of her 1841 *Poesías,* Josefa Massanés prefigured the defensive strategies that would characterize most of her generation's claims on behalf of women. Her opening paragraphs draw upon the rhetoric of enlightenment ideals associated with early Spanish liberalism:[1] all human beings must contribute to the construction of "civilización social" 'civil society,' and the march of progress; women's ignorance impedes "el movimiento de la general ilustración" 'the spread of general enlightenment' (iii). Emancipation is implicitly one of the general values she expects her reader to share, yet she is careful to qualify it in relation to women. Early on, she assures her readers that she seeks not the complete emancipation of women, "porque se opone a ello la naturaleza" 'because it is contrary to nature' (iv), but only their "intellectual emancipation." And this she justifies in terms not of women's innate right to self-realization but of their responsibilities as mothers and wives:

> Cuánto más cultivado sea el talento de la mujer, más conocerá las obligaciones que por la naturaleza y la sociedad le fueron cometidas, conocerá mejor el lugar que la corresponde en el mundo, y no haya cuidado; ella irá a ocuparle sin necesidad de enseñárselo. (xiii-xiv)

> The more a woman cultivates her talents, the better she will know the duties assigned to her by nature and society, the better she will recognize her place in the world, and don't worry—she will occupy it without having to be taught to do so.

Her representation of women's intellectual aspirations, her arguments in their behalf, are all shaped to reassure and propitiate a readership for whom women's subordinate, domestic role cannot be questioned. The anxiety that structures Massanés's apologia becomes explicit in the concluding paragraph:

> [E]l temor de que sea mirado como un crimen el que yo, joven y sin mérito alguno, entregue a la censura pública mis sencillas concepciones en un país en que (respetando sin duda la preocupación dominante) pocas mujeres se

atrevieron a otro tanto, me ha inducido a exponer las ideas que dejo vertidas en este discurso. (xv)

The fear that it might be regarded as a crime that I, young and without merit, should give to public censure my simple creations in a country in which—doubtless respecting the dominant prejudice—few women have dared to do as much has induced me to put forward the ideas expressed here.

The sense of cultural context that forced Josefa Massanés to whittle down her ambitions for herself and her sex—ambitions stimulated by liberal ideology—to fit acceptably within the dominant definitions of feminine nature and function characterized the whole tradition of women's writing that began in the 1840s. We have seen how the shadow of the domestic angel haunted the female-authored poetry and narrative of that decade; the influence of the stereotype only intensified after 1850. Indeed, the 1850s is the decade in which Geraldine Scanlon observes the beginnings of a proliferating literature of conduct manuals and psychological studies of women in Spain: the appearance of women as writing subjects in the 1840s stimulated a new written discourse aimed at defining and confining femininity (Scanlon 21). The accelerating pressures for female conformity took their toll. María del Carmen Simón Palmer, in her survey of the attitudes of nineteenth-century Spanish women writers, calls attention to their conservatism in comparison to women writers in the rest of Europe and in America. Of the more than 1,000 Spanish women who published in the nineteenth century, Simón Palmer says, "the immense majority opted to make themselves spokeswomen for the traditional values of the Christian family and defended the image of women as mothers and wives, hoping thus to be pardoned for the 'offense' of writing" (489). Such a strategy responded to the domesticating, repressive pressures that, as I noted in chapters 1 and 2, were applied to women writers by families, mentors, critics, editors, and general social opinion.

While recognizing the self-protective and therefore conformist bent of the Spanish tradition of women's writing that originated in the 1840s, however, we must not fail to take into account the opposing thrust of a rebellious and protofeminist consciousness in the roots of this same tradition. This other pole is already visible in Massanés's "Discurso" as her readiness to commit and justify the "crime" of claiming public attention for her writing, her eager insistence on gaining approval for some space in which women could exercise their intellectual power. This contestatory element is perhaps most fully represented in Gómez de Avellaneda's *Sab*. Under the influence of the liberatory Romanticism of the 1830s, Avellaneda's novel questions the racial hierarchy of European society while it vents in disguised form anger and frustration about the oppression of women as well. Echoes of such anger at women's exclusion from the larger world of the intellect and public activity reverberate in *Dos mujeres*, in the poetry of Carolina Coronado, and even—in a highly disguised and distorted form—in novels by such a conservative writer as Fernán Caballero. In all these examples, however, female protest is to some degree muted or concealed, reminding us that these texts constitute a compromise between an expanding female consciousness and that restrictive and threatening public opinion to which Massanés referred.

THE IDEOLOGY OF GENDER DIFFERENCE

An evolution in women writers' negotiation of these conflicting pressures becomes discernible if we compare texts written in the early to mid-1840s with those published at the end of the decade. Though the pressure of the developing ideal of the domestic angel left its mark on the early production of Gómez de Avellaneda and Coronado, the influence of Romantic ideas of poet and self was also powerful then. While *Sab* and *Dos mujeres*, published in 1841 and 1842 respectively, make concessions to the rising expectations that women behave like angels (Carlota and Teresa feel no anger; Catalina immolates herself to promote domestic harmony), the moving force of these novels is the Romantic subjectivity of its female—or, in the case of Sab, cryptofemale—protagonists, who chafe against social limitations and aspire to a transforming and transcendent passion. These novels offer an occasionally explicit critique of the limitations imposed on women by the domestic ideal and its central social institution, marriage.

Coronado was not so bold as Gómez de Avellaneda in her first major appearance before the public—her 1843 *Poesías*. Yet we have detected beneath the surface of this early poetry the female lyrical subject's will to define herself poetically by rewriting traditional representations of women. This implicit concern with the expression of a particularly female experience was more openly elaborated in the poems Coronado published during the middle of the decade. Her protests against women's lot in Spanish society focused, under the influence of Romantic artistic ideals, upon strictures against female creativity and self-expression. Such sentiments aroused passionate echoes from women poets around the peninsula:[2] the lyrical sisterhood of the mid-forties expressed a shared sense of women's victimization that was potentially a basis for challenging the domesticating ideology of motherhood and self-sacrifice to which they also adhered.

As the 1840s drew to a close, however, the conflicting impulses in women's writing tended increasingly to resolve themselves on the side of the culture's restrictive feminine ideal by conforming to the norms of the domestic angel rather than extending the Romantic quest to women. Gómez de Avellaneda provided one of the early signs of this shift. The play she wrote to gain success in the theater after the publication of her book of poetry and her first two novels gives evidence of deep anxiety that her female Romantic persona had offended patriarchal norms. *Munio Alfonso* (1844), acclaimed by Madrid critics as a much-needed rejection of Romantic dramatic models in favor of the high seriousness of classical drama, treated filicide as the tragically mistaken but heroic action of its protagonist. It is difficult from a twentieth-century perspective to read this highly ambiguous play as anything but an ironic indictment of Munio's hubris in deciding that honor requires him to murder his daughter.[3] Yet the drama's structure, by devoting the whole last act to the guilty father's expiation of his sin and attainment of full heroic status in the wars against the Moors, allows the legendary hero—whom Avellaneda regarded as her father's ancestor—to transcend the blot of daughter-murder. Avellaneda's dramatization of a paternal ancestor's filicide and her simultaneous rejection of Romantic aesthetics, immediately preceding her turn to religious poetry in 1846, signal her retreat from the feminist revision of Romanticism accomplished in her earliest publications. In the 1850s and 1860s Gómez de Avellaneda maintained a feminist stance in her unsuccessful campaign to be admitted to the Spanish Royal Academy and in her journalistic articles on women (Beth Miller 210–214), but she banished feminist concerns from her imaginative writing and excluded *Sab* and *Dos mujeres* from the edition of her complete works that she began to compile in the 1860s. Although she never advocated the role of domestic angel for women as other women of her generation did, Gómez de Avellaneda's literary production ceased to question that role after 1845.

Carolina Coronado's protests about women's social destiny also began to cool toward the end of the decade. In 1845 she characterized the domestic circle assigned to women as incarceration:

> Al cuerpo cuatro paredes
> Nos dan porque viva en calma,
> Mas como pudiera el alma
> Fugarse de tal prisión,
> En la ignorancia nos hunden,
> Sin pensamiento quedamos,
> Y así presas nos hallamos
> En alma y en corazón. ("A Luisita" 70)

To keep our bodies calm, they enclose them in four walls, but lest our souls escape this prison, they sink us in ignorance, denying us thought, and thus we are prisoners in soul and in heart.

However, by 1850, when Coronado began publishing a series of articles she had been compiling on contemporary Spanish women poets, she insisted from the outset that creative activity should in no way alienate women from their primary, domestic role. She established her own position on this matter in writing about her friend Robustiana Armiño:

> La señorita Armiño no ha querido adoptar la absurda y ridícula doctrina que pretende emancipar a la mujer de la antigua dependencia de sus consideraciones sociales; tal vez porque ha adivinado el lastimoso trastorno que ocasionaría en las familias esa especie de libertad que a trueque de romper los vínculos más sagrados, quisiera conquistar de las costumbres el genio de las mujeres. La señorita Armiño ha comprendido tal vez, que no se trata de variar la condición de la mujer, sino de mejorarla; que con el estudio no debe aspirarse a alterar el orden de su vida doméstica, sino a embellecerlo; la señorita Armiño . . . ha producido en [las costumbres feminiles] un adelanto, . . . logrando conciliar en la vida de una mujer el genio con la modestia, la meditación con la laboriosidad, y la instrucción con la sencillez. ("Galeria: Armiño")

Señorita Armiño has not wished to adopt the absurd and ridiculous doctrine that advocates emancipating women from their former dependence on social considerations, perhaps because she has guessed the sad upheaval that families would suffer as a result of the kind of liberty that female genius seeks to obtain at the cost of breaking the most sacred ties. Señorita Armiño has understood perhaps that it is not a matter of changing woman's condition but of improving it; that through study she should aspire not to alter the order of her domestic life but to embellish it; Señorita Armiño . . . has advanced [feminine customs] . . . by managing to reconcile in one woman's life genius with modesty, meditation with diligence, and learning with simplicity.

I have cited this passage at length because it so clearly spells out what seems to have been the consensus among women writers and their readers at the close of the decade we have studied: the angel of the hearth provided the essential model of womanhood, a model that advocates of female self-expression and education might refine in certain respects as long as they did not alter its basic outlines.

In 1849, when Cecilia Boehl entered the arena of publication, then, her conservative message about women's place found a receptive public, even though—ironically—she owed her access to that public to women's recent gains as producers of print culture in Spain. The power of the trend that made women writers primary exponents of the ideology of domesticity can be seen in the views expressed by Carolina Coronado in 1857, when, now a wife and mother, she renewed her series of biographical sketches of women poets. Although her return to this project, abandoned when she married, indicates a measure of continuing solidarity with other women writers, her attitudes about women's condition show a dramatic change.

She dedicated the first article in the series published in *La Discusión* to an explanation of her change of heart since the forties.

> [L]a severidad con que fui educada, y la índole del pueblo en donde nací, me hicieron formar la equivocada idea de que la mujer carecía en toda España de ilustración, de ánimo y de libertad para expresar sus afectos, tomando por intérprete a la poesía. . . . Así, yo me lamentaba en infantiles versos de la esclavitud de la mujer, de su soledad y su tristeza. ("Galería. Introducción")

> The severity with which I was brought up and the nature of the town in which I was born led me to form the mistaken idea that women all over Spain lacked education, encouragement and freedom to express their feelings, interpreted through poetry. . . . Thus, I lamented in childish verses women's slavery, their loneliness and sorrows.

But traveling to Madrid and then to France, she continues, convinced her of her error:

> Fuerza es confesarlo, en la sociedad actual hace ya más falta la mujer que la literata. El vacío que comienza a sentirse no es del genio, sino el de la modestia; la luz que empieza a faltarnos no es la luz de las academias, sino la luz del hogar. En Francia ha desaparecido la familia, y en España desaparecerá también, si seguimos tomando por modelo a nuestros vecinos.

> We must confess that today's society needs women more than it does literary ladies. The absence that is starting to be felt is not that of genius but of modesty; the light that we are beginning to need is not the illustration of the academies but the glow of the hearth. In France the family has disappeared and it will disappear in Spain, too, if we go on taking our neighbors as models.

Thus, some twenty-one years after Larra issued his warning, in his review of Dumas's *Anthony*, against liberating women from their subordination to reproduction (see chapter 1), his arguments were echoed by a Spanish woman writer whose existence, much less success, he could never have foreseen.[4] It is significant that Coronado, again like Larra, who saw Dumas's extreme individualism as a principle of social "disorganization," blamed the extremes of Romanticism for encouraging socially disruptive fantasies. Although Gómez de Avellaneda had abandoned the forms and language of Romanticism earlier, Coronado was more extreme in recanting Romanticism, as she was in condemning her earlier feminist preoccupations. Writing about Josefa Massanés as the only poet of the period—male or female—who had escaped contagion by the Romantic epidemic, Coronado asserted that "era aquella época del romanticismo una época bien desastrosa, no sólo para la literatura, sino para las buenas costumbres" 'the Romantic period was a disastrous one not only for literature but also for social morality' ("Las poetisas españolas"). The waning prestige of Romanticism and its imperatives of individual autonomy and unlimited space for subjectivity, then, coincided with the sweeping consolidation of a domestic, reproduction-centered definition of women even among writers who had previously contested that model to some degree.

It is only an apparent paradox that women writers should have espoused domestic ideology at precisely the point when they had firmly established writing as a viable female profession. This conjunction can in part be explained, as Simón Palmer suggests, by women writers' attempt to compensate ideologically for transgressing norms of feminine practice. The historical processes of gender differentiation themselves offer a more far-reaching explanation, however. As we saw in the introduction, in the broader context of Europe a redefinition of the differences between men and women accompanied the emergence of modern bourgeois Western culture, making the feminine complementary—rather than simply inferior—to the masculine. This new representational system permitted women a legitimate arena of self-expression and artistic authority in place of the silence that the sexual hierarchy of an earlier social formation had enjoined on them.

The impact of this shift began to be felt in Spanish literary culture precisely during the 1840s, a decade when the propertied classes retreated from the disruptions of the 1830s by appealing to ideas of order and hierarchy. If, as Bridget Aldaraca's study of the *ángel del hogar* argues, Fray Luis de León's sixteenth-century version of the "perfect wife" insisted on her silence, it was because as man's absolute inferior, she had nothing to say that he could not say better. The new bourgeois society that began to install itself definitively in Spain during the 1830s and 1840s, however, saw women as radically different from men, perfectly designed by nature for the reproduction and nurturing of the human species.[5] This redefinition, perceptible in the Spanish writing about women that I examined in chapters 1 and 2, implicitly granted women a kind of authority in the sphere for which nature had specialized them, a fact that the female authors of the period intuitively seized upon as a justification for engaging in writing, an activity still largely reserved for men. By making themselves mouthpieces for the ideology of women's "natural" domestic life mission, mid-nineteenth-century women writers in Spain laid claim to what the emerging society could not help but regard as a legitimate—and strictly limited—piece of terrain in written discourse.

The first generation of Spanish women writers, who began writing under the stimulus of the Romantic cult of subjectivity, mapped in their texts not only the points of opposition between the bourgeois feminine ideal and the Romantic overreacher but also the points where these two apparently competing models for representing the female self could be articulated in the new bourgeois image of female subjectivity. When in 1857 Carolina Coronado confirmed her complete adherence to the dominant scheme of gender difference by declaring that she was "persuadida de que el juicio en la mujer es una cualidad tan rara como la sensibilidad en un hombre" 'persuaded that good judgment in a woman is as rare a quality as sensibility in a man' ("Las poetisas españolas"), she indicated the fundamental point at which the Romantic validation of feeling was integrated in the new representation of woman as endowed with a superior sensitivity and emotional responsiveness in accordance with her maternal function. Coronado's generation had won a tenuous social acceptance for women's authority—and authorization to write—with regard to the tender emotions (see Deville's comments on women's poetry cited in chapter 2) at the price of ultimately attaching that authority to the bourgeois ideal of domestic womanhood.

FEMALE SUBJECTIVITY AND DESIRE

As the pioneering women writers of the 1840s adapted Romantic models to develop a discourse of female subjectivity that eventually supported and received support from a reconstruction of sexual difference as asymmetrically complementary (that is, the woman's sphere was qualitatively different from but still subordinated to the man's), they encountered one intractable problem in particular. That problem was the place of desire in the Romantic schema of the self. The Promethean drama of the Romantic self in Europe and in Spain specifically was the drama of desire itself, reaching toward what the subject does not possess. Yet the complementary system of representing sexual difference that was in place in European culture by the early nineteenth century regarded desire as exclusively an attribute of the male. Thomas Laqueur has shown that in the accounts of sexuality offered by medical science, increasingly thought to be an authoritative version of objective reality, female pleasure was no longer considered to be necessary to reproduction by the mid-eighteenth century (1–3). Moral and political discourse about women increasingly pointed to women's lack or transcendence of sexual appetite as a distinguishing feature. In Spain, where the cult of the Virgin Mary was deeply ingrained in the religious tradition, the ideal of woman as a sexless mother was readily accepted. Indeed, nineteenth-century Spanish culture regarded any form of desire as incompatible with true femininity, and this prohibition dogged women writers' efforts to incorporate Romantic subjectivity in images of the female self.

Despite notable differences among the three women writers whom I have discussed in detail, their texts construct remarkably similar relationships between the female subject and desire. For all of them, woman's desire is dangerous and destructive to her; as writing subjects, these women disavow, disguise, sublimate, or condemn female impulses toward self-gratification. Although female sexual desire is presented—always indirectly—as most destructive, the lust for preeminence, achievement, or power also has distinctly negative consequences for the female subject. The sexual desire of Cecilia Boehl's Marisalada is inherently self-destructive, while her ambition—with which the narrating subject identifies at one point in the novel—destroys family and friends. Carolina Coronado's feminized sunflower, longing for a sun that signifies both sex and glory, consumes itself in death-bound obscurity.

It is in such treatment of desire that the women Romantics' representations of the self, produced within the cultural horizons imposed by the dominant ideology of gender differences, most consistently differed from those of their male colleagues. While male versions of the Romantic self suffered too as a consequence of their Promethean desire—

Espronceda's Lucifer, for example, burns in hell—that suffering marks them as heroic, the undaunted victims of an unjust and inferior social authority. Male desire, in and of itself, is mostly presented as a positive value, instigating man's ceaseless quest for knowledge, producing the utopian vision that moves mankind forward, driving man to make his own destiny. For the Spanish women Romantics, in contrast, desire is a curse that the female subject must contend with, the enemy of her self-possession and wholeness. Gómez de Avellaneda's "Amor y orgullo," whose self-alienated subject experiences sexual love as a painful decentering, exemplifies the female self's struggle against the sundering ravages of desire. To the extent that Avellaneda and her women contemporaries could not divorce the textualization of the female subject from the cultural context in which writer and reader operated, self-gratifying desire—forbidden to women by deeply rooted social codes—remained a disruptive though ever-present element in the configuration of the female self.

The women Romantics could not eliminate desire entirely from their self-representations, partly because the creative ambitions that led them to break social taboos by writing left their mark on the texts produced by this act of rebellion. Although the women writers we have studied treated sexual desire only with extreme circumspection and ambivalence, they all made space in their texts for women's creative aspirations and powers. Paradoxically, the writer who explicitly granted artistic talent to her female protagonists in *Elia* and *La gaviota* was the same Cecilia Boehl who preached adamantly against women's aspiring to achievement in their own right. Avellaneda and Coronado found rather more oblique forms of making poetic power an attribute of the female subject. Uniting Carlota's superior sensibility with Teresa's intelligence and Sab's passion, imagination, and energy, the three-personed protagonist of *Sab* forms a composite image of the novel's narrating subject—that is, the three protagonists constitute a "superior soul" whose vision of justice, love, and beauty projected within the novel's degraded world figures the poetic power of the female author. Coronado's early poetry metaphorically characterizes the female lyrical subject in terms of the bee, granting the female poet a creative activity that, while distinguished from that of the high-soaring male genius, nevertheless in its own earth-bound arena has validity as an encounter of mind and world. Her later poetry vacillates between rebellious attempts to break out of the limitations of female poetic authority and expressions of the anxiety produced by such impulses.

In their personal lives, these writers varied considerably in their ability to reconcile their identity as women with their vocation as writers. As we saw in chapter 7, Cecilia Boehl believed the two to be entirely incompatible and remained painfully in conflict about her writing until the end of her life. The young Carolina Coronado, in contrast, evinced skepticism about the popular wisdom that writing defeminized women. In a letter to Hartzenbusch she declared: "[M]e he convencido de que es fábula y enredo lo que algunos decían de que no se pueden conciliar los dos extremos de la pluma y el dedal. . . . [H]allo que puede una mujer estar escribiendo toda su vida sin renunciar a su sexo, como tantos pretenden" 'I'm convinced that what they say about not being able to reconcile the two extremes of the pen and the thimble is a deceitful fiction. I find that a woman can write her whole life long without renouncing her sex, as so many claim' (Cartas, carta 219). Despite such differences in attitudes and experience, however, the writing produced by these women shows that, caught as they were in the crosscurrents of the conflicting discourses of gender ideology and Romantic poetic individualism, they could not always successfully negotiate a coherent image of the female subject in their texts. In some cases a chasm of silence separates a mysterious female figure—Coronado's Rosa Bianca or Boehl's Elia—from the verbal power associated with masculine and worldly authority. More frequently, female subjectivity is represented as internally heterogeneous, divided between femininity and genius in some form or another. Such division is evident in the anxious vacillation of Coronado's lyrical subject between root and wing, for example, or in the more complex identity-hostility between the narrating subject of La gaviota, transgressor as well as voice of virtue, and its protagonist, an antiheroine and an artist.

The complex and ambiguous images of female subjectivity produced by the Romantic women writers disappeared from discourse about women in the literature of mass consumption after 1850. During decades of disturbance and revolution (1850–1880) when Spain's propertied classes were divided to the point of fragmentation by political, economic, and regional differences, the image of the naturally domestic, virtuous, and submissive woman seemed to become particularly important as a shared cultural norm that preserved traditional gender—and class[6]—hierarchy. In periodicals and serialized fiction, as Andreu has shown, the female subject was represented in terms of the normative and reductive Virtuous Woman, in whom desire, creative imagination, and conflict had been entirely eliminated. However, although

popular literature showed no trace of the more complex female subjectivity of the 1840s, the legacy of the Romantic women writers was preserved in the high culture of late nineteenth-century Spain, in women's
poetry, and, in particular, in the realist novel, the art form *par excellence* of bourgeois culture.

THE LEGACY OF THE ROMANTIC
FEMALE SUBJECT

It was in the realist novel's representation of subjectivity and women
subjects that the dominant literary tradition most clearly echoed the
women Romantics. Realism, the successor of Romanticism as the
privileged aesthetic of bourgeois culture, inherited the focus on individual subjectivity and the language for representing it that made the
Romantic revolution part of the larger cultural revolution supporting
the emergence of modern capitalism in the West. However, the realist
novel submitted the Romantics' ever-expanding self to the constraining
pressures of society and history, and in this way opened itself to the
problematics of self and society that concerned the women Romantics.
For one thing, domestic life and feminine subjectivity became indis-
pensable to realism's project of representing the totality of social forces
operating in individual experience. For another, the femininization of
the Romantic subject responded to problems closely related to the
realist preoccupation with how society limited and conditioned the individual subject. For these reasons, it should come as no surprise that
figures of the self developed in the 1840s by Gómez de Avellaneda,
Coronado, and Fernán Caballero reappeared in the realist novels of the
1880s written by both men and women.

Gómez de Avellaneda's conflation of the Romantic *alma superior,*
whose subjective powers place it in conflict with social norms, with the
alma sensible that tagged the subject as female (see chapter 2) anticipated one of the Spanish realist novel's most significant figures. As Noël
M. Valis points out, one important character type in the late nineteenth
century embodies Romantic sensibility, usually in terms of an aspiration to a poetic existence frustrated by an irremediably prosaic milieu:
"The very triviality of the type and the sheer repetitiveness of its successive appearances should not blind us to a significant fact: its prolon-
gation within mainstream realism in Spanish letters" (300). In many
cases, especially when this type was embodied in a male character, the
realist novel treated the pretensions and values of the Romantic soul

with a corrosive irony that seems designed to castigate the Romantic sensibility (and perhaps its associated connotations of femininity) lingering on in writers and readers. This is, for example, one of Valis's arguments in her analysis of Emilia Pardo Bazán's novel *El cisne de Vilamorta*. The realist novel's tendency to parody the type in question is one manifestation of a maturing and self-protective bourgeois culture's anxiety to control and limit the Romantic subjectivity that characterized an earlier, more militant and radical moment in its own formation. Nevertheless, just as the discourse associated with Romantic subjectivity remained alive and meaningful in late nineteenth-century culture, so also the image of the superior soul mired in a degraded world retained its power to mobilize meaning.

Novelists found the superior soul image particularly suggestive when embodied in a female protagonist. Indeed, this image provides the fundamental structure of one of Spanish realism's most influential novels, Leopoldo Alas's *La regenta,* which centers on the oppressive impact of a stagnant provincial milieu upon Ana Ozores, a woman of superior intellect, imagination, and feeling. Gómez de Avellaneda's innovation in *Sab* and *Dos mujeres*—endowing female characters with Romantic longings for transcendence that are frustrated by social limitations imposed specifically on women—receives in *La regenta* the exhaustive elaboration permitted by realist techniques. The novel's account of Ana's education, adolescence, and marriage reveals in detail how in provincial society her class position and gender force upon her the empty conventions of the domestic angel and condemn her to a life devoid of meaningful activity. Ana's plight is echoed in the tragedy of Fermín, the priest who loves her, a Promethean overreacher who recognizes in Ana a kindred "superior soul." Although Fermín can use the power of the Church to satisfy his ambitions, ecclesiastical constraints on his sexuality feminize him (the Church literally puts him in skirts), making him impotent to realize his deepest longing for transcendence through love. Thus, the Romantic self as female or feminized became for the realist novel a sign connoting the universal impotence of the individual in contemporary society.

Other important novels—those of Benito Pérez Galdós above all—register the suggestive power of women's struggle to define themselves as subjects in the face of prescriptive social objectification. I am not thinking only, or even primarily, of *Tristana* (1892), which makes that struggle its explicit thesis. Although earlier works such as *La desheredada* and *Fortunata y Jacinta,* monuments in Galdós's exploration of the interaction of human experience and history in contemporary Spain, do not specifically refer to a feminist thematic, they do center on what was the essence of the drama enacted in the writing of the women Romantics: the never entirely successful efforts of female protagonists to redefine according to their own sense of self the meaning society has assigned them. Galdós has in this sense replaced the novelistic paradigm of the male Romantic subject trying to make his way in a prosaic world, like Balzac's Lucien de Rubempré, with female protagonists, who embody for him the most poignant contradictions of consciousness and world. It is true, as Andreu argues (100–103, 130), that while Galdós represents the subjectivity of such women characters very differently from the pulp fiction that monolithically propounded the norm of the *ángel del hogar,* the implications of his narrative support the ideal of the domestic woman. The writing of the women Romantics did not reject basic tenets of that ideal, either. But what permits us to see in Galdós's novels a preservation of certain meaning clusters generated in the earlier elaboration of a female writing subject is the location of the struggle for consciousness and self-definition— *the* essential human project for Galdós—in the female subject and its specific dilemmas.

Though the realist novel drew on Romantic paradigms for representing subjectivity, it went much further that the principal Spanish Romantics in making problematic the unity and autonomy of the subject of consciousness. Galdós, for instance, was much concerned with the phenomenon of false consciousness, with desires that, appearing to spring from the deep recesses of the soul, received their shape and content from inappropriate social ideologies: for example, Isidora Rufete, determined to shape her destiny according to her idea of herself, self-destructively follows the program outlined in her mad father's antiquated fantasies.

In its attention to the social determinants of desire and the inherent division of consciousness, the Spanish realist novel repeated and elaborated in new ways patterns that had emerged in the women Romantics' construction of the female subject. Increasingly, these late nineteenth century novels portrayed characters as split between contradictory desires, much like the lyrical subject of Coronado's poetry or the writing subject of Cecilia Boehl's *Gaviota.* There are many instances in the works of Alas and Galdós of characters whose actions express wishes that they have repressed as unacceptable. It was the woman novelist Emilia Pardo Bazán, however, who followed up most consistently on the female Romantics' image of divided consciousness, giving the un-conscious manifestations of desires prohibited by social norms a central place in several of her novels. In *Insolación* the female protagonist, Asís, acts out her powerful sexual attraction to a handsome young An-dalusian, while her consciousness, represented in interior monologue, only registers the internal echoes of social disapproval of feminine sex-uality. The split subject in *Los pazos de Ulloa* is Julián, a young priest who has without difficulty banished all thought of sexuality from his mind. Yet by depicting Julián's sudden, unexplained moments of un-easiness and anxiety around women and his disturbing dreams, the narrative shows that he has not yet mastered his unconscious sexual fantasies.

If the latter half of the nineteenth century preserved in its liter-ary discourse traces of the language and figures of female subjectivity elaborated by the women writers of the 1840s, it also produced direct descendants of those same writers, as the reference to Emilia Pardo Bazán reminds us. Among the hundreds of women writers who fol-lowed in the career path that the pioneers of the 1840s had opened up to women, two major Spanish writers stand out: Pardo Bazán and the poet Rosalía de Castro, neither of whom followed the dominant trend of adopting the protective coloring of the domestic angel. In this sense, both Pardo Bazán and Castro carried on—though in different ways—the contestatory impulse that glimmered in the women's writing of the early 1840s.

The intrepid Pardo Bazán, who parlayed the privileges of her class position in the aristocratic, capitalist Spanish oligarchy into relative sexual freedom in her personal life, became in the 1890s an outspoken advocate for feminist reforms, joining her voice with that of the inde-fatigable Concepción Arenal. While Pardo Bazán textualizes important aspects of female experience—including (in *La tribuna*) women's po-litical activity—she does not offer an unequivocal critique of oppres-sive class and gender ideologies. Yet as an active propagandist for a bourgeois feminist perspective, as the first female Spanish university professor, and as a living model of an unintimidated woman, she played a major role in establishing the groundwork from which twen-tieth-century Spanish feminism could rise.

Rosalía de Castro, in contrast, was not an activist in terms of pub-lic or even private demonstrations of feminist convictions. Her writ-ing, however, powerfully registers her lack of conformity with a gender system she perceived as unjust and with a social system she saw as exploitative and inhumane. As a poet, she was a direct heir of the liberal Romantics: Espronceda's influence was very strong in her first book of poetry, *La flor* (1857), whose title, by calling attention to an important motif in the poetry of the women Romantics, indicates that she was also conscious of inscribing herself in a female tradition. Indeed, in the prologue to her first novel, *La hija del mar* (1859), she designated the line of women writers that made it possible for her to dare to present a book to the public. Although she does not mention Coronado or Gómez de Avellaneda, Castro claims the same foremothers they also had claimed, naming Sappho, Saint Teresa, Mme de Staël, and George Sand (whose influence on Castro was pervasive). In an early article—"Leiders" (1858)—she echoes the Romantic rhetoric of liberation as appropriated for women by Avellaneda and Coronado:

> Sólo cantos de independencia y libertad han balbucido mis labios, aunque alrededor hubiese sentido, desde la cuna ya, el ruido de las cadenas que debían aprisionarme para siempre, porque el patrimonio de la mujer son los grillos de la esclavitud. (2: 1524)

> My lips have babbled only songs of independence and freedom, though since the cradle I might have heard around me the sound of the chains that were to imprison me forever, for the shackles of slavery are woman's patrimony.

The great poetry in Galician written by Rosalía de Castro in the 1860s and 1870s far surpassed earlier Spanish Romantic models in capturing popular traditions and language and in speaking for a marginalized group—the common folk of impoverished Galicia. The female perspective is an essential part of this poetry, which refers repeatedly to the double burden carried by Galician women, responsible both for working the fields and for raising the children while their husbands were at sea or seeking work in other parts of the peninsula. In a cycle such as "As viudas dos vivos e as viudas dos muertos" 'The Widows of the Live and the Widows of the Dead,' from *Follas novas* (1880), the social situation of Galician women reverberates powerfully with the intimate desolation expressed by the female lyrical subject. Castro's novels deal undisguisedly with such issues as the objectification of women by male sexual obsession, the debilitating effects of women's economic and emotional dependence on men, and the unsatisfactory alternatives available to independent-minded women. Rosalía de Castro's writing, then, picked up and raised to new levels of literary discourse the awareness of women's oppressive social destiny, the empathy with the marginalized, and the aspiration for free self-expression and self-determination that had characterized Spanish women's writing of the early 1840s. Critics are only now beginning to realize that her poetic achievement, increasingly valued in the twentieth century for its innovativeness and evocative power, was profoundly rooted in her gender identity.[7]

The same factors that slowed and attenuated the development of capitalism and the bourgeois revolution in Spain, and thus delayed the rise of a modern press and the institution of universal, state-run education, also affected the formulation of women's claims to the rights and privileges such a transition extended to men of the propertied classes. Spanish feminist scholars have been understandably disheartened in their search for a submerged tradition in the nineteenth century that might reinforce twentieth-century Spanish feminism. Matilde Albert Robatto confesses to "the deep disappointment I have felt on confirming . . . that in Spain there was not the slightest sign in the nineteenth century of the formation of a feminist movement comparable to the ones that developed in England or the United States" (36). María del Carmen Simón Palmer, looking for signs of feminist advocacy among Spain's many nineteenth-century women writers, concludes, "It is clear that literature did not serve our authors as a means of going from their own experience to denounce a collective situation, as occurred in other countries" (484). As both scholars then point out, the particularities of Spanish history and culture gave Spanish feminism a different shape and timetable from that of England or France. But, as I hope this study of Spain's women Romantics has made clear, Spain developed its own unique women's tradition in response to the shaping forces of its culture.

The preceding chapters have demonstrated that as soon as historical circumstances were the least bit propitious—that is, as soon as the press began to expand, as soon as reforms benefiting bourgeois men were underway and the ideology of individualism was gathering momentum—Spanish women were ready to explore that narrow opening to opportunity through the only means open to them at the time—writing. At a moment when Romanticism was at its peak in Spain, these women revised its model of the self, and, resisting the various cultural trends that would objectify them or confine them in domestic servitude, created a literary language expressive of a complex female selfhood.

The texts produced during this early moment of women's participation in print culture were submerged, however, by the sweeping mid-century triumph of the model of the *ángel del hogar*. Female as well as male authors adopted the reductive model of woman as domestic angel along with other conservative social ideologies that reflected the anxiety of Spain's propertied classes for order and hierarchy. Even pioneering women writers of the 1840s collaborated in the repression of their early, protofeminist works: Gómez de Avellaneda's *Sab* and *Dos mujeres* were not reprinted until 1914, when a Cuban edition of her complete works came out. Carolina Coronado, who lived until 1911, made no attempt to reverse the exclusion of her most explicitly feminist poetry from anthologies and republications of her work, an exclusion that has persisted until the present day. The scattered publications of the *hermandad lírica* are lost among the archives of nineteenth-century periodicals, ignored by literary historians. And until recently, critics have not known how to decipher the signs of Fernán Caballero's repressed feminist impulses. Despite the continued dominance of ideologies of women's subordination and the blindness of official culture to the origins of a literature of female—if not precisely feminist—consciousness, however, that tradition survived in the flow of culture itself, reemerging with Rosalía de Castro and Emilia Pardo Bazán in the next generation of women writers and subtly enriching the expressive and critical capabilities of the prestigious and lastingly influential realist novel of the late nineteenth century.

Appendix

Texts of Poems Not Available in
Twentieth-Century Editions

BY GERTRUDIS GÓMEZ DE AVELLANEDA

A él
[*Poesías,* 1841 ed.]

Era la edad lisonjera
En que es un sueño la vida,
Era la aurora hechicera
De mi juventud florida,
En su sonrisa primera:
    Cuando contenta vagaba
Por el campo, silenciosa,
Y en escuchar me gozaba
La tórtola que entonaba
Su querella lastimosa.
    Melancólico fulgor
Blanca luna repartía,
Y el aura leve mecía
Con soplo murmurador
La tierna flor que se abría.
    ¡Y yo gozaba! El rocío,
Nocturno llanto del cielo,
El bosque espeso y umbrío,
La dulce quietud del suelo,
El manso correr del río.
    Y de la luna el albor,
Y el aura que murmuraba,

Acariciando a la flor,
Y el pájaro que cantaba—
Todo me hablaba de amor.
    Y trémula, palpitante,
En mi delirio extasiada,
Miré una visión brillante,
Como el aire perfumada,
Como las nubes flotante.
    Ante mí resplandecía
Como un astro brillador,
Y mi loca fantasía
Al fantasma seductor
Tributaba idolatría.
    Escuchar pensé su acento
En el canto de las aves:
Eran las auras su aliento
Cargadas de aromas suaves,
Y su estancia el firmamento.
    ¿Qué ser divino era aquél?
¿Era un Angel o era un hombre?
¿Era un Dios o era Luzbel...?
¿Mi visión no tiene nombre?
¡Ah! nombre tiene... ¡Era *él*!

*   *   *

299

El alma guardaba tu imagen
     divina
Y en ella reinabas ignoto señor,
Que instinto secreto tal vez ilumina
La vida futura que espera el amor.
     Al sol que en el cielo de Cuba
          destella,
Del trópico ardiente brillante fanal,
Tus ojos eclipsan, tu frente descuella
Cual se alza en la selva la palma
     real.
     Del genio la aureola, radiante,
          sublime,
Ciñendo contemplo tu pálida sien,
Y al verte, mi pecho palpita, y se
     oprime,
Dudando si formas mi mal o mi
     bien.
     Que tú eres no hay duda mi sueño
          adorado.
El ser que vagando mi mente buscó,
Mas ¡ay! que mil veces el hombre,
     arrastrado
Por fuerza enemiga, su mal anheló.

          *   *   *   *   *   *

     Así vi a la mariposa
Inocente, fascinada
En torno a la luz amada
Revolotear con placer.
     Insensata se aproxima
Y le acaricia insensata,
Hasta que la luz ingrata
Devora su frágil ser.
     Y es fama que allá en los bosques
Que adornan mi patria ardiente,
Nace y crece una serpiente
De prodigioso poder.
     Que exhala en torno su aliento
Y la ardilla palpitante,
Fascinada, delirante,
Corre... ¡y corre a perecer!
     ¿Hay una mano de bronce,
Fuerza, poder, o destino,
Que nos impele al camino
Que a nuestra tumba trazó?
     ¿Dónde van, dónde, esas nubes

Por el viento compelidas?...
¿Dónde esas hojas perdidas
Que del árbol arrancó?
     Vuelan, vuelan resignadas,
Y no saben donde van,
Pero siguen el camino
Que les traza el huracán.
     Vuelan, vuelan en sus alas
Nubes y hojas a la par,
Y a los cielos las levante
Ya las sumerja en el mar.
     ¡Pobres nubes! ¡pobres hojas
que no saben dónde van!...
Pero siguen el camino
Que les traza el huracán.

                              (1840)

                  A la poesía
              [*Poesías,* 1841 ed.]

     ¡Oh tú, del alto cielo
Precioso don al hombre concedido,
Tú de mis penas divina consuelo,
De mis placeres manantial querido;
Deja que pueda mi dorada lira
Cantar la gloria que tu fuego
     inspira.
     ¡Ardiente poesia!
¡Alma del Universo! De tu llama
Al incendio feliz, el alma mía
En entusiasmo férvido se inflama,
Rasga la mente su tiniebla oscura
Y el rayo brota de tu esencia pura.
     ¿Qué canto desusado
Exhalan, lira, tus templadas cuerdas
Que al pecho palpitante y abrasado
Pasadas dichas y placer recuerdas,
Volviéndole ¡ay! las emociones
     gratas
Con que los días de su abril
     retratas?
     ¡Salve, salve mil veces!
Musa de la ilusión, que adormecida
Estabas en mi mente! Resplandeces
Astro de paz en mi agitada vida,
Y al noble fuego de tu amor fecundo

Llenaré de tu gloria el ancho
  mundo.
  Mas no: tú misma vuela
Y al orbe tus misterios celestiales
Con abrasada inspiración revela,
Comunica tu fuego a los mortales
Y haz circular tu soplo blandamente
De región en región, de gente en
  gente.
  Asaz el monstruo impío
Que en sangre hirviente sus laureles
  baña,
Al viento dio su pabellón sombrío,
Asaz ardiendo en inclemente saña
El numen ¡ay! de la nefanda guerra
Con su cetro feral rigió la tierra.
  De la ambición insana,
Del odio y la venganza acom-
  pañado,
Al Orco torne, en impotencia vana,
Quede su solio impuro derrocado,
Y el funesto laurel que altivo ostenta
Marchito caiga de su sien sangrienta.
  ¡Genio de la armonía!
No a la posteridad des la memoria
De esos hombres de sangre, ni a su
  impía
Fama le prestes tu fulgente gloria:
Tu carro triunfador no cuesta llanto
Ni el laurel que conquistas con el
  canto.
  No envidies sus blasones
Ni del poder la efímera grandeza
Que hinchada ves de impuras
  oblaciones:
De tu destino la inmortal belleza,
Tu sublime misión, ¡oh poesía!
Ni acero ha menester ni tiranía.
  ¡Oh! nunca profanada
La altiva frente ante los tronos bajes,
Ni sea tu voz por la ambición
  comprada,
Ni cubras la impiedad con tus
  celajes:
¡Nunca el magnate o el feroz soldado
A sus pies vean tu laurel hollado!
  Tu genio independiente

Rompa las nieblas del error grosero,
La verdad preconice, y de su frente
Temple con flores el rigor severo,
Dando al mortal en dulces ilusiones
De saber y virtud gratas lecciones.
  A ti ofrece natura
Su más variada pompa y su
  grandeza,
A ti los cielos brindan su hermosura,
Y el aura de la noche su pureza;
Y el himno entonas que al Eterno
  sube
En las zafíreas alas del Querube.
  Hablas: todo renace.
Tu creadora voz los yermos puebla,
Espacios no hay que tu poder no
  abrace,
Y rasgando del tiempo la tiniebla,
Luz celestial, descubres e iluminas
Las mutiladas silenciosas ruinas.
  Por tu acento apremiados
Preséntanse del fondo del olvido
Ante tu tribunal siglos pasados,
Y el fallo que pronuncias, trasmitido
Por una y otra edad en rasgos de oro
Eterniza su gloria o su desdoro.
  Al héroe que se inmola,
Y a quien su patria ingrata
  desconoce,
Le ciñes tú la espléndida aureola,
Y haces que el sabio la esperanza
  goce
De que si el odio empaña su
  memoria
Tú cantarás al porvenir su gloria.
  Mas si entre gayas flores
A la beldad consagras tus acentos,
Haces nacer los célicos amores,
Haces brotar purísimos contentos,
Que de tu voz la Omnipotencia
  blanda
Con ley de paz los corazones manda.
  Así Petrarca un día
Sintió de amor las penas, los
  encantos,
El puro fuego que en su pecho ardía
Admira el mundo en sus divinos

cantos,
Y aun en la orilla de Valclusa el aura
Murmura triste el nombre de su
    Laura.
    Y vosotros, de España
Vates ilustres, dulce Garcilaso,
Tierno Meléndez, ¿la iracunda saña
De altivos héroes celebráis acaso?
No, que la gloria en vuestra lira
    hermosa
Sólo enlaza los mirtos con la rosa.
    ¡Oh! si dado me fuera
Vuestro dulce cantar, vuestra
    ternura,
O el plectro ardiente del sublime
    Herrera,
O del culto Rioja la tersura,
Entonces ¡ay! el fuego que me anima
Extendiera mi voz de clima en clima.
    Mil veces desgraciado
El que insensible a tu divino acento,
Con alma yerta, y corazón gastado,
No siente hervir el alto pensamiento;
Que es el mundo sin ti templo vacío,
Cielo sin claridad, cadáver frío.
    Mas yo doquier te miro:
Si de la noche con el fresco ambiente
De puras flores el aroma aspiro,
Al murmurar de la sonora fuente;
Tú respiras allí, y en leda calma
La dulce inspiración viertes al alma.
    Si con la blanca aurora
Despertando natura, se engalana,
Y de záfir y rosa se colora,
Rica de juventud, de amor ufana,
Tú con su brisa en lánguidos
    desmayos
Giras del sol en los primeros rayos.
    Si al huracán violento
De la borrasca el manto denegrido
Enluta el éter, y en su firme asiento
El cerro tiembla en hórrido
    estampido,
Trémula siento palpitar mi seno
Y oigo tu voz al retumbar del
    trueno.
    También, también un día
Del ancho mar en el inmenso llano

Tu faz sublime con placer veía,
Ora silbase el aquilón insano,
Ora gimiese en la extendida lona
La brisa pura de la ardiente zona.
    Aun en la tumba helada!—
Aun en la tumba, sí, pálida y bella
Te vi borrar, de adelfas coronada,
De la muerte cruel la triste huella,
Y de tu santa inspiración el vuelo,
Llevar el alma del sepulcro al cielo.
    De la fortuna ciega
Nunca imploré los miserables dones,
Ni de las dichas que el amor me
    niega
Me adularán mentidas ilusiones.
Eres tú sola, ¡oh musa! mi tesoro,
Tú la deidad que sin cesar imploro.
    Y no ambiciosa aspiro
A conquistar el lauro refulgente
Que humilde acato y generosa
    admiro,
De Homero o Taso en la radiosa
    frente,
Ni invoco, ¡Byron! de tu gloria
    esclava
El numen de dolor que te agitaba.
    Como rosa temprana
Que troncha el cierzo, o marchitó el
    estío,
Pasa veloz la juventud lozana,
Y la árida vejez, su aliento frío
Al exhalar marchita cuanto alcanza,
Gloria, placer, ternura y esperanza.
    Dame que pueda, entonces,
¡Virgen de paz! ¡Sublime poesía!
No transmitir en mármoles y bronces
De un siglo en otro la memoria mía,
Sólo arrullar, cantando, mis dolores,
La sien ceñida de modestas flores.
                                    (1840)

A una mariposa
[*Poesías*, 1841 ed.]

Fugaz mariposa,
Que de oro y zafir
Las alas ostentas,
Alegre y feliz.

Cual siguen mis ojos
Tu vuelo gentil,
Que al soplo desplegas
Del aura de abril.
    Ya rauda te lanzas,
Al bello jardín,
Ya en rápidos giros
Te acercas a mí.
    Del sol a los rayos
Que empieza a lucir,
¡Con cuánta riqueza
Te brinda el pensil!
    Sus flores la acacia
Desplega por ti,
Y el clavel fragante
Su ardiente rubí.
    Abre la violeta
Su seno turquí,
La anémona luce
Su vario matiz.
    Ya libas el lirio,
Ya el fresco alelí,
Ya trémula besas
El blanco jazmín.
    Mas ¡ay! cuán en vano
Mil flores y mil,
Por fijar se afanan
Tu vuelo sin fin!
    ¡Ay! que ya te lleva
Tu audaz frenesí
Do ostenta la rosa
Su puro carmín.
    ¡Temeraria, tente!
¿Dó vas, infeliz?
¿No ves las espinas
De punta sutil?
    Torna a tu violeta,
Torna a tu alelí,
No quieras, incauta,
Clavada morir.

                        (1838)

A mi jilguero
[*Poesías,* 1841 ed.]

No así las lindas alas
Abatas, jilguerillo,

Desdeñando las galas
De su matiz sencillo.
    No así guardes cerrado
Ese tu ebúrneo pico,
De dulzuras colmado,
De consonancias rico.
    En tu jaula preciosa
¿Qué falta a tu recreo?
Mi mano cariñosa
Previene tu deseo
    Festón de verdes hojas
Tu reja adorna y viste:
Mira que ya me enojas
Con tu silencio triste.
    No de ingrato presumas,
Recobra tu contento,
Riza las leves plumas,
Da tus ecos al viento.

        Mas no me escucha
    Que tristemente
    Gira doliente
    Por su prisión.
        Troncha las hojas,
    Pica la reja,
    Luego se aleja
    Con aflicción.
        Ni un trino solo
    Su voz exhala,
    Mas bate el ala
    Con languidez;
        Y tal parecen
    Sus lindos ojos
    En sus enojos
    Llorar viudez.

    Ya conozco, infelice,
Tu pena punzadora:
Tu silencio la dice,
Mi corazón la llora.
    Cuando el dolor te oprime
Y cuando callas triste
¿No echas de menos, dime,
El campo en que naciste?
    ¿Y el prado lisonjero,
Y el bosque silencioso
Do ensayaste primero
Tu vuelo temoroso?

¿El árbol cuya rama
Meció tu blando nido,
Y el agua que derrama
Tu manantial querido,
    Donde a beber llegabas
Del lago cristalino,
Y a la sombra posabas
Del centenario pino?
    ¿Y recuerdas la amena
Pradera, con sus flores,
De los cantares llena
De tus tiernos amores?
    ¿Y el séquito canoro
De lindos pajarillos,
Las espigas de oro
Robando de los trillos?
    ¡Por eso ya no canta
Tu pico enmudecido,
Que en desventura tanta
La voz es un gemido!
    Yo tu suerte deploro;
Y en triste simpatía
Cuando tu pena lloro,
Lloro también la mía;
    Que triste, cual tú, vivo,
Por siempre separada
De mi suelo nativo,
De mi Cuba adorada.
    No ya, jilguero mío,
Veré la fértil vega
Que el Tínima sombrío
Con sus cristales riega,
    Ni en las tardes serenas
Tras enriscados montes
Disipará mis penas
La voz de los sinsontes,
    Ni harán en mis oídos
Arrullo al blando sueño
Sus arroyos queridos,
Con murmullo halagüeño.

        Ni verá el prado
        Que vio otro día
        La lozanía
        De mi niñez,
            Los tardos pasos
        Que marque incierta

Mi planta yerta
Por la vejez.
    Ni la campana
Dulce sonora,
Que dio la hora
De mi natal,
    Sonará lenta
Y entristecida
De aquesta vida
Mi hora final.
    El sol de fuego,
La hermosa luna,
Mi dulce cuna,
Mi dulce hogar....
    Todo lo pierde,
Desventurada,
Ya destinada
Sólo a llorar.

    Pues somos en desventura,
Pájaro infeliz, iguales,
Cantarás tú mi amargura
Y lloraré yo tus males.
    Nacidos en cruda estrella,
Unidos por el destino,
Trina al son de mi querella
La canción del peregrino.
    Mas tu mirar angustiado
En mí fijas con tristura
Y tal parece que osado
Me atribuyes tu amargura.
    ¿No es igual mi cruda pena
A la que te agobia impía?
¿No nos une la cadena
De una triste simpatía?
    "No, porque en extraña tierra
Tus cariños te han seguido,
Y allí la patria se encierra
Do está el objeto querido.
    De una madre el dulce seno
Recibe tu triste llanto,
Y yo de consuelo ajeno,
Solo lloro, y solo canto.
    Eres libre, eres amada,
Y yo, solitario, cautivo,
Avecilla abandonada
Para divertirte vivo.

¡Ah! no, pues, mujer ingrata,
No te compares conmigo,
Tu compasión me maltrata
Y tu cariño maldigo."
   Esto me dicen tus ojos,
Esto tu silencio triste.
Ya comprendo tus enojos,
Ya, jilguero, me venciste.
   ¡Libertad y amor te falta,
Libertad y amor te doy!
Salta, pajarillo, salta,
Que no tu tirana soy.

   Salida franca
   Ya tienes, mira,
   Goza, respira,
   Libre eres ya;
      Torna a tu campo,
   Torna a tu nido,
   Tu bien querido
   Te espera allá.
      Mas no me olvides
   Y a mi ventana
   Llega mañana
   Saliendo el sol:
      Que yo te escuche
   Sólo un momento
   Cantar contento
   Tu dulce amor.
      Corriendo el llanto
   Por mi mejilla,
   Dulce avecilla,
   Te envidiaré:
      Y el eco triste
   De mis lamentos
   Con tus acentos
   Confundiré.

Y luego, caro jilguero....
¿Mas, dónde está?... Ya se lanza
Donde mi vista no alcanza,
Donde no llega mi voz:
   ¡Así me deja el ingrato
Sin escuchar mis acentos,
Y ya en las alas de los vientos
Se precipita veloz!
   Adiós, pajarillo hermoso,

Adiós, ingrato querido;
Los bienes que habías perdido
Te restituye mi amor.
   ¡Así a mí quiera la suerte
Volverme en hora dichosa
Mi Cuba dulce y hermosa
Y su cielo inspirador!

                              (1839)

              En una tarde tempestuosa
                      Soneto
              [*Poesías*, 1841 ed.]

   Del huracán espíritu potente
Que hoy libre dejas la región precita,
¡Ven, con el tuyo mi furor excita!
¡Ven con tu fuego a coronar mi
      frente!
   Deja que el rayo con fragor
      reviente,
Mientras cual hoja seca, o flor
      marchita,
Tu fuerte soplo al roble precipita
Roto y deshecho al bramador
      torrente.
   Ven a librarme de la pena extraña
Que a un alma altiva con baldón
      devora
Y el brillo puro a la razón empaña.
   Ven, y al inerte pecho que te
      implora
Da tu poder y tu iracunda saña,
Y el llanto seca que cobarde llora.

                              (1841)

                   El insomnio
              [*Poesías*, 1841 ed.]

De la noche el negro manto
Envuelve a la tierra ya,
Natura en su seno tranquila reposa
Y el sueño entre sombras se siente
      vagar.

Sus alas, que lento bate
De la brisa al susurrar,

Vertiendo en el sueño beleño
   dichoso,
Del triste suspenden cuidados y afán.

Calladas su lento vuelo
Las horas siguiendo van,
Y trémulas lanzan del cielo enlutado
Las tibias estrellas su lumbre de paz.

Las flores plegan sus hojas;
Y cual llanto celestial
Benigno las riega nocturno rocío,
Que torna la aurora cuajado cristal.

Las aves guardan su nido,
Callan el viento y el mar,
Y en grato silencio, y en calma
   apacible,
Ostenta la noche su adusta beldad.

Sola yo en sosiego tanto
Velo y sufro sin cesar,
Y el sueño que imploro con lánguido
   acento
Mis votos desoye con cruda
   impiedad.

¿Por qué bárbaro no alivias
De mi mal la intensidad?
El llanto que abrasa mi rostro
   marchito
Tú puedes, piadoso, con flores secar.

Suspende ¡sueño! suspende
Un instante mi penar,
Y halaguen mi mente doradas
   quimeras
Que el luto me oculten de triste
   verdad.

Verterá el sol en oriente
De sus luces el raudal,
Y lánguidos ¡sueño! mis ojos
   cansados
Sus fúlgidos rayos con pena verán.

¡Muévate mi acento amargo!
¡Templa mi insomnio fatal!
¡Oh padre precioso del mudo
   sosiego!
Tu néctar divino me da por piedad.

Basten al dolor los días
Y su infausta claridad,
Sin que de la noche de penas
   consuelo,
Los ayes del triste perturben la paz.

Desciende, ¡sueño! propicio,
No alargues tu ausencia más,
Y sin preguntarme cuál es mi agonía
Piadoso me otorga tu dicha falaz.

Todos duermen, y en el seno
Del reposo universal
Un ser no se encuentra que gima mi
   pena
Y quiera sensible mi canto escuchar.

¡Mas no! que suena a deshora
Con lastimoso compás
Un eco lejano cual canto de muerte
Y en alas del viento meciéndose va.

¡Ay, tu arrullo lamentable
Conozco, tórtola, ya!
Amores llorando del bien que
   perdiste,
Al cielo en la noche le cuentas tu
   afán.

¿Mas qué vale tu lamento,
Tu pura fidelidad,
Oh pájaro triste, si el cielo impasible
Ni escucha tu queja ni alivia tu mal?

¡Ay! si algún consuelo puede
Simpático afecto dar,
Saber que tus penas comprendo y
   deploro
Alivio es que nunca faltarte podrá.

¡Halague el sueño al dichoso!
Nosotras para llorar
Velando pasemos la noche sombría,
Velando aguardemos la luz matinal.

Mi compasión a tus ansias
Alivio dulce dará;
Un pacto sellemos de amor y tristeza
Unidas por siempre con fiel amistad.

Tú sola la confidente
De mis pesares serás...

Tu pecho abrasado, de amantes
    modelo,
Del mío el secreto merece guardar.

¡Mas no digas a los vientos
Mi tierna pena jamás!
Me basta que quieras, sensible a mi
    pena,
Si el sueño me deja conmigo velar.
                                        (1840)

BY CAROLINA CORONADO

(Untitled)
[Cartas, carta 196, 31 Dec. 1842;
also Fonseca 179]

Yo en tristísimo gemido
desahogara mi cuidado
si el temor de ver reído
por otros mi mal llorado
no acobardara el sentido.
    Bien pueden los que un azar
sufrieron de la fortuna
sus desdichas lamentar
y sus lamentos alzar
sobre el cerco de la luna.
    No haya miedo, ría el mundo
de su amarguísimo lloro,
que es un dolor sin segundo
el fiero dolor profundo
que al hombre le arranca el oro.
    Los que en el mundo perdieron
riqueza, honores, poder,
ésos tan sólo sufrieron,
ésos solos consumieron
la fuente de padecer.
    Esos en el mundo son
no más los graves cuidados
que agitan el corazón,
sin ellos no hay aflicción,

desdichas ni desdichados.
    Si llora joven doncella
es necia puerilidad,
y al exhalar su querella
risas excita la bella
en la grave ancianidad.
    Que miden sus corazones
por la miseria las penas,
la dicha por los doblones,
y ellos no ven más cadenas
que el hierro de las prisiones.
    Los hombres, libres azores,
la estrecha jaula no miran
do encerraron con rigores
sus egoístas amores,
las palomas que suspiran.
    Que de su fuerza al abrigo
dieron al mundo esta ley,
como con genio enemigo
dieron el hambre al mendigo
y dieron la hartura al rey.
    Diocesillos imprudentes
que alzando grandes ciudades,
fuertes muros, arcos, puentes,
legan a sus descendientes
miseria y calamidades.
    ¿Por qué necios trasplantaron
las rocas, por qué arrancaron

el oro de su manida,
y al fondo del mar bajaron
tras de la perla escondida?
   ¿Por qué, si no han de hallar
después de tanto afanar
entre ese rico montón
la piedra que te ha de dar
felicidad, corazón?
   ¡Ay! Si el oro ha de traer
sólo males, si han de ser
tiranos siempre los reyes,
valiera más no tener
reyes, tesoros ni leyes.
   Fueran menos desdichados
en salvaje soledad
los hombres abandonados,
que no mal civilizados
en dañina sociedad.
   Mas, al fin, pájaros son
que alas tienen, tienen viento,
la mujer en su aflicción,
¡ay! no tiene ni un acento
para llorar un momento
los hierros de su prisión.
   Que el temor de ver reído
por otros mi mal llorado
en el corazón herido
tiene el dolor comprimido,
tiene el llanto sofocado.

A la soledad
[*Poesías,* 1843 ed.]

Al fin hallo en tu calma,
Si no el que ya perdí contento mío,
Si no entero del alma
El noble señorío,
Blando reposo a mi penar tardío.
   Al fin en tu sosiego,
Amiga soledad, tan suspirado,
El encendido fuego
De un pecho enamorado
Resplandece más dulce y más
    templado.
   Y al fin si con mi llanto
Quiero aplacar ¡ay triste! los enojos

Del íntimo quebranto,
No me dará sonrojos
El continuo mirar de tantos ojos.
   Danme, sí, tierno alivio
La soledad del campo y su belleza,
Y va el dolor más tibio
Su ardiente fortaleza
Convirtiendo en pacífica tristeza.
   Plácenme los colores
Que al bosque dan las luces
    matutinas;
Alégranme las flores,
Las risueñas colinas
Y las fuentes que bullen cristalinas.
   Y pláceme del monte
La grave majestad, que en las
    llanadas
Como pardo horizonte
De nubes agolpadas,
Deja ver sus encinas agrupadas.
   Allí con triste ruido
De las sonoras tórtolas, en tanto
Que posan en el nido
Bajo calado manto,
De una a otra encina se responde el
    canto.
   Tal vez mis pasos guío
Por los sombrosos valles,
    escuchando
Al caminante río,
Que con acento blando
Se va por los juncares lamentando.
   Ya entonces descendiendo
De su altura va el sol, cansada y fría
Claridad esparciendo,
Y a poco entre armonía
Cierra sus ojos el señor del día.
   Y los míos acaso
Alguna vez, del sueño sorprendidos,
Dejaron que en su ocaso
Pararan confundidos
Afanes del espíritu y sentidos.
   Si sola y retirada,
Aun me entristece más noche
    sombría,
La luna con rosada
Faz, por oculta vía

Sale a hacerme amorosa compañía.
　Y al fin hallo en tu calma,
¡Oh soledad! si no el contento mío,
Si no entero del alma
El dulce señorío,
Blando reposo a mi penar tardío.

Al jazmín
[*Poesías*, 1843 ed.]

　Orgullo de la enramada,
Blanca y leve florecilla
Más que todas delicada,
Y más que todas sencilla.
　Muestra el lirio temblorosa
La faz cristalina y pura;
Y ostenta encendida rosa
La peregrina hermosura.
　Alza bella la azucena
La copa tersa y nevada
De ricos ámbares llena,
De mil abejas cercada.
　Pero ¿quién tu brillo iguala,
Viva flor del cano estío,
Que luces entre su gala
Como espuma en claro río?
　Por sencilla y delicada,
En el jardín entre ciento
Fijas tú, flor, la mirada,
Y fijas el pensamiento.
　Y por el seno argentino
Que blando perfume expira,
Do bebe néctar divino
La abeja que en ti respira.
　¡Flor graciosa y nacarada,
La más tierna de las flores!
¡Oh mil veces bienhadada
La que roba tus amores!
　¡Bienhadada mariposa
Que tu pétalo estremece,
Cuando a tu lado reposa,
Y en tu aliento se embebece!
　Por delicada y sencilla,
En el jardín entre ciento
Se fija en ti, florecilla,
Mi vista y mi pensamiento.

A mi tío don Pedro Romero
[*Poesías*, 1843 ed.]

　Si para entrar en tan difícil vía
El aliento a mi numen no faltara,
Ya de la patria nuestra lamentara
Los males en tristísima elegía.
　Y la virtud ya el genio cantaría,
Ya el vicio a deprimir me
　　consagrara;
Pero mi voz de niña desmayara
Y desmayara endeble el harpa mía.
　Más quiero, humilde abeja, aquí
　　en el suelo
Vagar de flor en flor siempre
　　ignorada,
Que al águila siguiendo arrebatada
Con alas cortas remontar mi vuelo.
Canto las flores que en los campos
　　nacen;
Cántolas para ti, que a ti te placen.

Cantad, hermosas
[*Poesías*, 1852 ed.]

　Las que sintáis, por dicha, algún
　　destello
Del numen sacro y bello
Que anima la dulcísima poesía,
Oíd: no injustamente
Su inspiración naciente
Sofoquéis en la joven fantasía.
　Si en el pasado siglo intimidadas
Las hembras desdichadas,
Ahogaron entre lágrimas su acento,
No es en el nuestro mengua
Que en alta voz la lengua
Revele el inocente pensamiento.
　Do entre el escombro de la edad
　　caída
Aún la voz atrevida
Suena, tal vez, de intolerante
　　anciano,
Que en áspera querella
Rechaza de la bella
El claro ingenio, cual delirio insano.

Mas, ¿qué mucho que sienta la
    mudanza
Quien el recuerdo alcanza
De la edad en que al alma femenina
Se negaba el acento
Que puede por el viento
Libre exhalar la humilde golondrina?
    Aquellas mudas turbas de mujeres,
Que penas y placeres
En silencioso tedio consumían,
Ahogando en su existencia
Su viva inteligencia,
Su ardiente genio, ¡cuánto sufrirían!
    ¡Cuál de su pensamiento la
        corriente,
Cortada estrechamente
Por el dique de bárbaros errores,
En pantano reunida,
Quedara corrompida
En vez de fecundar campos de
    flores!
    ¡Cuánto lozano y rico entendi-
        miento,
Postrado sin aliento
En esos bellos cuerpos juveniles,
Feneció tristemente,
Miserable y doliente,
Desecado en la flor de los abriles!
    ¡Gloria a los hombres de alma
        generosa,
Que la prisión odiosa
Rompen del pensamiento femenino!
¡Gloria a la estirpe clara
Que nos guía y ampara
Por nuevo anchurosísimo camino!
    Lágrimas de entusiasmo agra-
        decidas
En sus manos queridas,
Viertan los ojos en ofrenda pura:
Pues sólo con dejarnos
Cantando consolarnos,
Nos quitan la mitad de la tristura.
    ¡Oh cuánto es más dichosa el alma
        mía
Desde que al arpa fía
Sus hondos concentrados senti-
    mientos!

¡Oh cuánto alivio alcanzo
Desde que al aire lanzo,
Con expansión cumplida, mis
    acentos!
    Yo de niña en mi espíritu sentía
Vaga melancolía
De secreta ansiedad que me agitaba;
Mas, al romper mi canto,
Cien veces con espanto
En la mente infantil lo sofocaba.
    Que entonces en mi tierra parecía
La sencilla poesía
Maléfica serpiente, cuyo aliento
Dicen que marchitaba
A la joven que osaba
Su influjo percibir sólo un momento.
    ¿Cómo a la musa ingenua y
        apacible
Bajo el disfraz terrible
Con que falsa nos muestra antigua
    gente
Su cándida hermosura,
Pudiera sin pavura
Conocer y adorar antes la mente?
    ¡Qué rara maravilla y qué alegría
Sintió mi fantasía
Cuando mudada vio la sierpe fiera
En niña mansa y pura,
Tan llena de ternura
Que no hay otra más dulce com-
    pañera!
    ¡Cuál mi embeleso fue, cuando a
        su lado
Mi espíritu mimado
Y en su inocente halago suspendido,
Suavísimas las horas
Tras de voces sonoras
Pasó vagando en venturoso olvido!
    Decid a los que el odio en ella
        ensaña
Que viles os engañan,
Esa deidad al calumniar osados;
Decidles que no es ella
La que infunde a la bella
Afectos en el alma depravados.
    Si brota en malos troncos
        enjertada,

Será porque arrancada
Del primitivo suelo con violencia
De la rama en que vive
A su pesar recibe
El venenoso jugo su existencia.
　　Empero, no esa flor alba y her-
　　　mosa
Aroma perniciosa
De la doncella ofrece a los sentidos;
A los que tal dijeron,
Decidles que mintieron
Como necios y torpes y atrevidos.
　　Y aquellas que sintáis algún
　　　destello
Del numen sacro y bello
Que anima la dulcísima poesía,
Llegad tranquilamente,
Y en su altar inocente
Rendid vuestro homenaje de
　　armonía.
　　Hallen los pensamientos op-
　　　rimidos
Que ulceran los sentidos
Giro en la voz y en nuestras almas,
　　　ecos,
Si con silencio tanto
De ese mudo quebranto
Los corazones ya no tenéis secos.
　　Cántenos su infortunio cada bella,
Que si la pena de ella
Penetra con su ciencia acaso el
　　mundo;
Mejor que los doctores
Explica sus dolores
Con agudo gemir el moribundo.
　　Dichas, amores, penas, alegrías,
Lloros, melancolías,
Trovad, al son de plácidos laúdes,
Mas ¡ay de la cantora
Que a esa región sonora
Suba sin inocencia y sin virtudes!
　　Pues en vez de quedar su vida
　　　impura
Bajo de losa oscura
En silencioso olvido sepultada,
Con su genio y su gloria,
De su perversa historia

Eterno hará el baldón la desdichada.
　　Cante la que mostrar la erguida
　　　frente
Pueda serenamente
Sin mancilla a la luz clara del cielo;
Cante la que a este mundo
De maldades fecundo
Venga con su bondad a dar con-
　　suelo.
　　Cante la que en su pecho fortaleza
Para alzar con pureza
Su espíritu al excelso templo halle:
Pero la indigna dama
Huya la eterna fama,
Devore su ambición, se oculte y
　　calle.

　　　　　　　　　　　　　　　　　(1845)

　　　　　Los cantos de Safo
　　　　　[*Poesías*, 1843 ed.]

　　　　　　　　I.
Como el aura suavísima resbala
De placer en placer fácil mi vida;
Entre el amor y gloria dividida,
¿Cuál es la dicha que a mi dicha
　　iguala?

Al lado de Faon, su amor cantando;
Con la luz de sus ojos fascinada;
Dicha inmensa es de Safo bien-
　　hadada
Perder sus horas en deliquio blando.

Dicha inmensa es de Safo venturosa
Que su amante en el aire que respira
Beba el acento de la tierna lira,
Que tan sólo por él suena amorosa.

¡Cómo a mis ojos inefable llanto
Gota por gota el corazón destila,
Si un instante su faz dulce y tran-
　　quila
Brilla gozosa al escuchar mi canto!

¡Si de su boca en lisonjero arrullo
La voz desciende a celebrar mi lira,

Y hálito vago que su labio expira
Mis sienes cerca entre el falaz mur-
    mullo!

Siento, Faon, tu delicado aliento
Bullir en torno de la frente mía,
Y en deliciosos tonos de armonía
Herirme el corazón tus voces siento.

El corazón sus golpes precipita
Al eco de tu voz apasionada:
A un suspiro, a un acento, a una
    mirada,
Como seno de tórtola se agita.

No temo entonces que por bella
    alguna
Perjuro olvides tu feliz cantora,
Ni atractiva beldad venga en mal
    hora
A destrozar mi plácida fortuna.

¿Y quién la flor de la ventura mía
Osara marchitar con mano aleve?
¿Quién a usurpar tu corazón se
    atreve
Y a reinar donde Safo reinó un día?

¡Ah! no soy bella: su preciosa mano
En mi rostro los dioses no impri-
    mieron;
Mas al alma benignos concedieron
De los genios el numen soberano.

Y citara en mis manos peregrina
Las hermanas de Febo colocaron,
Y de entusiasmo el corazón llenaron,
De amor ardiente e inspiración
    divina.

Goza de triunfos la beldad un día
Que el porvenir destruye rigoroso;
Cuando el genio entre aplausos vic-
    torioso
De la inmortalidad al templo guía.

Lecho de tierra y silencioso olvido
Sólo del mundo la hermosura al-
    canza:

El estrecho sepulcro a do se lanza
Los rayos borrará de haber nacido.

Cual sueño pasará, si el genio al-
    zando
La poderosa voz no la eterniza,
Su cantar que a los siglos se desliza
Vida preciosa a sus cenizas dando.

Yo también cantaré; también mis
    voces,
Tierno Faon, tu nombre repitiendo,
Con tu amor y mi amor sobrevi-
    viendo
Al porvenir sin fin irán veloces.

Yo a esa Grecia opulenta, sabia, y
    justa,
Arrancaré un aplauso duradero;
Una corona como el grande Homero
A mis sienes tal vez ceñiré augusta.

Y mírala, ¡oh Faon! y tu sonrisa
Premie el esfuerzo de tu Safo amada,
Más plácida a su ser que en la al-
    borada
Place a las flores la naciente brisa.

                    II.
Musas divinas, dioses del talento,
¿Qué me vale ceñir vuestra aureola?
Bella rival con su belleza sola
Alcanzó mi afrentoso vencimiento.

Lanzadla de ante mí, lanzadla,
    cielos;
Que al verla, el odio que me inspira
    crece.
Mi vista con su vista se oscurece,
Y hierve el corazón de envidia y
    celos.

Lanzadla lejos de él; no más admiren
Sus ojos a la bella enamorados;
Ni los míos en tanto ensangrentados
Por sorprenderlos incesantes giren.

Alma Venus, escucha tú mi ruego,
Y protege el amor que has encen-
   dido,
En el pecho cruel del fementido
Brote una chispa del extinto fuego.

Dame atractivos, dame esa ilusoria
Forma y hechizos con tu luz tocados;
¡Y quítenme los dioses irritados
Mi citara, mis cantos, y mi gloria!

III.
De Venus al oráculo las preces
De los augures fieles demandaron,
Y el fin de mis desdichas por tres
   veces
Y el triunfo de mi amor adivinaron.

Mas ¡ay! mintieron. Tú, roca insensible,
Desoyes mi pasión. ¡¡Ni una esperanza!!
¿No temes, di, que tu perjurio horrible
Provoque de los dioses la venganza?

¡Qué! ¿no temes que Venus indig-
   nada
A mis clamores presurosa acuda?
¿No temes que su cólera sagrada
Sobre tu frente criminal sacuda?

Amante diosa que al amor preside,
Tú la invocaste de tu fe testigo—
Mi injuriada pasión venganza pide;
Su hollada majestad pide castigo.

IV.
Tu juventud corría silenciosa,
Entre la oscura turba confundido.
Cuando uniendo a tu nombre su re-
   nombre
Safo su gloria dividió contigo.

La cantora de Grecia, descendiendo
De su altura hasta ti, quiso amorosa
Cantar tu vida y alumbrar tu frente
Con la radiante luz de su aureola.

Y a tu lado, Faon, si la voz mía
Se elevaba a cantar nuestros delirios,
Miel divina en mis labios derrama-
   ban
Solícitas las hijas del Olimpo.

¿Dónde la bella que, fingiendo
   amores,
Tu conquistado corazón me arranca?
Ayer mi seno de placer latía,
Y hoy de despecho y de dolor se
   abrasa....

El salto de Leúcades
El sol a la mitad de su carrera
Rueda entre rojas nubes escondido;
Contra las rocas la oleada fiera
Rompe el Leucadio mar embrave-
   cido.

Safo aparece en la escarpada orilla,
Triste corona funeral ciñendo;
Fuego en sus ojos sobrehumano
   brilla,
El asombroso espacio audaz mi-
   diendo.

Los brazos tiende, en lúgubre gemido
Misteriosas palabras murmurando;
Y el cuerpo de las rocas desprendido
"Faon" dice, a los aires entregando.

Giró un punto en el éter vacilante;
Luego en las aguas se desploma y
   hunde:
El eco entre las olas fluctuante
El sonido tristísimo difunde.

Una despedida
[*Poesías,* 1843 ed.]

Escuchad mis querellas,
Recinto y flores, del placer abrigo,
   Imágenes tan bellas
Como ese cielo que os protege
   amigo.

Asilo de inocencia,
Consuelo del dolor, bosque sombrío,
Ir quiero a tu presencia,
Y tu césped regar con llanto mío.

Y el agua de tu fuente
Beber acaso por la vez postrera,
Y respirar tu ambiente,
Besar tus flores, la gentil palmera

Que tu dintel guarnece
De lejos saludar entre congojas,
Y a la que en torno crece
Modesta acacia de menudas hojas.

Y a los álamos graves
El postrimer adiós dar afligida,
Y cantar con las aves
Tristísima canción de despedida.

Y en tu graciosa alfombra
Reposar halagada de ilusiones
Bajo la fresca sombra
De tus frondosos sauces y llorones.

Sus hojas se estremecen,
Y errantes sombras a mi planta
          evocan
Que en el viento se mecen,
Y mis cabellos con blandura tocan.

Desde aquí la pintura
Es más bello admirar de ese tu cielo,
Los visos y frescura
De las nubes cercanas a tu suelo;

Y al través de las ramas
Mirar el sol que su lumbrera humilla,
Y cual de rojas llamas
El occidente retocado brilla.

¿Ni qué música iguala
Al sordo vago suspirar del viento
Con que armonioso exhala
Un bello día su postrer aliento?

¡Ah! si mi vida entera,
Mi cara soledad, recinto amado,

Consagraros pudiera
El mundo huyendo y su falaz cui-
          dado!

Mas ¡ay! que la alegría
De contemplaros con la luz perece
Del presuroso día
Que a mis ansiosos ojos desparece.

Esas aves cantoras
Que de gozar la tarde fatigadas,
En tropas voladoras
Retornan gorgeando a sus moradas;

Cuando una sola estrella
Con apagada luz brille en el cielo;
Cuando la aurora bella
Ciña el espacio con purpúreo velo,

Y el nuevo claro día
Con sus tintas anime tu pradera;
Ellas con alegría
Volverán a girar por tu ribera.

En turba bulliciosa
Los bosques poblarán.... y yo en-
          tretanto
Lejana y silenciosa
Las horas contaré de mi quebranto.

¡Ay! ¡ellas tu hermosura
Gozarán y tu paz y sus amores!....
Yo gusté harta ventura:
Bebí en tus fuentes y besé tus flores.

En el castillo de Salvatierra
        [*Poesías*, 1852 ed.]

¿Por qué vengo a estas torres olvi-
          dadas
A hollar de veinte siglos las ruinas
Espantando al subir con mis pisadas
Las felices palomas campesinas?

¡Oh Walia! ¿no es verdad que pri-
          sioneras
La esclava del feudal y la del moro,

Pobres mujeres de remotas eras,
Regaron estas torres con su lloro?

¿Que perdido tu trono por Rodrigo
Y derrotado el moro por Fernando,
De tan largas batallas fue testigo
La misma torre donde estoy can-
tando?

¿Que inmóviles aquí tantas mujeres
Tanto llanto vertieron de sus ojos
Como sangre vertieron esos seres
Que arrastraron de Roma los des-
pojos?

¿Y que tendiendo sus amantes brazos
Al árabe y al godo que morían
Y arrancando sus tocas a pedazos
En inútil dolor se consumían?

¿Y que tras tantos siglos de combate
Que empedraron de fósiles la tierra
Subo a la misma torre de la sierra
Aún a pedir también nuestro rescate?

¡Ay! que desde aquellas hembras que
cantaron
Gimiendo, como yo, sobre esta al-
mena,
Ni un eslabón los siglos quebran-
taron
A nuestra anciana y bárbara cadena.

Y ya es preciso para hacer patente
La eterna condición de nuestras
vidas,
Unir las quejas de la edad presente
A las de aquellas razas extinguidas.

¿Quién sabe si en la choza y el castillo
Contemplando estos bellos hori-
zontes,
Fuimos por estas sierras y estos
montes
Más dichosas en tiempo más sencillo?

¿Quién sabe si el fundar el ancho
muro,
Que libertad al pueblo le asegura,
No nos trajo a nosotros más clau-
sura,
Quitándonos el sol y el aire puro?

Palomas que habitáis la negra torre,
Yo sé que es más risueña esta
morada,
Y ya podéis, bajando a la esplanada,
Decir al mundo que mi nombre
borre.

Yo soy ave del tronco primitiva
Que al pueblo se llevaron prisionera
Y que vuelvo a esconderme fugitiva
Al mismo tronco de la edad primera.

No pudo el mundo sujetar mis alas;
He roto con mi pico mis prisiones
Y para siempre abandoné sus salas
Por vivir de la sierra en los peñones.

Yo libre y sola, cuando nadie intenta
Salir de las moradas de la villa,
He subido al través de la tormenta
A este olvidado tronco de Castilla.

Yo, la gigante sierra traspasando,
Lastimados mis pies de peña en
peña,
Vengo a juntarme al campesino
bando
Para vivir con vuestra libre enseña.

Comeré con vosotras las semillas,
Beberé con vosotras en las fuentes,
Mejor que entre las rejas amarillas
En las tablas y copas relucientes.

Iremos con el alba al alto cerro,
Iremos con la siesta al hondo valle,
Para que el sol al descender nos
halle,
Cansadas de volar, en nuestro en-
cierro.

Nadie vendrá a decir qué fue de
    Roma
Ni llegará el guerrero a la montaña,
Y las nubes que bajan a esta loma
Me ocultarán también la faz de
    España.

Aquí no han de encontrarme los
    amores
Aquí no han de afligirme las mu-
    jeres,
Aquí no pueden los humanos seres
Deshacer de estas nubes los vapores.

Es un nido que hallé dentro una
    nube;
Mis enemigos quedan en el llano
Y miran hacia aquí... ¡miran en vano
Porque ninguno entre la niebla sube!

Yo he triunfado del mundo en que
    gemía,
Yo he venido a la altura a vivir sola,
Yo he querido ceñir digna aureola
Por cima de la atmósfera sombría.

Por cima de las nubes nos hallamos,
¡Libertad en el cielo proclamemos!
Las mismas nubes con los pies ho-
    llamos,
Las alas en los cielos extendemos.

Bajen hasta el profundo mis cadenas,
Circule en el espacio el genio mío,
¡Y haga sonar mi voz con alto brío
La libertad triunfante en mis al-
    menas!

Mas... ¿por qué me dejáis sola en el
    cielo
Huyendo del castillo a la techumbre?
¿Por qué se agolpa la muchedumbre
De pájaros errantes en el suelo?

¡Oh! ¿Qué estrépito es ese que ame-
    drenta?

La torre se estremece en el ci-
    miento—
He perdido de vista el firmamento—
Me envuelve en sus entrañas la tor-
    menta.

La torre estalla desprendida al
    trueno—
La sierra desparece de su planta—
La torre entre las nubes se levanta
Llevando el rayo en su tonante seno.

El terrible fantasma hacia mí gira,
Tronando me amenaza con su
    boca—
Con ojos de relámpago me mira—
Y su luz me deslumbra y me sofoca.

El rayo está a mis pies y en mi ca-
    beza;
Ya me ciega su lumbre, ya no veo.
¡Ay, sálvame, señor, porque ya creo
Que le falta a mi orgullo fortaleza!

Bájame con tus brazos de la altura,
¡Que yo las nubes resistir no puedo!
¡Sácame de esta torre tan oscura
Porque estoy aquí sola y— tengo
    miedo!

                     (1849)

La flor del agua,
a la sta. Da. Robustiana Armiño
[*El Genio* 2 Feb. 1845: 193–195]

¿Por qué tiembla? —No lo sabe.
¿Qué aguarda en el lago? —Nada.
De las aguas enlazada
A los hilos su raíz,
El movimiento suave
De la linfa va siguiendo,
La cabeza sumergiendo
Del agua al menor desliz.

Así la halló la alborada,
Así la encuentra el lucero,

Siempre el esfuerzo postrero
Haciendo para bogar;
Y en las olas la encallada,
Vaga y frágil navecilla,
Sin poder la florecilla
Impeler ni abandonar.

Movimiento que no cesa,
Ansiedad que se dilata,
Ni el agua que sus pies ata
Sostiene a la débil flor,
Ni deja, en sus olas presa,
Que vaya libre flotando,
Quiere que viva luchando
Siempre en continuo temblor.

¡Ya se inunda!... ¡Ya se eleva!...
¡Ya la corriente la traga!...
¡Ya navega... ya naufraga!
¡Ya se salva... ya venció!
¡Ya el agua otra vez la lleva
En sus urnas sepultada!...
¡Ya de nuevo sobrenada
En el agua que la hundió!...

Flor del agua, ¡cuántas flores
Viven en paz en la tierra!
Sola tú vives en guerra
En tu acuático jardín:
Te da la lluvia temores,
El manso pez te estremece
Y tu belleza perece
Sin gozar descanso al fin.

Robustina, flor del lago,
Por amante, por cantora,
Has venido en mala hora
Con tu lira y tu pasión;
Que en el siglo extraño y vago
A quien vida y arpa debes,
Donde quiera que le lleves
Fluctuará tu corazón.

Que las cantoras primeras
Que a nuestra España venimos
Por sólo cantar sufrimos,

Penamos por sólo amar;
Porque en la mente quimeras
De un bello siglo traemos
Y cuando este siglo vemos
No sabemos dó bogar.

Las primeras mariposas
Que a la estación se adelantan
Y su capullo quebrantan
Sin aguardar al abril,
Nunca saben temblorosas
Adonde fijar las alas,
Siempre temen que sus galas
Destroce el aire sutil.

Las ráfagas las combaten,
Las extrañan los insectos
Y de giros imperfectos
Si cansado el vuelo ya,
Sobre las plantas abaten
Buscando el capullo amigo
Hallan que néctar ni abrigo
La flor en botón les da.

Las orugas que encerradas
Aún están en sus clausuras
Mañana al campo seguras
Podrán sus alas tender;
¡Mas aquellas desdichadas
Que antes cruzan la pradera
Morirán, la primavera
Risueña sin conocer!...

¿Cuál es tu barca? —Una lira.
—¿Qué traes en ella? —Sonidos.
—Vuélvete, que no hay nidos
Para tus sones aquí;
Vuélvete, joven, y mira
Si en tu barca, más sonoro,
Puedes trasportarnos oro
U otro cargamento así.

¿Quién te llama? ¿A qué nos vienes
Con peregrinas canciones?
El trueno de los cañones
Del siglo el concierto es,

Y en vano sus anchas sienes
Pretendes ceñir de flores,
¡Ay! sus pies destrozadores
Hollarán cuantas le des.

¿Vienes de nuevo, alma mía?
¿Qué traes en la barca? —Amores.
Torna a otras tierras mejores,
Torna el camino a emprender;
Si es oro nuestra poesía
Nuestros amores son... nada.
Ve si la nave cargada
De cetros puedes traer,

Que, si no de amor, tenemos
Tan elevadas pasiones
Que sentimos ambiciones
De un cetro cada garzón;
Y cada garzón podemos
Con nuestros genios profundos
Media docena de mundos
Fundir en una nación.

¿Otra vez? ¿Qué traes ahora?...
Siempre en el mismo camino
Sobre el cauce cristalino
En su barquilla la flor:
Así la dejó la aurora,
Así la encuentra el lucero,
Siempre en el afán primero,
Siempre en el mismo temblor.

Robustina, flor del lago,
Por amante, por cantora,
Has venido en mala hora
Con tu amor y tu cantar:
Que en el siglo extraño y vago
A quien vida y arpa debes,
Dondequiera que la lleves
puede el alma naufragar.

Mas escucha, no estás sola
Flor del agua en el riachuelo;
Contigo en igual desvelo
Hay florecillas también
Que reluchan contra el ola,

Que vacilan, que se anegan,
Que nunca libres navegan
Ni en salvo su barco ven;

Pero enlazan sus raíces
A la planta compañera
Y viven en la ribera
Sosteniéndose entre sí:
Y cual ellas más felices
Desde hoy serán nuestras vidas,
Si con las almas unidas,
Vivimos las dos así.

El girasol
[*Poesías,* 1843 ed.]

¡Noche apacible! en la mitad del
            cielo
Brilla tu clara luna suspendida.
¡Cómo lucen al par tus mil estrellas!
¡Qué suavidad en tu ondulante brisa!

Todo es calma: ni el viento ni las
            voces
De las nocturnas aves se deslizan,
Y del huerto las flores y las plantas
Entre tus frescas sombras se reani-
            man.

Sólo el vago rumor que al arrastrarse
Sobre las secas hojas y la brizna
Levantan los insectos, interrumpe
¡O noche! aquí tu soledad tranquila.

Tú que a mi lado silencioso velas,
Eterno amante de la luz del día,
Solo tú, girasol, desdeñar puedes
Las blandas horas de la noche estiva.

*   *   *

Mustio inclinando sobre el largo
            cuello
Entre tus greñas la cabeza oscura,
Del alba aguardas el primer destello,
Insensible a la noche y su frescura.

Y alzas alegre el rostro desmayado,
Hermosa flor, a su llegada atenta:
Que tras ella tu amante, coronado
De abrasadoras llamas se presenta.

Cubre su luz los montes y llanuras;
La tierra en torno que te cerca in-
    flama;
Mírasle fija; y de su rayo apuras
El encendido fuego que derrama.

¡Ay, triste flor! que su reflejo abrasa
Voraz, y extingue tu preciosa vida.
Mas ya tu amante al occidente pasa,
Y allí tornas la faz descolorida.

Que alas te dan para volar parece,
Tus palpitantes hojas desplegadas,
Y hasta el divino sol que desparece
Transportarte del tallo arrebatadas.

Tú le viste esconderse lentamente,
Y la tierra de sombras inundarse.
Una vez y otra vez brilló en oriente,
Y una vez y otra vez volvió a ocul-
    tarse.

Al peso de las horas agobiada,
Por las ardientes siestas consumida,
Presto sin vida, seca y deshojada,
Caerás deshecha, en polvo con-
    vertida.

¿Qué te valió tu ambición, por más
    que el vuelo
Del altanero orgullo remontaste?
Tu mísera raíz murió en el suelo,
Y ese sol tan hermoso que adoraste

Sobre tus tristes fúnebres despojos
Mañana pasará desde la cumbre.
Ni a contemplar se detendrán sus
    ojos
Que te abrasaste por amar su
    lumbre.

Libertad
[*Poesías,* 1852 ed.]

Risueños están los mozos,
gozosos están los viejos,
porque dicen, compañeras,
que hay libertad para el pueblo.
Todo es la turba cantares,
los campanarios estruendo,
los balcones luminarias,
y las plazuelas festejos.
Gran novedad en las leyes,
que, os juro que no comprendo,
ocurre cuando a los hombres
en tal regocijo vemos.
Muchos bienes se preparan,
dicen los doctos al reino;
si en ello los hombres ganan,
yo, por los hombres me alegro;
Mas por nosotras, las hembras,
ni lo aplaudo ni lo siento,
pues aunque leyes se muden,
para nosotras no hay *fueros.*
¡*Libertad!* ¿qué nos importa?
¿qué ganamos, qué tendremos?
¿un encierro por *tribuna*
y una aguja por *derecho*?
¡Libertad! ¿de qué nos vale,
si son los tiranos nuestros
no el yugo de los monarcas,
el yugo de nuestro sexo?
¡Libertad! pues ¿no es sarcasmo
el que nos hacen sangriento
con repetir ese grito
delante de nuestros hierros?
¡Libertad! ¡ay! para el llanto
tuvímosla en todos tiempos;
con los déspotas lloramos,
con los tribunos lloraremos;
Que, humanos y generosos
estos hombres, como aquellos,
a sancionar nuestras penas
en todo siglo están prestos.
Los mozos están ufanos,
gozosos están los viejos,
igualdad hay en la patria,

libertad hay en el reino.
Pero os digo, compañeras,
que la ley es sola de ellos,
que las hembras no se cuentan
ni hay Nación para este sexo.
Por eso aunque los escucho,
ni me aplaudo ni lo siento;
si pierden, ¡Dios se lo pague!
y si ganan, ¡buen provecho!

(1846)

El marido verdugo
[*Poesías,* 1843 ed.]

¿Teméis de esa que puebla las mon-
    tañas
Turba de brutos fiera el desenfreno?
¡Más feroces dañinas alimañas
La madre sociedad nutre en su seno!

Bullen, de humanas formas reves-
    tidos,
Torpes vivientes entre humanos
    seres,
Que ceban el placer de sus sentidos
En el llanto infeliz de las mujeres.

No allá a las lides de su patria
    fueron
A exhalar de su ardor la inmensa
    llama;
Nunca enemiga lanza acometieron;
Que otra es la lid que su valor in-
    flama.

Nunca el verdugo de inocente esposa
Con noble lauro coronó su frente:
¡Ella os dirá temblando y congojosa
Las gloriosas hazañas del valiente!

Ella os dirá que a veces siente el
    cuello
Por sus manos de bronce atarazado,
Y a veces el finísimo cabello
Por las garras del héroe arrebatado.

Que a veces sobre el seno trans-
    parente
Cárdenas huellas de sus dedos halla;
Que a veces brotan de su blanca
    frente
Sangre las venas que su esposo es-
    talla.

Y que ¡ay! del tierno corazón llagado
Más sangre, más dolor la herida
    brota,
Que el delicado seno macerado,
Y que la vena de sus sienes rota.

Así hermosura y juventud al lado
Pierde de su verdugo; así envejece:
Así lirio suave y delicado
Junto al áspero cardo arraiga y crece.

Y así en humanas formas escondidos,
Cual bajo el agua del arroyo el cieno,
Torpes vivientes al amor uncidos
La madre sociedad nutre en su seno.

Rosa Bianca
[*Poesías,* 1843 ed.]

La luz del día se apaga;
Rosa bianca sola y muda
Entre los álamos vaga
De la arboleda desnuda,

Y se desliza tan leve,
Que el pájaro adormecido
Toma su andar por ruido
De hoja que la brisa mueve.

Ni para ver en su ocaso
Al sol hermoso un instante
Ha detenido su paso
Indiferente y errante.

Ni de la noche llegada
A las tinieblas atiende,

Ni objeto alguno suspende
Su turbia incierta mirada.

Y ni lágrimas ni acentos
Ni un suspiro mal ahogado
Revelan los sufrimientos
De su espíritu apenado.

¡Tal vez de tantos gemidos
Tiene el corazón postrado!
¡Tal vez sus ojos rendidos
Están, de mal tan llorado!

¡Tal vez no hay un pensamiento
En su cabeza marchita,
Y en brazos del desaliento
Ni oye, ni ve, ni medita!—

El poeta "suave rosa"
Llamóla, muerto de amores....
¡El poeta es mariposa
Que adula todas las flores!

¡Bella es la azucena pura!
¡Dulce la aroma olorosa!
Y la postrera hermosura
Es siempre la más hermosa.

En sus amantes desvelos
La envidiaron las doncellas;
Mas ¡ay! son para los celos
Todas las rivales bellas.

Viose en transparente espejo
Linda la joven cabeza;
Mas tal vez dio en su reflejo
Su vanidad la belleza.

¿Y qué importa si es hermosa?
Sola, muda y abismada
Sólo busca la apartada
Arboleda silenciosa,

Y allí cuando debilita
Su espíritu el sufrimiento,
En brazos del desaliento
Ni oye, ni ve, ni medita.

Ultimo canto
[*Poesías*, 1852 ed.]

Emilio, mi canto cesa;
Falta a mi numen aliento.
Cuando aspira todo el viento
Que circula en su fanal,

El insecto que aprisionas
En su cóncavo perece
Si aire nuevo no aparece
Bajo el cerrado cristal.

Celebré de mis campiñas
Las flores que allí brotaron
Y las aves que pasaron
Y los arroyos que hallé,

Mas de arroyos, flores y aves
Fatigado el pensamiento
En mi prisión sin aliento
Como el insecto quedé.

¿Y qué mucho cuando una hora
Basta al pájaro de vuelo
Para cruzar todo el cielo
Que mi horizonte cubrió;

Qué mucho que necesite
Ver otra tierra más bella
Si no ha visto sino aquella
Que de cuna le sirvió?

Agoté como la abeja
De estos campos los primores
Y he menester nuevas flores
Donde perfumes libar,

O, cual la abeja en su celda,
En mi mente la poesía
Ni una gota de ambrosía
A la colmena ha de dar.

No anhela tierra el que ha visto
Lo más bello que atesora,
Ni la desea el que ignora
Si hay otra tierra que ver:

Mas de entrambos yo no tengo
La ignorancia ni la ciencia,
Y del mundo la existencia
Comprendo sin conocer.

Sé que entre cien maravillas
El más caudaloso río
Gota leve de rocío
Es en el seno del mar,

Y que en nave, cual montaña,
Que mi horizonte domina
Logra la gente marina
Por esa región cruzar.

Mas ¡por Dios! que fue conmigo
Tan escasa la fortuna
Que el pato de la laguna
Vi por sola embarcación:

¿Qué me importa el Océano
Y cuántos ámbitos cierra?
¡Sólo para mí en la tierra
Hay diez millas de creación!

Mar, ciudades, campos bellos,
Velados ¡ay! a mis ojos;

Sólo escucho para enojos
Vuestros nombres resonar.

Ni de Dios ni de los hombres
Las magníficas hechuras
Son para el ciego que a oscuras
La existencia ha de pasar.

Tal ansiedad me consume,
Tal condición me quebranta:
Roca inmóvil es mi planta,
Aguila rauda mi ser....

¡Muera el águila a la roca
Por ambas alas sujeta,
Mi espíritu de poeta
A mis plantas de mujer!—

Pues tras de nuevos perfumes
No puede volar mi mente
Ni respirar otro ambiente
Que el de este cielo natal;

No labra ya más panales
La abeja a quien falta prado,
Perece el insecto ahogado
Sin más aire en su fanal.

(1846)

Notes

Nancy Armstrong's *Desire and Domestic*
olution of the English novel in terms of its

evolution as "that moment in which the
roduction becomes visibly antagonistic, their
center of political, social, and historical life"

s letter to Francisca Larrea, quoted by Javier

cation of woman's place by 'natural hierarchy'
liberal individualism—but the idealized senti-
l alternative. . . . Allegedly united in its affec-
sphere of life was held to depend for its health
en, suited for these special tasks on account of
em unsuited for the harsh world of commerce,

ribes this tendency, so pronounced in German
pply to the other Romanticisms as well: "[T]he
reflected is the human *Gemut,* that untranslatable
r psychological life in its totality and which is a
c generation. It is in activating and articulating the
es that romantic literature is often at its most proof romantic literature or art is often not the osten-
Gemut itself and its both individual and infinite

experience

6. Butler attributes the difference between mid-eighteenth-century sensibility and early nineteenth-century introspection to the development of literature as a commodity on an unprecedented scale: "In the long run the new conditions . . . probably tended to isolate the artist from his audience and thus to contribute to his solipsism. In this early state, the innovations surely seemed above all an opportunity. . . . [A]rtists were rising to the occasion, along with other entrepreneurs, responding to a new conception of a public which was potentially no less than mankind itself" (30).

7. Translations of this passage and all other passages from original French and Spanish texts are my own unless otherwise indicated.

8. "The sphere of spirit at this stage breaks up into two regions. The one is the actual world, that of self-estrangement, the other is that which spirit constructs for itself in the ether of pure consciousness. . . . This second world, being constructed in opposition and contrast to that estrangement, is just on that account not free from it; on the contrary, it is only the other form of that very estrangement, which consists precisely in having a conscious existence in two sorts of worlds, and embraces both" (Hegel 513).

9. Gilbert and Gubar (237–238) argue, for example, that "Victor Frankenstein's male monster may really be a female in disguise" (237).

10. Of the tendency to make the domestic woman bodyless, Armstrong remarks that "the rhetoric of the conduct books produced a subject who in fact had no material body at all" (136).

11. Although these Spanish women writers knew something of Mary Wollstonecraft—her name and her association with feminism, at least—I have found no evidence that they knew the work of her daughter.

1. LIBERALISM AND THE ROMANTIC SUBJECT

1. Vicente Llorens points out that though Alcalá's prologue, strongly influenced by English literature, was regarded as a Romantic manifesto, it had little real impact on Spain's Romantic writers, who were thoroughly indoctrinated by French ideas (80–81).

2. Larra's readers in 1836 had fresh in their minds his vehement satire in articles published just a few weeks before, such as "Dios nos asista" or "Los barateros," which made it clear that there was plenty of oppression in Spain. In "Los barateros" (April 1836), for instance, a personified Spanish Society points out its own deformities: "¿No ves que me falta la base del cuerpo, que es el pueblo? ¿No ves que ando sobre él, en vez de andar con él?" 'Don't you see that the base of my body, the people, is missing? Don't you see that I walk on it, instead of walking with it?' (2: 206).

3. Larra scoffs at Anthony for claiming that only those privileged by birth have access to society's benefits (2: 250) and adduces the case of Dumas himself as proof that modern society offers no obstacle to the success of a man of talent, no matter what his birth: "¿La literatura, la sociedad le han desechado de su seno por mulato? . . . Esa sociedad . . . de quien se queja, recompensa sus injustas invectivas con aplausos e hinche de oro sus gavetas. ¿Y por qué? Porque

tiene talento, porque acata en él la inteligencia. ¡Y esa inteligencia se queja y quiere invertir el orden establecido!" 'Have literature and society rejected him for being a mulatto? . . . The society he complains of repays his unfair invectives with applause and fills his pockets with gold. Why? Because he has talent, because it perceives his intelligence. And that intelligence complains and wants to upset established order!' (2: 251).

4. Alicia Andreu points out the redemptive character of the stereotypical feminine ideal that became dominant between 1840 and 1880: the very reason for the existence of "La Mujer Virtuosa" was to lead men away from immoral materialism. "Destined to be the carrier of the regenerative values that will lead Spain to its moral rehabilitation, woman will finally accomplish 'her sacred mission' here on earth" (91).

5. Bridget Aldaraca, in her study of the image of *el ángel del hogar,* shows how the nineteenth-century ideal incorporates the earlier view of female inferiority epitomized in the Renaissance treatise by Fray Luis de León, *La perfecta casada* (Aldaraca 72–73).

6. Among the various reforms enacted by the liberals in 1836 was the repeal of the law that restricted women to the gallery (termed the *cazuela,* or saucepan, in Spanish) in the theater.

7. Aldaraca dates the reign of the domestic angel "from the 1850s on" (63), while Andreu locates the apogee of the related stereotype, *la mujer virtuosa,* between 1840 and 1880 (71).

2. WOMEN WRITERS IN THE ROMANTIC PERIOD

1. According to Isabel Fonseca Ruiz (177), this undated letter was written in 1842.

2. Since no baptismal or other record has been found for Beatriz de Cienfuegos, some critics have suggested that the name was a pseudonym for a male writer (Perinat and Marrades 15).

3. An article in the *Revista Literaria del Español* (8 June 1845) cites and modifies a list of 108 names compiled by J. E. M.

4. A woman had already been granted a doctorate by the University of Alcalá, but she never attended the university. In 1875, Carlos III ordered that María Guzmán y de la Cerda, sixteen at the time, be awarded the degree after a public examination that was more of a social occasion than an intellectual exchange, according to Carmen Martín Gaite (227–230).

5. For more information on the history of the development of a women's periodical press, see Adolfo Perinat and María Isabel Marrades (17–34).

6. Andreu's analysis shows that the class basis of this manipulative image of women became ever clearer during succeeding decades as the bourgeois reaction grew (51–91).

7. The apparent contradictions between the journal's rather militant title and its defensiveness on the subject of feminism can be better understood in the context of a polemic raging at the time between two satirical journals. The democratic *El Sueco* scoffed at the post-1848 efforts to bring women into

French politics, while the Fourierist *El Toboso* urged Spanish women to become involved in politics. Cf. Perinat and Marrades (25) and Antonio Elorza (52).

8. Sappho is mentioned with some frequency in the press of the period. In the periodical press, she crops up in a satirical piece in 1836, in a short narrative of her life in 1846, and in Coronado's essay on her for *El Semanario Pintoresco* in 1850. Besides the loose translations or "imitations" of her poetry published by Romantic poets, a scholarly translation from the Greek by José del Castillo y Ayensa came out in 1832. The prevailing idea of Sappho was based not on the texts of her poems, however, but on a mythical tradition that envious persecution by other poets and her unreciprocated passion for Phaon led to her suicide, a leap into the sea at Leucades.

9. The general female readership seems to have been much interested in women of the past who had become part of literary history, for throughout the 1840s articles on Sor Juana Inés de la Cruz and Saint Teresa of Avila as well as on Sappho turned up in illustrated magazines and women's journals. There was considerable interest, too, in more contemporary writers like Mme de Staël and George Sand, although they were much more controversial. The creator of Corinne was praised for her learning and intelligence, but Spanish women were cautioned not to follow her example. Sand was repeatedly denounced as immoral.

10. Ellen Moers outlines this tradition in a chapter titled "Performing Heroinism: The Myth of Corinne" (173–210).

11. Joaquín Marco identifies three editions of *Lamentos de Corina dirigidos a su idolatrado Oswaldo* between 1835 and 1840 (299–305). Spain's Biblioteca Nacional has another, undated edition titled *Canción de la triste Corina, lamentándose de la ingratitud de Oswaldo* (Madrid: Juanelo).

12. More examples: "A mi querida amiga y hermana la poetisa Amalia Fenollosa," by Manuela Cambronero (20); "A la distinguida poetisa sta. doña Rogelia León," by Vicenta García Miranda (*Ellas* 30 June 1852: 164–165).

13. The initials are those of Dolores Gómez Cádiz de Velasco, who was named in 1845 as a collaborator in *La Ilustración de las Damas,* which Gómez de Avellaneda was to direct.

14. Gómez de Avellaneda followed Lamartine more closely in "Romance contestando a otro por una señorita," dated 1846, the same year in which Coronado published this paragraph. Avellaneda's text: "Canto como canta el ave, / Como las ramas se agitan, / Como las fuentes murmuran, / Como las auras suspiran" (*Poesías,* 1850 ed., 244). A translation of these lines is given below, in chapter 5.

15. "Biografía—Safo Cornelia," 23 May 1836: 3–4; "Una sesión en una asamblea de mujeres," 26 May 1836: 3–4; "Petición importante a S.M. por unas mujeres," 12 July 1836: 2–4; "Correspondencia de una Comadre de parir," 13 July 1836: 2; "Carta a *El Jorobado,*" 19 July 1836: 3–4.

16. In the prologue to this collection Balaguer describes women's condition as "a triple slavery with regard to their parents, their husband, and their children, [which] can only be solved if the problem is considered in its entirety" (Perinat and Marrades 20).

17. Aldaraca stresses the domestic angel's lack of individuality: "In a period of history in which the social individual is acquiring a new definition and importance, 'woman' is often perceived not as an individual but as a *genre*" (66).

3. PARADIGMS OF THE ROMANTIC SELF

1. In "Literatura," for example, he says of the new writer he envisions for Spain, "[N]o le será suficiente, como al romántico, colocarse en las banderas de Victor Hugo y encerrar las reglas con Molière y con Moratín" 'It won't be enough for him to line up under Victor Hugo's flag like the Romantics and lock away the rules with Molière and Moratín' (2: 134).

2. This tradition, which Larra explicitly traces back to Addison and Steele (see "Casarse pronto y mal" 1: 108), continued in France with writers like Jouy, or L'Hermite de la Chausée d'Antin, also explicitly mentioned by Larra, and in Spain with Mercadal in the late eighteenth century and Sebastián Miñano during the liberal Triennium. See José Escobar's *Los orígenes* for a detailed study of this tradition in Spain.

3. Larra, who had left Spain in discouragement in the spring of 1835, wrote to his parents from Paris when he learned in the following autumn that Mendizábal had been named prime minister, "[S]ince the moment has come when my party can completely triumph, I don't want to be detained here" (4: 278). The first articles he wrote on his return from France sparkle with the optimism and hope so evident in "Literatura" (Jan. 1836).

4. A good example of how Larra's biography became textualized as a general cultural type is found in the short fictionalization of his suicide published by Bernardo Núñez de Arenas (B. N. A.) six months later. The piece offers an interpretation of an engraving featured in the preceding issue of *El Observatorio Pintoresco*, in which a small girl asks her obviously depressed father, who is gazing at two pistols on a nearby table, "¿Por qué lloras, Papá?" 'Why do you weep, Papa?" Núñez de Arenas supplies an interior monologue for the suicidal figure, stressing his alienation from an injust society, his social isolation, and his unhappy love life. Both the engraving and the prose piece testify to the imprint of Fígaro's image on the popular imagination.

5. Vicente Llorens notes (154–156) the strong similarities of *Don Alvaro*'s plot to that of *Les Ames du Purgatoire*, by Prosper Mérimée, whom Rivas knew personally, as well as the likelihood that Victor Hugo provided the model for the play's scenes of lower-class life.

6. Ermanno Caldera (122) gives an account of the repeated performances of the drama.

7. In the periodical press of 1842, the obituary notices of Espronceda's untimely death give testimony of the high regard in which he was held by other writers. *Revista de Teatros* commented: "The younger generation, as González Brabo opportunely remarked, has been left without a leader. Castilian poetry has lost one of its favorite sons. The death of Espronceda has left a vacuum that no one can fill" (29 May 1842: 56). *El Corresponsal,* a daily paper, echoed these sentiments: "Spanish poetry has lost its most inspired lyric poet, the younger generation one of its noblest and most generous sons, and the staff of *El Corresponsal* a precious friend" (23 May 1842: 1).

8. For a stylistic analysis of Espronceda's versification and imagery, see Joaquín Casalduero 150–156. On diction, see Marrast 462.

9. Espronceda's imagination brought forth other representations of women as subjects besides Jarifa and Teresa. Elvira, of *El estudiante de Salamance,* and La Salada, of *El diablo mundo,* are important examples.

4. FEMINIZING THE ROMANTIC SUBJECT

1. In "Fígaro a los redactores del *Mundo,*" Larra satirized, for example, the liberal government's refusal in 1836 to extend the rights of the Constitution of 1812, which they had imposed on the queen-regent in a coup, to the Spanish colonies. Larra's fictitious correspondent from Havana complains that he didn't understand that constitutions were reserved for Spaniards and absolute governments for Cubans (2: 312).

2. In Cuba another abolitionist novel, *Francisco. El ingenio o Las delicias del campo,* by Anselmo Suárez y Romero, was finished by 1839, the same year in which the manuscript of *Sab* was completed. The Cuban novel, however, was not published until 1880, whereas *Sab* appeared in Spain in 1841 (Gutiérrez de la Solana 301–302).

3. For a discussion of how the metaphysics of desire in Espronceda's poetry resists the social explanations implied by his progressive political positions, see Thomas E. Lewis.

4. En route from Cuba to Spain, Gómez de Avellaneda and her family had spent several weeks in Bordeaux. After the French city, La Coruña was definitely a disappointment.

5. Larra summed up the feeling of Spanish intellectuals when he wrote in 1836: "Escribir como Chateaubriand y Lamartine en la capital del mundo moderno es escribir para la humanidad. . . . Escribir como escribimos en Madrid es tomar una apuntacion" 'To write like Chateaubriand and Lamartine in the capital of the modern world is to write for humanity. . . . To write as we write in Madrid is to take notes' (2: 290).

6. As Lucía Guerra Cunningham observes, "According to the traditional imperative of the genre, Carlos would find himself . . . before the opposition Good and Evil represented by the antithetical figures of the two women, and following the textual norms of edifying moralism, the conclusion of the novel would reaffirm the triumph of virtue and the punishment of vice" (3).

7. For a detailed discussion of this convention and its subversion by women novelists, see Nancy K. Miller, esp. 44–45.

8. Madelyn Gutwirth argues that de Staël's depiction of England corresponds to her conception of Switzerland: "For her, Helvetia was the land of exile where narrow, devout, earnest, well-intentioned people simply bored to lingering death people of talent, wit, temperament and ambition like herself" (218).

9. The 1842 article "La mujer," cited in chapter 1 as synthesizing the prevailing view that female nature subordinated all other feeling to love, was written by Pedro Sabater. It is an eloquent irony that Sabater was to become the first husband of Gómez de Avellaneda three years later.

10. So powerful is this narrative idea that it was later to structure the denouement of two of the nineteenth century's masterpieces—George Eliot's *Middlemarch* and Benito Pérez Galdós's *Fortunata y Jacinta*.

11. The novel was first advertised to the public under this title: "De un momento a otro debe publicarse el primer tomo de una novela que con el título de las *Dos hermanas,* acaba de escribir la distinguida poetisa señorita de Avellaneda" (*El Corresponsal* 3 June 1842: 2).

5. MODULATING THE LYRE

1. "A una literata," an 1845 poem by Josefa Massanés (*Flores marchitas* 85–91), for example, elaborates in bitter detail the additional afflictions that a literary vocation imposes on a woman.

2. The first edition of Gómez de Avellaneda's poetry was published in 1841. In 1850 she published another edition, amplified by the poems she had written since 1842, and in 1869, as one of the volumes of her *Obras completas,* she published her lyrical poetry, much of it extensively revised. In all three cases she preserved the original order of the 1841 edition and then added later poems in chronological order. Because I am interested in how women writers presented themselves as writing subjects during the first decade of women's active participation in Spanish print culture, I use the earliest accessible versions of Avellaneda's poems.

3. A good example is found in "Despedida a la Señora Da. D. G. C. de V.," dated 1843 in the 1850 edition (176–181).

4. As, for example, in an 1850 letter to Manuel Cañete, the literary critic for *El Heraldo*: "V. como poeta apreciará las dificultades vencidas en las nombradas combinaciones y en otras de mi invención que hallará en el libro, y como crítico dirá si valían la pena de aquel trabajo los nuevos metros que me atrevo a introducir en nuestra rica poesía" 'As a poet you will appreciate the difficulties overcome in the meters named and in others of my own invention that you will find in the book, and as a critic you will say whether the new meters I've taken the liberty of introducing into our rich poetry are worth the trouble they cost me' (qtd. in Cotarelo 436).

5. In the 1869 version, the speaking subject is also represented as feminine through the feminine ending of an adjective—"loca" (*Obras* 249). This version is much further from the original Hugo than the earlier versions; the changes are calculated to identify the speaking subject more closely with the Cuban-Spanish poet.

6. The addressee was undoubtedly Dolores Gómez Cádiz de Velasco, who was named in the announcement of *La Gaceta de las Mujeres* (26 Oct. 1845: 8) as a prospective contributor to the new journal to be edited by Gómez de Avellaneda under the title of *La Ilustración de las Damas*.

7. This metaphorical connection between a singing bird ambushed by a hunter and the dangers threatening a singing and desiring woman emerged in Avellaneda's radical rewriting of "A un ruiseñor," a poem from the 1841 collection, in the 1869 edition of her works. Elaborating on the earlier version's identification of the nightingale with the poetic and amorous part of the lyrical

speaker, the poet imagines the night as full of dangers for the singer: "¡Ay! ¿quién sabe / Si emboscado / Despiadado / Cazador / Lazo indigno / Te prepara . . . / Y ese canto / Te delata / En la ingrata / Lobreguez?" 'Ay, who knows whether in ambush a pitiless hunter lays an unworthy trap for you . . . and that song gives you away in the ungrateful darkness?' (*Obras* 261).

8. It is unlikely that the relationship between the two poems could be one of direct influence, for they seem to have been composed at about the same time. In the 1841 *Poesías*, "A él" is dated 1840. Espronceda's *El diablo mundo,* of which "Canto a Teresa" forms Canto II, did not begin publication until 1841. Although the elegy to Teresa may have been read or circulated in manuscript before then, it was not in print.

9. A note in the 1850 edition disclaims her agency in including the poem: "Las instancias de sus amigos [de la autora], prendados de la novedad y armonía que atribuían al metro de este trozo, lo salvaron de la destrucción a que fue condenado el resto de la obra" 'The urging of [the author's] friends, who were taken by the novelty and harmony they attributed to the meter of this passage, saved it from the destruction to which the rest of the work was condemned' (164).

6. WATERFLOWER

1. For example, *El Laberinto* announced in its first volume (1844) that Coronado was a contributor, and *El Semanario Pintoresco* (March 1844) carried an advertisement for *El Pensamiento* that named her as part of its editorial board.

2. P. D.'s review comments, "Some people have criticized the verses that we are commenting on for lacking the softness and tenderness that apparently should be the distinctive character of the fair sex's poetry" (17).

3. The Spanish term *soledad* is semantically related to another opposition besides 'solitude' / 'company,' for it also implies the arena of nature as opposed to civilization. Góngora's *Las soledades,* for example, refer to a pastoral world, closer to nature than to society. Thus, the "I" of Coronado's poem has no need to explain why her solitude brings with it the beauties of nature.

4. My thanks to Page DuBois for pointing out the connection.

5. See, for example, the sonnet "Lánguida flor de Venus, que ascondida" 'Languid flower of Venus, that hidden,' in which the blighted flower is the metaphorical equivalent of the poet's thwarted love: "Igual es, mustia flor, tu mal al mío" 'Your malady, withered flower, is like mine' (Blecua 246).

6. Coronado's accusation that male-dominated culture silences women resonates strikingly with late twentieth-century feminist arguments to the same effect. (See Kristeva; Cixous; and Gilbert and Gubar, for example.) It should be noted, however, that the latter regard this silencing to be the effect of the phallocentrism of dominant discourses, which make specifically female desire marginal to the symbolic order, while Coronado refers to the bourgeois social conventions that forbade the public expression of any vehement feeling on the part of a woman and that equated reticence with submissiveness.

7. It is not clear whether the Italianate form (Bianca) is a typographical error in the 1843 edition that was corrected in 1852.

8. "[W]omen from Jane Austen and Mary Shelley to Emily Brontë and Emily Dickinson produced literary works that are in some sense palimpsestic, works whose surface designs conceal or obscure deeper, less accessible (and less socially acceptable) levels of meaning" (Gilbert and Gubar 73).

9. Coronado explicitly pointed out Sappho's status as a myth in her 1850 essay on the Greek poet ("Safo").

10. A good example of this process can be seen in "A la señorita doña Encarnacíon Calero de los Ríos," first published in *En Pensil del Bello Sexo* in 1846 then revised and published in the 1852 collection as "A Elisa."

11. I have elected to cite from the version published in *El Genio* rather than the version collected in the 1852 *Poesías,* for although the two versions are very close, the latter, by eliminating specific references to Armiño, attenuates the immediacy of the poem's address of another woman poet.

7. DENYING THE SELF

1. Herrero (169–173) provides evidence from various travelers to Seville that family and friends read and celebrated Cecilia Boehl's manuscripts between 1828 and 1835.

2. Iris Zavala gives an account of the battles between liberal and conservative intellectuals about Boehl's novels (123–166).

3. For example, she wrote to Hartzenbusch in 1850, "¿[C]onque Fernán se ha atrevido a pegar a V? Esto es una infamia y un atrevimiento del que no tenía noticia Cecilia, que desde ahora intitulará a ese zoquete Fernán *no* Caballero" 'So Fernán dared to hit you? This is an infamy and an impudence that Cecilia was not informed of; from now on she will call that blockhead Fernán *no* Gentleman [Caballero]' (Montesinos, *Caballero* 112).

4. Herrero points out that in Germany only noblemen could purchase land; to this effect, Juan Nicolás was legally adopted by his stepfather, who had been awarded a title of nobility (46–47).

5. Julio Rodríguez-Luis's fine edition notes variations between the 1849 serialized version of *La gaviota* and two subsequent editions in 1856 and 1861. All versions coincide in these opening words; later citations will follow the 1856 version, since the author considered it to be the definitive one.

6. A letter to her mother accompanied by two short stories requested that they be put in the drawer where her father kept all her writings (Herrero 285).

7. According to Herrero (326 n. 18), J. N. Boehl used "romancesco" to denote the Romantic aesthetic he espoused. Dare we see unconscious hostility to her father in Cecilia's subversion of the meaning with which he used the term?

8. "The tendency of my little works is to combat the novelesque, a subtle poison in the good and plain path of real life," she wrote in a defense of her work published in *La Ilustración* in 1853 (qtd. in Montesinos, *Caballero* 35).

9. Rodney T. Rodríguez finds a precedent for novelistic realism in Spain

as early as 1827 with the publication of *Voyleano* by Estanislao de Cosca Vayo ("Continuity" 60) and points to novels written in the 1840s by Antonio Ros de Olano and Jacinto Salas y Quiroga, as well as by G. Gómez de Avellaneda, as fiction that focuses on the problems of contemporary Spain ("Las dos Españas" 192–197).

10. Herrero argues that it must have been completed before 1835 (333).

11. Such a plot line was, however, to become the standard one for Spanish fiction exalting the domestic angel, as Andreu points out (80). *La cruz del olivar* (published in 1867 in *El Correo de la Moda*), by Faustina Saez de Melgar, is an excellent example of the paradigm.

12. I refer to a trend in Anglo-American feminist criticism that, often applying the insights of Nancy Chodorow's feminist revision of object-relations theory, as well as Adrienne Rich's and Dorothy Dinnerstein's explorations of the mother-daughter bond, focuses on textual representations of mother-daughter and other woman-to-woman relations. See Judith Kegan Gardiner 133–135.

13. For example, Mme de Genlis in France and Fanny Burney and Maria Edgeworth in England.

14. Montesinos, Cecilia Boehl's most brilliantly insightful reader, remarks on her reluctant fascination with the erotic: "When one has read this author carefully, and I believe I have done so, one becomes convinced in the end that she lived obsessed—negatively obsessed, I would say, but it's the same thing— by that new eroticism that was taking over the new literature, and which she, despite all her scruples, was unable to hide from herself" (Prólogo 17).

15. Boehl insistently repudiated Sand as a precedent for her own writing. Montesinos quotes the following comment on *Lélia* from an 1842 letter by Boehl: "[Es] la obra más descocadamente mala que he leído, de bello lenguaje y bellos trozos, pero cuyo fondo es de un cinismo asqueroso. Si el talento superior de esta mujer sirve para escribir semejante libro, digo: gracias a Dios que me ha hecho negrito" '[It is] the most brazenly bad book I've ever read, with lovely language and lovely passages, but whose essence is of a nauseating cynicism. If the superior talent of that woman enables her to write such a book, "thank God I'm just a little black boy"' (Prólogo 15).

16. See Andreu (44–49) for an account of this process in slightly different terms. David Gies documents the popularity of melodrama combined with magic in the theater (65–80). Juan Ignacio Ferreras analyzes the plot structure of a significant portion of serial novels as based on the dual structures of good versus evil, with the action deriving from what he terms the "melodramatic triangle"—hero, villain, victim (female) (257–260). Umberto Eco points out the supernatural connotations given these characters (such as Superman or Satan) in order to enhance their impact.

17. Rodríguez-Luis also observes of Boehl that "in treating the love affair of the diva and the bullfighter, she adopts a dangerously melodramatic tone" (130).

18. Gilbert and Gubar, quoting Joyce Carol Oates to the effect that a writer may be closest to the characters whom he or she appears most to detest, note that this phenomenon is frequently found in women writers: "It suggests . . .

the self-dislike she may experience in feeling that she is 'really closest to' those characters she 'appears to detest.' Perhaps this dis-ease, which we might almost call 'schizophrenia of authorship,' is one to which a woman writer is especially susceptible" (69).

8. CONCLUSION

1. Her father, José Massanés Mestres, was a liberal who fought in the Spanish army against Napoleon and was persecuted by Ferdinand VII. He was also an architect who applied enlightenment ideas of urban space in the plan he designed for urban development in Barcelona. See Felió Vilarrubias 11–49.

2. As Coronado herself was later to observe in giving an account of how she conceived her project of writing the biographies of contemporary women poets: "Josefa Massanés . . . se quejaba como yo de la estrechez de nuestra vida; y algunas inocentes niñas, siguiendo nuestro ejemplo, llenaban las páginas de los periódicos literarios de lágrimas dolorosas por el común infortunio" 'Josefa Massanés . . . complained as I did of the narrowness of our lives; and some innocent girls, following our example, filled the pages of the literary journals with anguished tears for our shared misfortunes' ("Galería. Introducción").

3. See, for example, Hugh Harter's reading of the drama (86–89).

4. The echo, whether intended or not, was probably direct, for Coronado knew Larra well and admired him—and feared his imagined judgment. In "A Larra" (*Poesías,* 1852 ed., 92–93) she asks what Larra, who mocked women who wept, would think of women who sang.

5. This reconstruction of gender differences was perhaps most clearly manifest in medical science's representation of women. Thomas Laqueur argues that during the eighteenth century, European medicine abandoned the ancient view that female genitalia were simply inverted, inferior homologues of the male organs and adopted a model of physiological incommensurability between the sexes (4–18). Londa Schiebinger points out that until the eighteenth century it was not considered necessary to distinguish between male and female skeletons, for the sexes were regarded as physically different only in regard to genital organs. In the eighteenth century, however, as the view spread that the female organism is radically different from the male, anatomists began to interpret the female skeleton as designed primarily for reproduction, with a large pelvis and small cranium.

6. Cora Kaplan, pointing out that "[r]uling groups had traditionally used the sexual and domestic virtue of their women as a way of valorizing their moral authority" ("Pandora's Box" 165), argues persuasively that representations of sexual difference in nineteenth-century English literature also figured class and racial differences for their readers. Andreu shows the close connection between gender ideology and conservative bourgeois ideology in mid-nineteenth-century Spanish fiction (57–69).

7. See, for example, Matilde Albert Robatto's study.

Works Cited

PRIMARY SOURCES

Alcalá Galiano, Antonio. Prólogo. *El moro expósito*. By Angel Saavedra. Paris: n.p., 1834. Rpt. in *El romanticismo español—Documentos*. Ed. Ricardo Navas-Ruiz. Salamanca: Anaya, 1971. 107–128.

Arenal, Concepción. *La emancipación de la mujer en España*. Ed. Mauro Armiño. Madrid: Júcar, 1974.

Balaguer, Victor. "Melancolía—A mi amable amiga, la Sta. Amalia Fenollosa." *El Genio* 3 Nov. 1844: 42.

"Biografía—Safo Cornelia." *El Jorobado* 23 May 1836: 3–4.

Blecua, José M., ed. *Poesía de la edad de oro. II. Barroco*. Madrid: Castalia, 1974.

Boris de Ferrant, Natalia. "A mi amiga la sta. Angela Grassi." *Ellas / Album de Señoritas* 15 Mar. 1852: 51.

El Buen Tono: Periódico de modas, artes y oficios. Madrid, Jan.–Feb. 1839.

Byron, Lord George Gordon. *The Complete Poetical Works of Byron*. Boston: Houghton Mifflin, 1933.

Caballero, Fernán [Cecilia Boehl von Faber]. *Elia*. Madrid: Alianza, 1968.

———. *La gaviota*. Ed. Julio Rodríguez-Luis. Barcelona: Labor, 1972.

Cabeza, Felipa Máxima de, and María Paula de Cabeza. *La señorita instruída o sea Manual del bello sexo*. 2d ed. 4 vols. Madrid: Aguado, 1855.

Calero de los Ríos, Encarnación. "A la señorita doña Carolina Coronado." *El Pensil del Bello Sexo* 8 (11 Jan. 1846): 66–67.

Cambronero, Manuela. *Días de convalecencia: Colección de poesías y novelas originales*. La Coruña: Domingo Puga, 1852.

Castillo y Ayensa, José del, trans. *Anacreonte, Safo y Firteo*. Madrid: n.p., 1832.

Castro, Rosalía de. *Obras completas.* Ed. Arturo del Hoyo. Intro. Victoriano García Martí. Expanded 7th ed. 2 vols. Madrid: Aguilar, 1977.

"Congregaciones modernas: Los sansimonianos." *La Revista Europea, Miscelánea de Filosofía, Historia, Ciencias, Literatura y Bellas Artes* 1 (Feb. 1837): 219–248.

Coronado, Carolina. "A la señorita doña Encarnación Calero de los Ríos." *El Pensil del Bello Sexo* 25 Jan. 1846: 85–86.

———. "Al Sr. Director." *El Defensor del Bello Sexo* 8 Feb. 1846: 96–97.

———. "A Luisita." *El Defensor del Bello Sexo* 9 Nov. 1845: 70–71.

———. Carta a José de Souza. *El Defensor del Bello Sexo* 19 Oct. 1845: 45.

———. Cartas a Juan Eugenio Hartzenbusch. Ms. 20.806, cartas 195–230. Biblioteca Nacional, Madrid.

———. "La flor del agua, a la sta. Da. Robustiana Armiño." *El Genio* 2 Feb. 1845: 193–195.

———. "Galería de las poetisas: Introducción a las poesías de la señorita Armiño." *La Ilustración, Periódico Universal* 12 June 1850: 187.

———. "Galería de poetisas españolas contemporáneas. Introducción." *La Discusión* 1 May 1857: 3.

———. *Poesías de la señorita doña Carolina Coronado.* Madrid: Alegría y Charlain, 1843.

———. *Poesías de la señorita doña Carolina Coronado.* [Madrid]: n.p., 1852.

———. "Las poetisas españolas: Doña Josefa Massanés." *La Discusión* 21 June 1857: 3.

———. "Safo." *El Semanario Pintoresco Español* Nueva Epoca 5 (1850): 89–94.

El Defensor del Bello Sexo. Periódico de literatura, moral, ciencias y modas, dedicado exclusivamente a las mujeres. Madrid, 1845–1846. Weekly.

Deville, Gustave. "Influencia de las poetisas españolas en la literatura." *Revista de Madrid* 2d ser. 2 (1844): 190–199.

Durán, Agustín. *Discurso sobre el influjo que ha tenido la crítica moderna en la decadencia del teatro antiguo español. El romanticismo español—Documentos.* Ed. Ricardo Navas-Ruiz. Salamanca: Anaya, 1971. 54–100.

El Eco del Comercio 23 Mar. 1841.

"Educación de las mujeres." *El Español* 23 Feb. 1836: 2.

Espronceda, José de. "A Carolina Coronado después de leída su composición 'A la palma.'" Coronado, *Poesías* 1852 ed., 2.

———. *El diablo mundo. El estudiante de Salamanca. Poesías.* Ed. Jaime Gil de Biedma. Madrid: Alianza, 1966.

Fenollosa, Amalia. "La mujer." *El Genio* 27 Oct. 1844: 35–36.

Ferrer del Río, Antonio. *Galería de literatura española.* Madrid: Mellado, 1846.

Gaceta de las Mujeres, redactada por ellas mismas. Madrid. Sept.–Oct. 1845.

García Miranda, Vicenta. "A las españolas." *Gaceta del Bello Sexo* 15 Dec. 1851: 10–11.

———. *Notas biográficas y breve antología poética de Vicenta García Miranda, poetisa de Campanario.* Campanario, Spain: Fondo Cultural Valeria, 1981.

Gironella, Gervasio. "*Sab*, novela original." *Revista de Madrid* 3d ser. 3 (Feb.

1842): 209–211.

Gómez de Avellaneda, Gertrudis. *Autobiografía y cartas*. Ed. Lorenzo Cruz de Fuentes. Madrid: Imprenta Helénica, 1914.

———. *Dos mujeres. Novelas y leyendas*. Vol. 5 of *Obras de la Avellaneda*. Havana: Aurelio Miranda, 1914.

———. *Obras*. Ed. José M. Castro y Calvo. Biblioteca de Autores Españoles 278. Madrid: Atlas, 1974. Reproduces 1869 *Poesías*.

———. *Poesías*. Madrid: Prensa Tipográfica, 1841.

———. *Poesías*. Madrid: Delgras Hermanos, 1850.

———. *Sab*. Ed. Carmen Bravo Villasante. Salamanca: Anaya, 1970.

Gonzalo Morón, Fermín. "El destino de la mujer." *Revista de España y del Estrangero* 9 (1844): 474–480. First published as "La mujer." *El Iris* 29 Aug. 1841: 138–139.

Grassi, Angela. "A mi querida amiga Natalia Boris de Ferrant." *Ellas / Album de Señoritas* 8 Aug. 1852: 203–204.

Hartzenbusch, Juan Eugenio. Introduction. Coronado, *Poesías* 1843 ed., i–xii.

Hegel, G. W. F. *Phenomenology of Mind*. Trans. J. B. Baillie. 2d ed. London: Allen and Unwin, 1961.

Horace. *The Odes and Epodes of Horace*. Trans. Joseph P. Clancy. Chicago: University of Chicago Press, 1960.

"Jorge Sand." Signed "S." *El Pensil del Bello Sexo* 25 Jan. 1846: 81–83.

Lamartine, Alphonse-Marie-Louis de. *Oeuvres poétiques*. Ed. Marius-Francois Guyard. Paris: Gallimard, 1963.

Larra, Mariano José de. *Obras de Mariano José de Larra*. Ed. C. Seco Serrano. Biblioteca de Autores Españoles 127–130. 4 vols. Madrid: Atlas, 1960.

López Pelegrín, Juan. "De las mujeres. Primer artículo." *El Español* 14 June 1836: 3–4.

Massanés, Josefa. *Flores marchitas*. Barcelona: n.p., 1850.

———. *Poesías*. Barcelona: n.p., 1841.

Meléndez Valdés, Juan. *Poesías*. Ed. Emilio Prados. Madrid: Alhambra, 1979.

"El mundo al revés." Cartoon. *Revista de Teatros* 2 May 1841: 37.

Neira de Mosquera, Antonio. "De la novela moderna." *Revista de España, de Indias y del Estranjero* 12 (1848): 187.

Núñez de Arenas, Bernardo. "Su pensamiento." *El Observatorio Pintoresco* 15 Aug. 1837: 117–119.

El Observatorio Pintoresco. Madrid, Apr.–Nov. 1837.

P. D. "De las novelas en España: *Sab*, novela original por la Señorita Doña Gertrudis Gómez de Avellaneda." *El Conservador* 19 Dec. 1841: 11–16.

Pastor Díaz, Nicomedes. "*Poesías* de la Señorita Doña Gertrudis Gómez de Avellaneda." *El Conservador* 23 Jan. 1842: 14–18.

Periódico de las Damas. Madrid, 1822.

Pitollet, Camille. "Les Premiers Essais littéraires de Fernán Caballero: Documents inédits." *Bulletin Hispanique* 9 (1907): 286–302.

"La poetisa Saffo." *El Semanario Pintoresco Español* 2d ser. 4 (31 July 1842): 246.

"¿Por qué lloras, Papá?" Engraving. *El Observatorio Pintoresco* 30 July 1837: 100.

"Prospecto." *El Semanario Pintoresco Español* 1 (3 Apr. 1836): 1–8.

Quadrado, José María. "A Jorge Sand—Vindicación." *Revista de Madrid* 2d ser. 1 (1841): 199–211.

Rivas, Duque de. *Don Alvaro o La fuerza del sino. Lanuza.* Ed. Ricardo Navas Ruiz. Madrid: Espasa-Calpe, 1975.

Rodríguez Rubí, Tomás. "*Poesías* de Josefa Massanés." *Revista de Teatros* 1 Sept. 1841: 23–25.

Sabater, Pedro. "La mujer." *El Semanario Pintoresco Español* 2d ser. 4 (1842): 115–116.

Saez de Melgar, Faustina. *La cruz del olivar.* Ed. and intro. Alicia G. Andreu. Boston: *Anales Galdosianos,* 1980.

Sand, George. *Indiana.* Ed. Pierre Salomon. Paris: Garnier, 1962.

——. *Lélia.* Ed. Pierre Reboul. Paris: Garnier, 1960.

"Una sesión en una asamblea de mujeres." *El Jorobado* 26 May 1836: 3–4.

Souza, José de. Carta a Carolina Coronado. *El Defensor del Bello Sexo* 19 Oct. 1845: 46.

Valencina, Diego de, ed. *Fernán Caballero: Cartas.* Madrid: Sucesores de Hernando, 1919.

Wollstonecraft, Mary. *A Vindication of the Rights of Women. The Feminist Papers.* Ed. Alice S. Rossi. New York: Bantam, 1974. 40–85.

SECONDARY SOURCES

Abrams, Meyer H. "English Romanticism: The Spirit of the Age." Frye, *Romanticism Reconsidered* 26–72.

Albert Robatto, Matilde. *Rosalía de Castro y la condición femenina.* Madrid: Partenón, 1981.

Aldaraca, Bridget. "'El ángel del hogar': The Cult of Domesticity in Nineteenth-Century Spain." *Theory and Practice of Feminist Literary Criticism.* Ed. Gabriela Mora and Karen S. Van Hooft. Ypsilanti, Mich.: Bilingual Press, 1982. 62–87.

Andreu, Alicia G. *Galdós y la literatura popular.* Madrid: Sociedad General Española de Librería, 1982.

Arenal, Electa. "The Convent as Catalyst for Autonomy: Two Hispanic Nuns of the Seventeenth Century." Beth Miller, *Women* 147–183.

Ariès, Philippe. *Centuries of Childhood: A Social History of Family Life.* Trans. R. Baldick. New York: Vintage, 1962.

Armstrong, Nancy. *Desire and Domestic Fiction: A Political History of the Novel.* New York: Oxford University Press, 1987.

——. "The Rise of the Domestic Woman." *The Ideology of Conduct.* Ed. Nancy Armstrong and Leonard Tennenhouse. New York: Methuen, 1987. 96–141.

Barbéris, Pierre. *Balzac et le mal du siècle.* Vol. 1. Paris: Gallimard, 1970. 2 vols.

Beauvoir, Simone de. *Le deuxième sexe.* Vol. 1. Paris: Gallimard, 1949. 2 vols.

Bloom, Harold. "The Internalization of Quest-Romance." Bloom, *Romanticism and Consciousness* 3–23.

——. *The Ringers in the Tower.* Chicago: University of Chicago Press, 1971.

————, ed. *Romanticism and Consciousness*. New York: Norton, 1970.

Butler, Marilyn. *Romantics, Rebels and Reactionaries: English Literature and Its Background, 1760–1830*. Oxford: Oxford University Press, 1981.

Caldera, Ermanno. *Il dramma romantico in Spagna*. Pisa: Universitá di Pisa, 1974.

Campo de Alange, María. *Concepción Arenal: 1820–1893. Estudio biográfico documental*. Madrid: Revista de Occidente, 1973.

Capel Martínez, Rosa María, ed. *Mujer y sociedad en España: 1700–1975*. Madrid: Dirección General de Juventud y Promoción Socio-Cultural, 1982.

Carnero, Guillermo. *Los orígenes del romanticismo reaccionario español: El matrimonio Böhl de Faber*. Valencia: Universidad de Valencia, 1978.

Casalduero, Joaquín. *Espronceda*. Madrid: Gredos, 1961.

Chodorow, Nancy. *The Reproduction of Motherhood: Psychoanalysis and the Sociology of Gender*. Berkeley, Los Angeles, London: University of California Press, 1978.

Cixous, Hélène. "Castration or Decapitation." Trans. Annette Kuhn. *Signs* 7 (1981): 41–55.

Cotarelo y Mori, Emilio. *La Avellaneda y sus obras: Ensayo biográfico y crítico*. Madrid: Tipografía de Archivos, 1930.

Cott, Nancy F. "Passionlessness: An Interpretation of Victorian Sexual Ideology." *Signs* 4 (1978): 219–233.

Criado y Domínguez, Juan P. *Literatas españolas del siglo XIX*. Madrid: Pérez Dubrull, 1889.

Darrow, Margaret H. "French Noblewomen and the New Domesticity, 1750–1850." *Feminist Studies* 5 (1979): 41–65.

de Man, Paul. "The Rhetoric of Temporality." *Interpretation: Theory and Practice*. Ed. Charles S. Singleton. Baltimore, Md.: Johns Hopkins University Press, 1969. 173–209.

Descola, Jean. *La vida cotidiana en la España romántica: 1833–1868*. Trans. Oscar Collazos. Barcelona: Argos, 1984. First published as *La vie quotidienne en Espagne au temps de Carmen*. Paris: Hachette, 1971.

Domínguez Ortiz, Antonio. *Hechos y figuras del siglo XVIII español*. Madrid: Siglo XXI, 1973.

Eagleton, Terry. *The Rape of Clarissa*. Minneapolis: University of Minnesota Press, 1982.

Eco, Umberto. "Rhetoric and Ideology in Sue's *Les Mystères de Paris*." *International Social Science Journal* 19 (1967): 551–569.

Elorza, Antonio. "Feminismo y socialismo, 1840–1868." *Tiempo de Historia* 3 (1975): 46–63.

Escobar, José. *Los orígenes de la obra de Larra*. Madrid: Prensa Española, 1973.

Espresati, Carlos González. *La juventud de Amalia Fenollosa, poetisa romántica*. Castellón de la Plana, Spain: Sociedad Castellonense de Cultura, 1965.

Ferreras, Juan Ignacio. *La novela por entregas: 1840–1900*. Madrid: Taurus, 1972.

Fonseca Ruiz, Isabel. "Cartas de Carolina Coronado a Juan Eugenio Hartzenbusch." *Homenaje a Guillermo Gustavino*. Madrid: Associación Nacional de Bibliotecarios, 1974. 171–199.

Fontana, Josep. "Formación del mercado nacional y toma de conciencia de la burguesía." *Cambio económico y actitudes políticas*. Barcelona: Ariel, 1975. 13–35.

———. *La quiebra de la monarquía absoluta, 1814–1820*. Barcelona: Ariel, 1971.

Fontanella, Lee. "Mystical Diction and Imagery in Gómez de Avellaneda and Carolina Coronado." *Latin American Literary Review* 9 (1981): 47–55.

Frye, Northrup. "The Drunken Boat: The Revolutionary Element in Romanticism." Frye, *Romanticism Reconsidered* 1–25.

———, ed. *Romanticism Reconsidered*. New York: Columbia University Press, 1963.

Furst, Lilian. *Romanticism in Perspective*. London: Macmillan, 1969.

Gallagher, Catherine, and Thomas Laqueur. *The Making of the Modern Body: Sexuality and Society in the Nineteenth Century*. Berkeley, Los Angeles, London: University of California Press, 1987.

Gardiner, Judith Kegan. "Mind Mother: Psychoanalysis and Feminism." Greene and Kahn 113–145.

Gies, David Thatcher. *Theatre and Politics in Nineteenth-century Spain: Juan de Grimaldi as Impresario and Government Agent*. Cambridge: Cambridge University Press, 1988.

Gilbert, Sandra M., and Susan Gubar. *The Madwoman in the Attic: The Woman Writer and the Nineteenth-Century Literary Imagination*. New Haven, Conn.: Yale University Press, 1979.

González Palencia, A. *Estudio histórico sobre la censura gubernativa en España. 1800–1833*. Vol. 2. Madrid: Tipografía de Archivos, 1935. 3 vols.

Greene, Gayle, and Coppélia Kahn, eds. *Making a Difference: Feminist Literary Criticism*. London: Methuen, 1985.

Guerra Cunningham, Lucía. "Transgresión femenina del folletín en *Dos mujeres* de Gómez de Avellaneda." Unpublished manuscript.

Gutiérrez de la Solana, Alberto. "*Sab y Francisco*: Paralelo y contraste." *Homenaje a Gertrudis Gómez de Avellaneda*. Ed. Gladys Zaldívar and Rosa Martínez de Cabrera. Miami, Fla.: Editora Universal, 1981.

Gutwirth, Madelyn. *Madame de Staël, Novelist: The Emergence of the Artist as Woman*. Urbana: University of Illinois Press, 1978.

Hagstrum, Jean H. *Sex and Sensibility: Ideal and Erotic Love from Milton to Mozart*. Chicago: University of Chicago Press, 1980.

Harter, Hugh A. *Gertrudis Gómez de Avellaneda*. Boston: Twayne, 1981.

Hartman, Geoffrey H. "Romanticism and 'Anti-Self-Consciousness.'" Bloom, *Romanticism and Consciousness* 46–56.

Hauser, Arnold. "A Flight from Reality." *Romanticism: Problems of Definition, Explanation and Evaluation*. Ed. John B. Halsted. Boston: Heath, 1965. 67–76.

Herr, Richard. *The Eighteenth-Century Revolution in Spain*. Princeton, N.J.: Princeton University Press, 1958.

Herrero, Javier. *Fernán Caballero: Un nuevo planteamiento*. Madrid: Gredos, 1963.

Homans, Margaret. *Women Writers and Poetic Identity: Dorothy Words-worth, Emily Brontë, and Emily Dickinson.* Princeton, N.J.: Princeton University Press, 1980.

Jameson, Fredric. *The Political Unconscious: Narrative as a Socially Symbolic Act.* Ithaca, N.Y.: Cornell University Press, 1981.

Juretschke, Hans. *Origen doctrinal y génesis del romanticismo español.* Madrid: Ateneo, 1954.

Kaplan, Cora. Introduction. *Aurora Leigh and Other Poems.* By Elizabeth Barrett Browning. London: The Women's Press, 1978. 5–36.

———. "Pandora's Box: Subjectivity, Class and Sexuality in Socialist Feminist Criticism." Greene and Kahn 146–176.

King, Edmund L. "What Is Spanish Romanticism?" *Studies in Romanticism* 2 (1962): 1–11.

Kirkpatrick, Susan. "The Ideology of *Costumbrismo.*" *Ideologies and Literature* 2 no. 7 (1978): 28–44.

Kristeva, Julia. "Women's Time." Trans. Alice Jardine and Harry Blake. *Signs* 7 (1981): 13–35.

Laqueur, Thomas. "Orgasm, Generation, and the Politics of Reproductive Biology." Gallagher and Laqueur 1–42.

Lazo, Raimundo. *Gertrudis Gómez de Avellaneda: La mujer y la poetisa lírica.* Mexico City: Porrúa, 1972.

Lewis, Thomas E. "Contradictory Explanatory Systems in Espronceda's Poetry: The Social Genesis and Structure of *El Diablo Mundo.*" *Ideologies and Literature* 17 (1983): 11–45.

Llorens, Vicente. *El romanticismo español: Ideas literarias. Literatura e historia.* Madrid: Castalia, 1979.

López-Cordón Cortezo, María Victoria. "La situación de la mujer a finales del antiguo régimen (1760–1860)." Capel Martínez 47–107.

Manzano Garías, Antonio. "Amalia Fenollosa." *Boletín de la Sociedad Castellonense de Cultura* 38 (1962): 38–80.

———. "De una década extremeña y romántica." *Revista de Estudios Extremeños* 24 (1969): 1–29.

Marco, Joaquín. *Literatura popular en España en los siglos XVIII y XIX.* Madrid: Taurus, 1977.

Marrast, Robert. *José de Espronceda et son temps: Littérature, société, politique au temps du romantisme.* Paris: Klincksieck, 1974.

Martín Gaite, Carmen. *Usos amorosos del dieciocho en España.* Madrid: Siglo XXI, 1972.

Menhennet, Alan. *The Romantic Movement.* London: Croom Helm, 1981.

Miller, Beth. "Gertrude the Great: Avellaneda, Nineteenth-Century Feminist." Beth Miller, *Women* 201–214.

———, ed. *Women in Hispanic Literature: Icons and Fallen Idols.* Berkeley, Los Angeles, London: University of California Press, 1983.

Miller, Nancy K. "Emphasis Added: Plots and Plausibilities in Women's Fiction." *PMLA* 96 (1981): 36–48.

Moers, Ellen. *Literary Women.* New York: Doubleday, 1976.

Montesinos, José F. *Fernán Caballero: Ensayo de justificación.* Berkeley and Los Angeles: University of California Press, 1961.

———. Prólogo. *Elia*. By Fernán Caballero. Madrid: Alianza, 1968. 7–25.

Morse, David. *Perspectives on Romanticism*. London: Macmillan, 1981.

Muñoz de San Pedro, Miguel. "Carolina Coronado: Notas y papeles inéditos." *Indice de las Artes y las Letras* 64 (1953): 1, 21–22.

Okin, Susan Moller. "Women and the Making of the Sentimental Family." *Philosophy and Public Affairs* 11 (1981): 65–88.

Perinat, Adolfo, and María Isabel Marrades. *Mujer, prensa y sociedad en España: 1800–1939*. Madrid: Centro de Investigaciones Sociológicas, 1980.

Pescatello, Ann M. *Power and Pawn: The Female in Iberian Families, Societies and Cultures*. Westport, Conn.: Greenwood Press, 1976.

Poovey, Mary. "My Hideous Progeny: Mary Shelley and the Feminization of Romanticism." *PMLA* 95 (1980): 332–347.

———. *The Proper Lady and the Woman Writer: Ideology as Style in the Works of Mary Wollstonecraft, Mary Shelley and Jane Austen*. Chicago: University of Chicago Press, 1984.

Rajan, Tilottama. *Dark Interpreter: The Discourse of Romanticism*. Ithaca, N.Y.: Cornell University Press, 1980.

Rodríguez, Rodney T. "Continuity and Innovation in the Spanish Novel: 1700–1833." *Studies in Eighteenth-Century Spanish Literature and Romanticism in Honor of John Clarkson Dowling*. Ed. Douglas Barnette and Linda Jane Barnette. Newark, Del.: Juan de la Cuesta, 1985. 49–63.

———. "Las dos Españas: Two Approaches in the Novel of the 1840s." *Estudos Ibero-Americanos* 4 (1978): 191–203.

Rodríguez-Luis, Julio. "*La gaviota*: Fernán Caballero entre romanticismo y realismo." *Anales Galdosianos* 8 (1973): 123–136.

Romero Tobar, Leandro. *La novela popular española del siglo XIX*. Madrid: Ariel, 1976.

Sandoval, Adolfo de. *Carolina Coronado y su época*. Zaragoza: Librería General, 1929.

Scanlon, Geraldine M. *La polémica feminista en la España contemporánea: 1868–1974*. 2d ed. Madrid: Ediciones Akal, 1986.

Schiebinger, Londa. "Skeletons in the Closet: The First Illustrations of the Female Skeleton in Eighteenth-Century Anatomy." Gallagher and Laqueur 42–82.

Shaw, Donald L. *Historia de la literatura española. El siglo XIX*. Esplugues de Llobregat, Spain: Ariel, 1973.

Silvert, Eileen Boyd. "*Lélia* and Feminism." *Yale French Studies* 62 (1981): 45–66.

Simón Palmer, María del Carmen. "Escritoras españolas del siglo XIX o el miedo a la marginación." *Anales de Literatura Española de la Universidad de Alicante* 2 (1983): 477–490.

Stone, Lawrence. *The Family, Sex and Marriage in England: 1500–1800*. New York: Harper and Row, 1977.

Valis, Noël M. "Pardo Bazán's *El cisne de Vilamorta* and the Romantic Reader." *MLN* 101 (1986): 298–324.

Van den Berg, J. H. "The Subject and His Landscape." Bloom, *Romanticism and Consciousness* 57–65.

Vilarrubias, Felió A. *Noticia de una colección de papeles de José Massanés (1777–1857) y Josefa Massanés de González (1811–1887)*. Barcelona: Diputación Provincial de Barcelona, 1966.

Woolf, Virginia. "Professions for Women." *Women and Writing*. Ed. Michèle Barrett. San Diego, Calif.: Harcourt, Brace, Jovanovich, 1979. 57–63.

Zavala, Iris. *Ideología y política en la novela española del siglo XIX*. Salamanca: Anaya, 1971.

Index

Designer:	U.C. Press Staff
Compositor:	Prestige Typography
Text:	10/13 Sabon
Display:	Sabon
Printer:	Braun-Brumfield, Inc.
Binder:	Braun-Brumfield, Inc.